Psychology Revivals

Methodologies of Hypnosis

Originally published in 1976, this title looks closely at the current nature of controls in hypnosis research at the time and tries to assess what they contributed to our knowledge of hypnosis. Specifically, the book analyses the contributions to our understanding of hypnotic phenomena offered by the application of six contemporary methodologies, or paradigms, of hypnosis. The primary concern is with those paradigms that are experimental, rather than clinical, in orientation, and which had emerged over the previous decade as coherent programmatic collections of procedural strategies, all of them associated with distinct and important views of how hypnotic behaviour can best be explained.

Methodologies of Hypnosis

A critical appraisal of contemporary paradigms of hypnosis

Peter W. Sheehan
Campbell W. Perry

Routledge
Taylor & Francis Group
LONDON AND NEW YORK

First published in 1976
by Lawrence Erlbaum Associates, Inc.

This edition first published in 2015 by Routledge
27 Church Road, Hove BN3 2FA

and by Routledge
711 Third Avenue, New York, NY 10017

Routledge is an imprint of the Taylor & Francis Group, an informa business

A Library of Congress record exists under ISBN: 0470150289

ISBN: 978-1-138-88495-3 (hbk)
ISBN: 978-1-315-71576-6 (ebk)
ISBN: 978-1-138-88499-1 (pbk)

Methodologies of Hypnosis

A critical appraisal of contemporary paradigms of hypnosis

Peter W. Sheehan
Campbell W. Perry

Routledge
Taylor & Francis Group
LONDON AND NEW YORK

First published in 1976
by Lawrence Erlbaum Associates, Inc.

This edition first published in 2015 by Routledge
27 Church Road, Hove BN3 2FA

and by Routledge
711 Third Avenue, New York, NY 10017

Routledge is an imprint of the Taylor & Francis Group, an informa business

A Library of Congress record exists under ISBN: 0470150289

ISBN: 978-1-138-88495-3 (hbk)
ISBN: 978-1-315-71576-6 (ebk)
ISBN: 978-1-138-88499-1 (pbk)

METHODOLOGIES OF HYPNOSIS

A Critical Appraisal of Contemporary Paradigms of Hypnosis

PETER W. SHEEHAN
UNIVERSITY OF QUEENSLAND

CAMPBELL W. PERRY
CONCORDIA UNIVERSITY

LEA LAWRENCE ERLBAUM ASSOCIATES, PUBLISHERS
1976 Hillsdale, New Jersey

Lawrence Erlbaum Associates, Inc., Publishers
62 Maria Drive
Hillsdale, New Jersey 07642

Distributed solely by Halsted Press Division
John Wiley & Sons, Inc., New York

Library of Congress Cataloging in Publication Data

Sheehan, Peter W
Methodologies of hypnosis.

Bibliography: p.
Includes indexes.
1. Hypnotism–History. I. Perry, Campbell W., joint author. II. Title.
BF1125.S5 154.7 76-3543
ISBN 0-470-15028-9

Printed in the United States of America

Contents

Preface

Recently there has been an immense growth in the sophistication of our knowledge about hypnotic phenomena. Those who are researching hypnosis are far more timid in their inferences than they used to be. The once easy, sweeping generalizations of old are no longer viable. The borderlines between current disputes in the hypnotic literature are typically blurred, concepts held to be important in hypnosis now are clearly pertinent to other areas of psychological inquiry as well, and hand in hand with our growth in the knowledge of what to look for there has been an increasing awareness of the subtleties of method that are needed to evaluate the phenomena themselves. This book attempts to represent the state of the "contemporary methodological art," as it were. It looks closely at the current nature of controls in hypnosis research and tries to assess what they contribute to our knowledge of hypnosis. Specifically, the book analyzes the contributions to our understanding of hypnotic phenomena offered by the application of six contemporary methodologies, or paradigms, of hypnosis.

Our primary concern is with those major paradigms of hypnosis that are experimental, rather than clinical, in orientation, and which have emerged over the last decade as coherent programmatic collections of procedural strategies, all of them associated with distinct and important views of how hypnotic behavior can best be explained. They offer a representative survey of current accepted procedural practices aimed towards providing very stringent tests of certainty about what hypnotic data mean. The paradigms also illustrate the typical tools of the trade, as it were, of a sample of significant researchers in the field whose viewpoints represent some of the best accepted traditions of modern scientific research. Understandably enough perhaps, each of the models we take up seems best equipped to solve those particular problems it considers most important to investigate. The distinctive orientations of the various paradigms, however, reinforce Scheffler's (1972) point that the real issue among scientists is probably not one of uniformity (for such would seem impossible), but objectivity—a criterion demanding reasoned and informed discussion of the comparative merits of separate approaches to knowledge. The search for objectivity, in this sense, is a goal that strongly motivates our endeavors in this book.

Each of the hypnotic theorists (and researchers) we consider in this text, perceive the study of hypnotic phenomena somewhat differently, but the observations that all of them provide are valuable. The proponents of the various paradigms stress different issues and often see variables in different relations to one another, but the understanding that emerges from viewing their diversity of stance leads us to a richer, fuller awareness of the phenomena at issue and towards a more sensitive appreciation of the difficulties any theorist faces who chooses to work in the field of hypnosis. In the following pages, some paradigms survive scrutiny better than others as far as their rigor, consistency of logic, and even accuracy, are concerned, but no single methodology associated with the study of hypnosis (or any other domain of psychological investigation, for that matter) guarantees us the path to truth. Each paradigm is useful in alterting us to separate problems that need to be solved, and each focuses on discrete sets of procedures that are potentially valuable for promoting fresh insights into hypnotic phenomena.

We have been especially concerned throughout this book with approaching individual paradigms by trying to tease out their particular assumptions and the logic that underlies them. Accordingly, our evaluation of any one methodology has not been based on the assumption that another point of view is a priori better or more favorable in any way. We have found it impossible, however, to be completely lacking in bias, and we can only apologize in advance for the personal prejudices that no doubt display themselves in our text. We hope, though, that our evaluation of the separate methodologies of hypnosis that we investigate represents a fair and impartial assessment of the precision of thinking that lies behind the accepted logic of each. Our essential yardstick for evaluating the accuracy of inferences associated with each paradigm has been to ask whether the controls that are adopted typically by its proponents are adequate, and, in this important sense, the primary orientation of the book is methodological, not theoretical. Comprehension of phenomena is limited, however, by focusing on method alone, and we consistently attempt to evaluate the theoretical frameworks within which the methodologies are embedded.

In our preoccupation with analyzing experimental techniques we have sought to recognize the essential limitations of the method of laboratory testing itself. The strengths and weaknesses of that method have to be assessed if we are ever to arrive at the true meaning of findings collected within the traditional research context. The laboratory test setting is integrally associated with each of the methodologies we consider, and analysis of the social psychology of that setting is highly pertinent to evaluating each paradigm's contribution to knowledge.

Exact specification of test procedures is a major goal of the good researcher. The solution to design problems lies not in inventing increasingly complicated methods of control to cope with the growing number of difficulties that an experimenter observes, but in knowing the precise limitations of the methods one wants to employ. In the area of hypnosis, perhaps especially, one of the major limitations that derives from what the researcher does is the difficulty he faces in knowing how important private experience is to the understanding of what he is studying. The impact of subjective testimony seems obvious, yet we must somehow come to grips with the basic problem that private report can interfere with the very process of our coming to know (Skinner, 1975).

We hope that the book will have meaning for researchers working in fields other than hypnosis, for it seems to us that many of the problems we have isolated in this book pertain as much to the methodology of the social sciences as they do to the study of a particular set of defined phenomena we have chosen to categorize descriptively as "hypnotic." Pertinent to any prediction in science, the adequacy of the various hypotheses or theories covered in this book (considered in terms of the orientation of one paradigm or another) has been consistently judged according to how well the hypotheses suggest distinct criteria for acceptance and supply ready means of confirmation. Put in another way, they needed to establish their own method of developing the truth. The fact that many hypotheses in the book conflict theoretically with others is, of itself, relatively unimportant. The lesson of science clearly is that later explanations may be as good or better than early ones. We asked, though, that each hypothesis should supply the means to demonstrate its own falsity. The bias we adopt in this respect is shared by many others as well.

It is important to assess how far we have come from the assumptions held by the earlier historical theorists, and in some respects it is sobering to realize how slight has been our advance when one contrasts the concepts of old with those emerging now among contemporary researchers. An historical introduction to the book (Chapter 1) makes this point. Perhaps one of the most enduring notions lying behind work in hypnosis, and which can be traced through the writings of many of the early investigators, is the assumption of stable individual differences in hypnotic responsivity. The analysis of Hilgard's orientation, which focuses on this assumption and incorporates it within a well-defined framework of research strategies, thus provides a suitable first methodology for review (Chapter 2). An analysis of Barber's paradigm follows (Chapter 3) and presents us with the most critical attack on the concept of hypnosis that modern literature provides. Barber asserts that the concept of hypnosis itself is expendable. He argues militantly against a state account of hypnosis and offers us distinctive methods for analyzing suggestion phenomena. Similarly, Sarbin's model, which follows in the next chapter, argues distinctively for a nonstate orientation to hypnotic phenomena and overlaps in emphasis with Barber's paradigm in several important respects.

The methodologies of Sutcliffe and Orne are analyzed in Chapters 5 and 6. Both these theorists accept the notion of state, and their methodologies have been grouped together because of their primary reliance on role-playing as a major technique of control comparison. The methodology of London and Fuhrer is taken up in Chapter 7, and this paradigm draws our attention somewhat distinctively to the relevance of situational analysis of hypnotic events and to the importance of such an emphasis for the proper understanding of hypnotic events; discussion of this methodology leads us to contrast the influence of "situation" with the alternative accounts covered by earlier chapters in terms of "trait" and/or "state." The organization we have followed for each of the paradigms has been to outline initially the theory behind the methodology, survey distinctive procedural practices, outline the problems that appear to be especially associated with it, and evaluate the evidence in support of it. Finally, for each methodology considered, we offer an overall evaluation of the paradigm and point out some of the directions in which future research might meaningfully move if the implications of the paradigm's application are to be pursued.

Chapters 8 and 9 which conclude the book attempt to integrate and summarize the preceding material. In Chapter 8 we outline some of the major sources of artifact that consistently beleaguer hypnotic researchers (and other investigators testing human subjects) who choose to work within the confines of the laboratory test setting. In this chapter we discuss some of the ways in which the problems created by artifact might be alleviated and attempt to illustrate our argument by taking two of the models considered earlier and analyzing the consequences of their application when both are brought to bear upon the same problem. In Chapter 9, we bring together some of the central issues and problems in the field and survey the various collections of strategies that have been analyzed previously to arrive at some recommendations or guidelines for future, systematic research. As far as possible in this pursuit, we have tried to maintain an open attitude. Our recommendations for procedures are intended to represent less a dogmatic set of principles than tentative suggestions to researchers who wish to increase the precision of their thinking and who want to assess the potential inaccuracy of many of the inferences that can be too easily drawn about the data they collect. Finally, we would assert that although the application of these guidelines may allow for systematic control of subsequent observations, it should be remembered that the act of observing is itself a variable that may influence outcomes. The researcher is obligated to evaluate carefully the potential effects of all his experimental intrusions.

We owe our deep gratitude to many. In particular, we would like to thank Lawrence Erlbaum for the enthusiasm he imparted concerning the project and for the continuing support he has given us over the last two years while the book was being written and in preparation. We wish to thank also William Coe for his detailed comments on the manuscript, Ernest Hilgard for his helpful remarks on

Chapter 9, and the students of hypnosis at the University of Queensland, and Concordia University, Montréal, for their de facto evaluation of many of the ideas that now measure our thinking. Finally, our thanks go to Jan Stewart, May Lundquist, Christine Poirier, Alison Cavaye, and Denise Hokin for their invaluable help in getting the manuscript to print.

PETER W. SHEEHAN
CAMPBELL W. PERRY

METHODOLOGIES OF HYPNOSIS
A Critical Appraisal of Contemporary Paradigms of Hypnosis

1
Historical Antecedents and Perspectives

> If it is to illusion to which I owe the health I believe I enjoy, I humbly entreat the experts who see so clearly, not to destroy it; that they may enlighten the universe, that they leave me with my error, and that they permit my simplicity, my frailty and my ignorance to make use of an *invisible agent, which does not exist but which cures me* [Testimony of a satisfied patient in *Supplément aux Deux Rapports de MM. Les Commissaires* (1784) (quoted by Podmore, 1909, p. 65)].

Methodologies come to exist in science when the true nature of a phenomenon is not immediately obvious. Their heuristic purpose is to provide an investigator with a framework for making planned observations pertinent to the questions he or she feels are relevant. They are intimately linked with what are variously called theories, models, and paradigms. Thus, methodologies may mislead as well as clarify, since they depend upon an investigator's ability to know what the relevant variables are which determine a phenomenon's occurrence.

Hypnosis is one such phenomenon for which these preliminary comments are particularly valid. Currently, there are several major approaches seeking to elucidate its essential parameters, which are in conflict on certain substantive issues. Much of the reason for this conflict stems from differences in theory from which the methodologies obtain their rationale. Their theoretical underpinnings did not develop in a vacuum but, rather, follow a long tradition of attempts to unravel paradoxes about hypnosis that have existed for virtually two hundred years.

The history of hypnosis in Europe begins in the France of the 18th Century. It is important for many reasons. As a history of trial and error, interspersed with a modicum of success, it is of interest, in its own right, in the same way that many periods in the history of science, literature, the arts, politics, and social affairs are absorbing. But beyond its immediate appeal, it is informative, and gives many insights into issues that remain controversial in current hypnotic research.

Part of its relevance to present day thinking is that by "a gradual correction of errors [Hull, 1933, p. 18]" it tells us, unequivocally, some of the things that hypnosis is *not.* It permits us to rule out a number of possible explanations of the nature of hypnosis, thereby reducing the range of presently plausible models. Thus, for instance, although it took almost a century to demonstrate, no current investigator can expect to be taken seriously if he advances a model predicated on Mesmer's assumption that hypnosis is a matter of animal magnetic forces or fluids in the universe which, when harnessed appropriately, can effect substantial changes in human behavior, particularly in a curative context. Likewise, the belief shared by both Mesmer and de Puységur that hypnotic phenomena depend upon special skills or supernormal powers of the hypnotist can be safely dismissed in equivalent fashion. This can be done without denying that in some situations, particularly clinical ones, special technical and interpersonal skills which communicate competence and trust to the hypnotized person are mandatory. Other alternatives can be ruled out, as the result of extensive inquiry throughout the nineteenth century, which is often dismissed prematurely as a period of sterility in the history of hypnosis (Hull, 1933). Thus no present day theory which conceives of hypnotic behavior as in some way fraudulent or as sham behavior can expect to be taken seriously. One can do this without denying that hypnotic behavior may have components of role enactment (in a sense that is not to be confused with social compliance) or fantasy behavior. Likewise this can be said without rejecting the view that it may be possible to formulate state theories of hypnosis more fruitfully in other terms.

Finally, the history of hypnosis is important because it provides a social history of a phenomenon over a prolonged period. It involves investigators operating at different points of time under often markedly different conditions of belief in the society, and in intellectual circles. It involves also some major differences in induction procedure. There is a great distance between the methods used by Mesmer to evoke the phenomena associated with the *baquet,* and the present day practices associated with administering the Stanford Hypnotic Susceptibility Scale: Form C (Weitzenhoffer & Hilgard, 1962) under laboratory conditions. While there are differences in the manifestations of hypnotic phenomena elicited by the respective induction procedures, there are no serious doubts that, in each case, we are dealing with the same basic phenomenon. By concentrating on such variations in social and scientific belief, and in induction procedure we may come to better understand the nature of hypnosis through a study of its history.

This historical account is deliberately selective mainly because several good historical accounts already exist. It places its emphasis on certain periods, investigators, and induction procedures which appear to illuminate certain parameters of hypnotic responsivity. As a result, many investigators over the last 200 years receive less than due acknowledgment of their contribution to what we now think we know about hypnosis. More substantial documentation of certain points can be found in the historical treatments of Binet and Féré (1888), Bramwell (1906), Podmore (1909), Janet (1925), Hull (1933), Darnton (1968), Ellenberger (1970), and Sarbin and Coe (1972). Tinterow (1970) is an invaluable source of many of the more important (and difficult to obtain) original writings on hypnosis of the 18th and 19th centuries.

ANIMAL MAGNETISM

Mesmer's Antecedents

The early history of hypnosis in Europe developed from naturalistic methods of inquiry, which contrast markedly with the formalized laboratory test procedures used by the researchers we will later evaluate in this book. The naturalistic method, however, yielded a rich variety of phenomena which, even now, must be explained. The procedures that were used also generated many false positives mainly because many very basic hypnotic phenomena were ignored because they were not in accord with prevailing theories of the period. Observation then, as now, tended to be grouped around what investigators believed was intrinsic to hypnosis. Hypnosis was stumbled upon by people, using patently false theories about the nature of the universe, who sought miraculous cures of physical illnesses that had defied treatment by orthodox medical means. Since it appeared to produce miraculous cure of physical disorders it became intimately linked with miraculous psychic phenomena. As a result, naturalistic methods were slow to yield the basic observational data. Nevertheless, both the valid observations—and the errors—provide a starting point, even today, for scientific inquiry and both give a perspective to many prevailing contemporary problems.

Hypnosis is ordinarily dated as beginning in Paris in the 1770s with Franz Anton Mesmer. However, two of Mesmer's contemporaries, Father Gassner and Father Hell, used methods of curing physical ailments which influenced Mesmer's techniques significantly. Both Gassner and Hell represented certain approaches to cure and used certain practices that had existed for many of the preceding centuries. In the case of Gassner, who began as an obscure country catholic *curé*, and enjoyed a brief period of prominence, it was the practice of utilizing catharsis as a means of treating physical illness. The particular variant of cathartic cure practiced by Gassner was the exorcism rights of the Catholic Church. Father Hell's approach, by contrast, was based upon the very ancient belief that the human body has magnetic properties, and that the magnet itself could be curative of physical illness. Mesmer's contribution was to coalesce these two traditions and to produce a form of treatment that was uniquely his own. There is also a strong suspicion from the early literature on animal magnetism that he produced, in the process, a more powerful method of cure than had existed hitherto when either magnets or catharsis were separately used. In this, as we shall see, he was probably aided by certain unique social factors existing in European culture, and particularly that of Paris, during the late 18th century.

Father Johann Gassner (1727–1779) was ordained into the Catholic priesthood in 1750. As the result of what looks to have been certain psychosomatic disorders—severe headaches, dizziness, and other disturbances which were exacerbated when performing his priestly duties of saying Mass, hearing confession and preaching—Gassner came to suspect the work of the Devil. He proceeded to treat himself successfully using the Church's methods of exorcism and prayer. From his own experience of successful self-treatment, Gassner proceeded to apply his techniques to others with considerable success, so that by the early 1770s he had created a considerable reputation as a healer.

Gassner's method of healing by exorcism showed one remarkable similarity to the methods soon to be made famous by Mesmer. The exorcism of physical disorders was mediated by convulsive crisis. His treatment procedure followed a typical course. Dressed in ceremonial garbs, Gassner would have the prospective patient kneel before him. The patient would be asked his name and to describe his illness. Having ascertained that the patient had complete faith in Jesus, a precondition which Gassner considered essential for successful treatment (and probably was, for reasons unsuspected at the time), Gassner would proceed to elicit an agreement that anything he would order should happen. Having obtained consent, Gassner would pronounce in Latin "If there be anything preternatural about this disease, I order in the name of Jesus that it manifest itself immediately." Ordinarily, the patient experienced convulsions, that were often quite severe, which to Gassner was proof that the illness was due to evil spirits rather than natural causes. Gassner would proceed to demonstrate his power over such malign forces by directing the convulsions to various parts of the body. Following which, having tamed the Evil Presence, Gassner would culminate the treatment by expelling the evil one, usually through the toes or fingertips.

There is one further feature of Gassner's treatment worthy of special note. The Abbé Bourgeois, a contemporary observer, asked one of Gassner's patients, a nun, who had just been exorcised "whether it had been very painful; she answered that she had only a vague memory of what had happened, and that she had not suffered much [Ellenberger, 1970, p. 54]." Contemporary accounts of these early treatments are scarce; however, there is evidence from this, and from a few observers of Mesmer's techniques that spontaneous amnesia sometimes followed the convulsive catharsis elicited by these methods. Spontaneous amnesias do not appear to have been widely noticed at this time, since contemporary observers appeared much more distracted by the seemingly miraculous cures of hitherto stubborn physical ailments.

The second and more major component of Mesmer's thinking stems from an ancient belief in the curative powers of the magnet, which still existed, with some added refinements, in the Middle Ages. The use of magnetized rings worn around the neck or on the arms, and of talismen and magic boxes were common practices used to cure illness (Binet & Féré, 1888). Gradually, theoretical models to explain the potent effects of magnets developed. Not unnaturally, it was reasoned that if magnets could cure, it must be because the human body had magnetic properties.

In his thesis (*De planetarum influxu*) for which he received his medical degree from the Faculty of Vienna in 1766, Mesmer drew upon these beliefs, and the further notion, which was also current, that planetary rotation was somehow involved in the process. He argued for the existence of a universal fluid which he conceived of as a kind of impalpable and invisible gas in which all bodies were thought to be immersed. It was through this fluid, which Mesmer believed to have many of the attractive qualities of a magnet, that the planets influenced the body. He believed that human beings were constructed like a magnet, with the left side containing poles in opposition to those of the right side. Disease, he believed, was simply a disharmony in the distribution of these fluids and could be cured by magnetism, through the reestablishment of harmony.

In the years that followed his doctorate, he lived in Vienna practicing as a physician and achieved considerable social prominence. As a continuation of the interests expressed in his doctoral thesis, Mesmer kept himself informed of ongoing experiments in France, Germany, and Britain which were using magnetic methods to treat physical ailments. One such investigator in this area was Father Hell, a Jesuit whose specific hypothesis concerning the contradictory findings that were accruing in this area centered upon the nature of the magnets used. He believed that more consistent manifestations of healing by magnetic methods could be obtained if magnetic steel plates were custom-made to be attached, and fit closely to the diseased body site. Hell settled in Vienna in 1774 upon being appointed Professor of Astronomy. Mesmer met Hell socially and was able to induce him to have his craftsmen make a number of such plates specially designed to be applied to the appropriate bodily area. Shortly afterwards, Mesmer began treating his first patient by magnetic means. Fraulein Oesterlin, a 29-year-old patient, suffered from a convulsive malady with such symptoms as severe toothache and earache, delerium, rage, vomiting, and swooning. Using astronomical criteria, Mesmer felt he was able to predict the occurrence of these various disorders. He then proceeded to attempt to modify their incidence. Armed with a set of Father Hell's plates, Mesmer set about altering the course of her condition by attempting to establish a magnetic tide inside her body. One day, when the patient had a renewal of her usual attacks, Mesmer had her swallow a preparation containing iron and proceeded to attach magnets to her stomach and to each leg. Mesmer (1779) describes what ensued:

> Not long afterwards, this was followed by extraordinary sensations; she felt inside her some painful currents of a subtle material which, after different attempts at taking a direction, made their way towards the lower part and caused all the symptoms of the attack to cease for six hours. Next day, as the patient's condition made it necessary for me to carry out the same test again, I obtained the same success with it [pp. 37–38].

The remissions of symptoms obtained using these methods with this patient were frequently accompanied by what Mesmer called beneficial crises. It is difficult to ascertain whether such crises were coincidental to the therapeutic techniques used, or were the results of Mesmer communicating his belief in the efficacy of crisis through his procedures, or even whether they were based upon cultural beliefs shared by doctor and patient as to the nature of cure. But it is clear that Mesmer at this early stage, considered them important. Further, he quickly decided that his success with Fraulein Oesterlin could not have been caused by the magnets themselves. Rather, it reinforced his belief about the influence of the "General Agent"–that animal magnetism could be accumulated in his own person and then transferred to patients with ensuing curative effects.

In the meantime a rancorous dispute developed with Father Hell, who insisted on credit for the discovery, and claimed that Mesmer was stealing his work. Hell's position was that he had made a major breakthrough; he asserted that by tailoring his magnets to fit various parts of the body so that they agreed with the magnetic vortex, he was obtaining the success that had eluded the magnetic experimenters in England, Germany, and France by virtue of their less-perfected magnets. In defense of his own position, Mesmer proceeded to demonstrate in meticulous detail that the magnets had no effect in themselves. He kept in touch with Father Hell and conducted many tests in his presence. To show that the magnets were not the crucial factor in the cure, he demonstrated that almost anything–other metals, paper, wool, silk, stone, glass, and water–could conduct the magnetic forçe. This elaboration of orthodox magnetic doctrines into a belief in a general magnetic force, and in the curative effects of cathartic crises formed the cornerstones of Mesmer's subsequent practices. As we have seen, neither idea was at all new. Mesmer's unique contribution was to bring the two traditions together, and to modify them. In particular, his ability to obtain similar effects (and possibly more profound effects) by the use of contact and passes instead of magnets represent a major development, even though the phenomena he elicited would appear to be more based upon (the then unsuspected) placebo effects than the magnetic force he postulated.

Mesmer in Paris

Mesmer moved to Paris in 1778 and was to remain there for at least the next seven years. Starting with a house in the Place Vendôme, he rapidly developed a following by the publication of his theory in the form of 27 propositions in 1779, by the use of pamphlets to popularize his works, and by a gradually increasing magnetic practice. The latter indeed had become so extensive that by around 1780–1781, Mesmer was obliged to institute a *valet toucheur* to magnetize on his behalf, and subsequently the *baquet* as a method of group magnetism. Soon after Mesmer bought the Hôtel Bullion, and installed four *baquets,* one for the free use of the poor. Later still, a tree was magnetized for their collective use when the free *baquet* proved insufficient to the demands placed upon it.

This bare chronology of events scarcely conveys Mesmer's fame in Europe during his Paris sojourn, which was immense. Some of this may be attributed to a dominant personality, influential patrons, and to the inherently dramatic nature of the phenomena with which he dealt. However, certain social factors in Paris at this time appear also to have contributed to his success, particularly when it is realized that the official scientific bodies–Académie des Sciences, Société Royale de Médecine, and the Faculté de Médecine–were antagonistic to his claims. Certain features of late 18th century Paris which were conducive to a favorable reception of magnetic doctrines have been emphasized by various other authors (Darnton, 1968; Ellenberger, 1970; Podmore, 1909). The American War of 1776 marked the beginning of a chronic national financial crisis which was ultimately to prove a factor contributing to the outbreak of The French Revolution. The brunt of the country's malaise was carried by the poorer classes; the aristocracy enjoyed excessive privilege. Graft and speculation was endemic (Rudé, 1964). There was a general unrest, which some have called a mass hysteria. One way in which this manifested itself was a rush by the general public to embrace successive fads and crazes.

Equally as important were the breakthroughs in science which occurred during this period. Newton's doctrine of gravity, initially dismissed for many years by orthodox French science, was becoming known through the efforts of Voltaire. The discovery of electricity by Benjamin Franklin excited popular imagination through public demonstrations. The helium balloons of the Charlières and Montgolfières brothers made man airborne, for the first time. Likewise, Lavoisier was in process of demonstrating that water, hitherto thought of as one of the four basic elements, was actually a compound of hydrogen and oxygen. The fact that a basic element, which could be seen and touched, and under some conditions smelled, could be broken down into finer constituents that were barely (if at all) perceptible, constituted a startling departure from conventional wisdom.

The effect on the lay public of all these discoveries must have been profound, and may have increased susceptibility to animal magnetic forces. The scientific innovations of this era were widely perceived to mean that man could understand and harness invisible forces; forces which controlled human life in hitherto unconceived ways. Seen in this social context, Mesmer represents a meeting point of science and religion (Darnton, 1968). In addition, these events coincided with the period of Enlightenment, which with its emphasis on reason as opposed to tradition and supersitition, was making its presence felt at all levels of society. This process was undoubtedly accelerated by these selective demonstrations by science of its ability to harness invisible forces. Such forces had hitherto been the almost exclusive monopoly of the Church, which had never made very strong claims of being able to harness them; it claimed only to know about them better than the average person and to have the authority to negotiate divine intervention without any guarantees of success. The Church at this time was suffering from a general erosion of credibility for other reasons;

the various scientific innovations of this period that were occurring only served to further expose its vulnerability in a number of areas and to challenge its authority. It is for these reasons that Mesmer received great recognition, while Father Gassner and Father Hell lapsed into obscurity and are now, at best, considered as historical curiosities. Mesmer was able to produce identical phenomena, and with seemingly greater regularity and intensity. His theory, though equally as invalid as theirs, had greater plausibility. This is so, particularly in the case of Father Gassner, whose explanations of his cures were based upon religious premises at a time when orthodox religion was suffering a number of temporary set backs. Indeed Mesmer believed that Gassner was practicing the principles of animal magnetism without being aware of it.

It was demonstrable that electricity (an invisible force) could be harnessed, and that helium could lift a balloon. It was thus totally reasonable to believe that an invisible animal magnetic force might also exist, and be capable of curing physical illness. The plausibility of such a belief could only be reinforced by the fact that animal magnetic procedures often cured or substantially relieved illness after other more orthodox methods had failed. Such cures reflected, in part, the inadequate state of traditional medical diagnosis and practice of the period–it was an era where the medical profession was satirized regularly (often without mercy) on the Paris stage. Further, many illnesses treated by Mesmer would now be more easily recognized as having psychosomatic components, and (sometimes) origins. Given this, Mesmer undoubtedly achieved sufficient ameliorations and cures to provide apparent validation of his theories.

Mesmer's successes illustrate certain fundamental propositions about the nature of cure by essentially psychological means. He was able to obtain cure and amelioration of illness using a patently false theory, which had plausibility only because it was consistent with certain emerging scientific beliefs about the nature of the universe. At the very least, his magnetic treatments illustrate the point that therapeutic success does not validate a theory. Equally significant, they demonstrate the importance of prevailing social climates in determining what will be believed about the nature of a phenomenon, which in turn may act as a condition of its occurrence. The fact that all of the professional medical societies were antagonistic to Mesmer's claims does not mitigate these conclusions–there was always enough doctors and scientists sympathetic to Mesmer's doctrines, and it was possible to turn the disapproval of the professional societies to advantage.

The Baquet

Because of the exigencies of a rapidly growing practice within a few years of arriving in Paris, Mesmer was obliged to develop group methods of treatment. It is difficult to reconstruct the motives which led him to choose the *baquet,* since he had satisfied himself some years prior to arrival that magnets were extrinsic to the process. The use of this apparatus had, of course, obvious metaphorical associations with the physical magnetism he had previously rejected. The *baquet* also possessed some similarities to the Leyden Jar, so that it probably looked scientific.

Mesmer's methods of magnetizing, using the *baquet,* are of interest not merely for the phenomena it produced, but for the behaviors that were not recognized until a later, less flamboyant, era of hypnotic treatment emerged. The *baquet* was a circular oak cask, 12–18 inches high, of sufficient size for up to 30 people to be able to sit around it. At the bottom of the *baquet* lay a bed of powdered glass and iron filings on which bottles of mesmerized water were arranged in various ways. It was covered by a lid pierced with holes from which protruded movable metal rods positioned so as to be applicable to different parts of the body. The patients sat around the *baquet* in several rows, with those in the front row in direct contact with the *baquet* through the metal rods. To transfer the effects to the whole group, patients were connected to each other by cords passed around their bodies and by linking thumbs and index fingers with each other. Magnetic influences were heightened by other features of the decor. The room was hung with thick curtains so that only subdued light illuminated the room, the floors were thickly carpeted, and astrological motifs hung from the wall. Since propositions 15 and 16 of Mesmer's statement of 1779 stated that animal magnetism could be transmitted and augmented by mirrors and music, mirrors were strategically placed around the room and soft music came from a wind instrument, a pianoforte, or a glass harmonica played by Mesmer.

The patients themselves sat in silence. This procedure in itself was sufficient to induce a crisis in some of them, and they would be carried off into an adjoining padded *Chambre de Crises* where they could convulse freely without self-injury. For others, the approach of Mesmer and his assistants was necessary for the crisis to manifest itself. He carried a long iron wand with which he touched the diseased parts. At other times he would magnetize patients by eye fixation. Still yet another more controverisal method (which was to be the subject of a confidential report to the King of France on the moral aspects of magnetism in 1784), involved massaging the hypochondriac (ovarian) region and the lower abdomen, sometimes for hours. As Binet and Féré (1888, p. 19) have observed, "young women were much gratified by the crisis" which ensued from the latter treatment "that they begged to be thrown into it anew; they followed Mesmer through the hall, and confessed that it was impossible not to be warmly attached to the magnetizer's person." In short, magnetic treatment was not a unitary thing, which can be seen also from the fact that magnet practice involved, in appropriate cases, the administration of cream of tartar (a laxative) to induce evacuation. Success often followed this procedure in cases where cream of tartar alone had been ineffective.

Individual differences in response to the *baquet* and magnetizing procedures were noted, even at this early stage. Mesmer, indeed, observed that some people were insensitive to magnetic persuasion. There are, he said "some, although very few, whose properties are so opposed that their very presence destroys all the effects of magnetism in other bodies. This opposing property also penetrates all bodies . . . this constitutes not merely the absence of magnetism, but a positive opposing property [Mesmer, 1779, p. 55]." Other individual differences in response to the *baquet* were observed, the most detailed of which comes from the commission of 1784, charged by the King of France to inquire into animal magnetism. The Commissioners themselves used the term crisis to refer to convulsive, drowsy, or lethargic symptoms, produced by animal magnetism, thereby recognizing a multiplicity of behavioral effects.

In their descriptions of patient response, they noted that:

> Some of them are calm, tranquil, and unconscious to any sensation; others cough, spit, are affected with a slight degree of pain, a partial or a universal burning, and perspiration; a third class (of patients) are agitated and tormented by convulsions. The convulsions are rendered extraordinary by their frequency, their violence, and their duration. As soon as one person is convulsed, others presently are affected by that symptom. . . . These convulsions are characterized by precipitate and involuntary motions of all of the limbs or of the whole body, by a contraction of the throat, by sudden affections of the hyperchonders and the epigastrium, by a distraction and wildness in the eyes, by shrieks, tears, hiccuppings, and immoderate laughter. They are either preceded or followed by a state of languor and reverie, by a species of dejection, and even drowsiness [Benjamin Franklin *et al.*, 1784, p. 87. This and all subsequent quotations from this source are taken from the first English translation of 1785].

The impression left by the Commissioners was that the convulsive crisis was the most general aspect of the cure, despite their distinguishing three types of response (no response; motor response such as coughing, pain, etc.; and convulsive response). However, there remains some doubt as to the incidences of various behaviors in response to the *baquet*. There is a suggestion in their report that magnetic practice altered between the time of Mesmer instituting the baquet (circa 1781) and the Commissioners' investigation of Deslon's practice in 1784. They report that although Deslon had installed a quilt-lined *chambre des crises*, he did not use it. Further, in the controversy following the publication of the Commissioners' report, an anonymous pamphlet appeared compiling case histories of patients treated from 1782 to 1784, which suggested that the crisis was not a prominent feature of the magnetic cure. Later a document was published entitled *Doutes d'un Provincial* (believed to have been written by Antoine Servan, former attorney general to the Parlement of Grenoble), who had found relief through animal magnetism after 20 years of failure with orthodox medicine. He reported that, in the provinces, convulsive crises occurred no more than 5–6 times in 50 cases, and that such crises were all relatively mild (Podmore, 1909). Interestingly enough, this figure of 10–12% is not unlike the figure for high hypnotic susceptibility which is regularly reported by modern laboratory investigators using unrestricted samples of college students.

Background to the Commission of Enquiry of 1784

From the time of his arrival in Paris in February, 1778, Mesmer sought to obtain official recognition from the major scientific and medical societies—Académie des Sciences, Société Royale de Médecine, and Faculté de Médecine. In all three cases he failed. An attempt to obtain Royal approval in 1781 suffered a similar fate. Soon after, Mesmer in conjunction with some of his wealthier patients, developed a plan whereby Mesmer would give a course in the principles and practice of animal magnetism, in which he would reveal the secrets of his discovery. This offer was conditional upon Mesmer obtaining one hundred students at 2400 livres each, a condition that was easily met. From this money-making scheme developed a series of magnetic societies, first in Paris, and later in all major provincial cities of France. They were known as *Sociétés de l'Harmonie,* and quickly flourished. The activities of these groups (many of which became Jacobin groups during the French revolution) were the decisive factor in the King of France's decision of 1784 to institute two official inquiries into animal magnetism.

It is often implied by histories of hypnosis that these two Commissions constituted an act of benevolence by the French monarchy, which only wanted to ascertain the truth of a highly visible and contentious debate within the scientific establishment. In actuality, a secret report of the Paris police to the effect that some magnetists were injecting radical politics into their public lectures appears to have been the main cause of official concern (Darnton, 1968). Magnetism by this time was spreading rapidly throughout Paris and the provinces, attracting people of every social class. Probably most disquietening to the Government, however, was that magnetism was taking a strong hold among the wealthy. What Mesmer had been unable to do in his approaches to the scientific establishment, now became possible with the spread of his influence through the *Sociétés de l'Harmonie* and the official fears of its political intent.

Accordingly, on March 12, 1784, the King of France appointed two commissions of enquiry into animal magnetism. The main enquiry consisted of nine members, five of them drawn from the Académie des Sciences, with four medical representatives from the Faculté de Médecine. This group consisted of some of the most distinguished scientists of this period. It was chaired by Benjamin Franklin, who at that time was American Ambassador to France. The other 4 Académie members were Lavoisier, Bailly (the noted astronomer), Leroy (Director of the Académie), and de Bony (who died shortly after the investigation commenced). The four medical representatives were Majault, Sallin, D'Arcet, and Guillotin. The second commissions, chosen from the Société Royale de Médecine, carried out parallel but independent investigations. Both submitted their findings almost simultaneously five months later.

Needless to say it was the Benjamin Franklin report signed on August 11, 1784, which attracted the most public attention. However, a report dissenting from the conclusions of the Société Royale, drawn up by de Jussieu, which was generally ignored at the time, is of some significance.

The Commissions of Inquiry of 1784

The experimental program for the Benjamin Franklin Commission was drawn up by Lavoisier, and it is believed that the final report may have been written by him, although it is usually attributed to Bailly who was appointed as reporter for the commission. The commissioners' investigation has variously been described as a model of the application of the scientific method, and as a futile endeavor; depending upon what aspect of the report one is evaluating, both judgements have validity. Certainly the experimentation of the commissioners had an elegance which qualifies their report as a natural starting point for any discussion of experimental hypnosis. The disappointment of the report comes from the narrow frame of reference the commissioners set themselves. They saw their task as being to "inquire into the possibility of the existence and utility of animal magnetism." They noted that "the question of its existence is first in order; that of its utility was not to be examined until the other shall have been fully resolved. The animal magnetism may indeed exist without being useful, but it cannot be useful if it does not exist [Benjamin Franklin *et al.*, 1785, p. 89]."

In their initial phase of investigation, the commissioners determined, by use of an electrometer, that the baquet contained no electrical or magnetic properties. They concentrated upon Deslon's practice, despite an open letter from Mesmer to Franklin disavowing Deslon's particular practice of magnetism. Then, having studied Deslon's *baquet* they proceeded to investigate his therapeutic practice. However, they quickly decided that the supercharged atmosphere of the *baquet* was unconducive to experimentation. As they explained:

> the multiplicity of the effect is one obstacle; too many things are seen at once for any of them to be seen well. Beside, the patients of rank on account of their health might be displeased with the investigations of the commissioners. The very act of watching them might appear a nuisance; and the recollection of this might be burdensome, and impede the commissioners in their turn [p. 88].

The commissioners' enquiry covered four distinct areas of evidence: (a) they investigated the effect of magnetism on themselves, (b) they studied it using 14 sick people, (c) they examined magnetic phenomena practiced by Jumelin who produced effects identical to Mesmer but did not distinguish magnetic poles in the human body, which were thought to be essential by the magnetists, and (d) finally, they examined people in blindfold and other conditions where the person did not know if he was being magnetized at any particular time. Of these, the latter experiments involving blindfold and other conditions where the patient was unaware of when he was being magnetized, are of greatest importance. They provided decisive evidence for the nonexistence of animal magnetism, and strong evidence for an alternative explanation of magnetic phenomena which formed the basis of their final conclusions.

In the first three groups of observations the commissioners performed essentially naturalistic observations under poorly controlled conditions. From these they developed a strong conviction that imagination was the major ingredient of magnetic practices. However, up to this point, they had not been able to reproduce in their studies the conclusive crises they had observed in the public demonstrations of magnetism. The purpose of the final series of experiments was thus to examine the effect of a subject's not knowing when magnetic stimulation was being applied. This was done in a rigorous experimental fashion using blindfolds and partitions between the subject and the magnetic source. Only subjects whose susceptibility to magnetism had been predetermined by Deslon were used. The commissioners conducted experiments on five different "susceptibles." In all cases, identical outcomes were observed. The tests and procedures that they used are of considerable interest.

A typical experiment, involving a 12-year-old boy, was conducted in Benjamin Franklin's garden at Passy. An apricot tree was magnetized and the boy, blindfolded, was taken from tree to tree in the garden, embracing each successive tree for 2 minutes in the manner prescribed by Deslon. At the first tree, after 1 minute the boy reported profuse perspiration; he coughed, spat and reported a slight pain in his head. This tree was 27 ft from the magnetized tree. At the second tree, 36 ft from the magnetized tree, the boy reported stupefaction and increased headache. At the third tree even further away (38 ft) the boy reported increased headache and stupefaction and said he believed he was approaching the magnetized tree. At the fourth tree, 26 ft away, the boy fell into a crisis—he fainted and his limbs stiffened. Deslon attempted to explain this contrary finding by noting that all trees by their very nature, participated in the magnetism. To which the commissioners dryly observed that "a person, sensitive to magnetism could not hazard to walk in the garden without the risk of convulsions [p. 108]." Numerous other, often ingenious, blindfold tests were performed with the other four patients and yielded similar results.

On the basis of such tests, the commissioners concluded that the effects attributed to animal magnetism, the existence of which they clearly refuted, could be explained alternatively by touch, imagination and imitation, with particular emphasis being placed on the role of imagination. As they pointed out, imagination alone often produced a crisis. By contrast, they saw pressure and touch as preparatives, and imitation as the means by which the effects were communicated and extended. The parallel with emphases in modern day theorizing is an obvious one.

It is perhaps one of the great ironies of the history of hypnosis that these conclusions are only now, almost 200 years later, beginning to be taken seriously. As we note in Chapter 9, a number of the theorists discussed in this book, of often widely different theoretical and methodological stance, are beginning to converge upon very similar formulations of hypnosis, each of which emphasize the role of imaginative processes. There is continuity with the Benjamin Franklin commission findings in such conceptualizations of hypnotic processes as "believed-in imaginings" (Sarbin & Coe, 1972; see Chapter 4 of this book), "imaginative involvement" (Josephine Hilgard, 1970; see Chapter 2), "vividness of imagery and proneness to fantasy" as preconditions of "delusion" (Sutcliffe, 1965; see Chapter 5), and "thinking with and vividly imagining suggested effects" (Spanos & Barber, 1974; see Chapter 3).

Aftermath of the Commissions of 1784

There has always existed a certain amount of cleavage between clinical and experimentally oriented investigators of hypnosis, which exists to the present day. The origins of this cleavage are to be found in the Benjamin Franklin commission's report of 1784. While its inquiry into the existence of animal magnetism represents an immaculate conception for experimental hypnosis, the opposite must be said on the conclusions it drew on the therapeutic value of animal magnetism. The commissioners revealed an unwillingness to treat the issue in a depth similar to which they had examined the question of animal magnetisms existence. On the one hand, they readily admitted to the therapeutic value of faith in the recovery from illness and in religion. This kind of faith they saw as a constructive product of imagination. However, they saw imagination which led to convulsions as an almost invariably destructive consequence of induced imagination. They painted a frightening picture of convulsions, regularly produced, being so violent as to cause the patient to rupture blood vessels and spit up blood. They further raised the spectre of the crisis state, through produced voluntarily at first, becoming habitual. Thus they begged several questions in concluding "that the existence of the fluid is absolutely destitute of proof, and that the fluid, having no existence, can consequently have no use [p. 126]." The commissioners further advised that both the practice and (because of the likelihood of imitation) the witnessing of the practice were dangerous and likely to produce the most pernicious effects. In a secret report to the King, the commissioners outlined the potential moral dangers posed by the magnetic practice of applying touch to the abdomen and to the hypochondriac (ovarian) region.

The report of the commissioners of the Société Royale de Médecine was made public on August 16, 1784, five days after the Benjamin Franklin report. It likewise saw dangers in magnetic cures both with respect to the health of persons treated and with respect to the general public resulting from imitation. However, this commission attempted in the five months allotted to it to evaluate the cures claimed by the magnetists. They distinguished between "illnesses where the diseases were evident and having a known cause" and illness where the diseases were slight and symptoms were vague and of undetermined causes. For the former, this commission reported observing no instance of cure or of even significant improvement. For the latter, significant improvements were reported by patients in many cases. The commission attributed these to hope, regular exercise and (presumably much to the embarrassment of the medical profession) abstinence from the remedies previously taken.

The two reports led to a polarization of public opinion in the years following their publication. Though Mesmerism was ridiculed in many segments of the press and on the stage, the defense of it was spirited. In a deluge of pamphlets, the magnetists reiterated four main lines of criticism of the Benjamin Franklin Commission's handling of the inquiry. They maintained that (a) it had refused to investigate orthodox Mesmeric methods by confining itself to Deslon's practice, which had been denounced by Mesmer, and thus revealed its bias; (b) sheer imagination alone could not produce the extraordinary effects the magnetizers claimed; (c) the commissioners had totally neglected the fact that hundreds of people had been cured by magnetism, and (d) medical practice at this time was dangerous.

Perhaps the most major attack mounted upon the commission by the magnetists was the anonymous publication of 1784 of the *Supplement aux Deux Rapports de MM. les Commissaires* which consisted of a compilation of 115 cases treated by magnetic methods, mainly by Deslon. The list of disorders for which relief and/or cure was claimed is formidable; in particular, animal magnetism was reported to be especially effective in the treatment of gout and rheumatic afflictions. In addition, there were cases recorded of head pain, sciatica, skin disease, congested spleen, convulsive asthma, tumors, body burns, putrid fever, catarrh, and after effects of stroke, various diseases of the abdominal viscera, and various eye diseases. Even allowing for errors of diagnosis by the doctors that patients had seen prior to magnetism and to psychosomatic involvement in many cases there is little reason to doubt that magnetic methods produced a considerable number of successes.

One final aspect of the mesmeric period deserves emphasis, and concerns the subjective and behavioral phenomena induced by magnetic prodcedures. The subjective phenomena most frequently elicited around the *baquet* were sensations of warmth, tickling, and pain. The most common behavioral phenomena observed were vomiting, expectoration, sweating, evacuation, various convulsive behaviors, and a multiplicity of responses that were loosely defined, even by the Benjamin Franklin commission, as "crises." There is however, evidence that certain behaviors that were elicited were overlooked in the general excitement of the mass therapeutic convulsive crisis. Laurent de Jussieu, in his dissenting report from the Société Royale de Médecine Commission's findings, reported the occurrence of both noncathartic crises and more important, of posthypnotic amnesia:

> A young man who was frequently in a state of crises became in that state quite silent, and would go quickly through the hall, often touching the patients. These regular touches of his often brought about a crisis, of which he would take control without allowing anyone to interfere. When he returned to his normal condition he would talk again, but he did not remember anything that had taken place, and no longer knew how to magnetize. I draw no conclusion from this fact, of which I was a witness on several occasions [quoted by Podmore, 1909, p. 70].

Likewise, hypnotic analgesia was not taken seriously (although some reports suggested that it occurred), until it drew attention in some of the Paris hospitals in the early 1820s.

ARTIFICIAL SOMNAMBULISM

Although the experimentation of the commission had settled certain questions about animal magnetism, it was naturalistic observation which provided the next major extension of knowledge about its phenomena. Amand-Marie-Jacques de Chastenet, Marquis de Puységur (1751–1825), who came from one of the most distinguished families of the nobility (one noted for its philanthropic activities) had paid his 2400 livres in 1784 to learn Mesmer's techniques. Feeling that he had failed to comprehend Mesmer's great secret he retired to the family château at Buzancy, about 150 miles from Paris. Here, he proceeded to apply certain variations of Mesmer's methods to the local peasantry with little expectation of success.

From the beginning of his magnetic training, de Puységur had been antipathetic to the magnetic crises produced around the *baquet.* He believed they were the main reason for much of the discrediting of magnetic practices that existed at the time. Even more important, he regarded them as artifactual of the large number of patients that Mesmer had to treat, often single-handed. Because of this, de Puységur reasoned that under such circumstances the crisis, being unsupervised, became more extreme than it need be, because it could not be guided and quietened by the magnetist. He quickly met with success. Two women, suffering from toothache were magnetized without crisis and their condition quickly alleviated within a few minutes. Shortly afterwards, de Puységur had the opportunity to practice this alternate approach to magnetism further and proceeded to stumble across phenomena that had been ignored totally by Mesmer and his followers.

One night he visited Victor Race, a 23-year-old peasant of his estate, who had been suffering inflammation of the lung for the previous four days. De Puységur arrived to find the fever subsiding and proceeded to magnetize him. To his surprise, Victor began speaking in a manner that was more like that of an equal, despite the fact that Victor was, ordinarily, barely articulate in the presence of a superior. Perhaps the most striking feature of Victor's "sleep," from the viewpoint of modern hypnosis, was his inability to recall its events when subsequently awakened. On one occasion Victor, while in "sleep," entrusted a paper of considerable personal importance to de Puységur's safekeeping. On the following day, de Puységur found that Victor had spent the day anxiously looking for this paper. De Puységur labeled this condition artifical somnambulism because of its many superficial similarities to sleepwalking. There is evidence that similar posthypnotic amnesia occurred at times around the baquet; indeed, the Mesmerists made this claim following circulation of de Puységur's experience with Victor. However, they did not give it much attention, and clearly did not see it as integral to magnetic behavior.

The dynamics of Victor's spontaneous posthypnotic amnesia are worth speculating about seeing that spontaneous amnesia is now relatively rare. It is possible that it was very much a product of the type of hypnotic relationship that de Puységur developed with Victor in which rapport was one of the most prominent features. Around the *baquet,* rapport among patients was commonly reported. Once, however, magnetic treatment became established on an individual basis, it was found that the magnetized patient could hear no voice but that of the magnetizer and was exclusively under his influence. Indeed, de Puységur took exclusive rapport as diagnostic of the magnetic state. The transition from a master–peasant relationship to one of close rapport and apparent, though temporary, equality may have created such discontinuity in their relationship as to produce conditions favorable for spontaneous amnesia, at least in a person who had what would now be called hypnotic ability.

De Puységur's work with Victor and other patients laid down some other traditions in the hypnotic literature of a less generally believable kind. He found that Victor and others could diagnose their own ailments, while magnetized, to predict their course and date of final cure, and to prescribe appropriate treatment. Indeed, when the sheer volume of patients became prohibitive, de Puységur like Mesmer before him, magnetized a tree in the public square of Buzancy, and used magnetized patients to diagnose and prescribe for the illness of others.

In 1785, de Puységur took Victor to Paris and demonstrated him to several audiences. A worsening of Victor's condition occurred, which was explained by Victor during magnetic sleep as being directly due to being placed in front of audiences that were often unbelieving. This occurrence strengthened de Puységur's belief in the importance of rapport factors upon the magnetic state—from there onwards he refused all requests to give demonstrations and performances, and would only use magnetic sleep for curative purposes. It also highlights the hypnotized person's awareness of extraneous cues in the induction situation, and echoes the sentiment expressed by the Benjamin Franklin Commission of 1784 that it had decided to visit Deslon's practice as infrequently as possible through fear of offending the patients of rank, since "the very act of watching them might appear a nuisance; and the recollection of this might be burdensome [Franklin *et al.*, 1785, p. 88]."

Throughout his life, de Puységur proclaimed himself as a loyal disciple of Mesmer and never attempted to publicly refute him in any way. However, his own observations of artificial somnambulism led him to articulate principles of magnetism which differed from Mesmer's public pronouncements, though they may indeed have been identical to what Mesmer regarded as the great secret he would never tell. Initially he adopted a variant of mesmeric theory and postulated a fluid composed of dephlogistinated air. From 1785 onwards he began to modify the purely physical theories of Mesmer in favor of a belief in a form of mental transference from the magnetist to the subject, in which primary emphasis was placed upon the magnetist's powers. Such a theory was not altogether divorced from Mesmer's belief in his own ability to harness magnetic forces from the atmosphere, to concentrate them in his person and to transfer them to another person. Both the doctrines of de Puységur and Mesmer explicitly postulated the existence of supranormal powers and abilities possessed by the magnetist, a view that was to haunt the study of hypnosis for much of the nineteenth century.

Although de Puységur, like Mesmer, was led astray on some points by naturalistic observation, these very methods also led to an extension of knowledge as to the nature of magnetic phenomena. His initial belief, and demonstration, that the convulsive crisis could be moderated, provides a starting point for the observation that variations in induction procedure lead to corresponding alterations in the hypnotized person's behavior. This finding, at best implicit during the magnetic period, provides the basis for many modern conceptualizations of hypnotic behavior as having a role-enactment element to it. There is considerable disagreement as to whether role aspects are central to an understanding of hypnosis (see Sarbin, Chapter 4) or are more peripheral in nature (see Orne, Chapter 6). However, there is a general consensus that such role-related behavior is a part of hypnotic phenomena, and the starting point for this belief comes from de Puységur's demonstrations that the convulsive crisis could be assauged, and that the *baquet* was not integral to producing hypnotic phenomena. While he wavered on this point (magnetizing a tree when the volume of patients became excessive), his discovery parallels Mesmer's earlier insight that magnets were not essential to the production of the healing crisis.

There are other modern viewpoints that can be traced to de Puységur's work; for instance, the now generally accepted view that hypnosis required the development of interpersonal rapport and trust in order to be properly effective (see Chapter 8). Likewise, Barber's rejection of state theorizing (see Chapter 3) depends in part upon historical demonstrations (some of which were provided by de Puységur) that hypnotic manifestations vary as a function of the manner in which hypnosis is represented to the subject. As Barber (1969) notes, behaviors such as limpness–relaxation, psychomotor retardation, lack of spontaneity, and fixed facial expression have often been considered as unique to hypnosis but, in fact, tend only to occur when hypnosis is induced using suggestions of relaxation, drowsiness, sleep, and passivitiy. Further, such behaviors are not manifest when suggestions of this type are not administered.

Much of de Puységur's impact was long term and was not well-recognized during his lifetime. Nevertheless, his immediate effect was significant both in terms of the innovations he brought to induction techniques through the moderated crisis and the uncovering of posthypnotic amnesia as a phenomenon integral to hypnosis. The fact that the magnetists subsequently claimed to have observed posthypnotic amnesia but had not perceived its significance illustrates again the way in which methodologies for investigating hypnosis can be affected by the underlying theoretical assumptions of their proponents.

LUCID SLEEP

Commencing around 1813, a third figure began to exert a significant influence upon the history of hypnosis. The Abbé José Custodio di Faria (1756–1819) was a Portuguese priest, who claimed to be a Brahmin. He is a neglected figure in the history of hypnosis; Binet and Féré (1888), for instance, dismiss him as a "thaumaturgist." In his own time, too, he fared little better, partly because of his poor French (although this had not hampered Mesmer) but mainly because of an incident at one of his demonstrations where he failed to recognize the deception of an actor. On the basis of this incident, Faria became the object of ridicule and his ideas were not taken up by many during his lifetime. Most subsequent historians have given credit to Alexandre Bertrand, for ideas that originated with Faria. This is mainly because Faria, unlike Bertrand, lacked medical training, and was taken less seriously in scientific circles (Podmore, 1909). In addition, the widely circulated report of his being deceived by simulation did not add to his credibility.

It is surprizing that Faria remains undervalued and that his contributions are often credited to Bertrand despite the fact that the sequence of events is well-documented. From 1813 onwards, Faria gave public demonstrations of mesmerism which he preferred to call lucid sleep and in 1819 published a book entitled *De La Cause du Sommeil Lucide,* which was intended to be the first part of a longer treatise. His death that year prevented this major project from being carried out. In his first book *Traité du Somnambulisme* (published in 1823) four years after Faria's death, Bertrand was still defending orthodox magnetic doctrines, such as the patient's power to see the interior of the human body and his ability to predict the course of a disease. At this stage he believed that such phenomena could be explained by an instinctive perception of organic processes, which he considered to be a human equivalent of the nest building and migratory instinct in birds. It is not until his book *Du Magnétisme Animal en France* (published in 1826) that Bertrand specifically repudiated the central magnetic doctrine of an external force, and attributed the phenomena of magnetism to imagination. Further, one of Faria's subjects, Général Noizet in his *Mémoire sur le Somnambulisme et le Magnétisme Animal* (written in 1820 but not published until 1855) stated that he became convinced of the correctness of Faria's position and passed his views on to Bertrand. It may be true that Bertrand's notions of the central role of imagination in hypnosis express a more sophisticated doctrine than Faria's; nevertheless, the original debt is to Faria. Bertrand's contribution was important nevertheless, in its amalgamation of Faria's theories with the conclusions of the Benjamin Franklin commission. To fully appreciate the extent to which Faria's thinking departed radically from contemporary beliefs, it is necessary to look briefly at certain early 19th century developments. The French Revolution temporarily halted the further spread of animal magnetism. The Sociétés de l'Harmonie disappeared, except for those which became Jacobin societies in 1789. Many of the aristocrats who had adopted magnetism were either executed or fled the country; three of the Commissioners of 1784—Bailly, Lavoisier, and Thouret—were guillotined.

The main preoccupation of this period continued to be with the conclusions of the Benjamin Franklin Commission of 1784. Because it had failed to come to grips with the fact that many cures were obtained using magnetic techniques, a number of animal fluidic theories (as opposed to magnetic theories) developed in the early 19th century. All attempted to provide alternate explanations of the Commissioners' conclusion that animal magnetism was no more than a matter of imagination, imitation, and touch, and hence could not be curative.

Thus, there existed at this time a variety of beliefs such as that of de Jussieu that the phenomena elicited by Mesmer could be explained in terms of animal heat, which was conceived of (in terms as equally broad as animal magnetism) as a principle underlying the universe. Likewise, Pétetin in his book *Electricité Animale* (published in 1808) believed that magnetic phenomena could be explained in terms of accumulations of animal electric fluid in the body, and the notion that disease drove vital fluid from the peripheries to the brain and nervous system. He supported this conclusion with a series of remarkable experiments on transposition of the senses in cataleptic patients. In the cataleptic state, these patients could not seemingly hear, but could reply to questions addressed to the pit of the stomach, the fingertips and/or toes. Such patients were often found to be able to taste, smell, or see in these regions exclusively. There were many other theories at this time proposed in similar vein. The observations on which they were based indicate some of the excesses and errors of the naturalistic methods of the period.

Given this historical context, it is not surprizing that Faria's views about magnetism were neither welcomed nor appreciated. This is especially so since he expressed them with little respect for the Magnetists' sensitilities. The last two chapters of his book *De la Cause du Sommeil Lucide* (1819) were variously entitled "On the absurdity of the action of an external will in the provocation of lucid sleep" (which attacked the view that magnetists possessed special skills to command external forces) and "On the futility of the supposition of a magnetic force," in which his rejection of magnetic theories was uncompromising:

> I am not able to conceive how the human species can be so bizarre that it has to search out the cause of this phenomenon in a baquet, in some external force, in a magnetic fluid, in animal heat and in a thousand other ridiculous extravagances of this nature when this type of sleep is common to all human nature by dreams and to all individuals who get up, walk, and talk in their sleep [Faria, 1819, p. 33; for this and all subsequent quotations from Faria].

Faria's views have a distinctively modern character, even though at times they are laced with large doses of the theology and medical science of his period. The latter was dominated by notions of spirits and sympathies and was due to a comparative lack of factual data on the nervous system and its disorders. To distinguish himself from the magnetic movement, he developed his own vocabulary. He referred to magnetism as *concentration,* performed by a *concentrationist* (magnetizer) upon a *concentrated* (subject). He referred further to somnambulism as *lucid sleep,* and to somnambulists as *époptes,* a term coined from Greek.

He believed that "the supposition of a magnetic fluid is totally absurd, whether we consider its nature, its applications, or its results [p. 360]." The main basis for this conclusion was his observation that there were individual differences in response to the techniques for inducing lucid sleep. He had not been the first person to notice this; Mesmer had been puzzled by individual differences in response to the *baquet,* but Faria was the first to emphasize this fact, and to make it the cornerstone of his theoretical position. More important, Faria proceeded to document some of these individual differences. He observed (on the basis of experience with over 5000 people) that "experiments and observations demonstrated that lucid sleep, which adapts itself to climates, temperaments, and to the quality of foods, is in France in the ratio of one in five or six of the population [p. 142]." Similar individual differences in hypnotic response are still being observed over 150 years later.

Faria went on to state that animal magnetism was not the result of a magnetist having special skills in harnessing external forces and transferring them to sick people with curative effects. In flat contradiction of this belief, he was the first to argue that the magnetized person was the main active agent in what transpired; "We cannot induce concentration in individuals whenever we desire; rather we find people who are inherently susceptible [p. 34]." To emphasize the minor role played by the magnetist, he performed demonstrations in which children magnetized adults by the presentation of a hand.

His own theory was influenced by contemporary medicine, particularly the view that prevailed at this period that peripheral blood flow could be relatively thick or thin; though, in the arteries it was always thick. Faria seized this notion to explain the ability of *époptes*. He believed that thinness of the blood was a prerequisite condition for high hypnotic susceptibility. In support of this claim, he reported that he was able to modify hypnotizability in recalcitrant persons by extracting blood and rehypnotizing them successfully 24 hours later. He noted also, certain psychological characteristics that were conducive to hypnotizability, observing that women were more susceptible than men and that trained, experienced subjects were more susceptible than novitiates. Likewise, he noted that susceptibles were most often found among people who fall asleep easily, perspire profusely, and are highly impressionable. He also advanced an eye-movement criterion of susceptibility, believing that *époptes* could be distinguished by a rapid and sustained fluttering of eyelashes when the eyes are slightly closed.

These observations, based upon a mistaken physiology of the nervous system, led him to conclude that the most susceptible subjects for hypnosis were anemics, hysterics, and highly impressionable people. It is interesting that he considered a more likely theory and rejected it. This is the theory, first proposed by the Benjamin Franklin Commission and subsequently espoused by Bertrand, that lucid sleep was primarily a matter of the person's imaginative skills. His main reason for rejecting imagination was due to the close parallels he drew between lucid and nocturnal sleep, a view that affected much thinking about hypnosis until electroencephalographic methods were used in the 1950s to demonstrate their physiological dissimilarity. He felt it was sufficient to discount imagination as the decisive factor by simple recourse to the phenomenon of posthypnotic amnesia, observing that one remembers all that is imagined, whereas after lucid sleep one often forgets some or all of the events that have transpired.

Although he was mistaken about the causes of lucid sleep, his emphasis on individual differences and his belief that subject characteristics were responsible for these differences represented an important historical point in the history of hypnosis. This is especially so, given that he lived in an era where the magnetic movement was inclined to postulate progressively more esoteric external forces to explain the phenomena its adherents observed. For this alone, Faria would be important, but there were other views of his that merit attention.

Perhaps his most radical departure from the magnetic movement was the induction techniques he developed. The elaborate rituals of the *baquet,* of spells, and of magnetized trees were replaced by simpler, suggestive methods. Faria tended to choose subjects whom he considered had the requisite predispositions, as predicted by his theory. He would then seat them on a chair and ask them to close their eyes, and focus their attention on sleep. After a period of presumably progressively greater relaxation and concentration of attention he would instruct them with one word: "sleep." He would use this technique for up to three trials before concluding that the person lacked the requisite abilities. There were other variants used with recalcitrant subjects–at times he would use an eye fixation technique of having the person fixate on his open hand and gradually move the hand closer to the person's face. On other occasions he would lightly touch the person on various parts of the head, face, and body. To terminate lucid sleep he would simply tell the person to wake up.

It is clear that he regarded these techniques as primarily suggestive, but these in turn were effective only because of the powers of concentration possessed by *époptes.* He observed that "the sleep that results from the presentation of the concentrator's hand is only an effect of the *épopte's* concentration. At the sight of this behavior, the *époptes* see what is required from them and they immediately lend themselves to fulfilling these demands, and sometimes even in spite of themselves, by the power of conviction [p. 356]."

Faria's induction procedures produced at times, interesting behaviors. It is not certain whether these were based upon what was known by subjects of the effects of animal magnetism or were the result of Faria's subjects perceiving the simple instruction "sleep," as an authoritative command. But he notes that "it often happens that natural *époptes,* at the simple word *sleep,* given without any other elaboration, gestures or touchings, fall into a faint, manifesting abundant perspirations, feeling suffocations and palpitations of the heart, and if they achieve sleep it is only in the context of spasms and convulsions and without the intervention of intuition [p. 58]."

Faria thus gave little importance to the role of suggestion in producing the phenomena of lucid sleep, placing the main burden of explanation on the inherent abilities of *époptes.* Almost paradoxically, however, he made a number of crucial distinctions between different types of suggestions. He distinguished, for instance, between suggestions carried out in lucid sleep and posthypnotic suggestions. He also noted the existence of waking suggestion, even in naive subjects who had never experienced lucid sleep, noting that the experience of a waking suggestion was rarely as complete as that achieved in lucid sleep. Further, he accepted the existence of autosuggestion–he believed it to be one of the bases of posthypnotic suggestion, which might be also one of the mechanisms determining the success of a therapeutic suggestion. He also saw it as the main causal effect underlying the performance of fakirs and the manifestation of apparent miracles.

Perhaps most interestingly of all, Faria distinguished all of the previous types of suggestion from therapeutic suggestions. In his discussion of these he showed a conservatism that marked him off from the more florid claims of the magnetic movement and distinguished him as one of the first people working clinically with hypnosis to show a genuine understanding of the processes underlying cure. He emphasized that hypnotic techniques did not always work and indeed could be extremely dangerous if not fatal: "If one reviews past experience objectively, one should realize that concentration has produced both good and bad effects in susceptible people, and often no effect in people lacking the necessary disposition. Concentration can only be used with particular illnesses and by people who are familiar with it [p. 276]."

Some of Faria's observations showed an almost amazing awareness of placebo effects which are an important concern of the modern researcher. He recognized that an ineffective medicine, taken with confidence is more beneficial than effective medicine, and that such confidence could be induced by suggestion. He quite frequently used hypnotically induced placebos in his treatments. Thus, he observed that "a glass of water swallowed with the notion that it is eau-de-vie completely intoxicates; with the notion of an emetic it induces vomiting without effort or suffering. . . . The result is that a placebo ("poudre indifferente") .,. . can be as effective as medication, and this involves the *épopte's* control over the internal organs following the instructions of their concentrators [p. 6]."

Like de Puységur, Faria is important both for anticipating issues that continue to affect present-day thinking and for his further defining of the phenomena of hypnosis. His use of the simple command "sleep" provided, like artifical somnambulism, further observational data that hypnotic behavior can be elicited by a wide variety of induction procedures and can occur despite variations in the manner in which it is represented to the subject. Likewise, his analysis of cure by suggestive means demonstrated an appreciation of psychosomatic interaction and of placebo effects that is remarkable for its sophistication and insight into some of the mechanisms of suggestion.

At the same time Faria, as had de Puységur with posthypnotic amnesia, extended the range of hypnotic phenomena that need to be accounted for. Though ignored during his lifetime, he was the first to document the fact of individual differences in hypnotizability. Likewise his belief that hypnotizability depends upon abilities and skills of the hypnotized person continues to find a major place in the theorizing of modern investigators such as Hilgard (Chapter 2), Sutcliffe (Chapter 5), Sarbin (Chapter 4), and in the methodologies or procedural orientations of all investigators we discuss with the exception of Barber (Chapter 3). The use of experimental designs comparing subjects of high and low susceptibility testify importantly to the significance of Faria's observation of individual differences in hypnotizability, though as we shall see (in Chapter 9) there is still considerable confusion in the hypnotic literature as to how important is the skill of hypnotizability in determining hypnotic outcomes.

FLUID VERSUS FRAUD

Despite the Benjamin Franklin Commission's conclusion that animal magnetism did not exist, and despite Faria's work, which was ignored, the doctrine of animal magnetism continued to increase in respectability during the 1820s. This was entirely the result of the 1784 Commission's mishandling of the issue of cure. Magnetic journals were started, the Academy of Berlin offered a prize for the best essay on the subject, a Russian commission to the Tsar had reported favorably, and in Prussia and Denmark, laws had been passed to permit and confine the practice of magnetism to the medical profession. Experiments with magnetism began to be conducted in 1819 in two Paris hospitals—the Hôtel Dieu, and the Salpêtrière. Further, Bertrand, then a young physician, gave a popular series of lectures on the topic in the same year. As Binet and Féré (1888, p. 33) observed "in 1820 it might have been supposed that animal magnetism was about to enter upon a scientific era," but it was not to be.

The hospital experiments precipitated a renewed set of tensions within medical circles concerning the nature of magnetic phenomena. Nevertheless, the substantive issues were, in essence, a reformulation of the points of contention that had preoccupied investigators for the previous 35 years. The magnetists continued to use the many evidences of cure to buttress their claim that something more than imagination (a term which came to take on progressively more derogatory connotations) had to be involved. There seemed to be always enough cures to sustain this belief. The opponents of this doctrine seized upon a variant of the conclusion reached by the Benjamin Franklin Commission, and began to reformulate imagination in terms which equated it with fraudulence. In the short run this had a detrimental effect upon the study of hypnosis—an effect which was to persist until the 1880s. It recast the issues into an acrimonious dispute which was stated in terms of what Podmore (1909) has called the question of "fluid or fraud."

As a result, investigation was polarized between these two positions and other alternatives could not be considered seriously. This is the main reason for many subsequent historians considering the 19th century as one of sterility (Hull, 1933). But in actuality, the controversy had a very major and positive effect—the fact that adherents of the fraudulence viewpoint were never able to administer the *coup de grâce* necessary to uphold their position gave a certain long-term credibility to the belief that hypnotic phenomena have a certain reality, and are not simply artifacts of fallible verbal reportage, self-delusion or deliberate attempts at deception. In the short term, however, the failure of the fraud theorists to prove their case reinforced the magnetic position.

The experiments in the Paris hospitals which initiated this renewal of contentious debate usually involved female hysterical patients, who when magnetized, often gave seemingly dramatic evidence of being able to diagnose physical illness. One patient at the Hôtel Dieu for example, while magnetized was able to see her stomach filled with small red and white pimples which she pronounced incurable. At the side of her heart, she also saw a sac of blood and a fine thread which made her heart beat. She was able to prescribe for the latter and showed a rapid improvement of health. Experiments such as these began to become embarrassing, especially when the occasional patient (some of whom became mildly famous in medical circles in their own right) admitted to outright deception. The hospital council became alarmed and suspended the experiments. Nonetheless, the studies generated interest within the medical profession. Accordingly, a commission of inquiry was established by the Académie de Médecine in 1826 to investigate these phenomena and the claims made on their behalf. This commission, consisting of nine doctors, produced a report five years later in 1831.

The commissioners were concerned primarily with the question of whether animal magnetism existed as some kind of external force emanating from the magnetist. Unfortunately, they chose to test this hypothesis under poorly controlled conditions of observation using subjects who claimed to have extraordinary powers when magnetized. Thus, they concentrated on a very small sample of 12–14 persons who believed they had abilities such as visionless sight, prevision, and clairvoyance. The commission concluded that the majority of cases could be explained in terms of weariness, monotony, and imagination. It nonetheless gave support for the existence of an animal magnetic force—but by default. It concluded that some cases could not be explained in terms of imagination so that an animal magnetic force must exist as the only other viable alternative. This conclusion was based upon the performances of one or two patients, observed under inadequate control conditions. For instance, one of the subjects involved appeared capable of visionless sight. When observed, his eyes appeared to be so tightly shut, that his eye lashes interlaced. No attempt was made to apply a blindfold in order to eliminate the possibility of him being able to see something despite this interlacing. For various reasons, the Académie refused to publish the report.

A subsequent commission was established by the Académie in 1837. Its initial impetus seemed innocuous enough, stemming from a small number of reports of painless surgery effected by magnetic means. One of these involved a painless dental extraction by a member of the Académie, Oudet, after the patient had been magnetized by Hamard, a young physician. Another (some years earlier in 1829 by Cloquet), involved the excision of an ulcerated breast cancer in an elderly woman. Both reports were, naturally, of interest to the medical profession, but created considerable polarization within it. Certain critiques of the analgesic mechanisms involved in Cloquet's patients illustrate the over-commitment of some proponents of the fraud position. The patient's reports of painless surgery were dismissed by many proponents of fraud because, in addition to having a clearly diagnosed breast cancer, the woman had previously diagnosed herself, while magnetized, as having a diseased liver. She died of pleurisy three weeks after her breast surgery, and the subsequent autopsy revealed no such liver disease. Accordingly, many proponents of fraud believed that the woman in question was a pathological liar. They argued that a person who was capable of lying about her liver could not be trusted when she pretended to feel no pain during surgery. Others were apt to dismiss such testimony as merely indicating that pain can be suppressed voluntarily. One doctor even suggested that the patient's remorse for perpetrating a fraud had contributed to her death. Such views may now appear faintly ridiculous. However, it should be noted that certain propositions of the Gate-Control Theory (Melzack & Wall, 1965) which postulates a plurality of pain control mechanisms (including psychological ones) often elicit a similar disbelief.

The Commission of 1837, composed of nine doctors, set itself specific and scientifically legitimate terms of reference. These were based upon an offer by Berna, a young physician, to provide demonstrations; of somnambulism as a special state, of the insensibility of magnetized persons to pain, and of his ability to affect the patient's behavior by nonverbal means. This offer was received favorably, probably because it gave promise of shedding light on the pain issue. However, the investigation quickly became preoccuped with the nonverbal communication issue. As in 1831, the commission allowed itself to be sidetracked into issues concerning the ability of magnetized patients to transcend ordinary human faculties and to exhibit manifestations of the near miraculous.

The commission produced a report within a few months using two subjects tested over four sessions. In some respects the investigation of 1837 was slightly more methodologically sophisticated than the report of six years prior. Despite the small sample, at least blindfolds were used to investigate claims of visionless sight. The report itself was either negative or inconclusive on all of the terms of reference it had been given to investigate.

On the question of magnetic somnambulism as a special or altered state, the commissioners concluded that behavioral tests were negative and that all evidences for a special state were in the form of assertions by the magnetist that such was the case. They used pinpricks before and after induction of magnetism and found that the one magnetized subject used was equally insensitive to them on both occasions. By contrast the commission's conclusions concerning increased pain tolerance were inconclusive because the Académie placed so many restrictions on the type of experimental pain that could be attempted as to render the pain stimuli innocuous. On the nonverbal communication issue, the commissioners concluded that the patient's reports of leg paralysis and alterations of sensibility did not correspond with the occasions that the magnetist willed these phenomena to occur. All of these conclusions were based on one of the two patients used. A second patient was used to demonstrate visionless sight and clairvoyance with equally negative results; for instance, in the clairvoyancy test, this patient consistently saw objects different to those presented in front of her bandaged eyes.

Many of these conclusions were justified, given the nature of the questions being asked. However, because of the preoccupation with the issue of extraordinary powers, little attention was given to the less dramatic phenomena observed. The patient in the clairvoyancy test had described such objects as a gold watch in minute detail when only a railway ticket had been presented before her bandaged eyes. Interesting issues about hypnotic hallucination were thus ignored because questions concerning fluid, fraud, and clarvoyancy were at stake. Likewise, there is a pertinent fact underlying Berna's belief that he could influence conduct nonverbally; we are all now aware of how subjects can respond to implicit, nonverbal cues in the hypnotic interaction (Orne, 1959). Neither Berna nor the commissioners recognized the importance of these phenomena because the wrong questions were asked and because the only two answers that were possible (fluid or fraud) were both wrong.

The fraud position was predicated upon the basic fallacy that imagination (as expounded by the Benjamin Franklin Commission) could be reformulated to mean "not real." Just as the commissioners had mistakenly concluded that because an animal magnetic force did not exist, it could not have curative effects, the proponents of fraud assumed that imagination (redefined in this way) were merely a matter of deliberate falsification. Many present-day investigators have reasserted the importance of imaginational phenomena to hypnosis, and have emphasized their reality in the sense that imaginative phenomena appear to represent some of the more important ongoing internal processes of the person while hypnotized.

While this present-day trend has corrected the misrepresentation of a major issue by the nineteenth century proponents of fraud, some elements of this position continue to linger. Some critics of state theorizing in hypnosis appear to uphold a variant of the fraud position. Barber, for example (see Barber, 1969; also, Chapter 3), criticizes the notion of hypnosis as an altered state on the grounds that many behaviors thought to be unique to hypnosis can be obtained without it. By assuming that equivalent processes are operating in both hypnotic and nonhypnotic conditions, he comes close to asserting that nothing distinctive is in need of explanation. [See also a recent critique of hypnotic analgesia in surgery by Barber, Spanos, and Chaves (1974) which questions its reality using similar arguments.] Likewise Sarbin's rejection of the altered state notion, and his theorizing about hypnosis as a form of role enactment (see Chapter 4) has been misinterpreted to mean that he sees hypnosis as a form of sham behavior. Any modern-day account of hypnosis that views it as a form of extreme compliance likewise represents a carry over of the fraud position.

THE RISE OF SUGGESTIBILITY THEORY

The immediate effect of the two nineteenth century French commissions was to stifle investigation of hypnosis almost entirely for the next 50 years. The general tenor of thought can be seen by the fact that following the Commission of 1837, Burdin, a member of the Académie offered a prize of 3,000 francs to anyone who could demonstrate visionless sight under exacting experimental conditions. While there were several contestants, the prize was never awarded, and the study of hypnotic phenomena in France tailed off into a spiritualist movement, which had been gathering force gradually since the beginning of the century. The reasons for this are understandable. Given that some external force (magnetic or otherwise) might exist, it is natural that the spiritualists would want to know about it. While this development led to some highly creditable work by the Society of Psychical Research in England in the last decades of the nineteenth century, the general drift into spiritualism led to many important questions being held in abeyance for almost a century.

Fortunately there were a few honorable exceptions to this generalization. The Benjamin Franklin Commission contained the beginnings of a large number of alternate explanations of magnetic phenomena that were primarily psychological in nature. These tended to be ignored in the ensuing controversies about the curative value of magnetic procedures. Faria's observations were likewise ignored as were those of Noizet (a layman). Bertrand, though held in personal respect in medical circles, fared little better. In all cases, the thrust of their thinking involved an attempt to explain animal magnetism in terms of the inner workings of the hypnotized person, rather than prevailing magnetic doctrines of external forces and fluids. These earlier investigators had a variety of different notions as to what psychological processes were involved. But regardless of whether primary attention was directed to imagination, to analogies with sleep and somnambulism, or to suggestion as the crucial factor, the emphasis in all cases was upon characteristics of the hypnotized person and/or the social interaction between hypnotist and subject. Each of these doctrines died with their originators only to be picked up and reformulated by later investigators. One such person was James Braid (1795–1860), a Manchester surgeon, who apart from coining the term hypnosis, is historically important for continuing and adding to this slowly emerging minority emphasis on the subject's internal processes which is now almost universal among present-day investigators.

James Braid and Neurypnology

Subsequent historians have been ambivalent in their evaluation of Braid's contribution to the history of hypnosis. To Binet and Féré (1888, p. 67) he is "the initiator of the scientific study of animal magnetism," a view shared by Bramwell (1906). In contrast Janet (1925, p. 156) considers his importance to have been overestimated and that "his works contain no essential new facts," by which he meant that Bertrand, Faria, and Noizet anticipated all that Braid had to say. In his lifetime, Braid was sensitive to the charge of "unacknowledged plagiarism" (Braid, 1843, p. 6) and in his book of that year took pains to differentiate his views from those of Bertrand and Faria. Certainly, it is true that Braid's ideas about the nature of hypnosis, and his induction methods, show striking affinities with the views of these earlier workers. While one is inclined to agree with Hull (1933, p. 10) that Braid's discoveries occurred "relatively independent and isolated" from those of the French investigators, he appears, nevertheless, to have read much of this literature. Initially Braid saw hypnosis as some form of sham behavior, a product of "collusion or illusion, or of excited imagination, sympathy, or imitation [Braid, 1843, p. 15]." He had come to this premature conclusion as the result of witnessing a demonstration by the French magnetist Lafontaine in 1841, though he returned for further sessions. As the result of observing the patient's inability to open his eyes, he became convinced that a physiological explanation of the phenomena was possible. At this stage, he believed that hypnosis consisted of "a derangement of the state of cerebro-spinal centres, and of the circulatory, and respiratory, and muscular centres, induced . . . by a fixed stare, absolute repose of body, fixed attention, and suppressed respiration, concomitant with this fixidity of attention [Braid, 1843, p. 19]."

Even at this early stage, one can see indications of a psychological notion of hypnosis in his references to fixidity of attention as an integral part of the process. Other anticipations of his later views are also to be found scattered through this earlier work. Thus, he gave some emphasis to the facts of individual differences in hypnotizability by observing that it is "unquestionable that there exists great differences in the susceptibility of different individuals, some becoming rapidly and intensely affected, others slowly and feebly so [Braid, 1843, p. 25]." Further, as part of his defense against the charge that he had plagiarized from Bertrand, Braid observed that Bertrand had invoked imagination to explain hypnotic phenomena, whereas he, himself, had never done so, and in fact believed that completely different processes were involved. Nevertheless, he was willing to concede that "the oftener patients are hypnotized, from association of ideas or habits, the more susceptible they become; and in this way they are liable to be affected *entirely through the imagination* [Braid, 1843, p. 36]." It is obvious that, from the beginning Braid's physiologizing was not thoroughgoing.

Braid like Faria, viewed hypnosis as analogous to sleep, and drew similar parallels. However, he preferred to call the phenomenon *nervous sleep* rather than *lucid sleep.* Like Faria, Braid also developed his own terminology to describe the phenomena, which has become the terminology of current usage. Initially, he used the term *Neuro-hypnology* (from the Greek *hypnos;* to sleep), which he contracted to *neurypnology* for a time, before setting on the less awkward terms of "hypnotize," "hypnotism," and "hypnotist." Many of his initial notions stemmed from the austere induction methods he developed (some of which were similar to Faria's). They involved having the subject fixate an object above eye level so as to produce a heavy strain on the eyes and eyelids. This ordinarily led to the following phenomena:

"In three minutes his eyelids closed, a gush of tears ran down his cheeks, his head drooped, his face was slightly convulsed, he gave a groan, and instantly fell into profound sleep, the respiration became slow, deep and silibant, the right hand being agitated by slight convulsive movements [Braid, 1843, p. 17]."

There may have been much implicit suggestion operating in this situation, but Braid, due to his medical training, initially saw such phenomena as primarily physiological in nature. In subsequent works (Braid, 1846, 1855), his position became progressively more psychological as he gave increasing emphasis to the role of suggestion in eliciting hypnotic phenomena. Indeed, he himself (Braid, 1855, p. 372) suggested that the term *psychophysiology* be used generically to describe all the phenomena of hypnosis which "result from the reciprocal actions of mind and matter upon each other," and which he believed were stimulated by suggestion. Many of these developments are seen in his pamphlet *The Power of the Mind over the Body* (Braid, 1846). This publication was concerned primarily with refuting the observations of Von Reichenbach, a magnetist. The latter had reported studies of individuals who, while magnetized, were able to see colored light waves and flames emanating from the magnets used by the magnetist and even from the magnetist's fingertips. Braid was able to demonstrate, using experimental techniques similar to that of the Benjamin Franklin Commission, that the phenomena reported by these "sensitives" were really hypnotic hallucinations. This particular study appears to have been crucial in leading Braid away from a predominantly physiological account of hypnosis to a more psychological one. This is probably because his earlier (1843) study was mainly concerned with the facts of hypnotic induction; in refuting the observations of Von Reichenbach the object of study was events occurring within hypnosis. A different approach was needed to understand a broader set of phenomena, and Braid was flexible enough to realize this.

Although theorizing was kept to a minimum in this paper (Braid, 1846), much emphasis was given to subject characteristics and to mind–body interactions in providing an alternate explanation of Von Reichenbach's experiments. "It is an undoubted fact," observed Braid (1846, p. 334), "that with many individuals, and especially of the highly nervous, and imaginative, and abstractive classes, a strong direction of inward consciousness to any part of the body, especially if attended with the expectation or belief of something being about to happen, is quite sufficient to change *the physical action of the part, and to produce such impressions from this cause alone, as Baron Reichenbach attributes to his new force.*" This emphasis is expressed more forcefully in *The Physiology of Fascination and the Critics Criticised* (1855) published five years before Braid's death. In this paper, he argued that hypnosis is a state of heightened concentration of attention (monoideism) in which imagination, belief, and expectancy are more intense than in waking.

Braid is also interesting for his view of hypnosis as being confined to those individuals capable of amnesia. "All short of this is mere reverie, or dreaming, however provoked [Braid, 1855, p. 370]." Thus, he recognized that there are differences in response to hypnotic instructions, but felt that only responsivity to the more difficult hypnotic items qualified as hypnosis. Within this group, Braid distinguished between two types of responsivity–*hypnotism* and *hypnotic coma.* This distinction reveals something of Braid's hypnotic techniques. People who were posthypnotically amnesic, but could retrieve the events of a previous induction in a subsequent induction were described as being in *hypnotism.*

Hypnotic coma was reserved for "deeper" cases whose posthypnotic amnesia could not be broken in subsequent inductions. The subsequent history of hypnosis has revealed that these phenomena are in part dependent upon the hypnotist's and subject's belief that the events of trance cannot be retrieved posthypnotically; amnesia itself has a suggestive component to it.

It may be true that everything Braid said was anticipated by Faria and Bertrand. Indeed his views on hypnosis constitute an interesting amalgam of Faria's analogy with sleep and Bertrand's emphasis on the role of imagination. In addition, he focussed upon suggestion as being an important determinant of the subjective phenomena elicited by hypnosis. His emphasis on expectations and beliefs of the hypnotized person draws attention to a greater range of mental processes that may be occurring within the hypnotized person than hitherto, and predates Barber's later concern with the role of motives, attitudes, and sets in determining hypnotic outcomes (see Chapter 3).

Although all subsequent historians have correctly pointed to Braid's importance, his contemporary impact was minimal. Throughout his career he was attacked both by the magnetists (whose ideas continued to dominate thinking about hypnosis) and by many of his medical colleagues who were unable to distinguish his views from that of the magnetists. His beliefs died in England with his own death but were retrieved, and added to, in France at around this same period. This occurred despite the fact that serious investigation of hypnosis in France was still suffering the negative affects of the two commissions of the 1830s.

Liébeault and Bernheim

Most of the initial historical debt for continuing the traditions of a psychologically oriented approach to hypnosis is to Auguste Liébeault (1823–1904). However, his contribution would probably have died with him, as with all previous proponents of this viewpoint, but for the fortunate accident of his geographic proximity to Hippolyte Bernheim (1837–1919), a medical professor at the University of Nancy, and for other reasons to be mentioned shortly.

In the period from 1860 to 1880, stage hypnosis flourished, and some work was carried out on so-called animal hypnosis in an attempt to circumvent the imputation of fraud, which lingered long after the inconclusive findings of the 1837 Commission. It was a period in which a doctor practicing hypnosis risked his professional career and his practice. Liébeault, a country doctor working for much of his career in a small village near Nancy, was one such practitioner. He appears to have read Noizet's book, and it is possible that he came into contact with Braid's views which were being disseminated in France by Azam and Durand de Gros during the late 1850s. Because of the dubious reputation enjoyed by hypnosis at this period, Liébeault made a bargain with his patients; he could either treat them with orthodox medicine for a fee or by hypnotic means without charge. He soon established an enormous practice, for which he received negligible income. Within the medical profession he was, accordingly, regarded as a fool, both for using hypnosis and for his refusal to take a fee. It was the temper of the times that were about to change. His book, *Sleep, and the state analagous to it, specially considered in the action of the morale of the physique* (published in 1866) sold only one copy. In it he emphasized the role of suggestion in producing hypnotic phenomena. Bernheim subsequently became interested in his work as the result of Liébeault successfully treating a patient by hypnotic means for a sciatica of six years standing which Bernheim had been unable to modify. He proceeded to adopt Liébeault's methods with similar success, and indeed rescued Liébeault from almost certain oblivion.

Bernheim's work represents the final emergence of the minority belief about hypnosis being a psychological phenomenon–a characteristic of the subject that can be set in motion by suggestion–and in his theorizing he gave suggestion a central, explanatory role. Whereas both Liébeault and Braid had regarded suggestion as causative but not explanatory of hypnosis, Bernheim regarded suggestion as both. Hypnosis, he believed was a form of activated and intensified suggestibility. Although this is essentially a circular view, it led to certain interesting implications. Bernheim took hypnotic phenomena to be magnifications of waking-life tendencies. He noted the incidence of spontaneously-occurring illusions, errors, and hallucinations. He also noted the tendency to act upon the ideas suggested in waking life; however the difference was that ordinarily one cognitated before acting, whereas, in hypnosis, such was not the case.

On Bernheim's view, suggestion caused people to enter hypnosis, and the state, once entered, further intensified the initial evoked tendencies. His recognition of "normal susceptibility to suggestion, which we all possess to some degree [Bernheim, 1890, p. 149]" further enabled him to account for individual differences in hypnotic depth. He argued that individuals are initially different in waking-life suggestibility, and will manifest the same degree of suggestibility in hypnosis which is itself a state of heightened suggestibility. It can be seen from this that Bernheim's views anticipate the current interest in "base-rates for hypnotic behavior"–a theme which is discussed in detail in other sections of this book (Chapters 2, 4, 7, and 9).

While the views of Liébeault and Bernheim can now be seen to have had a clear impact on present-day thinking, it took one further historical accident for the psychologically-oriented viewpoint to emerge as the potentially more plausible model for understanding hypnotic phenomena. It might have continued to remain a minority tradition for much longer, but for a unique set of circumstances which permitted a confrontation between magnetic and person-oriented views of hypnosis. While confrontations, as we have seen, had occurred sporadically in the preceding century, it was not until the 1880s that it occurred *within* the medical profession, between two highly respected physicians of equal prestige. Further, the substantive issues were such, that it was possible to make a clear choice between the two traditional ways of viewing hypnosis. All of these conditions were fulfilled in what has been subsequently referred to as the conflict between the "schools" of Nancy and the Salpêtrière. The result of this controversy was a clear refutation of magnetic doctrines.

THE DEMISE OF MAGNETIC DOCTRINES

The Salpêtrière Hospital in Paris had a long tradition of serious interest in hypnosis which dated back to the first decades of the 19th century. It was there that some of the experiments leading to the commission of 1831 were performed; also, Bertrand had delivered a series of well-received lectures on magnetism in 1819. In 1862, Jean-Martin Charcot (1835–1893) became medical director of one of the hospital's larger sections.

Charcot was a neurologist, and at the height of his fame was justly regarded as one of the great scientists of his era. As Ellenberger (1970, p. 94) has pointed out "he and Pasteur were to the French a proof of France's scientific genius, challenging Germany's alleged scientific superiority." His early work at the Salpêtrière from 1862–1870 which established his reputation as a neurologist, concerned diseases of the spinal cord. He thus brought to the study of hypnosis the training and preconceptions of one "accustomed to the examination of patients suffering from locomotor ataxia or from lateral schlerosis [Janet, 1925, p. 166]." In 1870, Charcot was given responsibility for a ward of the Salpêtrière consisting of female convulsive patients. The patient group composition was mixed; it consisted of epileptics and patients suffering from hysterical conversion reactions that were difficult to distinguish from epilepsy. Charcot began to seek distinguishing criteria using the methods that had served him so well in his earlier neurological studies. Thus he studied the reflexes and muscles of these two groups of patients using standard neurological tests to distinguish hysterical conversion from genuine impairment of the nervous system. Much of the work was done in conjunction with Paul Richet, a colleague who was meanwhile writing extensively on hypnosis. At a time when attitudes against hypnosis had hardened, as a result of the fluid or fraud controversy, Richet was laying a groundwork for its revival. His writings of this period centered around demonstrating that the phenomena of hypnosis could not be accounted for in terms of gullibility, fraud and the mutual self-deceptions of hypnotist and subject.

Charcot appears to have been greatly influenced by Richet's thinking and together they began to investigate hypnosis at the Salpêtriére around 1878. The purpose was to demonstrate hypnosis as a specific state which could be shown to have different stages. More important, they wished to show that these stages had characteristic symptoms which could be demonstrated, using precise and objective neurological and behavioral criteria. In this endeavor, Charcot thought he was using the same methods as had been brought to bear on the study of the spinal cord and the differentiation of hysterical from neurological epilepsy. However, he made the error of ignoring all he had learned about hysteria in these earlier studies, particularly the fact that hysterics often possess extraordinary abilities to mimic the symptoms of organic conditions, to the extent, often, of being able to deceive experienced medical practitioners for long periods of time. In addition, he made the fatal error of using a small sample of his most talented female hysterics.

Charcot can be regarded as representing a scientifically acceptable variant of the magnetic position, since he believed that he was inducing hypnosis by external mechanical means. Indeed it was believed at the Salpêtriére that hypnosis could be induced without the person even realizing it. At a later time, one other piece of magnetic lore also crept into the methods of the Salpêtriére. In some patients, a paralysis or muscle contracture existed on one side of the body. When this occurred, a large magnet was drawn across the body in such a way as to transpose the condition to the other side of the body. Seemingly, this procedure appeared to provide a bridge from the older discredited magnetic tradition to the modern, scientific study of hypnosis.

The classification of stages of hypnosis was in apparent obliviousness of the variety of implicit cues that may shape the patients' behavior. Hypnosis induced by such seemingly external means characteristically produced three distinct stages. The first state, *lethargy,* was produced by having the subject fixate on an object held near the eyes and slightly above them. This produced eye closure and the subject appeared to be deeply asleep and impervious to extraneous stimuli. The second stage, *catalepsy,* was brought about by the experimenter suddenly opening the patient's eyes. The patients now proceeded to manifest waxy flexibility of the limbs which could be molded into any position. This state could also be induced by the application of a sudden intense stimulus such as a bright light in a darkened room or the clanging of a Chinese gong. Indeed once at a patients' ball at the Salpêtriére, a gong was inadvertently struck, and many of the female hysterical patients immediately became cataleptically frozen into the position they were in at the sound of the gong (Ellenberger, 1970). A third state, *somnambulism,* could be induced by pressure to the vertex of the scalp, or by a slight friction. In this stage, the subject could hear and speak, was amenable to suggestion, and could display a variety of psychological phenomena. However, because Charcot had set himself the task of understanding the simple phenomena of hypnosis first, this latter stage was relatively neglected.

From this, Charcot deduced a patently false theory. All of these phenomena were produced in a minority of female hysterical patients, and could not be induced in any other type of patient. The condition was not present in all hysterics, but those who were able to produce the three stages were all found to be suffering from a severe form of the disorder. This led Charcot to equate correspondence between the extremes of hysteria with the extremes of hypnotic manifestations. Thus he took somnambulism induced by hypnosis to be symptomatic of a pathological condition. Charcot presented some of these findings to the Académie des Sciences in 1882. Although his findings were as equally spurious as those of the earlier magnetists, and although the Académie had three times previously in the prior century rejected magnetic claims, the paper was enthusiastically acclaimed. It is yet another irony of the history of hypnosis that scientific respectability came to hypnosis 98 years after the Benjamin Franklin Commission via the back door of the Salpêtrière by the use of observational methods that had only the appearance of scientific scrupulosity.

History has justly celebrated Charcot as a prime example of how a man of impeccible scientific credentials can lapse into the grossest of observer error. Much of his undoing was the result of his medical training; he approached the investigation of hypnosis in much the same way as a surgeon, even today, approaches the removal of a gall bladder. Just as a patient for surgery is prepared by paramedical personnel, whose job it is also to mop up after the surgeon has finished, so Charcot left the hypnotizing and dehypnotizing of patients to students. Only when the subject had been brought to an appropriate point of hypnotic responsivity would Charcot proceed to demonstrate and utilize its phenomena.

Further, Charcot, conscious of the long-standing imputation of fraud and self-deception to hypnotic behavior, stemming from the fluid or fraud controversy, sought to study hypnosis by concentrating on its simplest manifestations in the hope that more complex phenomena would become more readily understandable once the foundations of a theoretical edifice had been laid in this way. He believed that this had been the major error of the magnetic movement; they had prematurely sought to account for the complex without first considering the basic and seemingly simpler facts of hypnotic induction. Thus he did not deny the role of suggestion in evoking hypnotic phenomena, and indeed quite often utilized it clinically in the treatment of paralyses and various functional disorders. But he believed that such questions were complex and should be temporarily shelved until the parameters of the hypnotic state had been demonstrated. This in short meant developing a set of precise criteria, in much the manner of his work on epilepsy, that would distinguish hypnosis as a recognizable state. The results of this approach produced a disaster. Charcot seems to have been unaware of the possibility that his students and colleagues, realizing that they were working with one of France's most distinguished scientists, were inadvertently "discovering" patients whose behavior corresponded with the views of their *chef.* All seem not to have recognized the phenomena of hysterical contagion among their patients even though Charcot's ward of hysterical and epileptic convulsive cases was a potentially available object lesson. To complicate matters further, a number of students of the Marquis de Puyfontain, a well-known magnetist, sat in on Charcot's lectures and mingled with the patients, some of whom freely gave their services to de Puyfontain's magnetic experiments (Guillian, 1955). Thus many of the phenomena elicited in all innocence by Charcot were being strongly influenced by these external magnetic experiments. Further, Charcot believed that the hypnotized person is in some sense unconscious and cannot perceive what is happening in his immediate environment. This erroneous belief, which appears to have been a direct result of the equally erroneous belief in induction by purely mechanical means, led Charcot to freely discuss his doctrines in their presence, unaware of how this alone would have helped to elicit hypnotic behavior consistent with his theories.

Although Charcot's errors were gross, they are, unlike many errors, extremely instructive. Procedurally, they provide a series of elegant demonstrations of how the hypnotized person's behavior can be shaped by implicit (and at times extremely explicit) cues in the hypnotic situation. As well, they demonstrate the contribution of subject and hypnotist expectation in evoking hypnotic behavior. More rigorous demonstrations of how such factors may contaminate inferences about hypnosis have been subsequently provided by Orne (1959). In short, modern investigators owe Charcot a great debt for making the errors he did and providing an object lesson in experimental contamination. However, such errors might have been perpetuated for even longer than they were, but for the fact that they generated replicable conclusions about the nature of hypnosis. More important, the work of Bernheim and Liébeault at Nancy, carried out independently of Charcot's work during the same period, provided a decisive test of both the validity of Charcot's observations and a means of discrediting magnetic doctrines for all times.

The Nancy–Salpêtrière Controversy

Charcot's findings indicated that hypnosis could be produced by mechanical means, that three stages could be distinguished by objective criteria (seemingly), and that hypnosis was a morbid condition found only in a small minority of the most talented hysterics. These were testable propositions and were capable of refutation. The confrontation between the "schools" of Nancy and the Salpêtrière resulted from Charcot presenting these findings to the Académie des Sciences in 1882. Such observations were almost the exact antithesis of what had been observed and extensively documented by both Bernheim and Liébeault at Nancy. The battle was joined with the publication of Bernheim's book, *Suggestive Therapeutics,* which was published in 1884 and 1886 in two parts. Based upon his own experience with 700 patients, and upon a further 6000 treated by Liébeault, Bernheim was able to demolish Charcot's observation that somnambulism was a rare and morbid condition found only in a minority of hysterics. He was able to show that somnambulistic behavior occurred in 15–18% of the 6,700 cases observed, and that the phenomenon of somnambulism was not confined to hysterics.

Further he demonstrated that hypnosis was not produced by mechanical means, as Charcot had thought, but was rather the product of suggestion.

Somnambulism, for instance, could be obtained without rubbing the crown of the head, as at the Salpêtrière. For the induction of the first stage of hypnosis, he showed that it was not necessary to rely upon the eye fixation method practiced by Charcot. Fixation, passes, vocal suggestion, and simple closure of the eyelids all achieved the same effect. Further, and as equally decisive, Bernheim reported that of the several thousand patients observed at Nancy, Charcot's three stages of lethargy, catalepsy, and somnambulism had been observed only once, and this one instance was found in a former patient of the Salpêtrière.

In the often extreme antagonisms of the next few years between the Nancy and the Salpêtrière "schools" the views of Bernheim prevailed so that by 1892, at the time of the Second International Congress of Psychology, Charcot's position had already become an historical curiosity. It is believed that Charcot himself came to realize that his position on hypnosis and hysteria was untenable, and was in the process of beginning to revise his views at the time of his sudden death in 1893 (Guillain, 1955).

OVERVIEW

The history of hypnosis up to the beginning of the twentieth century was initially one of a gradual accumulation of knowledge of its basic phenomena. The methods of observation were naturalistic and the history illustrates both the strengths and shortcomings of such an approach. As Hull (1933) has observed, practically all of the phenomena of hypnosis had been observed during the first fifty years, between 1775 and 1825. However, as we have seen, some of its basic phenomena such as amnesia were not recognized immediately in the healing atmosphere of the *baquet* and indeed were only observed when de Puységur modified Mesmeric induction processes. Likewise, Mesmer observed individual differences in response to the *baquet* but gave them little emphasis. Again it was a radical departure from conventional induction procedures by Faria which led to the recognition of hypnotizability as a major area of scientific inquiry. In the 1830s, hypnotic analgesia came to be recognized (though reports of it occurred occasionally during the Mesmeric period) but it was given little importance. This is in part due to the fluid or fraud controversy which meant that the wrong questions were asked, though the discovery of chloroform in the late 1830s contributed also to the question being closed prematurely.

In addition to an accumulation of valid data on hypnotic phenomena, the early history of hypnosis suffered from the excesses of the naturalistic method. The animal electricity of Pétetin, de Puységur's belief in the ability of magnetized patients to diagnose and cure the illnesses of others, and the claims for supernormal powers during the fluid and fraud era (to mention a few of the early extravagent claims) diverted attention from more substantive questions.

This process was facilitated by an inflexibility within the magnetic movement which refused to take cognizance of the Benjamin Franklin Commission's findings (with *some* justification, given its mistreatment of the issue of cure). A similar inflexibility was shown towards the views of Faria and of Braid, though the justification was considerably less.

The century from 1825 onwards has been seen by Hull (1933, p. 18) as one of "remarkable sterility." Such a view fails to take account of the very illuminating conflict between two main ways of explaining hypnotic phenomena. The magnetic tradition saw hypnosis as a matter of external influence in the form of forces, fluids, and/or the hypnotist's powers acting upon the hypnotized person to produce alterations in his experience and behavior. The psychological (or person-oriented) tradition finally crystallized (through Liébeault and Bernheim) as suggestibility theory, but it is more accurate to think of it as one which emphasized the inner workings of the hypnotized person. Suggestibility is merely one of several possible internal processes that may be operating when a person is hypnotized. In the century leading up to Bernheim's confrontation with Charcot, various other mental processes were postulated as well and many of these continue to affect the thinking of current investigators.

The controversy between the Salpêtrière and Nancy "schools" was in some respects an historical accident, as we have seen. Nevertheless, it was important in at least two ways. It revealed through Charcot's errors that a scientist of the most impeccable credentials, using tightly controlled methods of observation, can commit the grossest errors of observation. And equally important, it freed subsequent investigators from having to refute theories which seek to explain hypnotic phenomena in terms of external, mechanical and esoteric forces.

In the chapters that follow, it is noticeable that many of the streams we chartered in this chapter continue to affect present-day thinking in various ways. We have already pointed to some of these in the course of this historical account and in the following section we describe some of the main issues, stemming from the history, which have maintained their influence.

Internal versus External Influence

Nineteenth century thinking about hypnosis was polarized between the magnetists' emphasis on external influence and the psychological emphasis on the subjects' inner processes. The discrediting of Charcot's position led to a decline of interest in external, environmental factors affecting hypnotic behavior for a considerable subsequent period. It is noticeable that this major issue of the nineteenth century has begun to appear in the theorizing of several of the investigators who are discussed in this book. Barber (Chapter 3) with his emphasis on the manner in which hypnosis is presented to the subject, and upon instructional variables represents one such attempt to account for part of the hypnotic variance in terms of factors external to the subject. Sarbin (Chapter 4), likewise, in stressing a variety of social role-related factors which contribute to hypnotic role enactment shows a comparable tendency, as do London and Fuhrer (Chapter 7) in their perception of hypnosis as having situational determinants. Orne (Chapter 6) likewise sees such factors as important but appears to follow the historical lesson of Charcot's errors and tends to treat such variables as contaminants of hypnotic essences rather than contributants. All of these investigators give varying degrees of emphasis to the importance of the subject's inner processes (in Orne's case, for example, it constitutes primary importance) but they indicate a continuity with the more defensible aspects of magnetic theorizing. Whereas the nineteenth century was polarized between external and internal accounts of hypnotic responsivity, present trends involve disagreements between investigators who place most of their emphasis upon internal processes and those who see hypnosis as a more complex product of interaction between person and situational variables. This interactionism (Bowers, 1973b; Ekehammar, 1974; Endler & Magnusson, 1974) parallels a similar current trend in personality theorizing in general.

The Inconstant Character of Hypnotic Events

A potentially major aspect of hypnosis, which can be abstracted from the foregoing account, concerns what we would call the inconstant or variable character of its manifestations. The descriptions we have provided of the effects of induction procedures used variously by Mesmer, de Puységur, Faria, Braid and Charcot indicate considerable variability of hypnotic effects. The cathartic crises of the *baquet* quickly gave way to a moderated crisis in the hands of de Puységur; indeed, the quilt-lined *chambre de crises* initiated by Mesmer in his early Paris days became obsolete within a few years. By contrast, the austere induction procedures of Faria produced perspiration, heart palpitation, spasms and convulsions. Shortly later, Braid, using similar methods to Faria, reported gushes of tears, slowed respiration, and slight convulsive movements of the hand. Later still, Charcot's procedures produced three seemingly distinct stages of lethargy, catalepsy and somnambulism.

Similar things can be said of the reports of amnesia that we have abstracted at various points. Its presence was observed and ignored during the Mesmeric period. To de Puységur, *spontaneous* amnesia was a central characteristic of hypnosis; by the time of Braid, some few decades later, the distinction had come to be between *hypnosis* and *hypnotic coma.* As yet another example of the changing nature in which hypnotic events manifest themselves, one can compare the intense interactions among patients around the *baquet* with the exclusive rapport that each member of an hypnotized group had with the hypnotist using de Puységur's techniques. It is of considerable interest that very few of these phenomena are encountered in current clinical and experimental practice.

Such observations fit well with distinctive emphasis on motives, attitudes and sets as major determinants of hypnotic outcomes (see, for example, Barber's model, Chapter 3), and as equally well with an alternative account of hypnosis in terms of role enactment (see Sarbin's model, Chapter 4). They mesh also, in a sense with modern attempts to separate artifact from essence in hypnosis (see Orne, Chapter 6)—a contrast that has lately come to be challenged by Sarbin. While it is clear that essences and artifacts should be separated (as was poignantly demonstrated by Charcot's failure to do so, and has been cogently argued by Orne subsequently), there is considerable merit to the suggestion that artifacts, once isolated, should not then be dismissed as necessarily counting for nothing. Sarbin argues, for instance, that many aspects of hypnosis usually thought of as artifacts, may in fact be role related variables which have considerable influence upon hypnotic behavior in their own right.

The issue is difficult to formulate clearly at this point, but all of the above observations to which we have alluded in the course of this historical treatment suggest a decidedly chameleon quality to the manifestations of hypnotic behavior, which needs to be understood more adequately than at present. Indeed, we propose that this characteristic may constitute a very neglected aspect of the study of hypnosis. The changing *zeitgeist* in many of its manifestations is puzzling, and we need to understand its variability better.

The Subjects' Mental Processes

Following the discrediting of Charcot's position, and of magnetism in general, the prevailing theory of hypnosis emphasized the role of suggestion in eliciting its phenomena. This is the theory of Clark L. Hull whose book *Hypnosis and suggestion: An experimental approach* (1933) placed the study of hypnosis on the sound experimental basis that is current now. Nevertheless, in our ensuing discussion of contemporary approaches, it is remarkable how small a role suggestibility plays. Historically, suggestibility theory provided a vehicle by which hypnosis could be studied as a phenomenon that is primarily psychological in nature. The tools of experimental psychology provided methods by which hypotheses from the suggestibility model could be tested. In the process, certain deficiencies in suggestibility theory became apparent, the most important of which is the theory's basic circularity. While this has not led to the total abandonment of the role of suggestion in the hypnotic process, it has led to a refocussing of attention by many investigators on other inner processes of the subject that have been historically influential. The role of imaginational processes, first proposed by the Benjamin Franklin Commission and later taken up by Bertrand and Braid, can be seen to varying degrees in the theorizing of such present-day investigators as Hilgard, Barber, Sarbin, and Sutcliffe. Dissociation, first proposed by Charcot's work with hysterics and subsequently taken up by

Janet, is strongly emphasized in Hilgard's most recent writings. The notion of delusion, which has connections with both of the foregoing concepts, is to be found both in the writings of Sutcliffe and Orne. Further, Braid's interest in the role of expectation and belief is paralleled by Barber's subsequent concern with motives, attitudes and sets. In contemporary study of hypnosis, then, the focus is clearly upon a wide variety of hypothesized mental processes that have important historical antecedents. In fact, much of what is being done currently can be seen as a sorting out of hypotheses that actually have been predominant in our thinking at various times in the past two hundred years.

Hypnotic Susceptibility

The Abbé Faria was the first person to see that individual differences in hypnotizability were an integral part of hypnotic phenomena. This influence is to be found subsequently in the writings of Braid, Liébeault, and Bernheim. Most present-day investigators accord it an important role. Some such as Hilgard, Sarbin, and Sutcliffe have emphasized it as a primary problem deserving of explanation. Others, such as Orne and the proponents of the London–Fuhrer design, give implicit acknowledgement to the problem by the use of designs which compare the performance of subjects who are high and low in susceptibility. Only Barber (though occasionally he also focuses on susceptibility) has given comparatively little emphasis in his technique and research to this aspect of hypnotic behavior. The methodologies we review in subsequent chapters can be seen as attempts to resolve the problem of what relative weights should be attributed to the role of hypnotizability (seen as a skill of the subject), the external environment, and the subject's "internal process workings." All of these issues here are evident in the history of hypnosis; present preoccupations are more with reconciling their respective contributions.

Methodologies of Hypnosis

We began by observing that the methodologies that have evolved from studying hypnosis always convey, as their basis, an underlying theoretical notion as to its nature. Variations in methodology depend, in part, upon what an individual investigator believes hypnosis is and methodologies develop as a way of ordering observations believed to be relevant to the question at issue. Thus the varying theoretical emphases of the investigators discussed in this book are reflected in their methodologies—in their choices of planned observations.

Historically, since the time of Mesmer, two main questions have evolved which can be seen in the terms of reference established by the Benjamin Franklin Commission of 1784. The Commissioners set themselves the task of inquiring into the existence of animal magnetism (a question of its nature) and its applications (a question of its curative value). The methodologies we survey in this book have all developed from the tradition initiated by the former question. The greater sophistication of present-day techniques as opposed to those used by the Benjamin Franklin Commission reflects merely the impact of growth in our knowledge of appropriate research strategies in determining specific hypnotic outcomes. However, what is currently lacking is the development of a set of methodologies to explore the issue of cure which, from the time of Benjamin Franklin, has been greatly neglected. While some present-day clinicians are sophisticated in experimental methods, the general trend of clinical research has historically developed, in fact, from the naturalistic traditions of the first hundred years of inquiry into hypnosis. Such practices continue to reflect the strengths and weaknesses of naturalistic methods and have recently raised issues as to whether the phenomena of clinical and experimental hypnosis are entirely identical (Thompson, 1970). More to the point, the general lack of a coherent set of strategies to investigate the mechanisms underlying this historically neglected issue of the therapeutic uses of hynosis may well mean that an important source of information as to the nature of hypnosis is being systematically ignored two hundred years after serious investigation first began.

We move now to our survey of contemporary approaches to hypnosis, all of which analyze the nature of hypnosis and its outcomes by application of sophisticated sets of standardized procedures. History bears obviously on the substance of what the modern theorists say, if not on the precision of their procedural applications.

2

Hypnosis as an Altered State of Awareness: The Methodology of Ernest R. Hilgard

> A man knows that he belongs to the human race because of his conscious experiences. . . . Why, then, are psychologists so timid in talking about conscious states, about awareness, when they are the initial subject matter [Hilgard, 1969, p. 68]?

One of the most influential workers in the field of hypnosis today and one who speaks outspokenly in defense of hypnosis as an altered state of awareness is Ernest R. Hilgard. Hilgard gives careful recognition to objective as well as subjective data, his philosophical position being a moderate one. He rejects the strict tenets of Watsonian behaviorism by saying there is much more to the study of hypnosis than the subjects' behavioral response to a hypnotic suggestion. Internal processes, inferred from subjective reports, are a prime part of his model's domain and the model claims that full understanding of hypnotic phenomena cannot be gained simply from specifying patterns of behavior in the hypnotic setting and isolating the social conditions that relate lawfully to them. At the same time, however, what the subject tells the hypnotist about his experiences is only one portion of the data to be collected. Objectivity is the paramount goal of the scientist but he cannot discard methodological caution to recognize only the value of talking about experience.

Hilgard (1969) labels his philosophical position "contemporary functionalism," a position occurring midway between the extremes of pure behaviorism and humanistic psychology. The philosophy can be termed alternatively one of enlightened operationism. It aims to retain objectivity (and the power of communication that accrues to that ideal) and yet at the same time acknowledges within its framework the special relevance of internal process constructs such as traits, and altered states of awareness. Miller, Galanter, and Pribram (1960) perhaps capture the flavor of the position most concretely with their term "subjective behaviorism"–a term that conveys the joint emphases of the model on what persons are doing and what they allege they are experiencing.

Because the model appeals to subjective events in the search for indices of hypnosis it should not be regarded in any way as an unsophisticated or unscientific model. The framework Hilgard proposes is both systematic in orientation and discerning in design. It asks specific questions about hypnotic phenomena and attempts to answer these questions in a precise way. The special design features of the model can really best be understood by first discussing Hilgard's theoretical position which is, in fact, a flexible one stressing the value of recognizing state, trait, and situational determinants of hypnotic responsiveness (Hilgard, 1975). It will be instructive to comment on the change in emphases his theorizing has taken through recent years; some of the changes–from early stress on individual differences to later emphasis on the dissociative process, for instance–have been relatively substantial ones.

THEORETICAL POSITION

Hypnosis Considered as "State"

An altered state of awareness may be generally defined as that which the individual or trained observer can recognize as representing a "sufficient deviation in subjective experience or psychological functioning from certain general norms for that individual during alert, waking consciousness (Ludwig, 1969, pp. 9–10)". Hilgard (1965a) conceptualizes hypnosis as an altered state of consciousness and lists the primary features of it in his major treatise, *Hypnotic Susceptibility*. In this book he argues that the hypnotized subject loses initiative and the willingness to act independently; the subject's planning function is turned over to the hypnotist, his attention is redistributed; and perception becomes selective according to the hypnotist's demands. Other characteristics listed are that the subject develops a heightened ability for fantasy production and a tolerance for reality distortion (illustrated by the acceptance of falsified memories). It is noted also that the hypnotized subject easily throws himself or herself into roles becoming deeply involved in them, and may develop amnesia for what transpired within the hypnotic state. A final characteristic and one which strongly dictates the nature of Hilgard's methodology is that a hypnotic induction supposedly leads to a small but significant increase in suggestibility over the level of response shown by subjects in the waking state. Although the link between "hypnosis" and "suggestibility" is an important one and Hilgard (1967) has defined hypnosis as a state of heightened suggestibility, the two concepts are not to be identified. There is a high correlation between responsiveness to suggestion inside and outside the trance state but subjective reports from subjects about their experience of trance forbid the simple equation of suggestibility and hypnosis. Hilgard reports evidence, for example, that subjects who were highly suggestible in the waking state did not feel as "entranced" as subjects who yielded the same objective suggestibility score following hypnotic induction.

In his early statements delineating the characteristics of the trance state, Hilgard placed particularly strong emphasis on the subject's "verbal report of being in hypnosis" and accepted such a report as being virtually the basic criterion of the state of hypnosis. In collaborative work with Tart (Tart & Hilgard, 1966), for instance, Hilgard formally endorsed subjective report as the essential criterion of hypnosis, and the subject's report about feeling hypnotized became "primary data about the presence or absence of hypnosis [p. 253]."

The early chapters of his text *Hypnotic Susceptibility* were largely responsible for others in the field (Barber, 1969, for example) viewing Hilgard as an extreme proponent of "state" theory. He was seen as one to whom the concept of state was crucial and who argued that hypnosis differed fundamentally from the waking state. In his later writings Hilgard (1969, 1971, 1973b) changed his emphasis on hypnosis as a well-defined state to stress the notion of "state as metaphor," a notion which values a descriptive (not causal) approach to hypnotic phenomena and firmly rejects any implication that hypnotic phenomena occur only as a consequence of hypnosis. The concept of state came to serve a more pragmatic role. One of its main functions was to help the investigator define the domain of hypnosis. Hilgard defined "domain" as the common patterns of behavior familiar in hypnotic lore which typically occur within the hypnotic setting–behavior, for instance, illustrated by hallucinations, posthypnotic response, and age regression. Generally, this approach to the domain of hypnosis is very much an empirical one where, conceptually speaking, the concept of "state" plays a less critical part. The domain concept was basically established to counter the assumption that the notion of hypnotic state is an expendable one, and that accepting the construct "hypnosis" commits one to adopting a causal position.

Defining the domain of hypnosis is a difficult task because behavior typical of hypnosis can sometimes occur without prior induction. It is necessary to carefully delimit the domain and Hilgard points to several reasons why the task is possible. First, hypnotic behavior clearly is not simply response to suggestion–instances of suggested behavior obviously include responses which do not belong within hypnosis (for example, forms of social suggestibility such as conformity and gullibility). A second point in defining the domain of hypnotic behavior is the stability of individual differences in those forms of suggestibility which do lie within the domain of hypnosis. This position is contentious. Evidence exists which suggests that the level of hypnotic susceptibility reached by subjects is persistent through time (Morgan, Johnson, & Hilgard, 1974), but recent studies on training for susceptibility have challenged the stability hypothesis (see Diamond, 1974; and Chapter 9 of this book). A third point relating to the domain of hypnosis is that experience reports given by subjects in the hypnotic setting support many of the phenomenological aspects of hypnotic-like behavior. Subjective and objective scores following hypnotic test procedures usually correlate highly together, one score confirming the other, but subjective scores can at times correct assessments made on the basis of objective scores where the latter are misleading. Hilgard claims, for example, that objective scores are spuriously high on some hypnotic scales because of pressure for compliance and an observed discrepancy between objective and subjective test scores illustrates this point. Recent evidence bears directly in supporting fashion on this claim (Ruch, Morgan, & Hilgard, 1974).

"State" considered as metaphor serves a useful classification function. Just as one can talk about waking and sleep as separate states of awareness and still not interfere with objective reporting of waking and sleep phenomena, so one also can discuss hypnosis as a particular state of awareness and still talk about hypnotic phenomena in an objective fashion. Labeling hypnosis as an altered state, though, offers no explanation of hypnotic phenomena. Hilgard (1967, 1973b) rejects unequivocally the temptation to use the concept of state by way of cause or explanation and he uses an analogy with sleep to make the point. Just as snoring and dreaming occur throughout sleep and it is not particularly helpful to say sleep causes them so too it should not be argued that hypnotic behavior is caused by an special hypnotic state. Genuine causal properties may eventually be attributed to the state but at the moment the more correct question to ask is "(Is) typical hypnotic behavior more likely when the conditions have been favorable for entering a hypothesized hypnotic state [Hilgard, 1969, p. 77]?" The concept of state, then, is viewed by Hilgard as a useful metaphor which helps in a "category" (but not "cause") sense to define the legitimate domain of hypnosis.

There are several points to make regarding Hilgard's emphasis on the "domain" of hypnosis as opposed to his early discussion (Hilgard, 1965a) of the characteristics of the "state of hypnosis." The first is that the model's theoretical investment in the concept of hypnosis as a special state has lessened; hypnosis is not too sharply differentiated from nonhypnotic activity. The second is that "verbal report of trance" is somewhat less crucial as a criterion of hypnosis; report of being hypnotized is one among many variables that can be used to validate the construct, hypnotic state. In search for the domain of hypnosis, Hilgard seeks to find lawfulness in interchange between public indications (for example, hallucinatory behavior, physiological stress response following suggestions of anaesthesia) and subjective report of hypnosis. Although the distinctive emphasis of the model is still on "internal processes" (Coe, 1971, 1973a), subjective report is recognized as limited datum. It was partly because of the possible invalidity of report data, in fact, that Hilgard expressed concern about the state concept. The whole issue of whether or not we can trust what the subject says about his being hypnotized is a particularly sensitive one. What, for example, are we to conclude about the subject who denies he is in trance yet continues to be unable to lift his arm when asked to do so? As Hilgard (1971) states, if we trust reports by subjects that they are hypnotized we ought to also trust reports that subjects are not hypnotized. Clearly, the issue of validity of self-report offers a major challenge to the model. Hilgard (1965a) reports that even among subjects who responded well on the appropriate tests only some two-thirds felt certain they could tell when they were actually in a state of hypnosis.

A third consequence of emphasizing the "domain" of hypnosis reflects another breakdown in importance of the state concept. Evidence has shown that in the presence or absence of induction there is highly consistent performance across different scales of susceptibility such as the Harvard Group Scale of Hypnotic Susceptibility (HGSHS:A) of Shor and E. Orne (1962), the Stanford Hypnotic Susceptibility Scale, Forms A, B, and C (SHSS:A and B, SHSS:C) of Weitzenhoffer and Hilgard (1959, 1962), and the Barber Suggestibility Scale (BSS) of Barber (1965, 1969). Though these scales are different in many ways they have much in common, and this is reflected in substantial correlations among them of the order of .70 (Ruch, Morgan, & Hilgard, 1974). Hilgard (1973b) states that the extent of commonality among them argues strongly that waking suggestion measured by the tests belongs within the domain of hypnosis. Any argument about the state of hypnosis is irrelevant to the point–waking suggestion of a certain kind is said to be of the domain of hypnosis as much as suggestion given following trance induction.

Hypnosis and "Open Inquiry"

The goal of attaining a reliable and valid index of hypnosis has not yet been reached by Hilgard's model or by any other framework. One might have assumed that the various features of the hypnotic state outlined by Hilgard in 1965 would have afforded appropriate indices of the altered state of awareness but few in fact have been researched comprehensively and those that have been researched have yielded controversial findings (see, for example, the investigation of trance logic by Johnson, Maher, & Barber, 1972, and the reply by Hilgard, 1972a).

In his early writings Hilgard set out the initial formulations of a developmental–interactive theory of hypnosis. The theory argued that early life experiences produced the necessary abilities for entering hypnosis and these abilities were released under the particular circumstances of interaction between subject and hypnotist (Hilgard, 1962; Hilgard, 1965a, b; J. Hilgard & E. Hilgard, 1962). The hypnotic state was viewed as characterized by various partial dissociations based partly on significant identifications with parental figures.

Delimiting the domain of hypnosis is a task that precedes formulations of these kinds. Before any agreement concerning indices of hypnosis, background experiences, cognitive organization, or personality processes can be reached, the proper area of inquiry for hypnosis must be firmly outlined. To achieve this end Hilgard moved away from outlining formal properties of the state and emphasized an "open inquiry" paradigm of research, which stresses the value of seeking converging approaches to the study of hypnosis—a theme which has been taken up by others, as well (see Sheehan, 1973c; Spanos & Barber, 1974). Hilgard (1971, 1972b) argued the position that an experimenter must be as open as possible in his inquiry in investigating whether or not changes specific to hypnosis occur. Sharply contrasting the particular features of his model with those proposed by Barber (reviewed in Chapter 3) Hilgard stated that the essence of the open inquiry paradigm was the advancement of an hypothesis followed by earnest pursuit to find evidence against the prediction as well as for it. Consistent with the logic of convergent operations (Garner, Hake, & Eriksen, 1956) the search should be for consistencies among measures: behavior, physiological function, observations made by the hypnotist, and self-report. Ideally, in the practice of this paradigm the experimenter should remain neutral about the outcome, and the conclusion of the study ought not to be anticipated in the design of the experiment. In summary, the strategy being proposed is basically one of sound, unprejudiced (ideally, nontheoretical) research aiming toward elimination of alternative hypotheses regarding the given construct, "hypnosis." The systematic elimination of threats to validity must be endorsed as a major goal of science—it represents a theme to which we return often throughout this book.

Hypnosis as Trait

People vary in the extent to which they respond to hypnotic suggestions and individual differences in hypnotic susceptibility are one of the most firmly established facts of hypnosis. These differences, though, can be highlighted or minimized in one's methodological approach to the study of hypnosis. They tend to be consistently recognized implicitly, for example, in Orne's (1959) experimental condition as he employs it in the real-simulating model of hypnosis, but variably acknowledged and underemphasized by Barber (1969) in his operational paradigm. The assumption of "stability of trait" relates to other models discussed in this book (see Chapter 4 on Sarbin, Chapter 5 on Sutcliffe, and Chapter 7 on London and Fuhrer). No model of hypnosis, however, more explicitly attempts to cope with the problem of individual variation in susceptibility to hypnosis than the framework proposed by Hilgard, though trait characteristics are recognized somewhere in most researchers' formulations about hypnotic events. Hilgard (1975) notes that there is a convergence of contemporary research upon the role played by the subjects' imagination and fantasy productions. And this increasing emphasis on imaginative involvement (for example, J. Hilgard, 1970, 1974) and absorption (for example, Tellegen & Atkinson, 1974) appears to call attention to enduring individual differences in particular skills and abilities.

Hypnosis, then, is basically conceived by Hilgard as reflecting a durable trait and the implications of that position clearly are that hypnotic susceptibility in any given subject should be (a) stable and consistent through time, and (b) should show at least some evidence of cross-situational consistency. Both these claims, related traditionally to trait theory, are rejected strongly by Mischel (1968) who thoroughly analyses the general trait position in very critical fashion.

High test–retest correlations for hypnotic susceptibility across a wide variety of scales obtained by Hilgard (1965a, b) argue in support of the stability of hypnotizability and for hypnotizability as a generalized trait. Recent evidence (Morgan, Johnson, & Hilgard, 1974) has shown that over a retest period of ten years the correlation found for college students was quite comparable to what one would expect to occur for intelligence test scores (r = .60). More persuasively, however, there is evidence to suggest that hypnotic susceptibility can be quite consistent over a variety of changing social conditions; measurement shows some degree of cross-situational consistency which Mischel (1968) argues is crucial for justifying the concept of trait. Ås, Hilgard, and Weitzenhoffer (1963), for example, found few substantial changes in their attempts to enhance the susceptibility of moderately hypnotizable subjects and high correlations over hypnotizability measures have been obtained when different induction procedures and item content have been employed (Hilgard, Weitzenhoffer, Landes, & Moore, 1961). Further, most contemporary research in hypnosis actually assumes considerable stability for hypnotizability as a measurable trait. The important issue of permanency of trait has focused around the question of how easily hypnotizability can be modified with training (Diamond, 1974). This issue is a very complex one, methodologically speaking, and we return to it in the final chapter of the book.

It is possible, as Hilgard (1971) suggests, that hypnotic abilities appear stable only because insufficient effort has been made to change them but this position is one that has more logical relevance than empirical justification. It is now widely accepted in the hypnotic literature that the subject brings with him or her the possibility of trance and it is hardly surprising that pronounced individual differences in the ability easily manifest themselves. The problem is not that the ability is there in varying magnitude so much as it is difficult to determine what is responsible for the ability in the first instance. Acceptance of the trait position does *not* necessarily commit one to a state position regarding hypnosis (Hilgard, 1975; see also discussion of this distinction in Chapter 9 of this book).

Both Hilgard and Sarbin (Chapter 4 of this book), for example, stress hypnotic ability and so embrace the notion of trait specifically, but only the former of the two theorists chooses to view hypnosis as an altered state of awareness.

Hypnosis and the Dissociative Process

As a result of a serendipitous finding Hilgard (1974a) developed a particular technique to explore the discrepancies that occur in hypnosis between physiological and verbal–behavioral evidence. Open, "aware" reports of pain, following suggested anesthesia, typically run counter to physiological indications; hypnotic subjects assert they feel no pain, but behave physiologically as if they do (see Chapter 5 of this book for detailed analysis of some of the implications of such a discrepancy). By means of automatic writing (and subsequently automatic talking for greater convenience), Hilgard has elicited reports of pain and suffering during testing for hypnotic anesthesia from what he has termed metaphorically, the "hidden observer." The special instructions for eliciting reports of this kind run typically as follows:

> Just as there are many things going on in our bodies of which we are unaware, under hypnosis there may be information processes of which we are not aware, things that the hypnotized part of you, to which I am now talking, does not know. If this is the case, when in a little while I place my hand on your shoulder, I can be in touch with this part of you that knows things the hypnotized part does not know, and it can talk to me. You will not know that this part is talking to me, or what it says, and when I lift my hand from your shoulder everything will be as it is now, until after you are out of hypnosis, I say to you 'now you can remember everything.' Then you will remember what you said, and we can talk about it [Hilgard, 1974a; similar instructions were also used by Knox, Morgan, & Hilgard, 1974].

Work with this technique has led to the formulation of a specific version of state theory which Hilgard (1973c, 1974a, b, 1975) terms a "neodissociation" account of hypnosis. Data show that the hidden observer reports feeling pain which is denied in conscious, open report by the same subject. Specifically, the theory postulates that a hierarchy of control systems exist which operate in any one instance for a given individual and hypnosis is an eminently suitable method for studying conflicting cognitive controls which can be characterized as dissociative. Hypnotic procedures alter the ordered hierarchy of the controls so that certain systems become differentiated or segregated from others. Features characterizing the process share something in common with properties of the process of "ego regression" formulated by Gill and Brenman (1961); in the shifting hierarchies of control that occur in hypnosis, the dominance of the normal executive ego is reduced. Other features, however, demarcate Hilgard's concept firmly from any traditional conceptions of the process of dissociation. Experimental evidence, for example, appears to negate quite clearly aspects of what the historically defined process would predict. Hilgard has found that performing a second task "out of awareness" actually creates more interference with an ongoing task than if it is performed simultaneously "in awareness" (Hilgard, 1975; Knox, Crutchfield, & Hilgard, 1973). Suggesting to a subject that he is unaware of the second task seems to have the effect of introducing a third task, namely *doing* something to keep the second task out of awareness. In summary, the technique associated with this specific account of hypnosis appears to index the operation of multiple cognitive control systems and highlights new and interesting procedures which are currently being explored.

Summary

Hilgard espouses both a state and a trait theory of hypnosis, but expresses clear concern about the causal implications of the state concept. Hypnosis as an altered state of awareness can be very meaningfully used in a descriptive, nonexploratory and classificatory sense and is held to be a particularly useful notion in outlining the domain of hypnosis and determining whether or not changes occur that are specific to hypnosis. The methodological ideal is the strategy of open inquiry where the investigator adopts procedures guaranteeing impartiality about the outcome of his experiment and the model aims toward looking for consistencies among the various measures–objective as well as subjective–which lawfully define the domain. As the concept of hypnotic state remains theoretically important so does the model continue to emphasize the value of gathering subjects' reports about their experience of trance. Consistent with the logic of convergent operations, however, subjective report is not necessarily the basic criterion of hypnosis. Rather, it should be used in conjunction with other measures to yield useful information and expand our knowledge about hypnotic phenomena.

Hilgard offers a sophisticated account of a state theory of hypnosis by his appeal to the concept of dissociation. New data on hidden observer effects return us, in a way, to primary reliance on subjective events. His neodissociative theory of hypnosis argues that the hierarchies existing among a subject's multiple cognitive control systems are reordered by hypnotic procedures, and there are some distinct advantages to this viewpoint over more general state theory. Primarily, as Hilgard acknowledges, we need no longer assert that hypnosis should be demarcated from other instances in which cognitive controls are modified; hypnosis merely helps us understand "the various dissociative processes that are, in fact, ubiquitous [Hilgard, 1973c, p. 213]." Further, attention becomes usefully focused on the cognitive effort of the subject in the hypnotic test situation. The theory derives from, but departs in many ways from Janet's early notions and Hilgard labels his account "neodissociative" to indicate explicitly that it should not be taken to imply equivalence with the historical concept.

In close accord with the notion of hypnosis as trait, Hilgard's model strongly emphasizes individual differences in level of response to tests of suggestibility. "Hypersuggestibility," formally listed by Hilgard (1965a) as a primary characteristic of the trance state, largely dictates the nature of the model's basic research design, the model introducing procedures designed explicitly to answer the question: What effect does induction have on the level of a subject's suggestibility? A question such as this reflects theoretical preferences of a distinct kind. The simple recognition of individual differences as major contributors to variance in hypnotic-like behaviors, and the model's particular concern about the specific effect of induction on suggestibility both express, at least implicitly, commitments of a theoretical nature. They highlight at least the fact that the "open inquiry" paradigm promulgated by the model describes more of an attitude of mind that the experimenter should cultivate than a framework which dictates specific research procedures matching the problems that arise.

With this account of Hilgard's theory of hypnosis before us we will now consider his model of hypnosis from the viewpoint of the methodologist. The model proposes detailed research procedures which differ distinctively in emphasis from those outlined by other models and these will be discussed by us in some detail. The work of Hilgard and his associates falls into at least four major categories (Spanos & Chaves, 1970), and these can be listed as: (a) the developmental (and other) correlates of hypnotizability; (b) the relationship of hypnosis and suggestibility; (c) the effects of hypnosis on pain–the problem of measuring pain and how effectively hypnosis reduces it; and (d) the development of instruments for measuring hypnotic susceptibility. The following section covers many aspects of Hilgard's work but concentrates mostly on Aspect (b) and to a lesser extent on Aspect (c). These aspects are considered to help us focus on those procedures that seem to reflect most appropriately the formal properties of his model.

SURVEY OF THE MODEL'S STRATEGIES OF RESEARCH

Analysis of the Same-Subjects Design

A very basic choice facing the researcher is whether subjects should act independently throughout the various experimental conditions or serve as their own controls. With respect to hypnosis, regardless of the decision that is made, the experimenter must then decide on the further problem of whether he should sample his subjects widely from the general population or stratify with reference to susceptibility. Four designs follow from the set of choices dictated by these two decisions and these are represented in Table 2.1. The table sets out the various design possibilities for stratified and unstratified samples performing either as their own controls or in independent groups. Hilgard's model explicitly rejects Designs 1 and 2 and accepts Designs 3 and 4 although in the model's initial formulation (Hilgard, 1965a) it was Design 3 that was clearly preferred.

TABLE 2.1
Possible Research Designs Relating to a Waking (W)–Hypnosis (H) Comparison

Independent groups		Subjects as own controls	
Design 1	Design 2	Design 3	Design 4
W H	W H	W H	W H
S_1 S_2	S_1 S_2	S_1	S_1
Unstratified with respect to susceptibility–random sampling from the general population	Stratified sampling: both S_1 and S_2 contain high and low susceptible subjects–random sampling from these populations of "selected" subjects.	Unstratified with respect to susceptibility–random sampling from the general population.	Stratified sampling: S_1 contains both high and low susceptible subjects–random sampling from these populations of "selected" subjects.

Note: The symbol "S" with different numbers (e.g., S_1 and S_2) represents the involvement of different samples of subjects. The term "stratification" here refers to selected sampling of diagnostic groups along the trait continuum "susceptibility to hypnosis."

No behavior following hypnotic induction can be attributed to hypnosis unless the investigator first knows that the response in question is not likely to occur outside of hypnosis in the normal waking state. Practically all hypnotic researchers argue the need for a waking control but they differ among themselves in how the control should be employed and what particular form it should take. Hilgard is adamant that subjects must serve as their own controls whereas other models (for example, Barber's operational paradigm and Orne's real-simulating model of hypnosis) state otherwise. The model is less clear, however, on the precise form the control should take. Whereas Barber's paradigm lays down in detail the nature of its set of Task Motivational (TM) instructions which constitute the model's major nonhypnotic control condition, and Orne's real-simulating model makes explicit exactly what are the procedures associated with simulating, insusceptible subjects who comprise its control group (for comparison with real, susceptible subjects), Hilgard's paradigm is relatively flexible about the nature of its controls. It seems relatively unimportant, for example, whether waking subjects are asked to imagine what the hypnotist is requesting or not, or whether waking subjects are led to expect or not to expect that hypnosis will be induced (see Hilgard & Tart, 1966; Tart & Hilgard, 1966).

Because there are wide individual differences in susceptibility, the model argues that selecting independent groups for comparison on a random basis will require large numbers of subjects before the mean differences between the groups will reach significance. Randomly selected, unstratified samples will contain at least some subjects who are insusceptible to hypnosis and for whom the treatment of hypnosis will have no effect. Treatment differences will also be small for those subjects capable of showing the hypnotic phenomenon without induction. When subjects are used as their own controls variability is reduced and the experimenter takes advantage of the correlation which exists between waking and hypnotic suggestion. The claim is that the design is much more economical and instructive than the independent groups design and gives precise recognition to the base level of a subject's suggestibility in determining the gains that are made from one condition to the other.

There are arguments for and against sample selection or stratification which the model does not seem to have resolved. On the one hand, Hilgard (1972b) argues that stratification must be employed because of the enormous variability among subjects in their natural tendency to experience the effects being studied. On the other hand, however, he argues (Hilgard, 1965a) that stratification eliminates the possibility of beginning an experiment with naive subjects thus creating the danger that the contrast between the waking and hypnotic conditions will be detected by the experienced experimental subject serving as his own control. The first of these arguments appears to be the more persuasive. If one is interested in a particular phenomenon there does seem some point in considering a sample of subjects who have the ability to experience the effect under investigation. Also, any advantage of naivety associated with the unselected sample is lost immediately the first condition is completed; the problems that may arise from using an "experienced subject" (one who has been exposed to procedures similar to those about to be employed) are merely introduced later rather than earlier in the research design.

The principle of employing subjects as their own controls protects Hilgard's model from the major methodological caveat stated by Barber (1969), Barber and Calverley (1962), Sutcliffe (1961) and others that a hypnotic condition should not contain just those subjects who are susceptible to hypnosis when the waking group compared with it is chosen haphazardly. The particular strength of Hilgard's model is that a number of variables distinct from those consequent upon the sequencing of experimental procedures do not contaminate the design, and the advantage gained is a substantial one. Barber and Calverley (1962) conducted an experiment on response to dreaming about suggested topics to demonstrate the methodological point. They especially selected deep trance subjects for their experimental group and compared the performance of these subjects with that of an unselected group of control subjects. Not unexpectedly, results showed greater responsiveness to the dream suggestion on the part of the hypnotic group. As the authors point out, and as the experiment was designed to show, it was inevitable that the hypnotic condition would be favored when such a comparison of independent groups was conducted.

While the independent groups design must ensure that the two samples of subjects in the waking and hypnotic conditions are truly comparable, the Same-Subjects design has no difficulty in this respect. The independent design has the advantage, though, that there are no order effects arising from employing one condition before another other than those that may arise from subjects' personalized cognitions concerning what comparisons the experimenter will be making when other subjects are tested as well. The problem of order effects is the main disadvantage of Hilgard's model and one which the framework handles relatively poorly. General discussion of the possible sequential effects involved will serve to raise several important methodological principles.

Sequence Effects

We know that when a number of treatments are administered in succession to the same sample of subjects, response to one may be highly dependent on the fact that prior treatment of some kind has preceded it. Sutcliffe (1961) addressed himself to the problem when he said that in this situation guarantees must be given that "the subject is not compromised, is not aware of the hypnotist's expectations, or such knowledge cannot affect the waking performance [p. 126]." When subjects are used as their own controls some security has to be given that initial treatment effects are temporary, the effects of each treatment being entirely dissipated before the next treatment is administered, and that subject's perceptions of the change that is implied by procedures being in sequence bear no relevance to the results. Additionally, the criterion measure for any person administered a particular treatment should not be affected or influenced at all by his experience of having been measured previously, the issue of measurement here being quite distinct from any actual effects of the prior treatments themselves (Lindquist, 1953).

Good hypnotic subjects may be so eager and willing to please that they strive to give the effects that the experimenter wants and such a danger obviously precludes using a single group of hypnotic subjects to act as their own controls. The most famous case in point is Pattie's subject who went to quite extraordinary lengths to prove to her hypnotist that she was blind in one eye. Additional data bearing on the same point have been amply provided by Wolberg (1948), and by Sears (1932) in a much discussed study on the effectiveness of anaesthesia suggestions on selected good hypnotic subjects serving as their own controls. In Sears' study there were strong discrepancies in the response of subjects to instruction in and out of hypnosis yet the same subjects earlier and in another context had shown waking behavior that matched their current hypnotic behavior. It seems that the good hypnotic subjects made relatively little effort to suppress their pain response when they were asked to inhibit it in the waking state—when the two conditions appeared in sequence.

The problem of subjects striving to please the experimenter in accord with the demands of the experimental situation is one that is by no means peculiar to good hypnotic subjects. And the issue is simply not resolved by randomly allocating unselected rather than susceptible subjects to comparison conditions. Orne (1959, 1962a) has conceptualized the problem under the general rubric, "demand characteristics of the experimental setting," and the problem is a pervasive one. Experimental subjects, regardless of the conditions being studied, may respond precisely according to their individual perceptions of the point of the experiment and the investigator's wishes. The act of pretesting itself, for example, can lead subjects to hold a clear expectation of improvement and data indicate that baseline testing then becomes a yardstick against which to define improved performance (Spanos, McPeake, & Carter, 1973).

Summary

Hilgard's design insists that subjects should act as their own controls rather than be allocated independently to separate experimental groups. The design is least costly in subject resources and eliminates completely intersubject variation which characterizes the independent groups design. Selected or unselected samples of subjects can be allocated to conditions (although the allocation should be random within each of the populations of "selected" subjects being considered). Naivety is preserved initially by Design 3 (represented in Table 2.1), but the advantage lacks permanency and is lost as soon as any experimental procedures are applied.

The demands of Hilgard's model are in fact quite simple. All that is basically required is a hypnotic condition incorporating the test procedures relevant to the hypothesis being investigated and a waking control condition omitting the treatment of hypnotic induction. The hypnotic and nonhypnotic conditions, however, should be identical with respect to such variables as "motivation to respond." When hypnosis is compared with a waking condition it is important, for example, that alertness and motivation are comparable across the two conditions or the comparison loses meaning. This point is particularly relevant when the waking control condition chosen for the comparison, such as a set of Task-Motivational (TM) instructions, is an especially motivating one. The simplicity of design structure is partly a function of Hilgard's concern to eliminate what he calls "noise" variables. Some variables are considered irrelevant by Hilgard (1972b) such as the form of the experimenter's question and the tone of his presentation, and these are normally controlled. Control, as opposed to systematic manipulation of them, aims to reduce the noise in the system and maximize the chances of obtaining meaningful differences. This distinction at the outset between "pertinent" and "nuisance" variables runs counter, it would seem, to Hilgard's paradigm of completely open inquiry, but the differentiation aims at minimum design complication in order to achieve the maximum of information about the specific questions the model raises.

The major problem the design has to cope with is obviously the possible order effects which can arise both from actual treatment influence of the prior condition(s) on the one(s) following and/or from subjects' cognitions of the cues for change emanating implicitly from the nature of the experimenter's procedures. When tested first in a waking condition and then in hypnosis, subjects may show superior performance in the hypnotic condition for a variety of reasons quite unrelated to the treatment labeled "hypnosis." In summary, the change may be due to the fact that a second testing simply implies that improvement of some kind is required; there may be actual practice effects arising from using the same measurement device twice; or the effects of first testing may actually carry over in some way to the second. Counterbalancing is one technique that can be employed to cope with these problems, but it is far from effective in some instances.

The following section of this chapter reviews the evidence in support of the model and attempts to illustrate in concrete fashion some of the methodological points that have been discussed above. Primarily, the evidence is considered in the light of Hilgard's claim that his is the preferred model for detecting small differences in suggestibility following hypnotic induction. As with any methodology of hypnosis the question that should be before us is whether the model accomplishes accurately and efficiently what it sets out to achieve.

EVIDENCE RELATING TO THE MODEL

Evidence for Hypersuggestibility

The basic question the Same-Subjects model is designed to answer is, "Does the induction of hypnosis measurably affect or influence hypnotic behavior, and if so, how much?" Long ago, Hull (1933) addressed himself to this question and found evidence of hypersuggestibility in the trance state. His studies were limited to the kinds of tests of suggestibility that he adopted and in the criterion he selected for the presence of hypnosis (eye closure), but they provided the first systematic test of the hypothesis. Three subsequent experiments analyzed the notion of hypersuggestibility closely (Hilgard & Tart, 1966; Tart & Hilgard, 1966; Weitzenhoffer & Sjoberg, 1961) and enlarged upon Hull's early findings. All of these three studies will now be examined in some detail as they represent a particular unit of research which highlights very distinctively the various strengths and weaknesses of Hilgard's model. As well, they appear to be dominant studies offering empirical justification for the framework.

Weitzenhoffer and Sjoberg (1961) tested two groups of subjects each consisting of 30 individuals. The sample comprised unsophisticated subjects who had no personal experience with hypnotic phenomena. One group (experimental) was tested first in the waking state and then in hypnosis, the other (control) was tested in the waking state on two successive occasions. In order to measure expectancy experimental subjects were asked whether they thought hypnosis would make a difference to their reactions to suggestion; the experimenter told them he himself did not know if hypnosis would affect their scores, or not. Experimental subjects knew that they would be tested both in and out of hypnosis and that they would be told when hypnosis was going to be induced; control subjects were told they would be tested twice on the various suggestions so as the experimenter could gain a good idea of their responsiveness. A subsample of the latter group was later recalled and underwent a hypnotic testing. Second testing always started two items prior to the first failed item in the waking test.

The crucial comparison was between the hypnotic test scores of the experimental sample and the second testing scores of the control sample. Both these groups had done the suggestibility test for the second time and the comparison contrasted reactions to suggestions inside and outside of hypnosis. Results showed that induction of hypnosis had a significant effect on subjects' test scores and that the two waking runs in the control sample yielded comparable results. The authors concluded from these data that hypnosis had a specific enhancing effect upon suggestibility and that no practice effect adhered to the test setting, although it was recognized not everyone who was tested showed a gain in suggestibility following hypnotic induction. Even though hypnotic and waking performance correlated as highly as .63 there was a nonsignificant correlation between waking suggestibility and actual hypnotic gain. The extent of increase in suggestibility attributed to hypnosis could not therefore be really accounted for in terms of subjects' level of waking suggestibility. The authors concluded that something else beside waking suggestibility determined hypnotic response and that the gain shown by subjects was a unique effect of the induction procedure.

Whatever the correct explanation is for Weitzenhoffer and Sjoberg's results their design is open to criticism. No effective control was instituted to study the possible demand characteristic effects arising from subjects serving as their own controls. Practice effect was studied within the design and procedures aimed at eliminating this source of error, but it is regrettable that in their control group the nature of the instructions they used heavily implied to subjects that no difference in response was expected of them. Control subjects were virtually instructed *not* to change their response from the level shown on the first testing occasions. On the other hand, subjects in the experimental group were told that their second condition would be quite different (concerned with hypnosis); thus, they were exposed to distinct demand characteristics for change rather than test consistency. Although Weitzenhoffer and Sjoberg obviously were concerned about possible expectancy efforts in their attempt to manipulate subjects' perceptions, their design assumed too much credulity on the part of the experimental subjects. Subjects could not be expected to believe that the experimenter really did not know if any difference would result when they were moved from waking to hypnotic test–the simple fact that on the second testing subjects took up where they had failed previously must have clearly suggested to experimental subjects that a definite improvement was expected. In summary, the evidence which Weitzenhoffer and Sjoberg put forward is consistent with their hypothesis but their design fails to overcome the essential difficulties outlined above that can arise whenever subjects are used as their own controls.

Hilgard and Tart (1966) took up the same question as did Weitzenhoffer and Sjoberg and applied similar strategies. The methodology of their experiment was more sophisticated, but it too serves to highlight some of the advantages and disadvantages of the "Same-Subjects" design.

This second study incorporated into its design the two alternative choice points–Same-Subjects, and Independent Groups–thus affording direct and useful comparison of the effectiveness of the two types of strategies. Separate independent groups of subjects were allocated on Day 1 to waking, imagination, and hypnotic induction treatment groups. On Day 2 all groups received hypnotic induction. Day 1 allowed comparisons across independent groups, and Day 2 provided the data on subjects as their own controls. An important part of the design and consistent with the model's emphasis on internal processes was the frequent collection of "state reports." Reports of how hypnotized subjects felt (as judged on an especially constructed rating scale) were gathered repeatedly throughout the session. Ten items on the SHSS:C were used for suggestibility testing on the first day and an equivalent form of the test was used on Day 2. The results of the experiment supported the same subjects design but not the independent groups design. Mean test scores for the groups did not differ on Day 1 but there were significant gains between the two days for the waking and imagination groups and no appreciable gain for the hypnotic induction groups. The experiment appears to show convincingly that small but statistically significant differences can occur when subjects serve as their own controls. But again no effective controls were adopted to systematically examine the many possible order effects that may have existed within the design.

A follow-up study did institute controls in an attempt to cope with possible biasing effects. Here, instruction conditions differed from those adopted earlier. Independent groups of subjects were allocated on Day 1 to an "imagination group with expectation of hypnosis," and "imagination group with no expectation of hypnosis," and a standard hypnotic induction group. Groups were subdivided on the second day. Half the subjects in each group repeated the same condition on Day 2 as they had completed on Day 1. The remainder of the subjects received hypnotic induction. For the subjects who were given an induction on Day 1, consistent with the other groups, half the subjects repeated the same condition on Day 2; the other half, however, switched to an imagination (no expectation of hypnosis) condition. Overall the design repeated the same basic format of the earlier study but the subdivision of groups–where half the subjects repeated their conditions–allowed for systematic investigation of possible practice effects. An additional feature of the design was that subjects were told explicitly whether or not they would receive a formal induction on the second day. In order to control for "holding back" (a phenomenon attributed to subjects who lower their pretreatment scores when they know that a hypnotic session is to follow) control subjects who received no hypnotic induction were told explicitly that they were control subjects and they would not be hypnotized on either of the two days. Also, as before, state reports were repeatedly taken.

Contrary to the results of the previous study there were significant differences among the three groups on Day 1. The authors made the point that particularly large samples of subjects were used in this study ($N = 30$) thus demonstrating that differences can show up with an independent groups design if the sizes of groups are extensive enough. Table 2.2 sets out the mean suggestion scores obtained in the study by control and experimental subjects on the two days. Control data show that there were no appreciable practice effects for any of the conditions across the two days. Experimental groups, on the other hand, differed appreciably across the two days, and, as before, the gain consequent upon hypnotic induction was significant. Some unreliability of the effect was evident, however, for the small sample of control subjects (not represented in the table) who were brought back for an unanticipated third session involving hypnosis; no appreciable hypnotic gain was observed. Additionally, state reports showed that the subjects who reported experiencing being hypnotized were in fact those who also displayed the highest suggestibility scores and this was so, regardless of instructions or order of treatment. Analysis of report data also indicated that some subjects in the imagination conditions reported being hypnotized and yielded suggestibility scores comparable to subjects receiving a formal induction. Results suggested then that some of the control subjects had actually become hypnotized.

As far as order effects are concerned the design employed in this study is not as conclusive as it at first seems. Strictly speaking, the controls incorporated within its framework are inadequate to satisfy the stringent demands of the Same-Subjects design. Consider first the fact that no practice effect appeared to be involved. Here it should be remembered that, as with Weitzenhoffer's and Sjoberg's study, control subjects knew they would be tested in the same condition again. A more appropriate control to answer this question of practice

TABLE 2.2
Mean Suggestion Scores for Control and Experimental Subjects on Both Days of Testing[a]

Control[b]		Experimental[b]	
Day 1	Day 2	Day 1	Day 2
1. Imagination–no expectation of hypnosis	Imagination–no expectation of hypnosis	Imagination–no expectation of hypnosis	Hypnotic induction
2.37	2.33	2.80	3.70[c]
2. Imagination–expectation of hypnosis	Imagination–expectation of hypnosis	Imagination–expectation of hypnosis	Hypnotic induction
2.73	3.23	4.00	5.13[c]
3. Hypnotic induction	Hypnotic induction	Hypnotic induction	Imagination–no expectation of hypnosis
3.83	3.77	5.03	3.53[c]

[a]From Hilgard and Tart (1966). Copyright 1966 by the American Psychological Association. Reprinted by permission.

[b]Control subjects received the same treatment across days; experimental subjects received different treatments.

[c]$p < .025$.

within the total cognitive framework of the experiment would have been for the experimenter to instruct subjects prior to Day 1 that they would, in fact, be tested in hypnosis on Day 2 and then for the experimenter to proceed by repeating the same condition on the second day. Deception is involved in the suggested strategy but such a design attempts to ensure that testing of control subjects is conducted in a similar cognitive context to testing of experimental subjects. In Hilgard and Tart's design results may demonstrate the absence of practice effect but equally well the inequality of cognitive contexts suggests that subjects expecting no change could be cognitively countering any tendency for small (but real) changes to occur across the two testings.

Hilgard and Tart especially concern themselves in their design with the phenomenon of "holding back" which Scharf and Zamansky (1963) and Zamansky,

Scharf, and Brightbill (1964) first demonstrated. This phenomenon is typified by subjects giving a particularly low "pretreatment" score in anticipation of the experimental treatment of hypnosis to follow. Results in Table 2.2 show little evidence of the phenomenon; experimental subjects did not demonstrate any tendency to give lower initial session scores than control subjects. One interesting comparison, though, is that between Experimental Groups 1 and 3 which provide the only counterbalancing encompassed in the design. Hilgard and Tart comment on the discrepancy between hypnotic scores for these two groups (3.70 and 5.03) and attribute it to chance differences in susceptibility among the subjects in the two samples. It seems plausible, however, that data could represent a subtle order effect quite different to the "holding back" phenomenon which is the obvious concern of the design. The mean hypnotic suggestibility score of 5.03 for Group 3 is quite comparable with the hypnotic score for Group 2 (5.13) so it is the score for Group 1 that seems at issue. It could be that the particularly low score for Group 1 is in part a function of the size of the initial test score given in the waking condition by the same set of subjects. This hypothesis argues plausibly that subjects may "hold back" pretreatment performance as the evidence of Scharf and his associates has indicated but also they may later adjust treatment scores in the knowledge of how they performed initially in the first session. Low pretreatment scores would imply lower subsequent performance than high pretreatment scores when modification is implied either by the experimenter's instruction to subjects and/or the nature of the conditions themselves. Subjects might adjust their performance "retrospectively" just as they can alter behavior in "anticipation" of what they are expected to do.

Overall, then, the results of Hilgard and Tart (1966) do not conclusively demonstrate "hypersuggestibility." The phenomenon may well exist, but the design they used yields results that are open to equivocal interpretation.

Tart and Hilgard's (1966) study is the final one in the series and raises a major question about the Same-Subjects design which merits serious discussion. The focus of this third study was on the tendency of subjects run under waking–imagination conditions to spontaneously enter the hypnotic state. Using stratified sampling procedures, High Waking Suggestibility (HWS)–High Hypnotic Suggestibility (HHS) and Low WS–High HS groups (preselected on the SHSS:C) each were tested under two conditions: waking–imagination, and hypnosis. The design differed in two basic respects from that used in the studies which preceded. A deception strategy was adopted and subjects were not told there was going to be a second condition. The authors argued that this strategy would eliminate the troublesome "holding back" phenomenon. Second, counterbalancing was systematically employed for the first time; half the subjects received the hypnotic condition first and the other half, the imagination condition. In an attempt to minimize experimenter bias, suggestions were also tape recorded (as before) and subjects' state reports were again carefully collected. If in the imagination condition subjects ever reported entering hypnosis they were immediately instructed to awaken fully, so as to prevent inadvertent induction of trance.

Checking on hypnotic selection, the authors found that the subjects in the study whom they had classified initially as high in waking suggestibility no longer appeared so. The present study took pains to prevent hypnosis occuring inadvertently in the waking condition whereas when the subjects were selected originally no such precaution was taken. Thus, data suggested that some subjects in the selection phase slipped into borderline hypnotic state when responding to waking imagination conditions and now were being prevented from doing so, thus creating an inconsistency in classification across the tests of waking suggestibility. A major inference from this work is that subjects who show high-waking suggestiblity might be performing as they do because they spontaneously enter trance under what is falsely assumed to be "nonhypnotic" instruction. It follows directly from this inference that for a state account stressing the relevance of "internal events" the absence of a formal induction procedure offers no firm guarantee that the conditions of an experiment are not trance inducing. The obvious relevance of subjects' subjective state reports gathered on all of the conditions adopted in this study led the authors to state that "report of feeling hypnotized" must be considered primary data about the presence or absence of hypnosis.

The fact that subjects showing high waking suggestibility may do so because they have entered hypnosis raises specific problems for Hilgard's model that the framework has not recognized fully nor has sufficiently dealt with. Past evidence (Hilgard & Tart, 1966; Weitzenhoffer & Sjoberg, 1961) established specific patterns of relationship between waking and hypnotic suggestibility. Data indicated that individuals fall into two categories; those who show an increase in suggestibility and those who do not and that people showing a high degree of suggestibility may or may not be hypnotized. The whole question of spontaneous entry into trance throws the data gathered in the earlier studies into new perspective. Conditions must be precisely defined whereby one can infer when a given condition is, or is not, "trance inducing," otherwise the relationship between hypnotic and waking suggestibility–and the issue of "hypnotic gain" which is germane to the model–remains indeterminate. Looked at within Hilgard's model the question of an "increase in suggestibility" can only be truly meaningful if the conditions used by the experimenter for his "waking" groups are *not* in fact trance inducing.

The model obviously views the collection of subjects' state reports as the appropriate solution to the problem. It is conceivable, for example, that data across conditions can be meaningfully compared for those subjects who do not report entering trance in the waking condition yet do report so in the hypnotic condition. This assumes, however, that verbal reports of being hypnotized are perfectly valid indicators of the presence or absence of hypnosis–a position

Hilgard himself has retreated from in his later writings. Research has also yet to resolve some paradoxical findings regarding the relationship between state reports and objective scores. In Hilgard and Tart's study (1966), for example, it is puzzling to note that subjects' reports of being hypnotized correlated significantly with suggestibility scores on an imagination condition where subjects had no expectation of hypnosis, but correlated zero with scores on the same condition where subjects actually expected that hypnosis would be induced. There is also something of a bind here for the state theorist which he has to be careful to avoid. If subjects' reports are equated with the presence of "hypnosis" he must be careful that the domain of procedures defining "trance inducing" does not expand to the ridiculous to include all kinds of events and occurrences as hypnotic in character. The problem of definition here, in research terms, is obviously a demanding one.

Two additional comments should be made about this final study of Tart and Hilgard (1966). The first concerns the counterbalancing that was employed. The study reported that there was no evidence or order effects and no data were listed for them. The sizes of the groups in the study, however, were very small and a maximum of three subjects would have been allocated to any given testing order. Both the paucity of numbers and the absence of data prevent one from assessing the adequacy of the counterbalancing strategy and from judging whether order effects within the design were effectively minimized by the strategy. The second point concerns the need for replication. The results from subjects' state reports appear to be crucial to the kinds of comparison the model is designed to make. Considering the importance of the findings and the fact that no more than six subjects were allocated to any one group, it is essential that the experiment be repeated with a much larger sample of subjects.

Following upon recent work conducted on the relevance of the processes of dissociation to hypnosis, Hilgard's "hidden observer" effects obtained in his research on pain need also to be evaluated in terms of the possible shortcomings of the Same-Subjects design. One implication of his novel technique is that the reports offered by the subject at different "levels," as it were, could reflect the subject's perception that varying pain reports are required of him–otherwise why would such an elaborate procedure be adopted by the experimenter? The paradox of the data is that open hypnotic reports of pain and suffering are consistent with the hypnotist's suggestions for anaesthesia, while the hidden observer reports pain and suffering that share characteristics in common with reports offered in a nonhypnotic baseline session (Hilgard, 1974a, b; 1975; Knox, Morgan, & Hilgard, 1974). The intelligent subject may know very well, though, how to cope with the unusual situation in which he is placed. Sacerdote (1970) puts the argument succinctly: "After all, the experimenter wants him (the subject) to have anaesthesia, wants him to deny anaesthesia; therefore, he does both things. In other words, he is complying very well; he is proving that he can use the dissociation to prove the point that the experimenter wants to prove, while at the same time being comfortable with his anaesthesia [p. 10] ." At this point, however, such a possibility yet remains to be tested.

Evidence for Specific Order Effects in Hypnosis

This seems the appropriate point to review the evidence provided by Scharf and his associates on the "holding back" phenomenon and to assess the relevance of these data to Hilgard's model. The phenomenon is one the model is particularly concerned to discount and the extent to which its procedures cope with the problem are therefore open to review.

Scharf and Zamansky (1963) conducted a series of experiments designed to investigate the effectiveness of hypnotic suggestions on the reduction of word-recognition thresholds. Twenty-four good hypnotic subjects were used and all subjects received three sessions in counterbalanced order: hypnotic suggestion, waking suggestion, and control. Each of the three sessions had a pretreatment (waking–no suggestion), a treatment (one of the above three), and a posttreatment (waking–no suggestion) phase. Results showed that pretreatment thresholds were associated with expectation of hypnosis. Apparently, subjects knowing that the experiment was concerned with hypnosis expected to be hypnotized in the suggestion sessions and consequently showed high initial word recognition thresholds. A second study was conducted to attempt to eliminate the troublesome variable. Using a similar design, with just a hypnotic and a control session, no indication at all was given to subjects that they would be hypnotized in one session and not in the other. To reinforce this change, procedures were employed to imply that the experiment was quite unrelated to the hypnotic screening that all subjects had undergone initially. The results of the study again showed high pretreatment thresholds and in a postexperimental inquiry conducted at the completion of the study 14 out of 24 subjects said they thought they might be hypnotized anyway during one or both of the sessions. The data are most relevant: attempts were made to prevent subjects associating the study with hypnosis but subjects still expected to be hypnotized regardless of what the experimenter did to control expectancy. Connors (1976) replicated the same effect in a quite different testing context. In the studies just reviewed, subjects gave high pretreatment thresholds in an attempt to "hold back" so as to allow improvement in the forthcoming treatment phase. In the light of such evidence it becomes critical to ask "how does one judge the effectiveness of hypnotic suggestions independent of behavior affected by expectancy of hypnosis?" Certainly, no simple manipulations on the part of the experimenter can be assumed to be adequate.

Procedures to control expectancies concerning hypnosis were contrasted directly in work reported by Zamansky, Scharf, and Brightbill (1964). Subjects were given explicitly differing information about hypnosis being part of the study and were tested in two sessions, a hypnotic and a waking one, receiving the two sessions in counterbalanced order. In the first of the two studies (Experiment 1) subjects heard no mention of hypnosis while in the other they were told that they would be hypnotized during the experimental (hypnotic) but not the control (waking) session. Results demonstrated a more general phenomenon than had been reported earlier. Across all pretreatment tests but one, subjects gave high thresholds which were reduced in the treatment phase. In the second study, however, where subjects were explicitly told hypnosis would be involved (Experiment 2) the control group *gave a low pretreatment threshold which rose rather than fell in the treatment phase.* The data for both of the experiments are illustrated in Table 2.3. The table shows control subjects in Experiment 2, yielding a rise in mean threshold from 170 to 200 msecs.

The results in Table 2.3 show that "holding back" fits part but not all of the data presented in the studies. The more general rule from this evidence appears to be that, when pretreatments are high thresholds are subsequently reduced, but when they are low they may later rise or remain unchanged. Results are consistent with our earlier discussion of the order effects appearing in Hilgard and Tart's (1966) study (see discussion above of the data in relation to Table 2.2). It seems that the nature of performance on one condition may in part dictate the extent of change that will be shown subsequently. It appears that "holding back" is only one of several possible order effects pertinent to the Same-Subjects design.

Now that the major studies illustrating the nature of Hilgard's model and the evidence relevant to order effects have been reviewed a more general evaluation of the model can be offered. Here, an attempt will be made to integrate the

TABLE 2.3
Mean Thresholds (Milliseconds) in Experiments 1 and 2 as Reported by Zamansky, Scharf, and Brightbill (1964)

	Pretreatment	Phase treatment	Posttreatment
Experiment 1			
Experimental	183	153	152
Control	185	140	134
Experiment 2			
Experimental	191	164	173
Control	170	200	161

[a]From Zamansky, Scharf, and Brightbill *Journal of Personality*, Vol. 32. Copyright 1964 by Duke University Press.

evidence available from the studies and to evaluate the model methodologically, overall.

SUMMARY EVALUATION OF HILGARD'S MODEL

Same-Subjects Design and Extraneous Influences

The major problem with a *Same–Subjects* as opposed to an *Independent Groups* design is the vulnerability of the former paradigm to systematic order effects reflecting influences that are extraneous to those the experimenter is really concerned about. Data suggest that three possible order effects may exist within the model: (a) a practice effect arising from repeated measurement on the test of suggestibility chosen by the experimenter; (b) "holding back" in the pretreatment phase on the basis of the expectancy that hypnosis will later be administered; (c) response to the demand characteristics for "change" reflecting the influence of "level" of performance of one condition on another where change across the two conditions is implied by the procedures adopted in the design.

Hilgard's model fails to adequately cope with these order effects. Across the major studies employed by the model, in fact, there is considerable methodological uncertainty as to what procedures in fact ought to be adopted. Systematic counterbalancing was employed in Tart and Hilgard's (1966) study but too few subjects were used to judge the adequacy of the control. The preferred strategy in the experiments that have used the model has been to manipulate the expectancy of subjects regarding what conditions will occur. In summary, Weitzenhoffer and Sjoberg asked subjects what expectancy they had and informed them that the experimenter had none himself; Hilgard and Tart (1966) investigated the possiblity of "holding back" by manipulating subjects' perceptions of change through the experimenter's instruction that a different condition would or would not follow; and Tart and Hilgard (1966) employed a deception strategy to control for the same phenomenon not instructing subjects at all concerning the fact a second condition would be run. All of these strategies, however, are suspect in the light of the evidence reported by Connors (1976), Scharf and Zamansky (1963), and Zamansky, Scharf, and Brightbill (1964). In these studies subjects developed expectancies about hypnosis quite independent of the experimenter's instructions (or lack of them). Postexperimental inquiry data revealed that the experimenter's manipulations were not at all being perceived by the majority of subjects as the experimenter had intended that they should.

The evidence suggests that the most likely form of artifact adhering to the model is that of a "change" in response following simply from subjects' perceptions of the experimental condition as different–change, though, that probably is dependent at least to some extent on the size or magnitude of scores given in the pretreatment phase. Practice effects are less likely to exist but they yet remain to be adequately investigated. Proper check on practice effects ought to repeat testing in the control group under conditions which are comparable (viz. in "cognitive expectancy of change") to those existing in the experimental group. The use of the Same-Subjects design as far as this particular order effect is concerned also requires the special construction of equivalent forms of the suggestibility test. Where more than two sessions are run, the cost of this work is high; the demand for alternative tests becoming especially prohibitive when there is a large number of repeated testings.

When the Same–Subjects design is employed, systematic counterbalancing should be a necessary feature of the design and when the strategy is applied the experimenter should carefully analyze the data for subtle order effects. Just how complicated these effects can become is well-illustrated in the research literature (see Chapter 7 for detailed discussion of some of these effects). Evans and Orne (1965), for instance, found unexpected demand characteristics operating in their counterbalanced design. Using a physical endurance task they found a significant interaction between condition of testing and the order in which the conditions were tested. Base-level endurance was significantly higher when waking base-level performance preceded hypnosis performance than when it followed hypnosis. There is no simple explanation of the effect and it obviously reflects a host of motivational and attitudinal variables that can operate within the social psychology of the psychological experiment. It is unfortunate that the Same-Subjects design has no well defined strategies to separately cope with the various effects which may arise and it is not strictly true to argue, as Weitzenhoffer and Sjoberg (1961) do, that an Independent Groups design suffers comparably from the same difficulties. Even if one group of subjects knows that another group is being hypnotized in the same study it seems a reasonable guess that the subjects involved have no real means of judging precisely what would be the nature of the performance of somebody else. "Expectation of change" is quite likely a much less relevant determinant of results when it is the hypothetical performance of other subjects that is being assessed.

The Nature of the Control Condition

One of the major assumptions behind Hilgard's model is that differences reflecting the effect of hypnotic induction are much less likely to emerge in an Independent Groups design than a Same-Subjects design, particularly when small numbers of subjects are tested. What has not been assessed with respect to the model and what appears very relevant to this assumption is that the likelihood of differences occurring with either design must depend on the exact nature of the nonhypnotic condition selected. Evidence relating to the Independent Groups design appears quite clear. When separate groups are used and a hypnotic condition is compared with a waking control defined simply as a "test of imagination" (for example, Barber & Calverley, 1962; for review of relevant studies, see Barber, 1969) differences usually appear, but where other control groups are used for comparison (for example, a TM condition defined also as a test involving imagination) the evidence inconsistently demonstrates the presence of differences. Sometimes, even the "nonhypnotic" condition yields a higher level of performance than the hypnotic one as shown, for example, by the data on subjective scores reported in the studies of Barber (1965), and Barber and Calverley (1962) where TM instructions were used. In general, a hypnotic procedure fails to produce an appreciable enhancement of suggestibility when compared to a set of instructions which informs subjects that previous subjects have performed well, that they should imagine vividly and should cooperate to the best of their ability. There are other matters raised by a comparison such as this one (motivational equivalence of the control and hypnotic groups easily may be lost, for example), but the general point can be made that the predictive power and efficiency of the Same-Subjects design must depend as it obviously does with the Independent Groups design on the exact specifications of the condition that is chosen for control purposes.

The evidence available on the Same-Subjects design suggests that defining the control condition as a "test of imagination" as compared to a "test of responsiveness to waking suggestion" or a test of relaxation (Edmonston, 1972) does make a considerable difference to the magnitude of the suggestibility test scores that are found (Hilgard, 1965a; Hilgard & Tart, 1966). One could well argue that all of these conditions constitute appropriate "nonhypnotic" controls yet some (for example, simple waking instruction) are much more likely than others (for example, imagination instructions) to yield significant differences from a hypnotic condition. In defense of his model Hilgard (1965a) makes the point that there is a lesson to be drawn from Barber and Glass (1962) employing a Same-Subjects design and finding significant differences, while Barber and Calverley (1962, 1963a) employed an Independent Groups design and generally did not. The differences in findings across studies, though, do not unequivocally support the efficacy of the Same-Subjects design. Results could be as much a function of the fact TM instructions were employed in the latter studies as the fact that the former study used subjects as their own controls. Barber and Calverley (1968) compared a variety of experimental conditions using both the Same-Subjects and Independent Groups designs and showed clearly that significant differences are obtainable using either methodological paradigm. The size of the differences that emerged, however, seemed to depend as much or perhaps even more on the nature of the control group adopted than on the fact that the same subjects performed across conditions. When comparing different models of hypnosis one obviously needs to keep very much in mind the fact that different models use varying kinds of control conditions. All inevitably carry distinctive consequences on their own.

Definition of "Nonhypnotic"

Very much relevant to our previous point regarding strict selection of control conditions is the observation made by Hilgard and his co-workers that some so-called "nonhypnotic" conditions are themselves trance inducing. It is not the procedural conditions per se that are important but whether or not the subject perceives them as part of a context that is "appropriate" for displaying hypnotic behavior. Something of the difficulties involved in such a position have already been mentioned.

A number of methodological observations seem pertinent. First, and most obviously, a condition which is intended as nonhypnotic but clearly is not should never be employed in an experimental design as a "waking" control. Second, while the likelihood of arousing hypnosis exists with some conditions and these conditions remain unspecified, the relationship between waking and hypnotic suggestibility (of major concern to the model) must remain indeterminate. The relationship cannot be outlined unambiguously in any exact fashion until further research isolates those conditions which are trance inducing from those conditions which are not. Finally, until such research is conducted it seems necessary to carefully investigate (at least with stratified samples of high waking suggestibility subjects) whether subjects report that they slip inadvertently into trance when so-called control conditions are employed. As an interim strategy Hilgard and Tart's "state report" procedure where subjects are alerted if they report feeling entranced seems a suitable procedure to adopt. The lowered responsiveness of subjects allocated to such a condition, however, is open to a number of interpretations. It is perhaps not altogether surprising, for instance, that subjects who are continually aroused when they start to become involved in their imaginings do not respond very well to suggestions. In the final analysis, what is needed is a parametric study of the characteristics of different sets of waking instructions in order to discriminate those sets of instructions that elicit trance reports from subjects. It is, of course, easier to raise the problem than to solve it—we are begging, for example, the very question "what is the essence of trance induction?" Even those who choose to formally apply the label "hypnotic induction" to their procedures are hard put to define what it is exactly that constitutes the category they adopt.

Need for Postexperimental Inquiry

An essential procedure which Hilgard's model has tended to neglect is a formal postexperimental inquiry into subjects' perceptions of the experimenter's manipulations. In a model which values the assessment of subjects' feelings about being hypnotized it is surprising that this more general inquiry has not been endorsed consistently. In none of the basic studies that have been reviewed, for example, was a formal postexperimental inquiry conducted, yet such an inquiry would have several important advantages: (a) it would validate the experimenter's assumption that any information fed to subjects to control their expectancies had the effect that was intended; (b) it would help the experimenter to explore subjects' individual perceptions of the demand characteristics carried by experimental procedures; (c) more importantly, it would enable the experimenter to evaluate much more precisely than the model does at present, whether or not the subject performed differently in the hypnotic conditions simply to match his perception of the need to change from how he had performed previously in the waking state; (d) finally, the inquiry would help to isolate out subjects who deliberately simulated performance in the study in order to please the experimenter.

"Verbal Report of Trance" as an Interactive Variable

As already noted, a very distinctive feature of Hilgard's model is its reliance on data gathered from subjective reports of subjects about the extent to which they feel hypnotized. The majority of models of hypnosis in the current literature underemphasize the value of verbal report; reliance on internal processes as implied by these reports runs counter, as it were, to the strict tenets of a truly objective, behavioristic approach to hypnosis. Stoyva and Kamiya (1968) in an important article looked specifically at the area of dreaming and showed how feasible it was to incorporate verbal report into the list of dependent measures in one's research design. Adopting the logic of convergent operations (which Hilgard, 1973b, formally espouses on his model) they drew attention to the scientific value of combining verbal report with other measures as a way of validating constructs symbolizing special states of awareness. Some attempt will now be made to extend the logic they put forward in order to point out the analytic possibilities of including subjects' verbal reports of hypnosis as primary research data. The full implications of the logic have not been discussed before with respect to hypnosis and the discussion serves to elaborate this very important aspect of Hilgard's model.

Let us assume for the purposes of argument that "trance logic"–the tendency some people display in the hypnotic setting to tolerate logical incongruities–is reliably associated with hypnosis. Orne makes the claim in his paper of 1959; and Hilgard (1965a) lists it as a primary characteristic of the trance state, and the issue has been a matter of sharp controversy in the recent literature (see Hilgard, 1972a; Johnson, Maher, & Barber, 1972). For the moment let us assume also that we are attempting to measure "hypnosis" by means of two measures:

"trance logic" behavior, and "verbal report of being hypnotized." At the outset, two rather extreme positions are indicated. First, one may argue that hypnosis can be defined strictly in terms of trance logic behavior: when behavior illustrating logical incongruity occurs following hypnotic induction then "hypnosis" can be assumed to be present; if the subject fails to report being in hypnosis, then it is his report which is in error. Alternatively, we can move to the other extreme and argue that the ultimate criterion is the subjective report. Here, the appearance of the logically incongruous response must first be validated against the report of trance and trance logic behavior is valuable only to the extent it correlates with the subject's verbal admission of trance. Consequently, if the subject shows the appropriate behavior but fails to report being in hypnosis then we can only assume that the special state of hypnosis has not in fact been induced.

There are difficulties with both these positions. As far as the first is concerned, it is hard to know what we ought to infer if trance logic-type behavior occurs in the absence of formal induction. We might want to conclude that "hypnosis" is indicated but if a subject gives the correct response and reports not feeling at all hypnotized we ought at the very least to be cautious before concluding that trance is truly present. There are difficulties also with the second position. At times, verbal report obviously seems limited as an accurate indicator of hypnosis. Consider, for example, a case where we administer an induction procedure and the subject then shows all the indications of a trance logic response. The subject subsequently develops amnesia for the events of trance and then goes on to deny that he experienced anything unusual. No one would be likely to accept this verbal report as a valid indicator of the absence of hypnosis. We know that if the amnesia was lifted and we asked the subject again he would respond differently. In this instance, we seem to be forced to accept the trance logic response (and justifiably so) as the more appropriate indicator of hypnosis.

A more moderate position is obviously called for, one that does not appeal exclusively to either measure. Such a position might be that hypnosis is a hypothetical construct indexed in an imperfect way by both trance logic behavior and verbal report of being in trance and a multitude of intersecting and overlapping observations bear upon it. The analytic possibilities afforded by this position are wide-ranging and they pose questions about the area of hypnosis that are rarely conceptualized and thus virtually ignored in the current literature.

Figure 2.1 illustrates this position diagrammatically and sets out the logical possibilities of interaction in a Venn diagram which depicts three circles. The first circle represents the ideal notion of "trance experience"; the second, the subject's verbal report that he is experiencing hypnosis; and the third represents the subject's demonstration of trance logic behavior—a subject incongruously reporting overlapping hallucinations after a hypnotist has given the suggestion to hallucinate and then presented the subject with the very object being halluci-

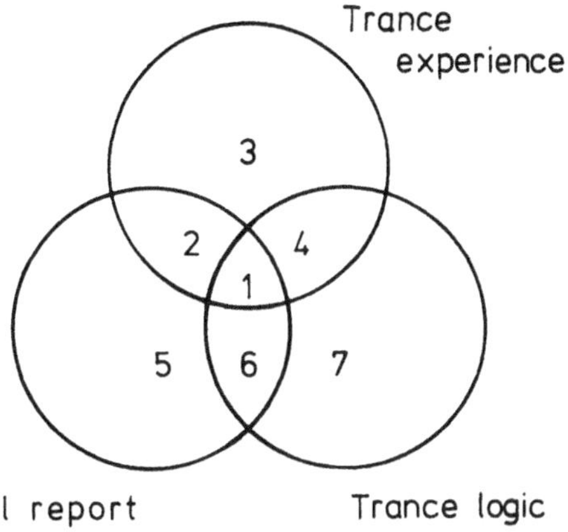

FIGURE 2.1 Venn diagram illustrating the logical possibilities resulting from the interaction of hypothetical trance experience, verbal report of hypnotic, and trance logic behavior.

nated, would be an example of this kind of response. The regions shown in the diagram are seven in number and are illustrated as follows:

Region 1. This is the ideal case where all the circles overlap. Actual experience, logically incongruous behavior, and verbal report of hypnosis are all congruent.

Region 2. Here, actual experience of trance occurs and the subject reports in accordance with the experience but no logical incongruity is displayed.

Region 3. Here, there is actual experience of trance but the subject does not report feeling hypnotized nor is there any evidence of logical incongruity.

Region 4. This is the case where trance is present and the subject shows evidence of logical incongruity but he doesn't report feeling hypnotized.

Region 5. Here, the subject mistakenly reports trance when it is not actually present and he shows no signs of logically incongruous behavior.

Region 6. This is the case where the subject mistakenly reports trance and also demonstrates logical incongruity.

Region 7. Here, logical incongruity is demonstrated but there is no report of hypnosis, nor is the state present in fact.

In setting out these regions, Figure 2.1 makes explicit the logical alternatives which pertain to the construct of hypnosis arising from attempts to measure it in two quite distinct ways. By means of the systematic exploration relatively neglected possibilities come to light—possibilities 5, 6, and 7 for example. Region 5 depicts the case where the subject is obviously responding purely to please the experimenter. Region 6 depicts a more unlikely instance but one that is still conceivable: the subject here is simply fabricating more intelligently than the other subject by manufacturing the behavior the experimenter is looking for in addition to reporting feeling hypnotized. Region 7 depicts the finding that so-called "trance logic" behavior is by no means unique to hypnosis; it occurs, for example, in other states of consciousness. Overall, the scheme allows us to know exactly the range of possibilities and helps to minimize the risk of bias in interpretation. It also encompasses the scattered observations which appear in the literature. Pattie (1935), for instance, comments on the fact many deep-trance subjects feel so little "entranced" that they may challenge the hypnotist as to whether they are in a hypnotic state or not–invalid verbal reports of the type indicated here are illustrated by Regions 3 and 4.

The framework outlined in Figure 2.1 is consistent with Hilgard's philosophical position and the salient principles as laid down by his model. The analysis recognizes verbal reports as potentially useful indicators of inferred mental processes, and the notion of "altered state of awareness" is conceptually incorporated into a full and complete framework of investigation. Also, new relationships can be investigated in the spirit of open, impartial inquiry. According to the scheme, hypnosis like any other state of awareness is an inferred process having a number of public accompaniments that are open to study and analysis. The measures themselves can be validated by experimental manipulation. If by some technique we could increase the amount of logical incongruity the subject showed in the hypnotic setting and at the same time we demonstrated that the subject reported an increase in "hypnotic depth" then here we are establishing more firmly than before the validity of trance logic as an indicator of the state of hypnosis.

The analysis that has been outlined, of course, represents an ideal case frustratingly far from reality–the question still very much remains open at the moment as to how useful the trance logic measure actually is and whether depth reports are thoroughly reliable. The suggested framework serves rather to point out the full relevance, conceptually speaking, of the verbal report measure and helps to illustrate just as Hilgard's model does, the respectability of holding to the state concept when it is analyzed within a framework based on the logic of convergent operations. Viewed as an interacting measure, "verbal report" does seem an entirely legitimate way of approaching the construct, "hypnosis."

IMPLICATIONS FOR FUTURE RESEARCH

This chapter has focused distinctively on Hilgard and the general model that he and his co-workers have investigated intensively. Methodologically speaking, the Same-Subjects design is clearly a very viable framework for research. Our analysis of the paradigm has focused on those studies that appear to have been the most influential in formally promulgating its essential features. In doing so, though, it was unfortunate that we bypassed the work of others in the field who have effectively used a similar design–workers, for instance, such as Reiff and

Scheerer (1959) who used subjects as their own controls in their classic work on hypnotic age regression.

Any model of hypnosis is inevitably associated with specific questions or issues in the field it is especially suited to answer. The issue that we have dealt with in this chapter and which has been proposed as the major one adhering to Hilgard's model is the detection of the possible differences in suggestibility between the effects of hypnotic induction and nonhypnotic instructions. The question is an entirely meaningful and legitimate one, but as we have seen, it is a difficult one to answer unequivocally. The nature of the inquiry almost dictates *à priori* the necessity of using subjects as their own controls. Where an "increase" in response from one condition to another is the point at issue, knowledge of the pretreatment rate of performance of a subject seems crucial in defining the true meaning of enhancement for any given subject. The argument is especially relevant where strong individual differences exist in the trait being measured—differences which, as Hilgard says, may swamp the very pattern of behavior that the experimenter is looking for were he not to choose to incorporate initial waking level responses of experimental subjects within the one design.

Many important areas of inquiry accrue to the model and fall naturally within the scope of its framework. The search, for example, continues for the correlates of hypnotic susceptibility. Though an unrewarding field of endeavor this topic of inquiry attempts to answer directly the primary question, "What makes one person more hypnotizable or susceptible than another?" "How modifiable is hypnotic susceptibility?" is another question which has led, like the personality issue, to contradictory findings in the literature (see Diamond, 1974; Hilgard, 1967, 1975). This latter question is especially important for the model, for it reflects in part the assumption of Hilgard's theory that hypnotizability is a durable trait changing rarely with differences in situational contexts. Finally, we are obliged to look also for adequate means of measuring "hypnotic depth." One of the basic tenets of Hilgard's theory is that hypnosis occurs in various degrees so this issue is a particularly significant one for the model; the inclusion of state reports as a standard feature of design attests the model's recognition of its relevance. All of these questions reflect areas of inquiry which deserve analysis and review in their own right. It is well to recognize, though, that as with the issue of "hypersuggestibility" none of them is the sole concern of Hilgard or the model that he has proposed. A multitude of workers in the field—using quite varying strategies—have attempted to investigate the correlates of hypnotizability, for example (for review of them see Deckert & West, 1963).

Independent of the logical relevance of the model to the specific questions it raises, we have asked method-wise what are the advantages and disadvantages, the strengths and weaknesses, of its strategies, and in the course of discussion a number of criticisms have come to light. First, there is the question of order effects. Conceptually speaking, the probable consequences of applying one treatment before another require exact formulation; the possible sequence effects adhering to the design are many and varied. "Holding back," for example, is just one aspect of the more general class of effects arising from performance on one condition affecting another preceding it, either through anticipation of what is to follow and/or knowledge of the performance that has already been achieved. The methodological uncertainty in the model concerning how best to cope with these effects has to be overcome; consistent, systematic use of counterbalancing at the very least is required.

Second, and related to the first objection, there is little formal attempt to adopt procedures that effectively achieve the control of subjects' expectations—a common problem through much of hypnotic research. Perhaps as Scharf and Zamansky (1963) suggest subjects ought to be told in the Same-Subjects design that no further testing will be conducted and wherever possible base-level responses ought to be taken before hypnotic screening is conducted. Always, a formal postexperimental inquiry should be instituted to examine subjects' actual perceptions of the procedures the experimenter has administered and, further, effective steps should routinely be taken to minimize intersession communication.

Third, the instructions used by the model (and any other model for that matter) should be carefully analyzed with respect to the specific attitudes, motivations and expectations they engender in subjects. More importantly, as far as this particular framework is concerned, they should be closely investigated for their potential to elicit verbal reports of hypnosis and those conditions which are found to facilitate feelings of being hypnotized should be classified separately from those which do not.

Finally, selectiveness of subject-sampling is an issue that requires formal resolution. At times, the model espouses subject selection; at other times it does not, arguing on the grounds that naivety of subjects is a design feature that ought to be preserved. Hilgard has often stated that a hypnotic study should obviously employ subjects who are capable of exhibiting the phenomena the experimenter is interested in—it seems reasonable, then, to say that stratified sampling is really the proper strategy to adopt. The question immediately arises, however, as to what particular groups should be chosen for comparison. There seems little cause for worry about selecting low waking suggestibility subjects; these subjects are the ones who are most unlikely to respond "hypnotically" in the waking condition and are also those who show the most gain following induction (Hilgard & Tart, 1966). The more obvious choice of high waking suggestibility subjects (obvious because this group offers the best guarantee that there will be a strong response following induction) presents us with some difficulties. Empirical research must either delineate conditions whereby it is known for certain that a highly suggestible subject's waking performance is truly nonhypnotic or effective procedures must be instituted (this is the solution preferred by the model) to guarantee that the waking subject does not slip inadvertently into hypnosis. This problem that state theory faces is a particularly vexing one.

The use of verbal reports in the attempt to validate the construct "hypnosis," is entirely consistent with the model's aims and represents a very positive strength of the framework. Consistent with recent formulations of the model, the logic of convergent operations offers us a sophisticated approach to the study of hypnosis as an altered state of awareness. Such logic, for example, forbids accepting verbal report as the sole criterion of hypnosis; use of verbal report within an analytical framework such as the kind set out in Figure 2.1 stresses the value of considering this particular measure, among others, as interactive variables. Such an approach is consistent with open inquiry as an essential feature of research endeavour; it embraces "internal processes" as usefully relevant to theorizing about hypnosis, and attempts to validate the construct at issue as a major methodological concern.

In conclusion, much remains by way of research to further our knowledge about Hilgard's model and new research indications have been opened up which are essential to explore. The notion that a plurality of functionally interdependent cognitive systems relate to hypnosis is an important one to consider, for example. The significance of the "hidden observer" approach lies not merely in its potential relevance for explaining currently puzzling hypnotic phenomena, but also in its relevance to a general psychology of how the mind works. Among other things, it has important implications for one of the unresolved problems inherent in Freud's earlier theory in which he divided the mind into conscious, preconscious, and unconscious systems and gave a dynamic role to a censor which had access to knowledge not possessed by conscious awareness; Freud was never able to specify how this could be so, and relinquished this theory in favor of the id–ego–superego formulation. However, the problem of cognitive processes showing a high degree of rationality (as exemplified by the Censor) that were not available to consciousness has continued to haunt cognitive psychology. By no means are all of the data on the "hidden observer" in, but current observations are sufficiently compelling to suggest that they may provide empirical underpinnings to an elusive concept. Further research must explore, however, the complex demand characteristics that obviously adhere to the technique. One might search, for instance, for ways in which the account can be distinguished from other explanations of hypnotic events such as that offered by role theory which appeals to the notion of "role involvement."

Hilgard's model of hypnosis like any other paradigm of research has both strengths and weaknesses. But, its weaknesses aside for the moment, such questions as those it raises highlight the essential productivity of the model. The very fact that problems like the ones that have been outlined can be formulated attests the model's scientific value and emphasizes its utility as a fruitful tool of theoretical and empirical inquiry.

3

The Operational Approach to Hypnosis: The Model of Theodore X. Barber

> "*Hypnosis, hypnotic state,* and related constructs are unnecessary and misleading . . . the phenomena that have been traditionally subsumed under these terms can be better understood by utilizing a different set of concepts that are an integral part of present-day psychology [Barber, 1969, p. iii].

No person in the field of psychology has done more to challenge traditional assumptions about hypnosis and to question the nature of hypnotic phenomena than Theodore X. Barber. An enormously productive worker, Barber has queried the very relevance of the term "hypnosis" as a necessary construct for explaining the multiple forms of behavior that typically occur within the hypnotic setting. Barber claims that the term "hypnosis" as it is ordinarily employed in the literature is ambiguously and tautologically defined and that research has been hindered much more than helped by continued appeal to the connotations that have accrued to this term through the years. His thinking challenges our most fundamental assumptions about hypnosis (Dalal, 1966) and in their place he has substituted searching empirical analysis of a multitude of factors that appear to bear upon "hypnotic" behavior.

Barber's model has isolated a host of variables which affect response to standard test suggestions. Responsivity to hypnotic instruction, for example, is functionally related to antecedent factors such as subjects' attitudes toward the phenomenon being investigated, the manner in which the context of testing is defined, and even the wording of suggestions and the tone of voice in which the suggestions are delivered. Looking at hypnotic phenomena in this way the model has no need for any special theoretical constructs such as "hypnosis" or "hypnotic state." Rather, it searches for the lawful functional relationships which exist between specifiable antecedent factors (such as the wording and tone of suggestions) and well delineated consequences that typify the various forms behavior may take in the hypnotic situation (viz. actual response to suggestion, "appearance" of trance, and testimony about being hypnotized).

Barber's proposed model, reflecting the basic tenets of scientific psychology, accepts the ultimate criterion of meaning as the testability of any statement that is made. In almost strict logical positivist fashion, the model attempts to rid hypnosis of its so-called "pseudoproblems"—those for which no empirical answers are available—and aligns the study of hypnosis firmly with the basic axioms of modern science. For the main part, Barber's account of hypnosis carries the characteristic hallmarks of strict operational thinking: the term "hypnosis" may denote something only if there are concrete criteria for its applicability; and propositions (about hypnosis) have empirical meaning only when the criteria of their truth or falsity consist of concrete operations performable upon demand (Stevens, 1939). Philosophically speaking, it is important to note that Barber's approach to the study of hypnosis is not an ultra-positivist one; his framework ultimately moves beyond the simple classification of concrete events. It is entirely consistent with the basic tenets of scientific empiricism, for instance, that the model recognizes the need for theoretical integration of data. It asserts, though, that hypothetical terms can only be allowed if they satisfy the basic criterion of meaning, that is, they are testable. Barber's major claim is that the theoretical concept of hypnosis, as we know it presently, is in fact untestable and hence the construct itself is expendable.

It is difficult to assess whether Barber's orientation is firmly behavioristic as well as operational. Strictly speaking, operationism ought not to deny the existence of a "hypnotic state" were we able to define this term in a satisfactory way. A strict behaviorist, though, might deny the concept in the first instance because of its mentalistic overtones and seeming adherence to internal, private rather than physical, public events. Perhaps the question the reader will find most provocative about Barber's model is whether its author rejects the concept of hypnosis solely on the evidence which is available or whether Barber considers the construct expendable because hypnotic phenomena can indeed be explained behaviorally without it. The distinction is a fine one. The first alternative places the onus on the scientist to prove that "hypnosis" is, or is not, a worthwhile concept regardless of its mental overtones. The second position assumes in the first instance that such a concept is not scientifically worthwhile and sets out to demonstrate that hypnotic events can be explained quite well without it in strictly behavioral fashion.

THEORETICAL POSITION

As Barber's notions about "hypnosis" have developed there have been subtle but quite distinct changes in his theorizing about hypnotic phenomena. These changes have to some extent gone unnoticed in the literature and it may be instructive to outline and discuss them at the outset. The general tone of the model that Barber has proposed has been one of extreme skepticism toward traditionalist claims about hypnosis and the model has consistently advocated a strong operational approach to the study of hypnotic phenomena. The changes in emphasis that have occurred in Barber's thinking about hypnosis date from the early formulations about hypnosis that he proposed in the late 1950s to his most recent statements (Barber, 1972; Barber & Ham, 1974; Barber, Spanos, & Chaves, 1974). One can discern three phases, as it were, in the development of his thinking and we turn now to discuss each of these briefly.

Early Development

In his earliest thinking on hypnosis Barber defined hypnosis primarily as a transactional process between subject and operator which itself was divisible into three quite separate and distinct processes: the hypnotic subject was viewed as selectively attuned to the words of the hypnotist, as accepting the words of the hypnotist as literally true, and as cognitively "set" to carry out the hypnotist's instructions and perform successfully. Although Barber was always careful to point out that hypnosis was not in fact a state (Barber, 1958a, b, 1960), state-like features clearly did characterize his initial conception of hypnotic events. The processes he proposed as explaining hypnosis overlapped considerably with those put forward by other theorists who firmly advocated the utility of the state concept. He showed no reticence about accepting the utility of the notion of "trance," for example. "Trance" was acknowledged as just one variable relevant to hypnosis and illustrated simply by an individual reading a book who suddenly realizes that he has no idea of what he has been reading (Barber, 1958a), but the significant fact is that the term was accepted at all. So readily was the term accepted as a legitimate concept, in fact, that Barber (1958b) talked of good hypnotic subjects obeying the hypnotist's suggestions to respond posthypnotically by going "deeper into trance" if and when necessary to properly carry out the suggestions they were given. Early formulations on posthypnotic behavior were also quite consistent with some of the notions of Erickson and Erickson (1941) who argued in traditionalist fashion (somewhat more unequivocally, though) that spontaneous entry into trance is a necessary prerequisite for successful posthypnotic performance.

One of the most salient features of Barber's early theorizing was his insistence on the literal acceptance of the truth or validity of the hypnotist's words by the subject being hypnotized. This process of coming to believe the hypnotist's statements are true bears striking similarity to the state-like conception of "delusion" put forward as a primary feature of hypnotic performance among susceptible subjects by Sutcliffe (1961) and Orne (1974b), and to earlier theoretical accounts of hypnosis as proposed by Arnold (1946). Considering also other notions about the good hypnotic subject that Barber proposed (for example, the susceptible person selectively attends to the hypnotist, decreases attention to "other" symbolic stimulation, increases relaxation, and is especially willing to respond), Barber's early account conflicts to a surprising degree with the thorough going skepticism of his overall general position. These early statements seem caught, as it were, between Barber's essential emphasis on social–transactional processes and surprising acceptance of many of the traditionalist inferences about primary "qualities" of the trance state.

So much, in fact, was common to traditionalist thinking that the lines of distinction between Barber's notions and those of the so-called "state" theorists were originally quite blurred. Barber (1960) saw the hypnotic subject as not the sole determinant of events (the hypnotist had to present his words skilfully enough so that the subject could, in fact, accept them as literally true), but Barber argued for hypnotic aptitude as a necessary condition for hypnotic behavior and for an attitude of "basic trust" between hypnotist and subject as important to the occurrence of hypnotic behavior. His concept of "hypnotic aptitude" predated Hilgard's formal emphasis on individual differences in susceptibility just as his listing of "selective attention" preceded Hilgard's (1965a) concentration on this particular attribute as a primary feature of the trance state. Some of Barber's notions are also quite consistent with others' state-like formulations about hypnosis (Shor, 1959, 1962). His account of "trance" is quite analogous, for example, to Shor's definition of the term as a generalized loss of reality orientation and the concept of "basic trust" is reminiscent of Shor's emphasis on the close personal rapport ("archaic involvement," as he terms it) which may exist between hypnotist and subject in the hypnotic setting. These similarities across theories diminished, however, as the model moved toward strict operational analysis as a framework of investigation. And, in doing so, it became a thoroughly distinctive model of hypnosis.

The Operational Phase

Empirical support for these early notions was weak; Barber relied predominantly on the behavior of selected groups of susceptible subjects and appealed strongly to the testimony of the subjects whom he tested. Later work, beginning in the early 1960s, quite sharply contrasted with his initial formulations and presented superbly systematic programs of research which now looked hard and analytically at the claims of the traditionalists (for example, Barber, 1962). Barber's theoretical conceptions inevitably changed. In reply to an attack on his methodology by Conn and Conn (1967), Barber (1967) challenged particularly the validity of his critics' statement that to understand hypnosis one must recognize factors such as the "exclusion of all extraneous stimuli except those which the operator brings to the subject's attention [p. 115]." In reply, he drew attention to the multitude of variables which affect subjects' testimony of trance and highlighted the fact that such reports may be elicited for quite extraneous reasons. It is significant to note that Barber's rebuke here is entirely at odds with his ready acceptance of the factor of "selective attention" as an integral part of his early formulations regarding the concept of hypnosis (Barber, 1958a, b). In the later work, Barber continues to stress that hypnosis is not a state, but his formal conclusions on the data are much more consistent with the avowed skepticism of his overall general position. This change in orientation is realized with maximum impact in his text, *Hypnosis: A scientific approach* (Barber, 1969). The book illustrates the essential operational character of his approach to hypnosis and represents in one volume a massive compendium of research which very seriously challenges the view that hypnotic phenomena ought to be explained as a function of a special state of consciousness.

The basic rationale for Barber's operational approach to hypnosis is that where alternative explanations hold, a hypothesis involving a theoretical term not defined independently of the behavior giving rise to it is always less satisfactory than a functional account which invokes no special concept at all. The essence of such a functional account of hypnotic phenomena is that concepts of any kind can only be employed when they lie close to observable events and are acceptable only if they are stripped of surplus meaning. The major intent of the framework is threefold. The model aims to: (a) isolate the dependent variables representing the phenomena to be accounted for; (b) specify the relevant antecedent variables related to these phenomena; (c) experimentally determine the functional relations holding between the two sets of variables (antecedent and consequent).

Table 3.1 sets out in illustrative form the various denotable variables, conceptualized by the model, that can be subsumed under the heading of "hypnosis." Examples of dependent variables are the standard measures of response to formal test suggestions, the appearance subjects put forward of being hypnotized, their reports of unusual experiences, and their actual testimony of having "felt" hypnotized. Many antecedent factors, procedural, and otherwise, are also present in the hypnotic context, and any one or more of them may be instrumental in producing the behaviors to be explained. Such antecedent influences include the nature of instructions given to subjects, the way in which the context of testing is defined, subjects' attitudes and expectations about testing, personality variables of both the subject and the hypnotist, and the social interaction between them. The construct "hypnosis" can be said, in fact, to be relegated within this scheme to the antecedent side of the functional equation (for further discussion of this claim, see Chapters 4 and 9 of this book).

The list of variables represented in Table 3.1 is far ranging, but not necessarily exhaustive and the table lists only some of the potential relationships requiring exploration. In essence, the model cogently argues it is the task of research, in fact, to find out which independent factors in particular have an observable effect on specifiable consequent variables, and what variables or combinations of variables most meaningfully relate to each other.

TABLE 3.1

Denotable Variables Subsumed under the Topic *Hypnosis*[a]

Independent (antecedent) variables	Dependent (consequent) variables
A. *Procedural variables* (instructions and suggestions) 1. Procedural variables subsumed under the term *hypnotic induction procedure* a. Statements which define the situation as "hypnosis" b. Motivational instructions c. Suggestions of relaxation, drowsiness, and sleep d. Statements that it is easy to respond to suggestions 2. Other procedural variables a. Specific wording of suggestions b. Experimenter's tone of voice in presenting suggestions c. Method used to present suggestions, e.g., spoken versus tape-recorded presentation d. Specific wording of the questions used to elicit subjective testimony	A. *Response to test suggestions* 1. Muscular rigidities 2. Analgesia 3. Visual–auditory hallucination 4. Age regression 5. Deafness, colorblindness, blindness, and other "physiological" effects 6. Amnesia 7. Postexperimental ("posthypnotic") response etc. B. *"Hypnotic" appearance* (for example, limpness-relaxation, lack of spontaneity, fixed facial expression, "trance stare," psychomotor retardation)
B. *Subject variables* (for example, subject's personality characteristics, and his attitudes and expectations with respect to the experimental situation)	C. *Reports of unusual experiences* (for example, changes in body image and feelings of unreality)
C. *Experimenter variables* (for example, experimenter's prestige, personality characteristics, expectancies, and attitudes)	D. *Testimony of having felt hypnotized*
D. *Subject–experimenter interaction variables* (for example, liking of experimenter for subject, and subject for experimenter)	

[a] From *Hypnosis* by Theodore Barber. © 1969 by Litton Educational Publishing, Inc. Reprinted by permission of Van Nostrand Reinhold Company.

Detailed discussion of one consequent and one antecedent variable might best serve to convey the essential character of Barber's model. The variables are chosen, however, to make explicit two basic rules of logic which appear to underly the paradigm, these being the *logic of alternative explanation* and the *logic of equivalence*. Discussion of the first variable touches more clearly on the former logic while discussion of the second variable more pointedly clarifies the latter.

Let us consider first the consequent variable "testimony of being hypnotized." Some investigators would undoubtedly claim that if subjects had received a formal hypnotic induction and later testified postexperimentally that they felt deeply hypnotized then the indications are clear that "hypnosis" was really present. Their inference may be correct but the power of Barber's model is that it points cautiously to a less traditional stance, one that specifies instead the many variables that functionally relate to the testimony of the subject in question. Evidence compiled by Barber (1969) indicates that whether or not subjects testify that they feel hypnotized depends on at least three sets of antecedent factors–subject's conception of what hypnosis is supposed to involve and his expectation about the depth of hypnosis he will experience, and degree to which he has actually responded to suggestions in the session, and whether the experimenter implies to the subject that he thought in fact he was in hypnosis. Barber, Dalal, and Calverley (1968), for instance, found that subjects' testimony was influenced by the hypnotist's expressed opinion of their performance and by the exact nature of the wording of questions asked of the subject concerning his experiences. Barber and Calverley (1969) also found evidence for a positive relationship between preexperimental expectations about hypnosis and subjects' later testimony of being hypnotized. Data, in all, suggest strongly that extraneous factors are powerful determinants of subjects' statements concerning their experience of trance.

One of the essential rules of logic underlying Barber's framework is what we will call in this book the *logic of alternative explanation*. This is an important rule of application for this and other models (for example, see Chapter 6 of this book) and it is a principle of logic attached to Barber's framework that is all too often overlooked.

Barber's model argues that operationally defined variables obviously play a part in determining whether or not subjects will testify that they are hypnotized. It asserts that it is more parsimonious and scientific to argue in terms of those functional relationships that are apparent than to appeal to concepts such as "hypnotic trance" which are difficult to index independently of the behaviors they are held to explain. Strictly speaking, this argument indicates that an "alternative explanation" is being proposed. One can attempt to explain hypnotic phenomena (here, subjects' reports of trance) by appeal to a special state of consciousness, hypnosis. But, alternatively, one can suggest that subjects' testimony of trance is itself influenced through suggestion implicitly afforded by "nonhypnotic" procedures, such as the way questions are phrased and the experimenter's opinion of subjects' performance. The latter of these two explanations makes the least assumptions and is the less contentious, but the evidence that is available does not prove the case for it, or disprove the possible relevance of "hypnosis" as an explanatory variable. There are indeed *two* explanations of the data each to be tempered, as we will see, with words of caution. The true nature of the logic of alternative explanation which adheres to the model can be readily missed. Chaves (1968), for instance, implies that Barber's data conclusively show that verbal report cannot be accepted as relevant to hypnosis since it is affected by extraneous variables such as the wording of the experimenter's inquiry. This inference is unjustified and far too strong for the data claimed to support it, as are statements such as those made by Field (1971) who criticizes Barber for turning verbal report into "just another dependent variable to be manipulated [p. 11]." The facts simply stated show that "testimony of trance" is a variable like any other dependent variable and it covaries as most such variables do with a considerable range of antecedent influence. The evidence is consistent it seems with both a hypnotic and a nonhypnotic account and does not unequivocally reject either, albeit one explanation at this moment looks much more respectable than the other.

We turn now to the second variable to be discussed, the antecedent factor of "Task Motivation (TM)." Table 3.1 lists the variable as one that is subsumed under the term "hypnotic induction procedure" and shows that standardized hypnotic induction procedures actually incorporate quite a number of "nonhypnotic" variables, including: (a) definition of the situation as hypnosis, (b) suggestions of relaxation, (c) cooperate–try instructions, and (d) statements that it is easy to respond to suggestions and to experience the suggested effects. Barber argues forcibly that high test response following induction may be due to the influence of one or more of these nonhypnotic variables rather than to the effect of any hypnotic elements assumed to be contained in the hypnotic induction procedure. In a series of studies testing this hypothesis, Barber and Calverley (1962, 1963a, b) randomly assigned subjects to one of three experimental treatments–Hypnotic Induction, TM instruction, and Base-Level instruction. Subjects assigned to the first condition were told they would be hypnotized and were given a standard induction. Subjects assigned to the second condition were given special imagination instructions designed to motivate subjects to respond particularly well; the instructions were especially intended to tap the nonhypnotic elements in the induction procedure labeled above as "cooperate–try" and "statements it is easy to respond." In the Base-Level condition subjects were simply instructed that they would receive a test of imagination. All subjects were then tested on the eight-item Barber Suggestibility Scale (BSS, Barber, 1965). Results for the three groups are represented in Table 3.2 which sets out the mean objective and subjective scores on the hypnotic-test scale. The results show a typical pattern of response which recurs throughout a

TABLE 3.2
Mean Objective (and Subjective) Scores on BSS Under Hypnotic Induction, Task Motivational Instructions, and Base-Level Conditions[a, b]

Test suggestion	Hypnotic induction	Task motivational instructions	Base level
1. Arm lowering	$.72_a$ ($.72_a$)	$.63_a$ ($.61_a$)	$.31_b$ ($.26_b$)
2. Arm levitation	$.72_a$ ($.56_a$)	$.63_a$ ($.56_a$)	$.27_b$ ($.24_b$)
3. Hand lock	$.84_a$ ($.69_a$)	$.76_a$ ($.81_a$)	$.58_b$ ($.40_b$)
4. Thirst "hallucination"	$.77_a$ ($.74_a$)	$.83_a$ ($.76_a$)	$.48_b$ ($.48_b$)
5. Verbal inhibition	$.85_a$ ($.64_a$)	$.74_a$ ($.69_a$)	$.43_b$ ($.27_b$)
6. Body immobility	$.82_a$ ($.63_a$)	$.67_{ab}$ ($.66_a$)	$.38_b$ ($.27_b$)
7. "Posthypnotic-like" response	$.60_a$ ($.29_{ab}$)	$.56_{ab}$ ($.42_a$)	$.40_b$ ($.14_b$)
8. Selective amnesia	$.53_a$ ($.35_a$)	$.44_a$ ($.39_a$)	$.21_b$ ($.13_b$)
Total scale mean:	5.8_a (4.6_a)	5.3_a (4.9_a)	3.1_b (2.2_b)
Total scale *SD* :	2.1 (2.3)	2.1 (2.3)	2.3 (2.1)

[a]From Barber (1965). Reprinted with permission of author and published from Barber, T. X. Measuring "hypnotic-like" suggestibility with and without "hypnotic induction," psychometric properties, norms, and variables influencing response to the Barber Suggestibility Scale (BSS). *Psychological Reports*, 1965, 16, 809–844, M3–V16.

[b]Objective scores in the same *row* containing a common subscript letter do not differ from each other at the .05 level of confidence. Similarly, subjective scores in the same *row* with a common subscript do not differ at the .05 level.

wide range of studies that have employed the operational paradigm (for detailed review of these experiments, see Barber, 1969). Hypnotic induction and TM instructional groups did not differ significantly from each other and both attained a high level of suggestibility response which was appreciably distinct from base-level performance.

The logic of inference that flows from the model's interpretation of this uniform but distinctive pattern of results is what we will term the *logic of equivalence.* The logic makes explicit the basic argument put forward by Barber's model for dispensing with the concept "hypnosis" and it runs as follows: If TM instructions designed to measure *nonhypnotic* variables, which are also contained within hypnotic induction, yield a comparable level of performance to that of induction then the results of the hypnotic group may also reflect nonhypnotic influences. Particular nonhypnotic variables (cooperate and try statements, and statements that it is easy to respond) are assumed to be equivalent across the two sets of conditions; therefore, identical behavioral effects surely indicate that these variables may be operating and we can dispense with the term "hypnosis" as necessary for explanation of what happens in the hypnotic condition.

Two logical assumptions are involved in this argument. First, there is an appeal to the logic of alternative explanation (discussed above) because results are taken to suggest an explanation other than one which uses the concept of trance. Second, the argument distinguishes the logic of equivalence—the model assumes that particular variables are equivalent under a hypnotic condition and another condition which is "nonhypnotic," and as a consequence comparable effects are deemed to reflect similar influence. It is important to keep these two rules of logic in mind when we move to evaluating the model, for they provide in fact the basic rationale for the operational paradigm's essential arguments concerning its data. The two logics should not be considered as independent of each other, for the logic of alternative explanation is clearly associated with the logic of equivalence; denial of the latter nullifies acceptance of the former. The logic of alternative explanation by its very nature implies that any inferences about hypnotic events that the model can make perforce are equivocal. The framework is soundly equipped not to prove the expendability of the concept, hypnosis, but to argue that explanations other than those using this concept equally as well explain the data; and it is in this way that the model precisely offers its distinctive challenge to the traditionalist stance. Equivalence of variables must be assumed in the first instance before the model's alternative account of the data can be maintained as valid, and any challenge to the logic of equivalence firmly undermines the basic utility of the model. If Barber's so-called "nonhypnotic" manipulations are not strictly comparable to those contained within hypnotic induction procedures then equivalent effects may obviously arise for a variety of different reasons. It is an important unstated assumption of the model, then, that nonhypnotic variables in the control comparison condition must be identical to variables contained within the hypnotic condition if explanation is to be offered for the results of the hypnotic group in precisely the way it is offered for the nonhypnotic group. This major point will be taken up in considerable detail below when we move to discuss the evidence that is available to support the model. For the moment, it is instructive to note, however, the complexity of logic that actually underlies application of the operational paradigm.

Recent Developments

Barber views it as more fruitful in science to proceed "gradually" toward broader theoretical principles of data integration. He argues that the psychology of hypnosis should depend ultimately on low-order theories based upon intervening constructs of an operational kind. In recent formulations about hypnosis (Barber, 1972; Spanos & Barber, 1974) he pointedly generalizes about hypnotic data and swings decidedly in the direction of acknowledging the value of experience. The good hypnotic subject who is responsive to test suggestions is formally conceptualized, for instance, as a member of an audience who comes to experience the feelings, emotions, and thoughts of the actors who are before him (Barber, 1972). The subject is said to have "positive" attitudes, motivations, and expectancies and he lets himself imagine and think along with the events as suggested; consequently he experiences the suggested effects. The subject who is responding to test suggestions is in a special state no more than a member of the audience who is responding to the communications of the actors, and the hypnotic subject experiences the events he does simply because he receives specific communications regarding them. This account of Barber's focuses specifically on attitudes, motivations, expectancies, and thinking with and imaging the events that are suggested. Just as attitudes, motivations, and expectancies reflect social influence processes in communications which are normally gathered under the rubric "social psychology" so these same mediating variables reflect influence processes in the field of hypnosis where the communications to the subject in the hypnotic setting are simply of a particular kind. Support for the theory comes directly from data showing that "hypnotic" subjects are positively motivated and are ready and willing to think with and imagine things as they are suggested. Recent work has focused, in particular, on the special relevance of imagination to hypnosis (Barber & Ham, 1974; Barber, Spanos, & Chaves, 1974; Spanos & Barber, 1974); the willingness of the subject to think and imagine with suggestions has, in fact, emerged as a critical theoretical concern of the model. Barber argues that his model has now reached a significant degree of agreement on constructs which integrate a variety of viewpoints and approaches to hypnosis; the hypnotic subject is conceptualized as someone who is willing to cooperate in fulfilling the aims of suggestions and the model argues that the cognitive processes involved can be subsumed under the construct "involvement in suggestion-related imaginings" (Spanos & Barber, 1974).

It is curious to note that in defense of these notions Barber appeals, among other things, to phenomenological evidence. He draws illustration, for instance (Barber, 1972), from his own personal experiences of response to test suggestions—"when I am having these experiences I feel as normal and as awake as when I am watching a movie, a stage play, or a television show [p. 132]." This "member of the audience" analogy puts acceptance of the operational model at some risk, however. First, it moves the model beyond the data to concern itself with the most appropriate classification of primary mediational variables. And, further, if members of an audience indeed experience events as Barber reports experiencing them we are still left with the testimony of subjects who color their personal account of being hypnotized with report to "compulsion to respond" and "involuntary tendency to react"—such reports occur regularly enough in the literature to require explanation and they may be a function of specifically antecedent influences, but the analogy in question appears to be poorly equipped to deal with them. The connotations of the analogy are elusive enough for Lieberman (1972, p. 230) to actually term them collectively, a "state theory of hypnosis." Laying aside the provocation of such a claim it is important to note that the model now accepts the theoretical relevance of hypnotic subjects' experience. Barber is in essential agreement, in fact, with state theorists on the point that hypnotic phenomena do involve genuine changes in subjects' experience and cannot be accounted for in terms of any appeal to voluntary response.

The move away from complete reliance on simple functional relationships has the advantage that specific predictions are made available for test. A subject, for instance, who has positive attitudes, motivations, and expectancies toward the test situation and who imagines the things that are suggested ought by reason of his cognitions to produce the overt responses and subjective experiences that are being suggested. Also, the model would predict that a subject with negative attitudes, motivations, and expectations toward the test situation will not respond positively to the test suggestions that are given. It is interesting to note that Barber's earliest formulations drew on the ideomotor theorizing of Arnold who emphasized the importance of subjects accepting the literal truth of the hypnotist's statements. Now the model moves back again to Arnold's (1946) theory to concentrate not on any "state-like" aspect of hypnotic response, but on the relevance of imagination processes to the occurrence of hypnotic phenomena (for further general discussion of the processes of imagination and their relation to hypnosis, see Sheehan, 1972). Important new directions in research have been opened up by this emphasis and have focused on forms of imagining such as "goal-directed fantasy"–a fantasy which represents for hypnotic subjects the imagining of a situation which, if it actually had occurred, would have resulted in the behavior that is being suggested (see Barber & Ham, 1974; Barber, Spanos, & Chaves, 1974; Spanos, 1971; Spanos & Barber, 1972, 1974). In studies by Spanos and Barber (1972), and Spanos, Spillane, and McPeake (1974), for example, evidence usefully reconciles the occurrence of imagination processes both in and out of hypnosis with the report of involuntary response that many susceptible subjects typically present. Data show that goal-directed fantasy and the experience of volition are positively related. When goal-directed fantasies occurred, no subject reported his response to suggestions as volitional; when goal-directed fantasies did not take place, however, the majority of subjects (60%) reported their behavior as under volunatry control (Spanos & Barber, 1972). Goal-directed fantasy (GDF) has also been shown to be positively related to amnesia (Spanos & Ham, 1973), although recent evidence implies that the response itself may be a suggested one (Buckner & Coe, 1975; Coe, Allen, Krug, & Wurzmann, 1974); GDF responses, for example, appear to be influenced substantially by the wording of the actual suggestions themselves.

The relevance of imagination processes to hypnosis that has been demonstrated reinforces the special claim by the model that the reported experiences and behavior of experimental subjects in the hypnotic setting are explained more parsimoniously and adequately on the basis of cognitive processes of the kind which are engendered by test suggestions, rather than by appeal to any special trance state. Theoretically speaking, the more recent work represents a decided move away by the model from central emphasis on the test setting to an expression of concern to detect general influences of cognitive strategies of control (see Barber, Spanos, & Chaves, 1974; Spanos, Barber & Lang, 1974). The move is made quite explicit by Barber, Spanos, and Chaves (1974, p. 20) whose text contains a modified version of Table 3.1 (which was selected from Barber's 1969 text). Their shorter, modified table specifically incorporates within it the category "mediating variables" and separately lists attitudinal and imaginal factors. Hypnotic test effects are explained as consistent with the growing body of literature claiming cognitive factors have a particularly important part to play in determining the effects of sensory input in general.

Looking in summary across these developments, one notes the definite progressions that have occurred in Barber's thinking. Barber initially proposed state-like notions (trance, selective attention, and delusional aspects of hypnotic response), but consistent with the thorough-going skepticism of his overall position these formulations gave way in much more decisive fashion to a strictly rigorous account of denotable variables in the hypnotic context. Extensive operational analysis led, then, to perception of the need to isolate basic integrative variables, and, most recently, Barber has attempted to classify those variables which are mediational in character and which most parsimoniously organize and account for the lawful empirical relations that have been isolated by the model. Generalizations concerning the data, though (albeit of a kind that lie close to the evidence), have implicitly introduced surplus connotations. The member of the audience analogy, as we have stated, is basically one that is oriented to internal processes and this excursion into theory by the operational model sacrifices something of the paradigm's essential character, appealing as it does to more than simple operational definitions and classification of behavioral correspondences. Emphasis on "involvement in suggestion-related imaginings" and "willingness to think along and imagine" has also rendered the model vulnerable to attack. Reyher (1975), for example, claims that these newly emphasized intervening variables, that have been chosen to integrate the data, are themselves difficult to assess in an independent and objective way. "Thinking along with," defined in terms of imaginative processes, implicitly represents quite a different kind of integrative construct than attitudes, motivations, and expectancies, and the former mediational account subsumes the latter, in so far as good hypnotic subjects who are positively motivated will think with and imagine events as they are suggested (Spanos & Barber, 1974). The model definitely seems to face some degree of vagueness with respect to how those internal processes it has chosen to emphasize can be indexed meaningfully, but threading through all of the developments in theory is Barber's essential insistence on the relevance of social psychological and cognitive–rather than "hypnotic"–analysis of trance events. Normal processes of social and cognitive psychology are considered perfectly adequate substitutes for the term "hypnosis."

We move now to consideration of the methodology implied by Barber's framework. As with other models we have analyzed, his methodology is distinctive and it argues for the acceptance of quite specific strategies of research.

SURVEY OF THE MODEL'S STRATEGIES OF RESEARCH

Coe (1971, 1973a) labels Barber's methodology as an "independent groups design." Taking his point, the major characteristic of Barber's model, as distinct from Hilgard's methodology say (see Chapter 2) is that independent groups of subjects are assigned randomly to different treatment conditions as opposed to subjects serving as their own controls. It is a feature of the operational model that the subjects assigned must be from the same population, whether it be a population of subjects who are selected or unselected for hypnotic susceptibility. In its basic form the model assigns sets of subjects to two groups–one receiving a standardized hypnotic induction procedure, and the other a procedure which in no way is hypnotic. The model nevertheless is quite flexible in the way that it operates and lends itself easily to factorial combination of different types of treatment. A study by Barber and Calverley (1966) illustrates the point; here, 16 treatment groups were employed in an attempt to determine the significant factors affecting amnesia. Considering, though, the multiplicity of comparison groups in this and other studies, the condition most "fraught with relevance" (Field, 1971) for Barber's system is the one labeled by the model, "Task Motivational (TM)." Comparison of this group with a group which has received a hypnotic induction provides, in fact, the most basic comparison of the model. The radical empiricism of the operational model argues in principle for the relevance of practically any manipulation, but, as Field (1971) points out, the model "hammers away at the task-motivational variable so repeatedly that it is plain this is an exception [p. 110]." The TM condition is clearly preferred, for example, to one which employs the use of faking subjects; as Barber (1969) states, "the most appropriate waking comparison group is *not* one that is asked to simulate hypnosis [p. 28]." Consistent, though, with the flexibility of the model in allowing a wide assortment of comparison groups, the framework does not exclude the possibility of using simulating subjects if they suit specific purposes of design (see, for example, Barber, 1972; Barber & Calverley, 1966). Barber legitimately cautions against using role-playing subjects for the reason that if they are employed, one must ask the question what consequences result from the hypnotic and nonhypnotic subjects (the role players) receiving totally different sets of experimental instructions.

In summary, then, selected or unselected subjects are allocated either to a formal induction condition or to a condition (that is, task motivational) which the model assumes is "nonhypnotic." Usually, a third group is also employed–a control condition where subjects are simply given suggestions without any special motivation for their task. The essential comparison is made between groups in test of the prediction that subjects in the hypnotic induction condition will behave differently from those in the control condition but in comparable fashion to subjects in the TM group. Support for this prediction is taken to indicate "trance" is not a necessary concept for explanation of what the hypnotic subjects do.

The rationale for choosing to use independent groups rather than subjects as their own controls has already been discussed in the context of Hilgard's model (see Chapter 2). Barber's model, more than any other framework, however, emphasizes the conditions of control to be fulfilled if separate groups are to be employed in proper fashion. Waking subjects must not be either less suggestible, less familiar, less in rapport, or less in motivation with the experimenter or his procedures than experimental subjects, and ideally all factors must be controlled that would discriminate waking and hypnotic subjects in terms of their willingness or motivation to carry out the experimenter's suggestions. Random allocation of subjects to conditions aims to control effectively for possible differences in prior practice and training, and subject variables of the kind evidenced by rapport are handled preferably by allocating *unselected* subjects to the various conditions. This practice is in contra-distinction to procedures adopted by others; Sutcliffe (1960; see also Chapter 5), for example, advocates the random allocation of selected (that is, hypnotizable) persons, as well, to the separate conditions. The model is especially demanding insofar as, in principle at least, it considers it necessary to randomize or hold constant a multitude of variables. One can perhaps sense the point of argument that has been made elsewhere about Barber's model (for example, Field, 1971) and about the operational approach to science in general (Marx, 1951): an operational framework fails in essence to outline the degree of relevance of the separate variables to be controlled. Some scheme for establishing "relevance" seems necessary when we consider that the differences among experimental treatments, whatever they be, are in fact limitless. It is small comfort to the researcher wanting to know what to control to be told that the possibilities of artifact in his experimentation are endless (Boring, 1969) even though the claim is perfectly correct.

One of the major limitations arising from solely relying on an Independent Groups design is recognized implicitly by Barber. This is the problem of knowing precisely what inferences to draw when the performance of subjects in a hypnotic (or TM) group differs from the performance of a separate group of control subjects. Although the control group provides a highly useful estimate of base-level performance there is still the possibility that the differences between groups are themselves accountable in terms of preexisting differences in responsivity among subjects. To answer this question irrefutably, base-line measurements of a nonhypnotic nature are needed for the same groups of subjects who are later tested experimentally under the various sets of instructions. If hypnotic or TM subjects differ in any way from control subjects in preexisting level of response then our inferences about experimental group differences must obviously be checked (see Fisher, 1962, for extension of this argument; and also Chapters 4 and 9 of this book). In this sense, the logic of the base-rates design is a very convincing one, as we argue elsewhere in this book.

In a series of studies (Barber & Calverley, 1964a, b; Spanos & Barber, 1968) Barber and his associates tested for base-rate levels of response prior to allocating subjects to experimental treatment conditions. The advantage gained from doing this is obvious as, for example, when the experimenter wants to draw unambiguous inferences about the significance of *enhancement* of visual hallucination response under hypnotic or TM conditions within the particular samples of subjects that have been tested (Spanos & Barber, 1968). Methodological risks are attached to such a design, however, and some attempt has to be made to cope with possible problems introduced by first testing subjects nonhypnotically. Spanos and Barber's study illustrates this point; inconsistencies they found among findings that are normally quite uniform when the operational model is applied suggest the presence of difficulties that yet need to be resolved. For subjects tested under conditions of no demand for honesty, Spanos and Barber showed no differences *between* experimental treatments—a rare finding when the operational model is applied. Results showed no evidence that hypnotic or TM performance differed from the level of performance shown by an independent group of control subjects, despite the fact that *across* conditions (considered separately) there was, in fact, a significant increase of visual-hallucination response for both the hypnotic and the TM groups. In another study (Barber & Calverley, 1964a) which used pre- and posttesting in analysis of enhancement of strength of endurance, results showed surprisingly that weight holding endurance was depressed for hypnotic subjects (as compared to base-level rate) but enhanced for TM subjects. It seems that before base-rate level of response can be included in a Barber-type design (or any other design) careful procedures need to be worked out for solving the artifactual problems that obviously arise from testing subjects prior to introducing the relevant treatment. Fisher (1962) suggests that one essential procedure for dealing with the problem is for base-line waking performance to be assessed prior to the experiment and in a context completely dissociated from it. The technicalities of achieving this in practice render this a very demanding solution, however.

The operational model advocates random allocation of subjects from the same population, but it expresses uncertainty on the issue of whether or not subjects ought to be selected for hypnotizability. The majority of studies employing the model have in fact used unselected subjects (for comprehensive review of these, see Barber, 1969) but there are others which have specifically assigned good hypnotic subjects to the various test conditions (for example, Barber, Chauncey, & Winer, 1964; Barber & Hahn, 1962). The whole issue of subject sampling is one that seems much more important to other theorists than to Barber, though recent work (for example, Gilbert & Barber, 1972) shows considerable concern for individual differences in susceptibility as a relevant variable for consideration. Hilgard (1965a, 1973b) and others (for example, Reyher, 1975) state that an unselected subjects design fails to provide the most favorable conditions for test of the traditional viewpoint and that a special degree of hypnotizability is necessary if one aims to investigate "hypnotic" reaction to test suggestions. The argument is not easily resolved. On the one hand, random allocation of subjects from the general population fails indeed to maximize the probability of obtaining the phenomena being investigated in as many subjects as possible and necessarily reduces the relevance of any trait account of hypnosis (Hilgard, 1971); on the other hand, employment of restricted samples of good susceptible subjects across experimental conditions places a special onus on the experimenter to ensure that his "nonhypnotic" condition is not in the least way trance inducing for subjects who have proven themselves to be highly susceptible to hypnosis and who may enter trance if the situation is defined appropriately. Translated into the arguments discussed earlier with respect to the Same-Subjects design (Chapter 2) another possible objection to stratified sampling is that susceptible subjects may actually have little room for enhancement when formal induction procedures are introduced by dint of the suggestibility they are capable of demonstrating in the waking state.

Some very positive features of the design that has just been outlined are that it makes no a priori assumptions about internal process constructs; it avoids the weaknesses involved in employing a concept like "trance" which cannot readily be defined independently of the behavior that gave rise to it; and it searches systematically for lawful empirical relations existing between antecedent and consequent variables. Perhaps the most provocative argument, however, that Barber brings to the defense of his methodology (and one to which we have already made reference) is that the operational model avoids the basic flaw of the tautology evident in traditionalist thinking about hypnosis. This accusation of circular reasoning is one that should be examined closely; the inferences that the traditionalists make about causality are actually much more complex than many of us recognize.

Barber (1969) claims that hypnotic-state theorists argue subjects are responsive to test suggestions because they are in an "altered state," the claim being also made that hypnosis is present because the subject passes the tests. The double causality posed here obviously involves us in a completely unacceptable, circular argument. The argument of the traditionalists, however, is something that can easily be misconstrued. They might well be implying that if "the subject passes the test" (A) because he is "hypnotized" (B), it is then legitimate to also argue that the subject is hypnotized (B) because he passes the test (A). Close analysis, however, shows that the causality of these two instances is really something quite different and the traditionalist position is not as naive as it first may seem. A suitably cautious proponent of state theory would not really wish to argue that the subject was hypnotized because he passed the test, for undoubtedly he would want to make the claim that the subject would be hypnotized even if he had not in any way been tested. Rather, the causality in question concerns "our knowing about the subject's state of hypnosis." It is much more logically correct therefore to say *A* causes *B*, and *B* causes our knowing about *A*. Two kinds of causality are involved here and three (not two) terms are relevant: the subject passing the tests (*A*), being hypnotized (*B*), and our knowing that the subject is hypnotized (*C*). In the first case it might be legitimate to say that hypnosis causes passing the tests, but in the second it is entirely illegitimate to argue that passing the tests causes hypnosis. Rather, A determines our knowing that the subject is in trance. The effect then really lies with our awareness or recognition that the subject is hypnotized, an effect comparable perhaps with our knowing that the subject is "intelligent," "dishonest," or "immature." Any possible confusion about causality aside, Barber's point is nevertheless well taken that scientifically viable concepts are best described independently of the behavior that gives rise to them. It is an unfortunate fact that hypnosis more often than not is invoked to explain behavior (for example, hallucination) that is also said to indicate it.

EVIDENCE RELATING TO THE MODEL

Barber's paradigm of hypnosis is in a peculiar position regarding its capacity to take up and solve particular research problems in hypnosis—the paradigm, by its very nature, has been designed to establish the expendability of the concept of hypnosis. Oriented toward the logic of "alternative explanation" (see above) it aims to show that explanations hold for understanding hypnotic events that have no need to appeal to special concepts like "hypnosis." There are specific problem areas, however, which nevertheless are its particular concern.

Very broadly speaking, Barber's model is concerned like all other models of hypnosis with establishing the empirical consequences of hypnotic induction procedures. Barber and Calverley (1963a), for instance, allocated subjects randomly to conditions where TM and trance induction procedures were either present or absent. The typical pattern of results that we have discussed emerged: the effects for both TM and hypnotic induction groups were greater than for the control group (no induction or TM instructions given) and both experimental conditions were comparable in effect to each other. The conclusion was drawn that a comparable level of "hypersuggestibility" was produced by administering TM instruction and a standardized trance induction. Chaves (1968) similarly concluded from an overall review of Barber's work that Barber's findings typically indicate that hypnotic induction yields an increment in suggestibility as compared with an unmotivated control treatment. Inferences of these kinds on the data may well be correct, but, strictly speaking, they cannot be drawn from application of an Independent Groups design, because such a design does not formally establish base-rate levels of response. Inferences about "hypersuggestibility" belong to comparisons *within* subject groups, and not to comparisons *between* subject groups which are the ones routinely made by the operational paradigm.

The study of the effectiveness of motivational instructions per se in creating effects comparable to those obtained with formal hypnotic induction procedures is perhaps the most singular concern of Barber's model. And such effectiveness is well established empirically. The comparability of behavioral effects of TM instruction and hypnotic induction across a wide range of test difficulties (see Table 3.2 for example) and hypnotic-test situations (Barber, 1969) establishes quite clearly that few, if any, behavioral effects are unique to hypnosis. Only in the rare instance are there data to show that the set of task motivational instructions employed by the operational model failed to yield significantly greater level of performance from that obtained by waking control subjects. Gilbert and Barber (1972) investigated the effects of cognitive performance (measuring visual–motor coordination, number facility, abstract reasoning and associative memory) of induction and motivational suggestions and atypically found no evidence of a significant main task instruction effect, but consistent in a sense with this finding was a similar absence of any effect for hypnotic induction. The general pattern of behavioral equivalence associated with this high motivation waking condition very convincingly counters the argument that hypnosis yields consequences that cannot be obtained in the waking state. Just as for the real–simulating model (see Chapter 6 of this book) comparability of results for highly motivated "nonhypnotic" and hypnotic subjects completely negate the hypothesis that "supranormal" patterns of performance are associated peculiarly with the trance state.

The emphasis of the model on motivational effects is a particularly important one for it serves to challenge many claims about hypnosis that are routinely reported in the literature. Brady and Levitt (1966), for example, found evidence of nystagmoidlike eye movements in a sample of highly suggestible subjects after they received hallucination suggestion, the response resembling that found when individual subjects actually inspected a rotating drum. Hahn and Barber (1966) found, however, that a comparable number of unselected subjects under waking conditions showed similar eye movements when they were instructed under task motivational instructions to simply imagine a rotating drum. Taken collectively, the evidence tells us that a small number of subjects show nystagmus when they are hallucinating under hypnosis, but any willingness on our part to appeal to hypnosis as a causative factor in explaining these results must be tempered with caution. It is possible (that is, an alternative account of the data is also available) that hypnosis is responsible but it may not be indicated, knowing as we do that comparable numbers of unselected people show nystagmus when motivated under waking conditions of the type presented in the TM context. Table 3.2, discussed above, tells us that even without special motivating instruction, more than an average of two out of eight items are passed by control subjects in an ordinary waking (base-level) condition. The data argue forcibly that the responses of subjects following induction can only properly be assessed after we have detailed knowledge of subjects' waking performance, motivated as well as unmotivated. It is very useful to know, for example, that variation in motivation among waking subjects can alone produce behavioral effects as discrepant as any performance difference between "hypnotic" and waking conditions.

In our description of the model above we saw how the operational framework builds its inferences upon the logic of equivalence and formulates its evidence in an alternative form that eschews all commitment to traditionalist notions about trance. We move now to consideration of two important questions pertinent to evaluating the adequacy of the model. First, we will consider what are the limitations of the logic of equivalence to which the model adheres; and, second, we will assess the evidence that is available to argue in support of the traditionalist stance—evidence, for example, that is difficult to explain in the kind of alternative way that the model prefers.

TASK-MOTIVATIONAL INSTRUCTIONS AND THE LOGIC OF EQUIVALENCE

Close review of the evidence reveals some anomalies as far as the results for TM subjects are concerned which threaten somewhat the assumptions underlying the logic of the operational paradigm. It is not strictly correct to argue, as Barber (1969) does, that the data represented in Table 3.2 above show that "response to test suggestions is facilitated to a comparable degree by task motivational instructions and by standardized hypnotic induction procedures" (Empirical Generalization 7, Barber, 1969, p. 52). Close perusal of the table suggests, for example, that the term "comparable" doesn't sufficiently recognize the fact that only *one* of the eight suggestions yielded a subjective score for the hypnotic condition that was greater than for the TM condition. This increase in subjective response for nonhypnotic as compared to hypnotic groups appears elsewhere in the literature and presents us with something of a puzzling finding. Barber and Calverley (1964c), for example, used a delayed auditory feedback situation and reported that 14% of their sample receiving waking suggestion were totally subjectively deaf while none of the subjects receiving hypnotic induction fell into the same category. Similar paradoxical effects occurred in Barber and Calverley's (1966) study on amnesia in which subjects who were instructed to "fake" amnesia reported at least twice as much subjectively real forgetting (after they were released from their faking role) as subjects who had received a formal hypnotic induction. The higher rate of reported subjective involvement for subjects receiving a condition assumed not to be hypnotically inducing legitimately raises the query that factors may be responsible for this level of response which are unique to these control test situations. The effects reported here may be chance events, but they seem to occur with enough regularity that we should ask ourselves, as Barber (1969) asks, "Of the many independent variables subsumed under the label(s) . . . *task motivational instructions* which are effective and which extraneous in facilitating response to test-suggestions? [p. 54]"

Many distinctive variables can be subsumed under the label "task motivational" (TM), and Barber and Calverley (1963b) have formulated some of the factors that are likely to be involved. Subjects given TM instructions are informed that: other subjects perform well on similar imaginative tasks (appeal to subject's self-esteem), they are expected to cooperate and try to the best of their ability (attempt to maximize motivation), they can perform as expected if they try to imagine well (definition of the task as one involving imagination), and if they don't try the experiment will be worthless and the experimenter will feel silly and disappointed (appeal to desire to please the experimenter). Theoretically, any one of the above factors might explain TM performance. In the relatively early stages of its development, proponents of the operational model (for example, Barber & Calverley, 1963b) argued the need to research into the exact nature of the antecedent influences that determine TM effectiveness, but to date this research has not been conducted by them. Rather, analysis has concentrated primarily on the hypnotic condition and the many variables which relate to it (for example, Barber & De Moor, 1972). The omission is important. Until we know precisely what variables account for TM performance we cannot argue (as the model does) in support of the logic of equivalence. Equivalent effects may in fact be obtained for the two conditions but if the variables of influence differ for the hypnotic and nonhypnotic conditions then comparability of effects may simply reflect similar behavioral consequences occurring for different reasons. Strictly speaking, the logic of equivalence under which the model operates assumes that subjects are responding in the nonhypnotic condition for the same reasons exactly as they could be responding in the hypnotic condition. For this logic to operate it is critically important to determine whether in fact the variables of influence within the set of instructions we know as "task motivational" are precisely the same as those occurring within the set of instructions labeled "hypnotic induction."

Two strands of evidence suggest quite strongly that extraneous factors adhere to the set of TM instructions which challenge the underlying logic of the operational model. The first to be discussed relates to work reported by Sheehan and Dolby (1974), the other comes from evidence across a series of studies that has appeared in the literature on the effect of "demand for honesty" on TM performance.

Sheehan and Dolby (1974) explicitly challenged the logic of Barber's paradigm. They tested the hypothesis that the standard set of TM instructions incorporated not only the variables "cooperate and try" and "statements it is easy to respond"–variables assumed by Barber to be also contained in hypnotic instruction–but also an artifactual variable labeled by them "behavioral constraint" argued to be relatively specific to the TM condition. The construct, in fact, highlights characteristics similar to those outlined earlier by others (Bowers, 1967). Close analysis of TM instructions indicates what appears to be strong social pressure on subjects to comply. Plapp (1972) takes the extreme position that the pressure is even reminiscent of the obedience evidence collected by Milgram (1963) in his classic program of work. An extract from the verbatim set of TM instructions (Barber, 1969) illustrates the point:

> In this experiment . . . everyone passed these tests when they tried. . . . If you don't try to the best of your ability, this experiment will be worthless and I'll tend to feel silly. On the other hand, if you try to imagine . . . you will be helping this experiment and not wasting any time [p. 46].

Sheehan and Dolby argued that pressure of this kind was relatively distinctive to the TM context; they asserted that hypnotic procedures might also carry social pressure but implications of this kind would be absorbed much more by the less emphatic context of hypnosis which stresses subjects' natural responsivity to test suggestions and their letting happen whatever is going to take place. Their argument was that, if the presence of such an artifact can be established, then the variables making up the set of TM instructions simply are not comparable to those contained within the total set of hypnotic induction procedures. The logic of equivalence is violated and the inference that flows from that state of affairs renders quite equivocal the formal assumptions of the model: if behavior is the same across the two conditions then TM subjects may be performing for reasons related to simple compliance while hypnotic subjects may be performing for reasons related to equally distinctive properties of their own particular treatment condition.

Two studies were conducted in the program of research to explore the logic of Barber's paradigm empirically. Study 1 presented three sets of instructions to subjects and asked them to rate the instructions according to the degree of social pressure that they felt the experimenter was placing on them to do what he asked simply because he was asking. The sets of instructions chosen were TM, hypnotic induction (both as used exactly by the model), and a third set labeled "modified hypnotic induction." This third set represented instructions which were designed to follow the basic procedures of standard induction, but in addition, were designed to socially pressure subjects noticeably more than the standard set. Fourteen subjects ranked the three sets for the degree of pressure they imposed. Results showed clearly that the set of TM instructions was perceived by subjects as appreciably more constraining than Barber's set of standard hypnotic induction instructions ($p < .01$) and the new set of modified induction instructions were seen as equally constraining as TM instructions. From subjects' testimonies, at least, it would seem that variables across the model's basic comparison conditions are not comparable. The model's two sets of instructions were perceived by subjects as differing quite markedly in the pressure they place on subjects to comply.

Table 3.3 sets out the mean objective and subjective scores on the BSS for subjects receiving the three sets of instructions. Scores are represented separately for easy (Items 1–3) and difficult (Items 4–7) items on the scale. (The final eighth item on the BSS was omitted because of an idiosyncracy of scoring.) The change scores (easy–difficult score) listed in the final column indicate the nature of the behavioral effect that emerged. The TM and modified hypnotic induction conditions differed significantly from the control condition ($p < .01$), but not from each other, while the control and the standard hypnotic induction groups did not vary from each other in magnitude of change across the different types of item. Results in Table 3.3 suggest that there are specifiable consequences associated with the variable "behavioral constraint." Similar behavioral change for the TM and modified hypnotic induction conditions both of which were shown in Study 1 to be equally socially pressuring—change not occurring to the same degree for the standard hypnotic induction condition—suggests that the artifact variable in question was responsible for the effects that occurred. The finding of interaction obviously needs replication but, considered collectively, the results of the two studies argue strongly for noncomparability of variables in the hypnotic and nonhypnotic test conditions of the operational model. It seems that Barber's model inadvertently admits to its set of TM instructions an

TABLE 3.3
Objective (and Subjective) Scores on the BSS for Easy (Items 1–3) and Difficult (Items 4–7) Tests of Suggestion for the *Task Motivational, Standard Hypnotic Induction, Modified Hypnotic Induction,* and *Control* Conditions[a]

Experimental group	Items: Easy	Items: Difficult	Change score
Task motivational	.80 (.68)	.51 (.30)	.29 (.38)
Standard hypnotic induction	.83 (.71)	.63 (.43)	.20 (.28)
Modified hypnotic induction	.87 (.76)	.56 (.39)	.31 (.37)
Control	.36 (.26)	.30 (.17)	.06 (.09)

[a] From Sheehan and Dolby (1974).

extraneous variable—one that can be defined explicitly in terms of a subject's feeling statement (on receiving the instructions) that he finds such instructions socially pressuring.

With this source of artifact acknowledged, the inferences that can be made about "hypnosis" from the model logically become quite complex. Even if the behavioral effects of TM instructions are the same as for Standard Hypnotic Induction instructions, the behavioral similarity that is found between the two conditions may not reflect similar influences. The performance of the hypnotic group may either be due to whatever is "hypnotic" or "nonhypnotic" about the induction procedures. The performance of the TM comparison group, on the other hand, may reflect the influence of what is common to hypnotic induction but equally well may reflect the distinctively pressuring quality of TM instruction. Argument of this kind necessarily limits the extent of our confidence in the model's alternative "nonhypnotic" account of the data. Confidence is reduced because the model's explanation of events occurring for the nonhypnotic group is itself equivocal.

Additional support for the above argument springs from the large body of evidence that has accumulated on the effects of "demand for honesty" on subjects' responsivity to test suggestions. Barber and Calverley (1964b) first started the argument rolling by demonstrating that base-level response to suggestions to hallucinate (both visually and auditorily) is augmented to the same degree by hypnotic induction and TM instruction. Arguing along similar lines to what has been just discussed, Bowers (1967) replied to the study by stating that subjects possibly felt compelled to report hallucinations under TM instruction in order to make the experiment a success. In his study, subjects unselected for susceptibility were told to hallucinate and pretest ratings were taken on the reality of visual and auditory hallucinations. All subjects were then given TM instructions to hallucinate. Before retest, however, half the subjects saw a second experimenter who demanded an honest hallucination report while the other half made their retest ratings in routine fashion. Results showed that for both sensory modalities the demand for honesty appreciably reduced the change in hallucination response from pretest to retest. Only when honesty was not demanded was there a significant change. Spanos and Barber (1968), in a much more comprehensive study than Bowers', followed up the problem by testing the effect of "demand for honesty" instruction on both TM and hypnotic response. The results for this experiment together with those from Bowers' study are reported in Table 3.4. Spanos and Barber showed that when honest reports were demanded, hypnotic induction, but not TM instructions, raised reports of visual hallucinations above base level; a comparable finding, however, did not emerge for auditory hallucinations. Taken collectively, the data summarized in Table 3.4 are consistent with the evidence of Sheehan and Dolby (1974). The evidence overall suggests that TM instructions transmit peculiarly strong pressure for

TABLE 3.4

Mean Base-Level and Posttreatment Auditory and Visual Hallucination Score[a]

	No demand for honesty				Demand for honesty			
	Base-level pretest	Post retest	Difference	*p*	Base-level pretest	Post retest	Difference	*p*
			Auditory hallucination scores					
Hypnotic induction	2.5	3.0	.5	<.08	2.3	2.5	.2	n.s.
Task motivational[b]	2.3	3.0	.7	<.01	2.2	2.5	.3	n.s.
	(2.65)	(3.30)	(.65)	(<.001)	(2.45)	(2.40)	(–.05)	(n.s.)
Control	2.2	2.5	.3	n.s.	2.5	2.4	–.1	n.s.
			Visual hallucination scores					
Hypnotic induction	1.8	2.5	.7	<.05	1.8	2.3	.5	<.05
Task motivational[b]	1.9	2.5	.6	<.01	1.7	1.7	.0	n.s.
	(2.05)	(2.65)	(.60)	(<.01)	(2.05)	(2.15)	(.10)	(n.s.)
Control	2.2	2.3	.1	n.s.	2.3	2.2	–.1	n.s.

[a]From Spanos and Barber (1968).

[b]Scores in brackets represent the mean hallucination ratings for "honesty" and "no honesty" instructions as reported by Bowers (1967) in his study.

compliance–pressure which is not carried to the same degree by standard hypnotic induction instructions. Hilgard (1973b) and Reyher (1965) pass similar judgment with respect to the model's procedures. Hilgard, for instance, comments on the compliance nature of TM instructions and remarks that Barber's set of motivational instructions produces "noise" in the system; responses scored as hypnotic-like contain several other kinds of responses among them.

Results are not altogether conclusive on the honesty issue. Spanos, Barber, and Lang (1974), for instance, have presented data to indicate that subjects' reports of pain in the hypnotic setting are less affected by demands for honesty than previously assumed; they reported no interaction between anesthesia instructions, hypnotic induction procedure, and demand for honesty. Despite such evidence, truthfulness of report is a claim that clearly should be established whenever TM instructions are employed. Hilgard (1975) has further drawn attention to the "false reference" information transmitted to TM subjects who are told (misleadingly) that everyone has done well; the effects of these cues need likewise to be determined. It seems also possible that these artifactual characteristics of TM instructions adhere to the wider context of the tests of suggestibility that normally accompany them. Evidence shows, for instance, that subjective test scores on the BSS are curiously lower than objective scores, implying that social pressure works to elicit behavioral conformity more than it produces effects which are confirmed through experience (Ruch, Morgan, & Hilgard, 1974).

TRANCE INDUCTION AND TASK MOTIVATIONAL INSTRUCTION

Many workers in the field (e.g., Barrios, 1973; Evans, 1968; Hilgard, 1964; Schneck, 1969; Watkins, 1972b) have leveled the criticism at Barber that the reason why his model yields such a high rate of response under TM instruction is that these instructions themselves are trance inducing. Tart and Hilgard (1966) reinforce the argument, asserting forcibly from data they collected that control subjects may spontaneously slip into hypnosis (for detailed discussion of their data, see Chapter 2). This particular criticism is the one most often raised in condemnation of the operational model. Barber has replied to it arguing that "testimony of being hypnotized" is itself functionally related to a whole series of denotable antecedent variables and it should not be assumed that subjects' report of trance when it does occur is necessarily related to the presence of hypnosis. Barber also claims that the criticism ridiculously forces psychologists, no matter what treatment they apply, to ensure that trance has not been induced.

In a somewhat overstated reply to his critics Barber ignores the fact that a given set of instructions cannot be assumed to be "nonhypnotic" just because the investigator fails to label it "hypnotic induction." There is some empirical evidence in support of Barber's position, however, which merits close consideration. Evidence suggests that TM instruction is actually effective for low-suggestible (poor hypnotizable) subjects as well as high-suggestible subjects (Barber & Calverley, 1965) and that TM subjects demonstrate a comparable response to that of hypnotic subjects even when they are told they are control subjects and are not going to be hypnotized (Barber & Calverley, 1963b). Both these sets of findings suggest that the arguments of Evans (1968), Schneck (1969), Watkins (1972b) and others are too extreme. The available facts are not explained adequately enough by saying that TM performance is like hypnotic performance simply because TM subjects are hypnotized.

Barber's model is open to attack on the issue nevertheless, but the criticism is most appropriately formulated in terms of the precise logic of Barber's model. This logic essentially claims that TM instructions are equivalent to hypnotic instructions on a limited number of variables which are in fact nonhypnotic. It is crucial therefore to the paradigm that the motivational control condition is truly "nonhypnotic." This is so because Barber's claim for the expendability of the trance concept derives from the inference that if procedural *nonhypnotic* variables in a waking condition lead to the same behavioral consequences as the hypnotic condition, and both conditions have these procedural variables in common, then the effects for the induction condition may be explained on the same procedural grounds. The assumption of "nonhypnotic" character for the TM instructional condition, then, is crucial to the basic logic of equivalence which underlies the paradigm.

With this logic in mind, the model is necessarily threatened by data indicating that subjects perceive the TM condition, in fact, as trance inducing. Sheehan and Dolby (1974) in their study asked TM and hypnotic subjects to rate on a seven-point depth scale the extent to which they felt hypnotized, and ratings of trance were associated appreciably with the TM condition. Additional evidence bearing on the issue comes separately from an altogether different approach to the problem by Connors and Sheehan (1976). In their study, they defined a test situation as measuring "hypnosis" or "influenceability" (not hypnotic) to independent groups of unselected subjects. Subjects in both context groups either received TM instruction or no TM instruction and each subject was tested on the BSS scale *without* induction. Results showed that the greatest behavioral effect of TM instruction (as indexed by BSS responsiveness) occurred in the context that was defined explicitly as hypnotic rather than the context defined nonhypnotically, but the extent of "compatibility" of the TM condition with the hypnotic context was not significant. Since the experimental contexts were systematically equated in terms of the model's accepted variables of influence (for example, positive attitudes, motivation, and expectancy) the results nevertheless suggest there is a need to explore carefully all of the cue characteristics that may adhere to the TM condition. Results further indicated the need to delineate the subjective and objective accompaniments of the TM treatment, in particular. Task-motivated subjects, for example, reported experiences of dissociation, involuntary response, and feelings of inner control (as measured by items on a self-report questionnaire designed to tap trance-type experiences–see Rawlings & Hammer, 1971) that differentiated them appreciably from nonTM subjects; following the session, TM subjects indicated significantly *more* feelings of dissociation and involuntary response and appreciably *less* feelings of inner control–a pattern of response that is entirely consistent with the test constructors' notions of susceptible subjects' probable response. Results do not indicate that TM instructions are trance-inducing, but neither do they easily conform to the formal assumption of the model that the treatment is completely nonhypnotic in character.

Subjects' personal ratings of trance depth–whatever such ratings mean–have to be dealt with at the level of a denotable variable with a potentially wide range of possible consequent effects. The implications to be drawn from the available evidence on the trance induction quality of TM instruction share much of the character of the implications drawn from our previous discussion of the factor, "behavioral constraint." Both represent unacknowledged sources of artifact and both similarly challenge the logic of the inferences that the operational model typically draws. Future exploration of the cues attached to TM instructions may resolve some of the inconsistencies of findings occurring in the literature. Spanos and Barber (1968), for instance, gathered hypnotic depth ratings from their own subjects who had either been given hypnotic induction, TM instruction, or no motivating instruction at all (control). Results from their study showed that the mean depth ratings of the TM and control groups did not differ significantly from each other while both sets of ratings were appreciably lower than the ratings obtained from subjects who had been given a formal hypnotic induction. Depth ratings satisfy the logical requirements of the model in the setting of Spanos and Barber (1968), but they differ markedly from the pattern of results found in the settings explored by Sheehan and Dolby (1974), and Connors and Sheehan (1976). Interlaboratory differences obviously exist, but the evidence gives too few clues as to what are the factors that are responsible.

We turn now to what empirical support there is available for the legitimacy of the construct, hypnotic state. Since the operational model aims to establish the expendability of the concept, its viability becomes a very relevant issue to this model in particular. Rather than exhaustively reviewing the hypnotic literature in search of confirming evidence which may equally as well fit a state model or an operational one, concentration will be more on those data which, at this stage of the model's formulation, are difficult to assimilate to the operational paradigm. The sources of evidence that will be examined will relate to some contemporary trends in hypnotic research, but for a very comprehensive survey of recent research developments, as such, the reader should consult the edited volume by Fromm and Shor (1972).

EVIDENCE SUPPORTIVE OF THE CONCEPT "HYPNOTIC STATE"

Testimony of Trance

Barber (1972) discusses the main sources of data which ostensibly support the traditional, hypnotic state, paradigm. Data can be drawn, for example, from the feats of stage hypnotists, the reports of amazing effects from subjects ostensibly in hypnosis, the testimony of subjects that they are experiencing a special state of consciousness, and the occurrence of "spontaneous" amnesia and "trance logic" in highly responsive subjects. Barber examines each of these (and other) sources in detail for evidence of a special state of consciousness, and in turn rejects them. The evidence is not perfectly clear, however, on several of the issues that he examines. Consider subjects' testimony of being in trance, for instance, which is a variable we have already looked at in some detail and we will not review again here. Report of being hypnotized is obviously a denotable variable influenced by a host of other variables including subjects' preconceptions about trance and the wording and tone of the experimenter's inquiry. There is a tendency in the research that has been conducted, however, to challenge subjective reports of hypnotic subjects as to their special validity but to overlook the necessity to challenge the validity of the report of nonhypnotic subjects at the same time. It can be cogently argued that comparable subjective reports from nonhypnotic and hypnotic subjects as to "subjectively felt" effects must inevitably lead us to query the claim that reports of hypnosis are distinctive to induction. Yet often it is not entirely clear whether or not the reports of a comparison group are in fact genuine and this indicates a problem with Barber's model. As we argued above, to be consistent with the logic of the paradigm the expendability of the trance concept is best indicated if we assume that comparable reports from hypnotic and nonhypnotic subjects are offered for similar reasons. But we have considered the possibility that nonhypnotic subjects yield subjective reports by reasons of social pressure whereas hypnotic subjects do not. If this is so, the status of susceptible subjects' reports of trance requires review; and it can be claimed that the model fails to pursue the full implications of the data. The substantially greater "subjective report of amnesia" by simulating subjects (as compared with hypnotic subjects) in Barber and Calverley's

(1966) study is paradoxical enough that a close, routine validity check ought to be conducted with respect to all conditions, hypnotic, and nonhypnotic alike.

Amnesia

Spontaneous amnesia has long been shown to be unreliable as an indicant of hypnosis, the evidence rather conclusively demonstrating that amnesia, where it appears spontaneously, is usually suggested (either explicitly or implicitly). Recent evidence, however, indicates there are aspects of amnesic performance that differentiate the susceptible person from the insusceptible person who is simulating hypnosis. Evans (1972), Evans and Kihlstrom (1973), Kihlstrom (1972) and Nace, Orne, and Hammer (1974) looked at the retrieval performance of those subjects displaying partial amnesia; studies found that hypnotizable subjects remembered events out of correct order whereas insusceptible subjects retrieved events in a much more segmental order. The method of analysis used for each subject was to calculate the rank order correlation between the order in which hypnotic test items were recalled and the order in which these same items were administered. Data showed that the mean rho scores of hypnotizable subjects were appreciably lower than the mean rho scores for insusceptible subjects; hypnotizable subjects characteristically remembered events out of correct order. Furthermore, there was no difference in the temporal sequencing of waking recall between the subjects who later (on screening) turned out to be susceptible and those who were found to be insusceptible. This research of Evans and his associates looks at the performance of the amnesic subject as a whole—the susceptible subject's failure to recall as well as his ability to forget—and it highlights in interesting fashion differences of style, although these differences admittedly have not yet been subjected to the stringent inquiry standards of the operational model's research strategies. At this stage the data clearly suggest that presence or absence of amnesia is not the only issue of concern to those who lay claim to there being distinctive effects associated with trance. Differences in "style" of recall may well indicate genuine attributes of hypnotic, as opposed to nonhypnotic, facilitation of amnesia.

There are further indications that in the search for differences investigators should look closely at qualitative features of subject's attempts to recall. Consistent with his emphasis on the memory retrieval process, Evans (1972) has reported that when a specific amnesia is suggested (for example, "forget that the number 7 exists") the hypnotized subject reacts to problems which require the use of the blocked content (the specific content is excluded from awareness) with different thought processes than those used by simulating subjects or subjects who are insusceptible to hypnosis. Evans argues that the hypnotized subject doesn't worry, for example, about finding a mathematically logical compromise solution to problems using the blocked number; and the whole issue is somewhat reminiscent of the trance logic controversy (Hilgard, 1965a, 1972a;

Johnson, Maher, & Barber, 1972; McDonald & Smith, 1975; Orne, 1959; Peters, 1973) which has yet to be resolved satisfactorily (for penetrating debate on the issue see Hilgard, 1972a; and Johnson, 1972). Amnesic subjects, as well as subjects who hallucinate doubly in trance, may simply be picking up cues telling them that the hypnotist permits them to perceive and express inconsistencies; subjects might be learning the intended thoroughness of their hypnotic performance (Fisher, 1962). The exact wording of suggestions, for instance, has been demonstrated before as a vital factor in determining whether, or not, a given hypnotic effect will occur and care must be taken to ensure that the way questions are asked is not merely responsible for the phenomena that are obtained. Subjects' pursuit of the intent of the hypnotist in this fashion fits the hypnotic data of Johnson, Maher, and Barber (1972) and McDonald and Smith (1975), but not the data of Evans (1972), nor entirely the data of Peters (1973). Johnson *et al.* and McDonald and Smith found that simulators in fact showed trance logic behavior (for example, "double hallucination response") equally as often as hypnotic subjects, while Evans reported logical problem solving among his simulators but not among his hypnotic subjects, the latter group displaying more logically incongruous forms of response. Peters (1973) found that simulators were differentiated from real subjects on a composite measure of trance logic but on very few of the individual items on which that composite was based. One must take into account, however, the defining features of the simulating technique when evaluating the evidence (see Chapter 6 for extended analysis of the method). Although Evans' and Peters' simulators responded more logically, that fact doesn't negate the possible differential effects of the special instructions simulators receive, any more, in fact, than the performance of the Johnson *et al.* (1972) simulators negate the possible effects of trance for hypnotic subjects. In both instances, causal relationships are far from indexed. It would indeed provide an easy solution to the hypnotic state controversy if one could be satisfied with simple demonstration of behavioral differences between simulating and hypnotic subjects. Differences between these two sets of subjects, however, may merely reflect the separate influences of varying kinds of instruction (see Chapter 6 for extensive discussion of this argument).

Preconceptions about Trance

One line of evidence that has emerged recently presents data which are difficult to assimilate to the operational paradigm; the results certainly are not readily explainable in terms of the social psychological processes favored by the model to date. Sheehan (1971b) found that hypnotic subjects will counter a preconception about trance if it conflicts subtly with the wishes of the hypnotist, whereas simulators, on the other hand, will not. In the series of experiments that he reports, both susceptible and insusceptible subjects initially viewed a demonstration of hypnosis which suggested that a good hypnotic subject should respond compulsively to a particular suggestion at all times. Simulating and real subjects were recruited from those attending the demonstration; simulating subjects then received instructions to role play, and all subjects were given a hypnotic induction and tested formally for the preconceived response. Toward the end of the session the hypnotist indicated he was about to lift all the suggestions he had given, but before doing so finally he informally used the cue word that previously had triggered the compulsive response. The dilemma for subjects created by these procedures was a subtle one. If subjects were to be influenced according to their preconception they ought still to have responded compulsively since the suggestion had not yet been finally removed; the hypnotist, though, clearly was about to remove the suggestion and could be taken to really not expect a response. When the hypnotist implied to subjects in this way that a response was no longer really necessary, real subjects stopped responding; the simulators, however, continued to respond as the demonstration had led them to believe they should and this was despite the fact that both groups had viewed exactly the same demonstration.

The data from this study are embarrassing to the operational model on two counts. First, Barber argues that hypnotic effects should accord with the expectations subjects have about hypnosis, and that hypnotic striving is more adequately explained in terms of role perception than special state concepts. It would seem to follow, then, that hypnotic subjects like other well-motivated subjects should respond according to their preconceptions about hypnosis where such expectations are clearly outlined, plausible and they have been firmly established. It seems that in this particular test situation strong role-perception as dictated by preexperimental expectations was actually ineffective, but *only* for those subjects who were susceptible to hypnosis and whose experiences in trance conflicted subtly with their preconceptions about "appropriate" ways of responding. An interpretation of this kind seems to obviously counter any simple operational analysis of susceptible subjects' behavior in terms of social influence processes of communication. Second, it was argued above that use of simulators is open to the criticism that differences between susceptible subjects and role players may simply be due to the different kinds of instructions the two groups receive in the experimental setting. The present study attempted to avoid the likelihood of this happening by replicating the entire experiment for both real and simulating subjects who received no prior demonstration at all about "appropriate" hypnotic response. Results for these groups showed an identical pattern of informal response (test was again made just prior to removal of the suggestion); both sets of subjects ceased responding compulsively in exact accord with what the hypnotist implied he wanted them to do. Previously obtained differences, then, could not have been due simply to one group receiving simulating instructions while the other group did not.

The distinctive behavior of real (susceptible) subjects in this research appears to index the consequences of susceptible subjects "becoming especially involved experientially in the events of trance." The pattern of response for susceptible subjects did not replicate for insusceptible role-playing subjects, nor could the pattern of response that was found be accounted for in terms of differing sets of instructions given to real and simulating subjects. Additional work in the series of experiments also determined that personality differences existed between those real subjects who countered the preconception and the real subjects who did not, but further work showed that these differences, in fact, were not responsible for the effect that was obtained. Role theory (see Chapter 4 for full discussion of such an account) has many traditional arguments which allow "escape" from attack and their possible relevance here lends some unequivocality to the present case for hypnosis. It could be claimed, for instance, that since hypnotic subjects operated under a different task definition (and consequently different role perceptions) than simulating subjects the data merely reflected the fact that simulators' distinctive interactions with the experimenter led them to distrust him personally, while the role perceptions of hypnotic subjects were such that the real group had no reason not to trust the hypnotist and so they became involved with him. Such an argument, though "post hoc," is plausible, but the elimination in this work of a variety of "nonhypnotic" explanations of the data–many of the kind the operational model normally selects as plausible "alternative accounts"–suggests strongly that it is premature for the model to argue, as it does, that concepts appealing to aspects of hypnotic consciousness are thoroughly expendable.

Attitudes, Motivations and Expectancies, and Imaginative Involvement

The final line of evidence to be reviewed which bears upon the operational model concerns the empirical effect of subjects' attitudes about hypnosis on their subsequent hypnotic response. This area of research should be viewed as being of primary importance to the model because it is to the variables of "attitude," "motivation," "expectancy," and "suggestion-related imaginings" that the model has appealed for higher theoretical integration of the facts that it has gathered. These variables have been chosen as "linking" constructs and provide the basic sources of mediational influence for the model. One of the major theoretical concerns of the model has been to show that positive attitudes, motivations, and expectancies about test situations lead in particular to equivalent effects in hypnotic and nonhypnotic contexts. The change in orientation of the model from a purely operational paradigm to an "integrative" one puts acceptance of the framework at much greater risk. The paradigm has come to make specific theoretical predictions that are open to test and consequently to refutation, and the accuracy of Barber's viewpoint therefore comes under additional scrutiny of a special kind. Empirical relationships are examined as before, but the *nature* of their outcome is now of much greater consequence to the model and necessarily determines much more the extent to which we accept it.

The validity of recent theoretical notions put forward by Barber (1972; see also Barber, Spanos, & Chaves, 1974; discussion above) depends heavily on support for the relevance of imagination to hypnosis, but also support for the prediction that positive attitudes toward the test situation are necessary for suggestible response to occur while negative attitudes toward the experimental situation effectively preclude successful response to test suggestions. Evidence to confirm such a position comes from studies conducted by Barber and Calverley (1964d, e) where a formal attempt was made to induce positive and negative test attitudes in subjects. In the first of these studies, one group of subjects was told the experiment tested imagination and another group was told the purpose of the study was to test gullibility. All subjects were then tested on the BSS. Results from the experiment showed a much higher rate of response to suggestion for the subjects who were told they were being tested for imagination. In the second of these studies a stronger negative attitude toward the test situation was induced by a much more convincing description of the study as a test of gullibility. Here, virtually all of the subjects in the negative attitude group failed to respond in any way to the BSS test suggestions.

Barber's interpretation of the evidence available from these studies is a little misleading. In the two studies just described, attitude to testing was clearly confounded with expectation of response and motivation to perform and so the influence of attitudinal factors per se cannot really be determined. Subjects led to believe they were being tested for gullibility would not only have had a negative attitude to testing, but would also probably have expected to respond poorly and would also probably be poorly motivated to perform well. Hypnotic subjects, on the other hand, could have had a positive attitude to testing but they might have differed markedly from their comparison group in expectation and willingness to respond.

In a study mentioned earlier, Connors (1972) attempted to unconfound some of these variables and investigated in more precise fashion subjects' cognitions about participating in an experiment on "hypnosis." Fifty-five subjects had the test situation defined to them as hypnosis, and 64 subjects had the situation defined nonhypnotically—as a test of influenceability (simply, "the ability to experience things that are suggested"). All subjects were asked to imagine themselves participating in an experiment defined in one of these two ways and they were given an extensive questionnaire which probed for the nature of their attitudes, expectancies and motivations concerning response. The major (and somewhat surprising) finding was that hypnosis was viewed by subjects as reflecting a trait they had no particular desire to have; subjects expressed negative attitudes about both hypnosis and influenceability. In a follow-up experiment different groups of subjects were drawn from the same general population of student volunteers and actually tested on the BSS under the two separate definitions of contexts. Data from the previous experiment had shown that "hypnosis" and "influenceability" engendered similar attitudes and expectancies of response so these variables, at least, were unconfounded. A control group of subjects was also tested for whom the context of testing was left totally undefined. Results overall showed an average rate of response of 37% but there were no behavioral differences on the BSS among the three context groups (hypnosis, influenceability, and control). As before, experimental subjects viewed the context of testing more negatively than positively while control subjects viewed their context in a positive fashion. Inquiry into the reasons for subjects' questionnaire responses indicated that subjects preferred to think for themselves and make up their own minds, the context of hypnosis implying to them that they might be prevented from doing this. Taken collectively, Connors' (1972) results appear to undermine the exact stated relevance of the principles chosen by the operational model for integrating its data. The facts demonstrate that defining the test situation as hypnosis does not, of itself, produce positive attitudes to the experimental situation as proponents of the model have tended to argue. Also, negative attitudes do not necessarily exclude response to test suggestion (although it should be stated that *strong* negative attitudes were not present in the studies just discussed). In the fact of data like these and the results from other studies which suggest that fantasy responses may themselves be suggested (for example, Buckner & Coe, 1975; Coe *et al.*, 1974), one can query the wisdom of the attempt to organize the data of the model through mediational variables of the kind that, as yet, have dubious or inconsistent effects.

SUMMARY EVALUATION OF THE MODEL

Few models of hypnosis have made so large a scientific contribution to the analysis of hypnotic phenomena as Barber's operational paradigm. His model has served to rigorously check our assumptions, sharpen our inferences, and strip the concept of "hypnosis" in much needed fashion of a veritable wealth of surplus meaning. In doing so, it has instituted new and important controls in the methodology of hypnosis that have influenced researchers enormously, the best known of these being the waking comparison, "Task Motivation." As Coe (1971) has stated, after familiarizing oneself with the operational model and its contribution to knowledge we have no option but to critically question the role of hypnotic induction in explaining the events of trance. More than any other paradigm it has specified a multitude of hypnotic events to be explained and a host of variables of antecedent influence to explain them, and has catalogued a great deal of evidence to suggest there are plausible alternative accounts of the data that have no need of special concepts such as "hypnosis," "trance," or "hypnotic state."

By its very nature the operational paradigm of hypnosis advocates systematic recognition of all factors of influence in the hypnotic setting and the model is peculiarly equipped to unravel much of the complexity of hypnotic events bypassed by those arguing for the "genuineness" of hypnotic response. As Chaves (1968) has pointed out, there is need for sorting out the criteria on which we attempt to argue that a response is truly hypnotic and it is in this regard that the operational model has contributed very usefully to our knowledge. Pain, for example, can be indexed in many ways–by physiological signs such as increased heart rate, blood pressure, and respiration rate; by gross signs of behavioral discomfort; or by verbal testimony of "feeling pain." The operational model argues unequivocally that these and any other consequences of noxious stimulation and suggestion–the so-called criteria of genuineness–must be outlined systematically and related lawfully to variations in antecedent influences. The advantage of the model is that logically all possible effects are opened to empirical examination. The advantage at times, though, becomes almost the model's weakness. All factors which potentially influence performance are required to be controlled but the model says virtually nothing about the relevance of each of the separate factors considered. "Which factors in the multitudinous array of variables ought to be controlled and which do not?" is a question the model finds very difficult to assess. There is no methodological principle guiding us toward especially important variables, or offering firm guarantee that the most relevant factors have not been overlooked; data do guide the researcher, but theory often serves more decisively to point the way. The ingenuity for deciding relevance stems from theorizing on the part of the researcher, and the model has only just begun to provide this in its most recent formulations concerning the particular significance of subjects' attitudes, motivations, expectancies, and "thinking along with suggestions" as the logical end of the antecedent chain of events. One of the major weaknesses of the operational paradigm, as with operationism, in general, as a movement within science, is that it does not tell us how to invent (Stevens, 1939) and invention at some point does seem necessary if knowledge is to advance significantly. Field (1971) expresses the same kind of concern when he states that the radical empiricism of Barber's model makes any variable worth the effort and there are no real criteria to guide the researcher as to the actual importance of the variables he is studying. The model may suffer from the simple fact there are relatively few indications as to which of the host of variables it has isolated are particularly worthy of notice, and which not; but, on the other hand, others may argue that the model generates its own distinctive criterion of importance through the sheer weight of the data it collects.

The basic thesis of this chapter has been that the inferences about hypnosis that are drawn from application of the model are drawn too strongly. The model operates as we have seen according to the logic of "alternative explanation" and the logic of "equivalence." It argues on the basis of comparability of hypnotic and nonhypnotic effects that alternative accounts of the data–in particular, explanations making no appeal to "hypnosis" as a causal variable–easily account for the evidence. Arguments about "the expendability of the trance concept" strictly speaking are illegitimate as far as the model is concerned. Where alternative accounts of the data hold, all that can be justifiably argued is that the concept of hypnosis may not be relevant even if the data appear to be consistent with theorizing about it (for discussion of further implications of the logic of alternative explanation and for cross-paradigm comparison concerning its application, see Chapters 6 and 8 of this book). The issue really becomes one of assessing which of the two alternative accounts–hypnotic or nonhypnotic–we prefer on other grounds that invariably revolve around the equivocality of our evidence, the adequacy and strictures of our control, and the reasonableness of our assumptions. The operational approach has very usefully highlighted just how much of the research in hypnosis fails to satisfactorily meet these standards of acceptance, but a close look at the paradigm reveals that it too has trouble satisfying the criteria we have just named. The logic of equivalence assumes comparability of variables of influence in the hypnotic and nonhypnotic conditions but there is a substantial body of evidence to suggest that this assumption is unjustified. Work on the effect of "demand for honesty." "behavioral constraint," and some of the paradoxical effects found for waking control subjects suggest, collectively, that hypnotic and waking effects might be reflecting quite different sources of influence, even if the effects in question look comparable. Artifactual variables appear to exist which the operational model has failed to recognize and to control. In principle, the criticism is easily met by the model, because any variable can simply be added to its comprehensive list of antecedent factors to be considered. Our discussion may help to indicate that there are weaknesses in the basic assumptions of the model which the future isolation of particular variables *may* not necessarily overcome.

Arguments about the trance-inducing quality of TM instructions serve to further highlight some of the specification problems of the model. The experimental group receives a hypnotic induction procedure, whereas the control (viz. TM) group does not. The inferences that the model purports to make regarding trance however, can only be accepted as valid and the adequacy of its nonhypnotic account can only be properly assessed if the control condition is thoroughly nonhypnotic. It is precisely the nonhypnotic variables relevant to both sets of conditions–control and experimental–that provide the special cogency of the model's alternative account and if any of these variables are challenged as to their nonhypnotic character then the logic of the model is undermined. There are two ways of looking at the data that have been reviewed: (a) aspects of subjects' patterns of behavior and testimony of trance following TM instruction indicate that TM instruction is, in fact, perceived as trance inducing by some subjects and may therefore evoke hypnotic response; and (b) the set of procedures labeled as "TM instruction" has been as yet specified incompletely and conclusions regarding the nature of its effects must perforce be equivocal. The first of these interpretations is compatible with the traditionalists' argument but their conclusion is too strong—testimony of trance, following TM instruction, for example, may be invalid and itself an artifact of social influence variables that to date have been undetected. The second interpretation is much the more defensible one and fits well into the general argument of this chapter. In summary, inferences from the model are considerably more equivocal than Barber would have us believe; unspecified variables adhere to the model's experimental manipulations and so complicate the logic of its inferences. Extensive analysis is obviously needed of subjects' "motivation for the experimental act"—nonhypnotic as well as hypnotic.

The operational model is one that is readily misunderstood, partly because people easily overreact to the strength of its attack. The model itself, however, tends to overstate the claims of the traditionalists and it is too uncompromising in its perception of the utility of the concept of hypnosis. The model assumes at times that adherents of hypnotic state theory advocate a single cause for behavioral patterns of the kind that are observable in the hypnotic setting. Multiplicity of causes, obviously, does exist; hallucinations, for example, can readily arise following induction procedures, sensory deprivation, cortical stimulation or even social pressure to respond, and in all these instances the experimenter has an obligation to research into the genuineness of the response. It does not follow, as the model would sometimes have us believe, that traditionalists are bound to the position that hallucinations (or any other hypnotic phenomena) produced by a variety of methods are necessarily equivalent or are produced by the same mechanism. There is no a priori threat to the traditionalist argument by Barber's demonstration that nonhypnotic procedures effectively elicit phenomena which are overtly similar to those observed in the hypnotic setting. As we have stated before, similar results produced by hypnotized and TM subjects may not necessarily arise through the operation of the same mechanisms and the claim that there are unique behavioral effects of hypnosis no longer really represents a sophisticated traditionalist stance.

Finally, the theoretical status of the operational model deserves additional comment. The model aims always to actively search for new variables and new relationships among variables but at the same time it seeks to find broad principles to integrate the large number of functional relations that have already been found. These principles have been sought in terms of the broader variables of attitudes, expectancies, and motivations, and willingness to think along with the hypnotist's communications. The inconsistencies in the data that are available on the operation of these variables, however, suggest that thorough integration of data in terms of them is premature. It seems likely that the mediational variables that have been selected are too superficial to account for the complexities of the evidence. Reyher (1975), for instance, has recently drawn attention to evidence which appears to challenge the integrative function of "willingness to imagine" as a prime theoretical construct. Items on a standard scale of hypnotic susceptibility which incorporated visual imaginal strategies were not found to be superior to a parallel form of the test which involved no visual, imaginal strategies. Findings like these, however, are rare. Subjects in hypnotic and TM treatment conditions tend to report visual imagery in response to hypnotic suggestions (Ham & Spanos, 1974), and results are much more consistent, than not, with the notion that response to suggestion implies the relevance of some generalized cognitive ability—one which Barber and his associates have called "involvement in imagining" (Barber, Spanos, & Chaves 1974; Spanos & Barber, 1974; Spanos, Barber, & Lang, 1974). In other respects, however, it is difficult to see how current formulations of the model can account for different kinds of evidence. The model, for example, cannot easily incorporate the finding that some hypnotic subjects actually counter predetermined expectancies about hypnosis when such expectations subtly conflict with those given by the hypnotist; role theory could assimilate the pattern of results, but its arguments are definitely "post hoc" and require predictive test. Further, other results indicate that hypnotic recruitment does not always engender positive attitudes, yet subjects' response to suggestion is nevertheless substantial.

Operational constructs of the type specified by Barber as necessary for the integration of data need to be supplemented by more penetrating processes of social influence, including, perhaps, interpersonal rapport. Barber's early theorizing emphasized interpersonal mediational processes which were dependent on reciprocal role playing, and his latest formulations have continued the trend by stressing the social psychological processes of influence communications. Both forays into theorizing, however, exclude any deep or thorough analysis of interpersonal interaction. Relationship factors are stressed as in the study of Troffer (1966; cited by Barber, 1969) who found that age regression-type behavior was more readily facilitated in subjects who were treated by the hypnotist as children than in subjects who were treated as adults. On the whole, though, studies of this kind have been the exception rather than the rule and the potentially dynamic nature of the subject–hypnotist interaction has been totally ignored. Too many aspects of interpersonal influence have been overlooked by the model, in fact, for its current theoretical orientation to be accepted as anyways near complete.

As has already been stated, lack of adequate theory does not pose any great crisis for the paradigm because the model's real strength lies in the support it gives to the thorough and systematic exploration of the functional relationships that exist between variables in the hypnotic setting and an exploration of this kind does seem essential before data can be integrated in proper theoretical fashion. There are dangers carried by theorizing, nevertheless and these occur implicitly within the paradigm even in the most operational of statements that it makes. For example, the model very consistently excludes the term "hypnosis" by substituting the term "suggestibility" in its statements of relationship. Yet "a 'type of suggestibility' (Barber, 1969, p. 54) demands specification of apparent meaning just as 'hypnosis' does, and 'suggestibility is facilitated' (Barber, 1969, p. 75) surely means more than the fact a subject is responding successfully to the experimenter's instructions [Sheehan, 1971e, p. 16]."

We turn finally to some suggestions for research which arise out of the particular way in which we have described and evaluated the operational model.

IMPLICATIONS FOR FUTURE RESEARCH

If Barber's model is correct in converging upon involvement in imaginative activities as a core construct for integrating hypnotic data (for similar emphasis see Chapter 4), then the research directions for his model come to differentiate it from other viewpoints. Despite such emphasis and its implications for considering internal processing, Barber's model continually focuses on situational and social psychological antecedents of hypnotic phenomena, while state theorists attempt to single out signs that experience in hypnosis has altered "fundamentally." Barber's task, in a sense, is much less formidable than the one which faces state theorists, but it too is still far from completed.

One of the most pressing areas for research effort as far as the operational paradigm is concerned is the systematic analysis of variables pertaining to its nonhypnotic comparison groups. The model has contributed vastly to our knowledge of the variables characterizing the hypnotic context, but in doing so it has instituted experimental manipulations of a "nonhypnotic" kind which themselves have not been subjected to penetrating analysis. A detailed examination of the model's instructions and procedures is necessary if the model is to continue to make the assumptions it does about its basic comparison conditions. The logic underlying the model's use of TM instruction should be opened wide to the scrutiny of the researcher. Experimentation might then decide what exactly are the variables which characterize TM instruction as distinct from induction and what precisely are the variables these two sets of procedures share in common. If it is found that the variables that differentiate TM from hypnotic instruction also yield similar consequent effects then the logic underlying the model is especially threatened. In their search for discriminating features researchers might well analyze further the possibilities of compliance that are directly or indirectly conveyed by TM instruction to a degree not comparably conveyed by hypnotic instruction; the work done to date on "behavioral constraint" and the effectiveness of "demand for honesty" instruction should be extended. Other variables also open to investigation are "appeal to the subject's competitive feelings," "appeal to self-esteem"; and subject's testimony of feeling hypnotized. This last variable as related to TM instruction is one which requires particularly thorough and systematic exploration. "Trance" is not a concept at all relevant to Barber's model, but the data nevertheless appear to threaten the basic logic of the model that is put forward. Future work needs to demonstrate (in support of the model) that reports concerning the presence of trance adhere invalidly to TM instruction and that the cue implications of TM instructions do not justify an appeal to hypnotic-type variables in any way. Barber himself has called for future research to consider carefully the implications of the wording of suggestions (for example, Barber, Walker, & Hahn, 1973). The need is evident though, for both so-called "hypnotic" *and* "nonhypnotic" procedures.

The strength of subjects' motivation relating to the various conditions that are employed by the model constitutes a related issue of some importance. One of the essential purposes of the main comparison condition of the operational model is to motivate the person who is not hypnotized as highly as the person who receives formal induction. It is surprising, though, that no real concern has been expressed by Barber as to whether this ought to be done by maximally motivating the subject who is not hypnotized. Waking motivational suggestions can be very effective in their influence (see Norris, 1973) and TM subjects, in particular, are very highly motivated to perform well—as, also, are simulating subjects in application of the real–simulating model of hypnosis (the logic underlying this model, though, is quite distinct and is the topic of a separate chapter, Chapter 6). If the logic of equivalence is to be applied to data associated with the operational model, the degree of motivation of control subjects should really be exactly comparable with that of experimental subjects. Precisely what extent of motivation is relevant to hypnotic subjects is an empirical question of paramount importance in its own right. Many workers in the field have assumed far too readily that the motivation of hypnotic subjects is intense (Fisher, 1962; Pattie, 1950; White, 1941a) and so have influenced the decision of researchers in hypnosis to demand maximal motivation from control subjects for purposes of comparison with hypnotic subjects. Undoubtedly, some susceptible subjects are especially highly motivated to respond, but it is risky to imply that intense striving at all times (Fisher, 1962) is a general characteristic of the susceptible person. Too much motivation of comparison subjects violates the strictures of adequate control every bit as much as too little. And the issue is not to be confused simply with the varying aptitude for trance that subjects may display. Research with the operational model should carefully determine what exactly is the level of motivation experienced by "hypnotic" subjects so that this level can then be matched exactly in its control conditions. The logic of equivalence demands this.

Empirically speaking, the operational model embraces all possibilities of lawful relation between antecedent and consequent variables. On the theoretical side, however, further work must decide what additional variables the model should endorse as mediational in character and which concepts it should select to integrate the data most parsimoniously. The results that are available suggest much more needs to be done to explore the contribution of "attitude," "expectancy," "motivation," and "involvement in suggestion-related imaginings" to hypnotic responsivity—for some hypnotic subjects positive expectancy of response has remarkably little effect (Sheehan, 1971b; Spanos, McPeake, & Carter, 1973) and lack of positive attitude to hypnosis is not as much as impediment to hypnotic response as we have been led to suppose (Connors, 1972; Connors & Sheehan, 1976). The interactions among these variables of influence also constitute an issue of some concern. Finally, the model appears only to have tapped the surface of the effects of processes of social influences. New directions in research, however, have focused valuably on processes that are obviously important. Analysis of the cognitive potentialities of the subject (for example, Barber, Spanos, & Chaves, 1974) including the various processes of imagination has constituted an important development in research and the knowledge gained from this advance has clearly enhanced the theoretical adequacy of the model and merged it closer in its formal orientation to other viewpoints.

In conclusion, it must be stated that there is much more to recommend about Barber's paradigm of hypnosis than to criticize. Its contribution to our knowledge about hypnotic phenomena has been immense and its scientific value is unassailable. The model has also had an overwhelming impact on the literature in the field. To accept or not to accept what Barber's operational paradigm has had to say about research into hypnotic phenomena is a dilemma that has dominated thinking in hypnosis for some years. Hopefully, this chapter has cast the operational model in a new and thoughtful light. We have tried to look aside from any simple account of the evidence which supports the model and have attempted to focus on the underlying assumptions of the model and the basic logic of its approach. Looked at in this way there seems much to justify the conclusion that the inferences which can be legitimately drawn from application of the operational paradigm are considerably more equivocal than the paradigm would presently have us believe.

4

Hypnosis as Role Enactment: The Model of Theodore R. Sarbin

> Mentalism is not the only thought model available to students of silent and invisible processes. An alternate way of thinking begins with guiding postulates quite different from those that influence the conclusions of traditional mentalists. The alternate view looks upon man as an active, exploratory, manipulating, creating, *doing* creature. In short, man is an actor [Sarbin & Coe, 1972, pp. 116–117].

To many of his colleagues, Theodore Sarbin's position, that hypnotic behavior can be thought of as a form of role enactment, appears to be an elaborate and futile exercise in linguistic philosophy. Sarbin has a keen grasp of the philosophy of science, and to such colleagues he appears to be excessively addicted to a facile logic, in which substance is secondary to style. The problem is compounded further by the fact that Sarbin sees a variety of psychopathologies (such as schizophrenia and depression) in similar role-enactment terms. Even more confusing, to some, is Sarbin's insistence that all theories in science are metaphors, including his own. Along with this insistence is an emphasis that theories as metaphors run the distinct risk of becoming reified, particularly if theory, conceived of in this way, is taken literally rather than as an "as-if" statement. Sarbin's theory is thus sometimes seen as an act of willful perversity for his advocacy of a role-enactment theory of hypnosis (which carries connotations of sham behavior), for his belief that all theories are metaphors, and for his recognition of the limitations of the role metaphor as theory. It is strange that this should confuse so many people, since the view that theories in science constitute convenient fictions or best guesses at the truth for want of more factual data has a long and honorable history in the philosophy of science, (Sarbin & Anderson, 1967). To say that all theories are metaphors, including one's own, is simply to subscribe to a common, and tenable belief.

There is the added problem of what Sarbin means by role. On this question Sarbin's position has undergone some subtle shifts in the last quarter century since his initial highly influential and innovative paper first appeared (Sarbin, 1950). In this endeavor, Sarbin has actively collaborated with his former student, William Coe, who has contributed much to the elaboration and empirical testing of role-enactment theory. We will begin by describing the basic aspects of his position that have remained unchanged over this long period before focusing upon this central issue of the cogency and pertinence of construing hypnotic behavior as role enactment.

In setting out the facts that a theory of hypnosis must explain, Sarbin is in agreement with the conventional wisdom of the last number of decades. In common with many theorists, he points to four types of observation that need to be accounted for: namely, the apparent discontinuity and apparent automaticity of hypnotic behavior, the large amplitude of hypnotic response to seemingly benign stimuli, and the presence of quite stable individual differences in response to hypnotic induction. In commenting on the apparent discontinuity of hypnotic response, Sarbin notes that the hypnotic behavior is different to what comes before and what follows a formal induction. The subject appears to be a "changed organism," whose responsivity is "qualitatively and quantitatively" different from customary baselines. It also appears to be *automatic*. The hypnotized subject *appears* to respond nonvolitionally, almost like an automaton, despite the fact that most behaviors exhibited in hypnosis are under voluntary control. This fact alone should make us careful in accepting hypnotic behavior at face value; the possibility of simulation, or some kind of elaborate game on the part of the subject, cannot be ruled out. And yet some hypnotic behaviors appear to be involuntary. For instance pain control appears to be beyond the realm of voluntary suppression of response, and often causes amazement when viewed in the hypnotic context. By contrast, similar pain control under conditions of high organismic involvement, such as the *stress* of combat appears comprehensible and explicable.

A cogent theory of hypnosis likewise needs to account for the amplitude of hypnotic response to seemingly benign stimuli. Many behaviors occur in hypnosis that might be expected to take place under antecedent conditions of stress fatigue, coercion, toxicosis, neurosis, and fever. And yet hypnotic behavior of the same magnitude frequently occurs simply as the result of the hypnotist talking to a subject in a pleasant and nondirective manner. Finally, there is a need to understand individual differences in hypnotic susceptibility, which have been reported for nearly a century (Bernheim, 1890). As we have noted, these individual differences appear to be quite stable, although current work on the modification of susceptibility (Diamond, 1974; Sachs 1971; see also Chapter 9 of this book) may lead ultimately to some reformulation of this belief. In common with several other theorists we discuss (notably Hilgard & Sutcliffe; see Chapters 2 and 5), Sarbin places strong emphasis on hypnotizability itself as a major phenomenon of hypnosis that needs to be explained by an adequate theory; his paradigm thus assumes the durability and stability of what appears to be an important trait characteristic of the subject.

These four classes of observation which an adequate theory of hypnosis must explain are not unlike what other theorists have emphasized; White (1941a) and Orne (1967), for example, list similar requirements. However, Sarbin's manner of summing up constitutes one of the most lucid statements of the problem facing a comprehensive theory of hypnosis. "*What,*" he asks, "*are the characteristics of those individuals who, in response to hypnotic induction procedures, exhibit conduct which is apparently discontinuous and apparently automatic?* [Sarbin, 1950, p. 257]." In answer to this question, Sarbin has taken the far from unique position that hypnosis, to be properly understood, has to be thought of as a specific instance of a broader class of psychological processes. Uniquely, however, he has chosen role behavior as the genus of the species. This means, among other things, that he sees hypnosis as an interaction between the hypnotized person and the hypnotist and he believes that concepts borrowed from social psychology are best able to deal with the facts of what is essentially a social interchange. Further, Sarbin has drawn as much upon the literature of the theatre as the social psychological literature on role behavior, in developing his position.

THEORETICAL POSITION

Early Theorizing

There has been a number of subtle shifts in Sarbin's theorizing over the past 25 years. These have been undertaken in the interests of formalizing the theory, and making it more rigorous and testable. Although much of the conceptual base has remained intact, Sarbin has been deeply concerned to operationalize which has led to certain changes in the formal aspects of his theorizing.

In his earlier approach, Sarbin (1950) sought to elucidate the main role-playing dimension that he believes underlies hypnotic behavior. He expressed it as a continuum which he characterized as a "conscious–unconscious" dimension. This first formulation clearly reflected the mentalistic orientation of dynamic depth psychology and, to a large extent, was a misnomer. It can be expressed better (as Sarbin subsequently has) as a dimension of self-awareness and organismic involvement in certain activities.

Sarbin drew heavily on the literature of dramatic acting which gives some emphasis to differences in the degree to which actors become absorbed in the dramatic roles they are playing. Some actors report becoming so immersed in their dramatic portrayal that they find it difficult to differentiate self from role. In particular he was attracted by the distinction between "heated" acting and "technical" acting. The difference between these two types of actors is not one of acting competence, nor of one actor being able to enact a particular dramatic role better than another, but rather is a matter of the subjective experiences they each report while acting.

The "technical" actor is one who reports that while on stage, he is relatively aware of himself, as a distinctive person, playing a part of another human being whose ideas and emotions and aspirations may be quite different to his own off-stage psychological makeup. By contrast, Sarbin was obviously intrigued by reports (such as provided by Archer, 1889) of some actors possessing almost quasi-dissociated selves. They gave frequent reports of losing themselves in certain roles so completely that they were relatively unaware of the audience, of other normally adequate peripheral stimuli and, most interesting of all, of themselves distinctive from the role they were playing.

Sarbin (1950) felt that these accounts of acting, particularly that of the "heated" actor, were not unlike those given of hypnotized subjects. He set out this hypothesized dimension of self-awareness and role immersion in diagrammatic form (which is reproduced in Fig. 4.1a) in which the overlap of lines is intentional. This initial model placed hypnosis midway on this continuum of role–self differentiation. Significantly, in terms of immersion–absorption, Sarbin saw hypnosis as being slightly more inadvertent behavior than "heated" acting, but as involving less self-role coalescence than hysteria. On this latter point the echoes of Charcot's earlier discredited theory which postulated complete identity of hypnotic and hysterical processes, are discernible (see Chapter 1).

In this earlier formulation, Sarbin was not content to leave matters at the point of drawing interesting parallels between hypnotic and dramatic performance. Further parameters still needed to be elucidated, and it is here that his flair for operationalizing concepts is manifest. Sarbin proceeded to elaborate three key concepts which would account for differences in both hypnotizability, and the intensity of hypnotic experience. Here again he drew heavily on the analogy of hypnotic behavior to "heated" acting:

> From this preliminary description, we submit that the role taking of the stage actor and the role-taking of the hypnotic subject embody the same characteristics:
>
> (a) Favorable motivation–the actor's self-concept and his perception of the part to which he is assigned must be congruent; if it is not, then his performance is unconvincing or he pays a terrific psychological price.
>
> (b) Role perception–the actor must first perceive the role he is to play–this is achieved partly by the actor's own experience with similar stage or real life roles, partly by the director's definition of the role.
>
> (c) Role-taking aptitude–needless to say, some actors can take a role more completely than others. Compare, for example, the performance of Barrymore as Hamlet with the efforts of a high school senior [Sarbin, 1950, p. 260].

Of these, he regarded role-taking aptitude as the most important–if one lacks the abilities specific to the task, no amount of favorable motivation or accurate

(a) States of ecstasy: mystical experiences;
Role and self undifferentiated

Hysterias

Hypnosis

"Heated" acting

Technical acting;
Role and self are differentiated

(1)

(b) Zero. Noninvolvement

I. Casual role enactment

II. Ritual acting

III. Engrossed acting

IV. Classical hypnotic role taking

V. Histrionic neurosis

VI. Ecstasy

VII. Object of sorcery and witchcraft
(sometimes irreversible)

Role and self differentiated	**Role and self undifferentiated**
Zero involvement	**Maximal involvement**
Few organic systems	**Entire organism**
No effort.	**Much effort**

FIGURE 4.1 Two conceptualizations of the dimensions of self-awareness and role immersion thought to underlie role enactment. (Part a from Sarbin, 1950. Copyright 1950 by the American Psychological Association. Reproduced by permission. Part b from Sarbin & Coe, 1972.)

role perception will compensate for the initial lack. Without it, one is in the position of the drama critic who can differentiate, with a high degree of accuracy, outstanding performances from the more routine, but could never perform at the requisite level himself.

In asking the further and final question—upon what does role-taking aptitude itself depend?—Sarbin proceeded to posit a view of hypnosis as constituting "as-if" behavior that has been a very influential one. It has affinities with the theorizing of Sutcliffe (see Chapter 5), whose notion of the hypnotic situation as involving an invitation to participate in "free play" or "directed fantasy" parallels the *as-if* formulation and constitutes an independent attempt to formulate hypnotic behavior in similar terms.

By *as-if* behavior, Sarbin sought to delineate situations where an individual responds to physically absent imaginal stimuli, as if they were actually present, even though at some level, the person is probably aware that they are not. As he put it then: "The *as-if* formulation may be seen not only in the drama, in hypnosis, but in fantasy, play, and in fact, all imaginative behavior. Imaginative behavior is *as-if* behavior [Sarbin, 1950, p. 267]."

Later Theorizing

We have dwelt upon Sarbin's earlier theorizing because it has provided the foundation for later developments. Some notion of the shifts in the theory can be seen in Fig. 4.1b (from Sarbin & Coe, 1972) which constitutes a more complex and more formalized version of the earlier model.

Many of these changes reflect Sarbin's deep concern to operationalize his concepts. This in turn is related to the fact that the role metaphor has been widely misunderstood to the extent that he has been accused, at times, of using role to imply that hypnotic behavior is akin to sham behavior. It should be clear that this is not so from even a cursory look at Fig. 4.1b. It can be seen that various classes of behavior, as in Fig. 4.1a have been ranged along a dimension of progressively greater organismic involvement which replaces the earlier "conscious–unconscious" dimension.

Further, there has been an attempt made to break down organismic involvement into its presumed constituent components–an attempt which involves certain assumptions. It can be seen from Fig. 4.1b that as the person moves towards greater organismic involvement, self and role become less differentiated. It is assumed further that with more organismic systems involved, greater effort is expended by the person as he moves further in this direction. Other aspects of Fig. 4.1b simply represent changes of terminology (viz. technical acting = ritual acting; "heated" acting = engrossed acting; hysteria = histrionic neuroses); the reasons for these changes we have already discussed. In the same vein, Sarbin now speaks of hypnosis not as role playing, but as role enactment, in a further attempt to limit reification of the role metaphor (Sarbin & Andersen, 1967).

Role enactment is conceived broadly in the sense that many kinds of behavior, including hypnotic behavior can be understood with reference to this central concept. It is seen by Sarbin as being affected by a number of underlying dimensions some of which he argues are highly pertinent to hypnosis, while others are less so. Thus people are thought by Sarbin to differ in the number of roles that they have available to them, and he reports evidence suggesting that the people who are more adept at taking new roles make better hypnotic subjects. At the same time, hypnotic performance does not appear to be related to the extensiveness of a person's role repertoire. By contrast *preemptiveness of roles* (the amount of time customarily spent in a role, for instance doctor versus spectator at a sporting event), is thought to be important for other behaviors, but is not especially relevant to hypnosis. The concept of *organismic involvement* is, however, central to role enactment. The greater the amount of effort and physiological participation expended by a person, the more likely it is that self and role will coalesce as in Fig. 4.1b. There are obvious and basic similarities between this position and Sarbin's earlier position (Sarbin, 1950).

Role enactment, then, concerns the degree to which a person becomes organismically involved in enacting a particular role and is itself affected by a number of underlying variables. These have been described in greater detail elsewhere (Sarbin & Coe, 1972). They are briefly summarized here to demonstrate the way in which the theory has developed over the years. There are six main variables affecting the quality of role enactment:

1. *Role location* is concerned with the person's ability to find a role that is appropriate to a specific situation. In the hypnotic situation it involves reciprocal acts by hypnotist and subject; the hypnotist, in establishing himself as competent and professional emits various cues to the subject, who in turn uses at least some of them to locate what is required of him as a subject for hypnosis.

2. *Self–role congruence* is the extent to which the person has self-characteristics which match the requirements of the role he is being requested to enact. This characteristic is seen by Sarbin as constituting a motivational variable. He sees the period of preparation of subjects for hypnosis, in which the subject asks questions about hypnosis and the hypnotist seeks to allay fears and to correct misconceptions about hypnosis as a means of establishing such self–role congruence. This procedure of preparing the subject for hypnosis, and winning his confidence maximizes congruence between self and role characteristics (to the extent that such exist) and is thought to motivate the person to perform optimally in the hypnotic role. This is particularly so on occasions where the subject finds that self and role characteristics correspond well.

3. *Role expectations* are related to the role location variable. They represent the degree to which a person develops accurate and favorable perceptions of a role and can then proceed to behave in a manner appropriate to what is required of him. For instance, a subject who perceives an arm rigidity suggestion as an implicit challenge, and proceeds to try hard, but fails to bend the arm will be judged as more convincing than a subject whose arm does not bend, but who expends little effort in the attempt to do so.

4. *Role skills* are a matter of the degree to which a subject possesses the requisite abilities demanded by a particular role, over and above his ability to locate it accurately, to develop appropriate expectations, and to match self and role characteristics accurately. In the hypnotic situation, role skills appear to be the most important variables determining successful hypnotic performance.

5. *Role demands* are conceived of as the actual demands of a situation. Sarbin regards Orne's notion of demand characteristics (the subject's perception of what is expected of him; see Chapter 6) as a limited example of a more global

notion. Basically, it concerns the extent to which any behavior is expressed in terms of societal norms and cultural mores. In most social situations there are limits placed upon the expressions of such behavior as modesty, aggression, and upon the types of communication permissible between participants; such demands exist also in the hypnotic situation and help to fashion the subject's responses to it.

6. *Reinforcing properties of the audience* concerns the extent to which the person(s) interacted with will give sustenance and support in their reactions to an individual's role behavior. In the hypnotic situation, the extent to which the hypnotist communicates his satisfaction with the subject's performance may significantly assist in maintaining successful performance, other things being equal.

It can be seen from this brief description that the factors underlying role enactment represent a more thorough elaboration of the earlier notions (Sarbin, 1950) of "favorable motivation," "role perception," and "role skills." The details of how all of these variables interrelate to produce variations in role enactment are provided elsewhere (Sarbin & Coe, 1972). As with Sarbin's earlier model, this specific approach leads to the adoption of a particular view of hypnosis, which in turn generates various research strategies.

Hypnosis as *State* or *Trance*

In his earlier writings, Sarbin (1950) referred to hypnosis as *as-if* behavior, which on further analysis, proved to be a matter of imaginative behavior. At this time, Sarbin showed some ambivalence to one of the most currently contentious issues in the field of hypnosis—the extent to which hypnosis can be conceived of as an altered state of the person. Terms such as "state," and "trance state" appear throughout the earlier paper (Sarbin, 1950) with no apparent negative connotation intended. But even at this earlier stage, Sarbin was clearly uncomfortable with the term, as in his occasional references to the "trance role" and in his formulation of hypnosis as *as-if* or imaginative behavior.

This dissatisfaction has been amplified in subsequent works. In his most recent writings Sarbin is at pains to reject the trance formulation and to present an alternative position which sees hypnosis as *believed-in imaginings*; in many respects this development of theorizing through time is reminiscent of the progression in Barber's conceptualization (see previous chapter). For Sarbin, the notion here is that in the fusion of role perceptions, locations, and skills with self–role congruence and other such moderating variables, self and role merge. From this ensues a process of role enactment at some level of self–role congruence.

This places Sarbin in a curious theoretical position that has been little appreciated. He tends to be characterized as rejecting state theory (as Barber does) for its implicit circularity, and certainly this is true. He maintains that "the circular use of the trance concept has been its greatest failure. Observed behaviors *X, Y, Z* (for example, catalepsies, rigidities, and amnesias) are the criteria that the subject is in a trance, but the subject must be in a trance in order to emit behaviors *X, Y,* and *Z*. . . . *The circularity follows from the lack of independent criteria to define the trance,* and bringing the circularity into the open has made it necessary to search for them [Sarbin & Coe, 1972, p. 108, italics added]."

As we noted in the previous chapter on Barber, many proponents of state theory take the above characterization as a misrepresentation of their position. They insist that one can promulgate a state/trance position without circularity, provided that one takes the testimony of the hypnotized subject as nothing more than a statement of his experience which itself needs explanation. They note, with some justification, that the fact that some formulations of state theory are circular should be no reason to conclude that the position, by its very nature, is circular. It is not often recognized that Sarbin, unlike Barber until fairly recently (Spanos & Barber, 1974), has consistently attempted to accommodate this point. Although Sarbin believes that state theorizing is of little value, he nevertheless holds to the position that some alteration of cognitive processes occurs during hypnosis. This view has affinities with state theorizing, but there are considerable differences in how Sarbin conceptualizes the matter. He has given extensive consideration to the problem of defining the characteristics of trance, and of setting out independent criteria which would make a state/trance position tenable. He has pointed out correctly that physiological indices have been rarely found, and that when reported, they have subsequently either failed to replicate, or else have been demonstrated to be experimental artifacts.

However, in common with state theorists, Sarbin accepts the point that the hypnotized subject's testimony of his experiences is a possible indicator of subjective alteration. He approaches this issue (Sarbin & Coe, 1972) by examining the sorts of verbal report that are acceptable to a state theorist as evidence that some form of altered experience has occurred. He proceeds to distinguish between two types of statement that a person might make of his hypnotic experience. On the one hand, a statement like "I was reminded of an incident that happened when my mother was alive" would tend not to qualify as evidence of a change in the individual's phenomenology. By contrast, the statement: "I clearly saw my mother, and I clearly heard her say 'James, do be careful'–my mother has been dead for 15 years" suggests an alteration in ongoing experience of a particular kind. On the basis of this distinction, Sarbin concludes that there are characteristic types of verbal report accepted by state theorists as indicative of hypnotic trance. He argues that a report such as "the sound of a fly buzzing around my face was real" (when there is no fly) had, like the statement of seeing one's mother, two distinguishing features. It is a report of an event that is (1) contrary to fact, and (2) is expressed with a high degree of credibility, if not complete conviction.

This position has been developed further by Sarbin and Coe (1972), who draw a very close analogy between these types of report that are used by state/trance theorists to justify their particular interpretation of hypnotic behavior, and the reports that are used to verify that a person has experienced an hallucination in a nonhypnotic context. The analysis follows Sarbin (1967, 1972) and Sarbin and Juhasz (1967), who argue that an hallucination is no more than the public reporting of *imaginings.* Further, such imaginings are of a special type; like reports of hypnotic experience they are counterfactual, and yet believed-in by the reporter as accurate descriptions of his ongoing subjective experience.

From this analysis, Sarbin and Coe (1972) draw a number of important and distinctive conclusions that can be summarized as follows:

1. The only real evidence for an hypnotic state or trance is the regular reportage of counterfactual statements expressed with great conviction.
2. Likewise a report of an hallucination in nonhypnotic contexts has similar characteristics; it too is a counterfactual statement expressed with conviction by the reporter of such phenomena.
3. The problem of defining hypnosis as a special state is that it utilizes a metaphor ("altered consciousness") that in itself would need explaining, and itself may interfere with understanding hypnosis as a naturalistic phenomenon, which can be analyzed without resort to discontinuous principles.
4. The problem with the current conception of hallucination is that it has become a pejorative term to cut off a certain class of people who, by their very reports of such imaginings, are classified as mentally ill, or as deviates from social norms. And yet for the imaginative reports given by such people there exists no defining characteristics which would distinguish their reports from nonpathological imaginative reports of poets, artists, and other creative people.

On the basis of such considerations Sarbin and Coe (1972) argue that it is more profitable to look at hallucinations and at reports of altered experience in hypnosis as believed-in imaginings for the simple reason that in each case certain implications do not have to be drawn. In the case of hypnosis, it is no longer necessary to infer a special underlying state or trance which may in turn lead to circularity. In the case of hallucination, one need no longer be embarrassed by the fact that some reports of hallucination are treated as pathological, whereas other similar hallucinatory material (when reported by artists and poets) is labeled as "creative" and nonpathological. The concept of believed-in imagining, in short, differentiates at a descriptive level between those who can distinguish the imagined from the real, as against those who cannot and avoids us making value-judgments.

This type of analysis, when related to hypnosis leads to a number of very important implications that may be of the most ultimate significance for the understanding of its nature. By reformulating trance as believed-in imaginings

Sarbin contends that one is able to ask more meaningful questions about hypnosis. Instead of asking what causes trance, one can, instead, inquire into the conditions that make some imaginings believable. Remembering that Sarbin sees all theories as metaphors, his position is that a better metaphor is provided by describing hypnotic experience in this way. Believed-in imaginings have the advantage of being obviously descriptive and are thus less likely to be formulated in the circular manner that has characterized many trance theories. But more than a substitution of metaphors is at stake. Sarbin argues that by replacing trance formulations with believed-in imaginings he is describing the same phenomena with considerably greater accuracy and clarity.

As a concept, "believed-in imaginings" has other advantages that fit Sarbin's notions of what an adequate theory of hypnosis must explain. In particular, he notes that individuals differ in the extent to which they believe their imaginings and in the circumstances under which this occurs. He is thus postulating a continuum of belief in imaginings which has continuity with the evidence of individual differences in hypnotic susceptibility. It thus provides the possibility of an alternative explanation of such differences.

At the same time, by posing the question in this way, Sarbin makes a strong distinction between the phenomenon that needs to be explained (hypnosis as believed-in imaginings) and the condition of the phenomenon's occurrence. In this respect his position is not unlike that of Sutcliffe who sees the subject, while hypnotized, as deluded in a descriptive sense and suggests that "the role of the hypnotic relationship and its procedures in the communication of delusory conviction remains to be clarified [Sutcliffe, 1961, p. 200]." In each case the emphasis is upon both the hypnotized person's subjective experience and the antecedents of such experience.

There are further implications of this position that deserves amplification. Sarbin's rejection of state theorizing is primarily on the grounds of circularity and parsimony. In his reformulation of state as believed-in imaginings he places great emphasis upon social antecedents, particularly situational, expectational, and role variables as being the most likely determinants of hypnotic behavior. In this respect he departs in his theorizing from many state theorists who place most, if not all, of their emphasis on the subjective phenomena of hypnosis. By contrast, Sarbin seeks to understand hypnosis not merely in terms of its subjective components, but in terms of the setting in which it occurs. This means more than merely the interpersonal transactions between hypnotist and subject; it includes also the broader social framework of belief, expectation and role-appropriate behavior in which hypnosis occurs. While many of these more global variables are dismissed by other investigators (notably Orne, see Chapter 6) as artifacts, and recognized as essential by others (see Barber, Chapter 3), Sarbin believes that they may be crucial determinants of hypnotic behavior in their own right.

It should be clear from the foregoing that while Sarbin rejects state theorizing, he does not reject the observations on which such theorizing is based. Indeed some of his theorizing retains vestiges of the altered-state notion. Although he sees hypnotic experience as believed-in imaginings, some of his descriptions of the processes involved have altered-state connotations, and appear to be intentional. Reference to Table 4.1b indicates some of the subjective accompaniments of the process "believed-in imagining," and shows some assumptions shared with state theorizing. It can be seen that as self and role become less differentiated, as the result of an interplay between certain already specified antecedent self and role characteristics (role skills, role congruence, etc.) there is greater organismic effort and involvement, and a greater number of organic systems become involved in the carrying out of behavior.

Such a view places him in greater agreement with state theorizing than is generally recognized; indeed, in common with such theorists he sees hypnosis as subjective alteration. But in his emphasis on role related social variables, this aspect of his work tends often to have been overlooked. This is, perhaps, because Sarbin has chosen to emphasize his points of departure from state theorizing on the assumption that the similarities would be manifestly obvious.

SURVEY OF THE MODEL'S STRATEGIES OF RESEARCH

Sarbin conceives of hypnosis as constituting one example of a general phenomenon of role enactment which is applicable to a wide variety of social situations. Much of his research has thus concentrated on the broader social framework. Though many of these studies are of interest in their own right we shall confine ourselves to those studies that are directly pertinent to the conceptualization of hypnosis as a role phenomenon. The strategies used by Sarbin in his hypnotic work are not easy to classify mainly because of the relative overall lack of formal testing of this aspect of role theory. One model (Sarbin & Coe, 1972; Coe, 1973a) has been taken by Sarbin to represent his most characteristic set of strategies, and has been labeled a *base-rates design.* It is characteristic only in the sense that it constitutes Sarbin's basic approach to the state issue in hypnosis. While rejection of state theorizing (as it presently stands) is central to Sarbin's own theoretical position, the base-rates approach does not give crucial evidence either way on the issue of hypnosis as role enactment.

For testing his central hypotheses on role enactment, a variety of strategies have, in fact, been used, depending upon the sorts of role-related variables under investigation at any given time. Of these, the most interesting and potentially most pertinent strategy is what we will call the *independent criterion groups* design. This design has been used in three studies (Coe, 1964; Coe & Sarbin,

1966, 1971). Each study compared groups of subjects who could be expected to possess above-average degrees of role-enactment skills (dramatic arts majors) with subjects appearing to have below-average amounts of such skills (biological and physical science majors). In other studies, comparisons between high and low scorers on specific role-related variables have been made within a single sample. For example, Coe, Buckner, Howard, and Kobayashi (1972) sought differences in hypnotizability within a group of dramatic arts students who had been partitioned into smaller groups in terms of various role-related skills; Sarbin and Lim (1963) related acting performance to hypnotizability within a group of subjects lacking acting experience.

In other studies (Coe, 1966; Coe, Bailey, Hall, Howard, Janda, Kobayashi, & Parker, 1970) which looked at the respective relationships of the role-demand and role-location variable to hypnotizability, no distinctive methodology is in evidence. In all, there has only been seven published experiments bearing on Sarbin's position on role enactment. In the remainder of the section, we will describe the base-rates design and the independent criterion groups design since they are the most germane to Sarbin's central concerns up to now. It is quite possible, however, that as investigation is extended to other role-related variables new strategies will be devised.

The Base-Rates Design

As indicated earlier, this design has been employed (though not frequently) to represent Sarbin's particular approach to the state issue in hypnosis. It takes its inspiration from a study by Barber and Deeley (1961). These experimenters enlisted ten subjects who walked past the experimenter's office to look at the plates of the Ishihara Test of Color Blindness. All subjects reported no prior experience with hypnosis and no known impairments of color vision. Their responses were compared with those of subjects in a previous study (Harriman, 1942) who had been tested on the Ishihara test following extensive hypnotic suggestions of color blindness. It was found that Barber and Deeley's (1961) sample of unhypnotized subjects gave as many color blind responses to the Ishihara as had Harriman's (1942) hypnotized sample, thus appearing to disconfirm the causal connection drawn between hypnosis and the color blind responses elicited in the earlier study.

The underlying rationale of the Base-Rates Design is to provide a means of demonstrating that many of the behaviors thought to be unique to hypnosis (hallucination, catalepsy, etc.) exist naturally (though with low frequencies of occurrence) in unselected samples. It does this by comparing base-rate frequencies found in unhypnotized, unselected groups with comparable frequencies found in highly-hypnotizable groups tested under conditions of hypnotic induction. There is some question as to whether the use of one group, and the comparison of its performance with experimental outcomes from prior studies, actually constitutes an experiment (Coe, 1973a). Be this as it may, there can be no question that the general issue of base rates touches upon some central concerns in hypnosis research (see Chapter 9 of this book for concluding comment on the issue).

Two experiments have been reported (Andersen & Sarbin, 1964; Sarbin & Andersen, 1963) to illustrate the use of this technique. The first of these (Sarbin & Andersen, 1963) sought to provide base-rate data as a means of evaluating a previous study by Underwood (1960), which had been concerned with the validity of visual hallucinations in hypnosis. Underwood reasoned that if hypnotic hallucinations constituted valid percepts there should be no difference in the magnitude of a visual illusion when it is perceived under normal viewing conditions as compared to when it is hallucinated. Essentially he found that very deeply hypnotized subjects made substantially larger errors than control subjects when the illusion was hallucinated. However, this deep hypnosis group made even larger errors when they viewed the illusion under a standard field condition. Indeed, in this condition, hypnotized and unhypnotized subjects performed comparably, as might be expected. It was concluded that hypnotic hallucination modified visual perception by distorting the perceptual field, although this distortion was not as great as that produced by the (unhallucinated) illusion itself.

Sarbin and Andersen (1963) repeated this experiment using 120 unhypnotized subjects. In the hallucination condition subjects were given extensive motivating instructions to imagine the parts of the visual illusion that had been hallucinated in the Underwood study. The 11 subjects who showed the largest "illusion" under this condition were compared with the subjects in Underwood's hallucination condition; the remaining 109 subjects were compared with Underwood's control group. In each comparison, the performance of Sarbin and Andersen's unhypnotized groups was identical to the comparable groups in Underwood's study.

From this, the main characteristics of the Base-Rates Design can be seen. Sarbin and Andersen (1963) were able to obtain data from an unhypnotized group which do not substantially differ from those obtained from Underwood's subjects who had been selected for hypnotizability and performed the illusion task under conditions of hypnotic hallucination. Since the two groups did not differ on *behavioral* criteria it was inferred that what is often thought to be an effect of hypnosis may be instead, a subject characteristic totally unrelated to hypnosis.

In a similar vein, Andersen and Sarbin (1964) administered items from the SHSHS:A (Weitzenhoffer & Hilgard, 1959) to a group of 120 Berkeley subjects, presenting the items as a set of "concentration or imagination tasks" They compared the performance of these 120 unhypnotized Berkeley subjects on eight items with the normative performance of 124 Stanford subjects who had been used to standardize SHSS:A under conditions of hypnotic induction. The comparison was, as before, between an unhypnotized group in an imagination condition and a normative group performing in an hypnotic induction condition. On four of the eight items (hand lowering, eye closure, verbal inhibition and arm immobilization) the two groups showed almost identical pass rates as scored by the SHSS:A criteria. On the other four items, the hypnotized group showed anything from an 11% (arm rigidity) to a 16% (hands moving together) superiority over the unhypnotized group. Andersen and Sarbin (1964) accounted for these latter findings in terms of differences in individual and group administration for the two samples, and in terms of volunteer bias in the Stanford sample. Although they regarded these arguments as convincing, the fact remains that they are based upon post hoc analysis rather than empirical data.

These two experiments underline the strengths and weaknesses of the base-rates design as practiced by Sarbin. Its potential merits are obvious. Like Barber's Independent Groups design (see Chapter 3 for full discussion of this model), it alerts us to the possibility that many hypnotic behaviors may have spontaneous base rates of occurrence in nonhypnotic situations for reasons that have not been overly pursued in the hypnotic literature. Its primary purpose is to provide evidence bearing on the state/trance issue which would favor an alternative explanation of behaviors thought to be exclusive to trance. However, as has been noted in the previous chapter in connection with Barber's operational model, it is premised upon a logic of equivalence. In each case it is assumed that if comparable behaviors are elicited in hypnotized and nonhypnotized groups, equivalent underlying processes are at work. Sarbin's use of base rates, however is more vulnerable to criticism than Barber's since he does not attempt to replicate the performance of hypnotized groups; instead he merely seeks to show that he can obtain comparable results to a previous study using an unhypnotized base-rate control. Further, the way in which Sarbin obtains base rates precludes an understanding of how unhypnotized subjects are able to duplicate hypnotic performance. No attempt is made to ascertain the determinants of unhypnotized performance by questioning subjects postexperimentally, or by comparing subjects in base-rate and hypnotic conditions. On the other hand, no special TM instructions are used by Sarbin to collect base rates. Thus, unlike Barber, his base rates cannot be criticized as containing a social pressure artifact. However, they may be contaminated by the perceptions of the experimental situation by subjects asked to imagine in the base-rates condition. Reports of visual illusion in Sarbin and Andersen's (1963) unhypnotized group may, in fact, be the result of different mechanisms to similar visual illusion reports under hypnotic hallucination conditions reported by Underwood (1960).

Sarbin's base-rate strategy is also less fully developed than that practiced by London and Fuhrer (see Chapter 7), even though results are often similar. Although the collection of base rates is an important part of understanding behavior in hypnosis, Sarbin's particular strategy appears to be more didactic than useful in practice since there are limits to the type of inference that can be drawn from it. While the design allows him to take a stand on the state/trance issue, it is essentially supplementary to the strategies he has used to test his hypotheses concerning hypnosis as role enactment.

The Independent Criterion Groups Design

This strategy shares one characteristic in common with the base-rates design. Using the base-rates paradigm, Sarbin attempts to show that certain differences in response to hypnotic stimuli are not the result of an hypnotic state, but rather, are due to preexisting differences in subjects that state theorists often tend to ignore. In the Independent Criterion Groups design, Sarbin attempts to demonstrate that crucial preexisting differences in role-related skills in interaction with other role variables lead to different hypnotic outcomes. Though each is addressed to different questions, they separately seek to demonstrate that hypnotic behavior is strongly influenced by preexisting differences within subjects and/or the experimental situation in which data are collected.

The design has not been used extensively—indeed the three main studies utilizing this approach (Coe, 1964; Coe & Sarbin, 1966, 1971) have all used the same two groups of 77 dramatic arts majors and 91 biological and physical science majors. The rationale is that since dramatic arts majors possess greater role-enactment skills, they should perform better on traditional scales measuring hypnotizability than do biological and physical science majors. The latter, as a group, are thought to possess less of this role-enactment characteristic. The design also attempts to specify the nature of the role-related skills that dramatic arts majors are thought to possess in greater abundance than control subjects. To date, inventory measures have supplied the means of providing these data.

Thus, in one study (Coe & Sarbin, 1966) all subjects prior to hypnotic induction using HGSHS:A (Shor & E. Orne, 1962), completed two brief inventories. The first was the *Congruence of Self and Role Scale* which consisted of questions concerning the degree to which subjects accept altered processes (for example, "I would find it interesting to see how my world would change with altered perception of it" (True) and "Would you like to get beyond the world of logic and reason and experience something new and different?" (Yes)). This scale also includes a *Role-Absorption Scale* (including items like "I usually have to stop and think before I act even in trifling matters" (False) and "I sometimes find that when I'm studying hard, I don't notice the passage of time" (True)). The second inventory was the *Role-Expectation Scale* which was based on the idea that subjects who know what is expected in hypnosis will perform better in an hypnotic situation. This scale also consists of two subscales, one measuring general expectations and the other specific expectations: (a) *The General Expectations Scale* (with items like "women who are hypnotized before childbirth often suffer a great deal of pain anyway" (False) and "I believe I can be cured of nearly any kind of psychosomatic illness through the use of hypnosis" (True)) is really a measure of the degree to which the subjects' attitudes towards hypnosis are favorable; and (b) *The Specific Expectations Scale* (with items like "the first signs of hypnosis are often slight changes in vision" (True) and "vivid thoughts brought about under hypnosis seem real to the hypnotized person" (True)) is a measure of the accuracy of subjects' perception.

This use of inventory material in conjunction with independent criterion groups permits refinement of the role-enactment variables into smaller components and allows independent analysis of their relative contributions to hypnotic performance. A summary of the model's main features which has been adapted from the text of Coe and Sarbin (1966), is provided in Table 4.1. As can be seen, the role-aptitude variable is operationalized in terms of the two criterion groups; role congruence and expectation are both assessed by questionnaires. While this analysis of variance design is not mandatory—other studies investigating fewer variables have used simple *t* tests—the flexibility of the model and the variety of

TABLE 4.1
Schematic Representation of Sarbin's Basic Model

Independent (antecedent) variables[a]	Measured by		Design[b]			
Role aptitude	Sampling of independent criterion groups	→	Drama students, actors, etc.		Science majors, unselected subjects, etc.	
Role congruence	Subjects divided into high and low on role-congruence questionnaire	→	High	Low	High	Low
Role expectation	Subjects divided into high and low on role-expectation questionnaire	High	*Dependent variable* $\bar{X}$ Score on HGSH:A for hypnotizability within each cell. . .			
		Low				

[a]Any other role-relevant variable can be incorporated into this design; the role-aptitude variable, however, remains a constant feature.

[b]More simple designs can be used, such as *t* tests for independent samples if fewer role-related variables are being considered.

main effects and interactions that can be evaluated are obvious. Also, it would appear that the role-aptitude variable, at this stage, has been given greater emphasis in the scheme of things, although Sarbin in much of his writing has given as great an emphasis to the contributions of situational effects to role enactment as to role aptitude.

The main potential drawback to the model, as it currently stands, concerns the types of inferences that can be drawn if differences between criterion groups (the role-aptitude variable) are found. Obviously other techniques are needed to explore the basis of such differences in greater detail. For instance, a finding that dramatic arts majors have significantly higher mean susceptibility scores than control subjects may be accounted for in a variety of ways. Dramatic arts students as a group may do better in hypnosis because of greater practice in adopting different roles as Sarbin believes. Alternatively, their superiority may be the results of individuals having natural role-immersion abilities being drawn to the profession of acting. A further possibility is that actors, because of their dramatic skills, may comply more readily with the requirements of the hypnotic role, without necessarily experiencing any greater subjective involvement. The model has sought to examine the first possibility by investigating such skill variables in groups that either possessed no acting experience (Sarbin & Lim, 1963) or consisted of actors of differing experience (Coe, Buckner, Howard, & Kobayashi, 1972). Clearly some such procedures are necessary to supplement findings based upon the application of independent criterion groups.

The model is less adequate in evaluating the possibility of greater compliance within acting groups, although only minor adjustments would be necessary in order to test for this possibility. Characteristically, the model examines the relationship of role-related variables to hypnotic performance by analyzing variations of hypnotic scale score means. The use of subjective scores (as practiced by Barber and Hilgard on many occasions, for example) in addition to the presently-obtained objective scores could help to illuminate this issue of compliance. Perhaps also, the use of postexperimental inquiries (as practiced by Orne, for example), and the taking of more than one hypnotic score would serve to strengthen conclusions.

The model, as it is presently practiced, serves itself least well in only examining differences in group means of hypnotic performance. The theory places great emphasis, for example, upon the ability of dramatic actors to become immersed in roles. It is believed that this process of immersion in both hypnosis and dramatic acting leads to progressively greater inability to differentiate self from role. On the basis of this, one would expect a greater number of dramatic arts subjects to score at the higher end of the hypnotic range, whereas more controls might be expected to score at the lower end. The model, while reporting differences in means does not analyze differences in score distributions to check this possibility. Yet such a finding would be of considerable theoretical importance, and would make it more difficult to interpret Sarbin's role-enactment notions in terms of social compliance.

In all cases—the obtaining of subjective scores, postexperimental inquiry data, and repeated hypnotizability measures, plus the examination of score distributions for dramatic arts majors and controls—only minor adjustments of the model's strategies are required. If hypnotic behavior is indeed related to various role antecedents the use of such additional strategies should help to identify the relevant variables more clearly and with relatively greater ease. Issues stemming from the failure of the model to utilize such strategies will be taken up in a later section when we evaluate the model as a whole.

EVIDENCE RELATING TO THE MODEL

It is unfortunate that the experimental literature bearing on hypnosis as role enactment is relatively sparse, given Sarbin's prodigality as a theorist and his long standing concern to operationalize his concepts. The most substantial data, as already mentioned, come from a group of 168 subjects (77 dramatic arts majors and 91 biological and physical science majors) whose performance has been analyzed by a variety of techniques and reported in three separate papers (Coe, 1964; Coe & Sarbin, 1966, 1971).

In the first of these studies (Coe, 1964), the two groups of dramatic arts and biological and physical sciences majors were compared for their performance on the HGSHS:A (Shor & E. Orne, 1962). For this, and two subsequent reports the subjects had no prior knowledge that hypnosis was going to be used in the experiment—they were told that it would be used only after arrival at the experiment, though they were given the opportunity to withdraw. This strategy appears deliberate, but the reasons for using it have always remained implicit. The performance of this California sample was compared with that of the normative Harvard sample (Shor & E. Orne, 1962). It was found that the California sample ($\bar{X}$ = 5.93) scored significantly lower on HGSHS:A Total Scores than did the normative Harvard sample (X = 7.39). Further, although the correlation of percentages passing each of the 12 items was high (r = 0.97), the Harvard sample always showed higher pass percentages than the Californian sample. These differences may reflect differences in recruitment procedure for the two groups, since the Harvard norms are based upon volunteer subjects who had been preinformed that the experiment involved hypnosis.

Upon further analysis, interesting differences were found between men and women from both the dramatic arts and science background. The findings were presented as percentages of subjects in each of the four groups passing each of the 12 HGSHS:A items. The data have been reordered in Table 4.2 to bring out the pattern of significant differences in HGSHS:A total scores, which were

TABLE 4.2
Statistically Significant Differences Between Dramatic Arts and Science Majors, Analyzed by Sex[a]

	HGSHS:A Group $\bar{X}$	Science men	Science women	Dramatic arts men	Dramatic arts women
Science–men ($N = 49$)	4.33	X			
Science–women ($N = 42$)	5.31	NSD	X		
Dramatic arts–men ($N = 34$)	6.41	$p<.05$	NSD	X	
Dramatic arts–women ($N = 43$)	8.00	$p<.05$	$p<.05$	$p<.05$	X
Total sample ($N = 168$)	5.93	NR	NR	NR	NR

[a]NSD = no significant difference; NR = not reported; $p<.05$ = groups differed at .05 level of significance or better.

reported by Coe (1964) in the text of his paper. It was found that there were no significant differences between science men and women and between science women and dramatic arts men. The dramatic arts women, however, scored significantly higher on HGSHS:A than any of the three other groups; the outcome appears to result primarily from the superior group's relatively high performance on the last three items (eye catalepsy, posthypnotic suggestion, and amnesia) which are more somnambulistic items. It can be seen, also, that the dramatic arts students scored above the group mean, while both science groups fell below it. The findings are consistent with the prediction of greater role skill for dramatic arts students, though some caution is necessary in interpreting this outcome. HGSHS:A is intended as a screening instrument and is loaded on ideomotor items. Its reported correlation with SHSS:C (an individually administered scale) has ranged from 0.59–0.72 (Bentler & Roberts, 1963; Evans & Schmeidler, 1966). Further, the HGSHS:A appears to be a more valid predictor of individually administered hypnotic scale performance for women than for men (Levitt, Aronoff, & Morgan, 1974).

The possible basis for the differences reported by Coe (1964) was investigated further in a subsequent study (Coe & Sarbin, 1966). In this study, performance on the Congruence of Self and Role Questionnaire and the Role-Expectation Questionnaire (both described in a previous section) was related to HGSHS:A performance. Further data on the performance of dramatic arts and science majors were also provided in the course of quantifying the Role-Aptitude variable. Since there were unequal numbers of men and women in the two student groups, and there were indications, already noted, that sex might be a moderating variable, the mean difference between the male and female hypnotic score in the total sample was added to each male score for purpose of statistical analysis, in an attempt to make it equivalent to an analysis of covariance. This procedure appears to have had the effect of stacking the analysis against the hypothesis since there were more males in the science group than in the dramatic arts group.

A three-factor analysis of variance indicated significant effects for Role Aptitude and Role Expectation but not for the Self–Role Congruence variable. However, when subjects were divided into highs and lows on the latter variable (by criteria not specified in the report) subjects with high role congruence scored significantly higher on HGSHS:A than low congruent subjects. Similar findings were reported for subjects high and low on both the Role Expectation and the Role-Aptitude variables. Of further interest was the finding that subjects high on all three role-enactment variables had significantly higher HGSHS:A scores than subjects who were high on two such variables, who in turn had significantly higher HGSHS:A scores than subjects high on one or zero role-enactment variables.

Rather surprising for the theory was the failure of the Self–Role Congruence variable to differentiate subjects in terms of their hypnotizability scores in the main analysis. This result may be due to the confounding of two separate variables in this inventory which consisted of an Acceptance of Altered Processes Scale, and a separate Role-Absorption Scale. There may not be a one-to-one relationship between accepting altered processes (which may be, for some people, an intellectual acceptance of subjective alteration regardless of their ability to engage in such alterations) and becoming absorbed in a role (seemingly an ability variable). Alternatively, as the authors suggest the self–role congruence variable may have already been confounded with the role-skill variable in that subjects had been preselected for their presumed difference on this characteristic.

Further evidence for a relationship between role skill and hypnotizability was sought by Sarbin and Lim (1963), utilizing two small student groups possessing no known special acting skills. In a pilot study 13 of the subjects were tested on the Friedlander–Sarbin Scale (1938), a forerunner of the Stanford and Harvard scales. In a subsequent session one week later the subjects had to improvise two pantomimed performances of coming home drunk and trying to find their door key without disturbing the neighbors, and of passing by the coffin containing the body of a recently deceased loved one.

The same design was used in the main study (N = 20), but a more neutral improvised pantomime performance was introduced; in this, subjects were required to portray a haughty egotistical person who had just been bumped at a social gathering, causing him to spill a cup of tea over his lap. In both parts of the experiment, the dramatic improvisations were rated on a 4-point scale of role skill by a panel of faculty members of the Dramatic Arts Department at the University of California. In the pilot study a nonsignificant rank order correlation between hypnotizability and role ability was found ($r = 0.39$). In the main experiment, a point biserial correlation of 0.52 was found between the same two variables ($p < .05$); and the two studies combined yielded a χ^2 significant at $p <$ .01.

As has been found in many studies investigating possible correlates of hypnotizability, the relationship between hypnotizability and role skill appeared to be nonlinear; some of the subjects low on role skill were highly hypnotizable. Conversely, all subjects rated high on role ability were also above the mean of hypnotizability.

The role-skill variable was investigated in a further study, this time using only dramatic arts students (Coe, Buckner, Howard, & Kobayashi, 1972). These investigators sought to determine whether the earlier reported relationship between role skill and hypnotizability was affected by practice in role enactment. Accordingly, 80 dramatic arts students were asked to provide information on the number of acting courses they had completed and on the number of acting roles in which they had participated on the stage. In the second part of the session, all subjects were tested on HGSHS:A without prior warning that this was to occur. Results indicated no relationship between the former variable and hypnotizability. However, the second set of observations gave support to the notion that practice may have been a moderating variable in the Coe and Sarbin (1966) study. The 80 dramatic arts students were divided into three groups in terms of acting experience; it was found that the group with no acting experience scored significantly lower on HGSHS:A than the other two groups whose prior acting experience ranged from 1 to 26 roles. When retrospective analyses were performed, it was found also that the acting experience variable correlated significantly with the Acceptance of Altered Processes Scale ($r = .34$), the Self–Role Congruence Scale total score ($r = .31$), the General Expectation Scale ($r = .25$) and the Expectations Scale total score ($r = .22$). Interpretation of this outcome is difficult. The results of the study suggest that practice in role portrayal on the stage affects the relationship of this measure of role skill to hypnotizability. However, as the authors recognized, the difference on the practice variable was between students with no acting experience and students who had participated in from 1–26 roles. It is thus possible that any acting experience, and the training that precedes it, facilitates hypnotic performance, although other (unmeasured) preexisting differences between subject groups may have affected this relationship also.

The main support for role theory provided by this study comes from the relationships found between acting experience and the various inventory measures of acceptance of altered processes, role congruence, and favorable expectations of hypnosis. Indeed, the general support provided by all of the studies which relate role skill to hynotizability underlines the need for further investigation. In particular, more concentrated effort needs to be directed towards distinguishing between "ritual" and "engrossed" acting (Sarbin & Coe, 1972). The latter concept appears to be at the core of Sarbin's thinking in his use of dramatic arts students to test these notions about role skill. The engrossed actor is postulated by the model to be more organismically involved and to achieve a more complete merging of self and role. The theory predicts that such characteristics (see Fig. 4.1b) are closer to the role skills required for hypnosis than those possessed by the ritual actor, but so far no test has been attempted. A similar point has been made by McReynolds (1967) who distinguishes between role portrayal and role empathy, and suggests that role empathy (the degree to which a dramatic role becomes subjectively real) accounts for the bulk of the variance.

In a factor analysis (Coe & Sarbin, 1971) of the data upon which earlier reports were based (Coe, 1964; Coe & Sarbin, 1966) three factors emerged. The first of these, though potentially interpretable also as a general factor, loaded most heavily on fly hallucination, vividness of the fly, type of academic major (dramatic arts versus science) and the Acceptance of Altered Processes Scale. The second factor loaded on a cluster of moderately difficult hypnotic items (communication inhibition, arm rigidity, arm immobiliation, eye catalepsy, and finger lock), while the third factor loaded on ideomotor items possessing relatively low item-difficulty level (hands together, hand lowering, head fall, and eye closure).

The authors interpreted these factor patterns as reflecting clusterings of items of similar difficulty which in turn could best be explained by the existence of the role-skill variable. They argued that certain kinds of cognitive processes are needed to progress from the less difficult to the more difficult items and that these cognitive processes involve the ability to continue to imagine in an "as-if" manner in the face of items that ordinarily become progressively less believable to a naive observer. In the course of their theorizing, they rejected alternate interpretations of the factor analytic data that appear equally plausible. Since the three factors isolated correspond fairly well to three levels of hypnotic susceptibility (high, medium, and low) it would be just as easy to interpret the factors in terms of an underlying trait of hypnotizability (as many investigators would tend to do), and/or a multiplicity of underlying mechanisms involved in hypnotic performance (Evans, 1968). Coe and Sarbin (1971) dismissed these alternative explanations on the grounds of parsimony and because of the factor saturation of type of academic major on their first factor. However, until the skills underlying the superior performance of dramatic arts majors to controls are better understood, this would appear to be shaving rather closely with Occam's razor. The factor analytic data are favorable to an interpretation consistent with role skill, but the evidence does not decisively rule out the other alternatives. Indeed, when the bases of role skill are better understood, they may even show some consistency with the alternate formulations in terms of trait, and of multiple mechanisms.

Two other studies have sought to evaluate the relationship to hypnotic performance of other role-related variables postulated by the model. Coe (1966), examined the role-demand variable, and Coe, Bailey, Hall, Howard, Janda, Kobayashi, and Parker (1970) investigated role location. In the former study 20 subjects were matched for self–role congruence, role expectation, role aptitude and HGSHS:A performance. In addition, an attempt was made to hold the role location and audience reinforcement variables constant, by having the hypnotist treat all subjects uniformly in the one case, and by utilizing the same standard verbatim instructions for all subjects in the other. Half of the subjects were then led to believe that their hypnotic performance was being observed by clinical psychology students through a one-way mirror; for the remaining subjects this one-way mirror was covered over. All subjects were tested on SHSS:C. In addition, an item of having the subject "flap his wings and crow like a rooster greeting the dawn" was inserted; this item was designed to make the subject look silly and was scored for the intensity of response. It was hypothesized that response would be less intense in the "audience" condition, thus supporting the belief that social propriety norms influence hypnotic outcomes. Subjects did not differ significantly on the "rooster" item, but the SHSS:C total scores of subjects in the "nonaudience" condition were significantly higher than in the "audience" condition, thus giving some support for the importance of the role-demand variable.

The role-location variables was investigated (Coe *et al.*, 1970) by using different hypnotists wearing either sports clothes or jeans and T-shirts, and by the use of differential prestige instructions. Half of the subjects in the two dress conditions were told that the hypnotist had considerable experience with hypnosis; the remainder were told that this was the hypnotist's first induction. In reality, all hypnotists lacked experience prior to the study. Significantly higher hypnotizability scores were obtained for hypnotists claiming greater hypnotic experience than for inexperienced hypnotists. There were no significant effects for the differential dress conditions and, contrary to prediction, no significant interaction between dress and instructions concerning prior experience.

The general direction of findings is consistent with a role-theoretical approach, and is encouraging for further research. Likewise, there is a certain consistency in the findings of some inventory-based studies performed by other researchers. In the course of investigating the occurrence of hypnotic-like experiences in every-day life, several independent experimenters have found moderate relationships between the report of "becoming" a person in a play, and hypnotic susceptibility (Ås & Lauer, 1962; J. Hilgard, 1970; Sutcliffe, 1965; Sutcliffe, Perry, Sheehan, Jones, & Bristow, 1963; Tellegen & Atkinson, 1974).

Much more empirical research is needed to clarify the effect of, and the interrelationships between the different role-enactment variables that Sarbin has identified. Up to this point, two main themes appear to be emerging from the studies that have been carried out. On the one hand, considerable emphasis has been given to the role-skill variable as being the main factor determining hypnotic performance. However, more recently, Sarbin appears to be saying that a number of other role variables such as the entire setting, the subjects' expectations, and role demands are of equal importance. These two types of emphasis may not be mutually exclusive but they create some problems for evaluation of the model.

SUMMARY EVALUATION OF THE MODEL

We began by noting that Sarbin's position has undergone a number of subtle shifts in the last 25 years. The model has always postulated that an interaction of various subject aptitudes (role skill) with broader social, situational variables produces hypnotic role enactment. The earlier writings (Sarbin, 1950) were nevertheless more person oriented in approach. To engage successfully in hypnotic role enactment the subject had to have favorable motivations and role perceptions, though it was thought that these attributes were obtained at least in part, from the social interaction of hypnosis. However, at this time, the burden of explanation for all that ensued in the hypnotic role was placed upon the role-skill variable. Without skill, favorable motivation and perception counted for little.

In his more recent writings (Sarbin & Coe, 1972), Sarbin appears to have modified this position. He now speaks in terms of a larger number of social antecedents (role location, self–role congruence, role expectation, role demands, audience reinforcement) and appears to relegate role skill to a less important position in the scheme of things. The position remains interactional in nature, but there are more variables interacting and there seems to be a reluctance to say that any one accounts for more of the variance than any other. At the time of role enactment, role-specific skills are said merely to become "more important" and contribute a "good deal" to the subject's involvement in the role.

Part of the reason for this shift of emphasis stems from Sarbin's concern with the extent to which verbal reports accurately reflect subjective experience. As he points out, hypnotic role enactment may cause the subject to have unusual experiences that are novel, or even strange and different for him. The extent to which he reports such experience may depend, often, upon what he believes is proper and appropriate for him to report, which in turn is related to role expectations, role demands, audience reinforcement and the like. While this is saying many things that are accepted by researchers in hypnosis of all persuasions, it poses problems for evaluation of the model. As with Barber's operational model (see Chapter 3), many factors are postulated as influencing hypnotic behavior; it is no consolation to an investigator to know that any one or more of them may be of greater importance on any particular occasion (even though such may be true).

A further problem is raised by this change of emphasis. In giving greater importance to the setting as a potentially major determinant of hypnotic role enactment, Sarbin has come to challenge the conventional wisdom concerning artifacts in hypnosis research. Most investigators employ a variety of strategies (for example, subjective scores, postexperimental inquiries, repeated hypnotic inductions, honesty reports, semiblind control groups) in an attempt to eliminate or neutralize factors assumed by them to contaminate experimental outcomes. Such artifacts are thought to stem, primarily, from the setting in which hypnosis is induced. By contrast, because he sees setting and situation as highly influential, Sarbin has shown a great reluctance to dismiss any such variable as artifact. Thus it is characteristic of the model that none of the above-mentioned strategies for controlling artifact are ever resorted to. Indeed to borrow Orne's (1959) distinction, Sarbin appears to give equal emphasis to both potential artifacts *and* essences of hypnotic behavior.

The point is well taken, and we discuss it further in Chapter 8. It implies a quite radical questioning of traditional beliefs concerning what constitutes an artifact (something that contaminates) as opposed to what is a variable which genuinely contributes to an hypnotic outcome. All roles presumably require some sorts of skills for effective enactment. It thus becomes appropriate to raise the question of whether (for example) practice of a skill is a confounding or artifactual variable, or something to be evaluated in its own right as a factor that influences hypnotic behavior. The dilemma is an important one for the model, since it challenges most of the current thinking on the control of artifact in hypnosis research.

The problem is represented diagrammatically in Table 4.3. It is well known that subjects with high role skill often perform less than optimally because of unfavorable setting variables (cell $S+\ E-$). Likewise, there are times when a subject of low skill performs at a high-hypnotic level because role demands, audience reinforcement and the like lead him to believe that he must comply with the hypnotist's requests, even if this involves not reporting his experience accurately (cell $S-\ E+$). Such situations are considered by other investigators as ones involving artifact that need to be controlled for in some manner. The problem posed by Sarbin's model is that since it never uses any of the conventional strategies to inquire into artifact, it can never determine whether certain procedures create contamination or contribute genuinely to hypnotic role enactment. Since it does not do so, a proponent of the model can never be certain whether a given incident of hypnotic role enactment is due to an artifact or to the influence of a setting variable.

TABLE 4.3
Possible Combinations of Role Skill and other Role-Enactment Variables (Role Demands, Role Location, Audience Reinforcement, etc.)[a]

		Other role-enactment (E) variables $E+$	$E-$
Role-skill (S) variable	$S+$	High level of hypnotic role enactment	Verbal report artifacts *may* influence performance
	$S-$	Verbal report artifacts *may* influence performance	Low level of hypnotic role enactment

[a]The pluses and minuses, though expressed as categories, are intended to express the notion that all role-enactment variables are continuous rather than dichotomous.

The issue is not unlike one we reviewed in the previous chapter when we discussed studies which demonstrated differences in hallucination reports between subjects who received Barber's TM instructions with and without demands for honesty (Bowers, 1967). Indeed the model appears to require some such similar strategy for investigating the importance of variables regarded by other researchers as artifacts if it is to contend that such variables actually play a crucial (as opposed to a contaminating) role in determining hypnotic performance.

The small amount of evidence to date indicates that role skill is an important ingredient of hypnotic role enactment. This is so even if other situational variables prove ultimately to be of comparable importance. A major task for the model, then, is to investigate the nature of the role skill variable in greater detail than has been attempted thus far.

In his theorizing, Sarbin has dwelt upon such concepts as organismic involvement, immersion of self and role, participation in *as-if* thinking, and believed-in imaginings. All can be seen as attempts to endow role skill with theoretical content and perhaps, surplus meaning. But greater empirical focus is required. This is especially so since the concept of role skill is what Ryle (1949) has called a dispositional concept. It describes certain "abilities, tendencies, and pronenesses to do" without specifying what such abilities actually are. Differences between dramatic arts majors and controls give role-enactment theory a tenability it would not otherwise have, if such differences could not be found. But since most people do not have dramatic acting experience, such a finding is of limited value if the nature of the skill cannot be specified more fully and generalized to the wider population of hypnotic subjects who have never acted on a stage.

In evaluating the findings that have accrued in favor of the model, one encounters again the problems we have discussed with respect to the issue of what constitutes an artifact. Differences between dramatic arts and science majors are extremely encouraging, but they invite a variety of alternative explanations. Since the model does not attempt to evaluate the accuracy of subjects' testimony of their subjective experience by questioning them post-experimentally, one cannot rule out differences in motives, attitudes and past experiences of dramatic arts students which may as equally contribute to their superior hypnotic performance.

Other variables in the hypnotic situation may exert a similar effect and lead to unintended consequences. For example, some studies (Klinger, 1970) have indicated that peer modeling has an effect on hypnotic performance. The model's practice is to recruit subjects at their regular classes and to test them in small groups. It is thus very likely that dramatic arts students undergo hypnotic testing in groups comprised of peers. This situation could be more conducive to entering into an *as-if* orientation appropriate to hypnosis but could as equally promote compliance to group pressure. The lack of a strategy to test for these possibilities does not enable one to choose between alternative explanations of the data. This problem has been recognized by Coe and Sarbin (1966), who suggest that the drama students may have perceived their performance on HGSHS:A as an attempt to evaluate their ability to concentrate, and hence performed better on the hypnotizability measure for this reason alone. However, they contend that such an alternative interpretation of the data "does not invalidate the experimental results, (though) it may weaken the theoretical conclusions [Coe & Sarbin, 1966, p. 405]." And yet when one considers that dramatic arts students are chosen by the model because "they have practiced attending to their gestural and other motoric behaviors and to internal stimuli [p. 404]" both experimental results and theoretical conclusions would appear to be put into needless jeopardy. While one can sympathize with the model's concern with the issue of artifact, procedures clearly need to be developed which reduce the number of presently available alternate explanations of existing findings.

A final issue that has been raised repeatedly about the model is one that takes up the question of whether Sarbin's reformulation of hypnosis into role-enactment terms provides anything more than a new terminology, which, while useful, provides no more than a verbal reassessment of traditional problems. Hilgard (1973d) has argued that role theory subtly leads a reader to believe that everything about hypnosis can be understood merely by reference to the interaction of the subject with a social setting. This should lead one to ask whether a role-theoretical account can provide any clearer understanding of a complex hypnotic behavior like amnesia than the noncircular variant of state theory which merely asserts that amnesia falls within the hypnotic domain, and is not yet fully understood.

Hilgard concludes that the role theoretical account of complex posthypnotic behaviors like amnesia

> . . . appears to fly in the face of facts in two ways: (a) by implying that the labeling of features of the subject–hypnotist interaction has explained the behavior and (b) by implying that the subject is not amnesic to himself, but only in his verbal behavior towards the hypnotist. Of course, if he is sufficiently 'organismically involved' he may be amnesic to himself. The authors (Sarbin & Coe, 1972) depend a good deal upon 'as-if' skills, but this question dodges the question of how convincing the 'as-if' experience is to the subject. *If it is accepted that he is amnesic to himself through organismic involvement, role theory and trance theory converge, with neither having an explanation of how, in detail, the amnesia is produced and relieved* [Hilgard, 1973d, p. 69, italics added].

Whether or not Sarbin's approach constitutes verbal sophistry will depend, ultimately, on his ability to demonstrate that the antecedents of role enactment (that is, coming to believe in one's imaginings) are of the character postulated by the model. In part too, it will depend upon his ability to uncover the types of mental processes that will enable role theory to adequately account for the more complex phenomena like posthypnotic behaviors. The task is clearly one of the more daunting ones in current hypnosis research, but also potentially one of the more fruitful ones. Through the challenge Sarbin has given to traditional assumptions of hypnosis he has had a significant impact in the field by forcing other investigators to carefully evaluate their positions.

IMPLICATIONS FOR FUTURE RESEARCH

Most of the theorists discussed in this book recognize a role component to hypnotic behavior. The general tendency has been to either consider role as a minor contributor to the total hypnotic variance, or else to dismiss it as an artifact of social compliance. Sarbin, by contrast, insists that the role metaphor is crucial to an understanding of behavior that is apparently automatic and apparently discontinuous. His theorizing has acted as a catalyst in hypnosis research for reassessing many traditional and basic assumptions. His experimental approach to hypnosis has not developed at the same pace, however, and there is presently a lack of rapprochement between what is postulated theoretically and the pertinent evidence which bears on his position. Nevertheless, the model has been prodigious in generating testable hypotheses which should ultimately lead to a considerable amount of important research data.

The main strategy up to now has been to employ criterion groups of dramatic arts majors and control subjects in an attempt to evaluate both the role-skill variable and the general position which equates hypnotic behavior with role enactment. While the small volume of available data is generally favorable to the central hypothesis, it is amenable to alternate interpretations and further refinements appear to be a major priority. Given that dramatic arts students have higher mean hypnotizability scores than science majors, more detailed experimental analysis is needed to flesh out the exact nature of the underlying variables involved.

As we indicated earlier, the model is basically equipped to disentangle this aspect of its theorizing in finer detail and to follow up the many promising leads thus far provided. Its failure to do so appears to result from an incomplete resolution of the artifact issue which in turn has led to a lack of development of practical strategies which would reduce the number of alternate explanations of present data. It may indeed be true that many relevant variables are currently mislabeled as artifacts by other investigators but such a proposition needs be stated in a form that is refutable by empirical test.

It is crucial for the model to determine whether differences among dramatic arts students and controls will continue to emerge under conditions of repeated testing for hypnotizability, whether subjective reports will substantiate the findings obtained from objective scores, and whether demands for honesty or postexperimental enquiry techniques affect conclusions. Within dramatic arts and control groups it is of equal importance to enquire into the degree of absorption, involvement, and immersion experienced by subjects of differential acting and hypnotic role skill. There is also the question of the degree to which changes in the total setting will affect hypnotic outcomes in subjects initially equated on skill (and indeed on a variety of other role-related variables). Artifacts may well be introduced by the utilization of some of the conventional control strategies that tend to be ignored by the model, but their use should help to evaluate the scope and nature of inferences derived from the model.

We began this chapter by noting that many of Sarbin's colleagues perceive his position on hypnosis as role enactment with a certain degree of disbelief, especially since his predilection for linguistic philosophy gives the appearance of verbal solutions to real problems. By now, we hope it is apparent that the model has not the superficiality of conceptualization and logic others so often attribute to it. Indeed, while some of Sarbin's solutions may turn out to be mistaken, his use of linguistic analysis has helped to clarify a variety of issues that hitherto have tended to remain implicit. Of all theorists in this book, Sarbin has presented the most detailed and systematic theory of hypnosis that is currently available. Role enactment may turn out to be the wrong metaphor for hypnosis, but in his formulation of hypnosis in such terms, he raises issues, and seeks solutions to problems that penetrate to the core of attempts to reach a proper understanding of hypnotic phenomena.

5

Credulous versus Skeptical Accounts of Hypnotic Phenomena: The Methodology of J. Philip Sutcliffe

> Methodological weaknesses render equivocal much of the available clinical and experimental evidence on . . . issues. Evidence alleged to support the credulous view can be shown to be consistent with the skeptical view and most points at issue remain unresolved. A necessary, albeit insufficient condition for resolution is improvement in the design of experiments on hypnosis [Sutcliffe, 1961, p. 190].

Of all methodologies of hypnosis the paradigm proposed by J. P. Sutcliffe is the most general of those considered in this book. The model is concerned primarily with scientifically indexing the "subjective experience" of the susceptible subject; it attempts to deal with the basic dilemma about how we know whether hypnotic experience is real or not. Understanding of the model is best approached through the historical survey Sutcliffe (1958, 1960) himself conducts into science's changing opinions as to the legitimacy of hypnotic phenomena.

Long ago, clearly impossible claims were made about hypnosis—somnambulists could accurately predict the future, see through opaque bodies, and do other equally amazing feats. Sutcliffe argues that even for more temperate claims the major problem in convincing people that statements about hypnosis were true was that the phenomena being reported were subjective and utterly private to those who were experiencing them. As reported by him, Binet, Féré, Charcot, and others came to recognize long ago that if the phenomena of hypnosis were to be legitimately established at all then some means of excluding deceit clearly had to be devised. Historically, skepticism came to be attached to the various claims made about hypnotic phenomena (see Chapter 1 of this book); the absence of any deception about what was happening came to be seen as a way of attesting the reality of private experience. The concept of simulation emerged as a key notion in the model as it is for many other theories of hypnosis (Dorcus, 1956; Orne, 1959; Pattie, 1933; Reyher, 1962; Sarbin, 1950; White, 1941a).

The philosophical tenets lying behind the model are reflected in the distinctions it draws between the verbal assertions of the hypnotized subject and the actual (reality) state of affairs. For Sutcliffe, objects exist independent of their being known, but they nevertheless may be known directly. The knowing of what exists in the real world, however, can itself be a legitimate object of knowledge. The scheme he proposes differentiates sharply between what is and what is not the case in the real world, and it discriminates between what happens in the real world and what the hypnotic subject simply asserts about it. Despite subjective conviction, what the hypnotized subject claims about hypnosis may either truly or falsely reflect what is happening in actual fact. The model thus acknowledges the importance of a subject's conviction about his experience while at the same time recognizing that this conviction may in fact be inaccurate. It analyzes experience in a methodological rigorous way by attempting to validate it against objectively defined patterns of behavior, both simulated and unsimulated.

Application of some of the formal tenets of the model to the problem of "fantasy" illustrates the essential emphases of the paradigm. Precisely because one individual cannot have someone else's experience, one person's private experience of fantasy means very little to others without some additional means of establishing communication. Although the experience is regarded as meaningful—reflecting a genuine area of scientific inquiry—the scientific status of it, simply judged privately, is viewed as suspect. The person who is dreaming or fantasizing, however, can verbally report on his experience and this testimony in itself helps to verify the phenomenon interpersonally. Verbal report is accepted by Sutcliffe not as a prime, or sole indicator of the reality of the experience, but as a guide—a very useful indicator, in fact—that the experience has truly occurred, the testimony about fantasy being preliminary to checking the experience by other means. The detail of the testimony may also usefully add to the value of the communication. Sutcliffe (1958) argues that if some fantasied event seems real to the subject then he ought to be able to describe it in detail just as one normally can describe any object in the external world in quite lengthy fashion. These notions about the status of verbal report as a measure of hypnosis contrast sharply with those of Hilgard (1965a). Faced with a discrepancy between absence of galvanic skin response (GSR) and a subject's verbal testimony of the subjective reality of pain, Hilgard's model challenges GSR as the accurate indicator of pain, while Sutcliffe's model would tend to argue strongly for the primacy of the more objective measure of response.

The ultimate yardstick for judging the reality of the event (in this case, fantasy) comes from a third way of looking at the phenomenon—consideration of its behavioral consequences. Certain stimulus–response associations have been established empirically in science—a strong shock delivered to a person, for example, immediately produces a variety of detectable physiological responses. If reality is to be accorded some fantasied event then the event should have objective consequences and they should be comparable to what happens in the real world.

In summary, the actual knowing of a private event such as the activity of fantasizing is important; the fantasy, however, must be recognized as an experience that may parallel the real world correctly or incorrectly. Testimony about the fantasy helps us to check on the veridicality of the experience, but reality can be firmly assessed only by comparing the behavioral consequences of the imagined events with the consequences of the unimagined, real stimuli which the fantasy is said to represent. If comparison of this kind demonstrates close similarity we may further increase our confidence about the experience by ascertaining whether the behavior we have isolated can indeed be faked.

We move now to consideration of Sutcliffe's theory of hypnosis. His theory as a whole is not easily gleaned from his published writings—it is revealed most fully in the unpublished manuscript that first reported the findings he collected (Sutcliffe, 1958). In the following sections we draw upon material from this source heavily.

THEORETICAL POSITION

The most important and best known distinction associated with this model is that between so-called "credulous" and "skeptical" accounts of hypnotic phenomena. Essentially, this distinction revolves around the question of whether suggested, hypnotic stimuli have identical sensory content to actual physical stimuli (the credulous position), or whether hypnotic behavior is a response to fantasy stimulation (the skeptical position). A *credulous* account of hypnosis is invoked when the perceptual process following hypnotic suggestion is assumed to be akin to that which is produced by the actual set of stimulus conditions—as when a subject who is asked to hallucinate the color red then sees a genuine negative afterimage (the color green) identical to what would result if the color red were fixated by that same individual actually. A *skeptical* account of hypnosis argues that a hypnotic subject perceives each situation as it really is while acting as if events are otherwise as suggested by the hypnotist—in the instance just cited, the hypnotized subject asked to hallucinate red would not actually see an afterimage, but he would report in testimony and behave as if he did.

The salient features of the credulous account are that the subject's testimony about the genuineness of his experience is perfectly acceptable, and hypnotic suggestions can be substituted for real stimuli as conditions of perception. According to the credulous account hypnosis should be considered as a special state which is able to produce changes in any mental or behavioral function and which can lead to a transcendence of normal capacity. In contrast with these characteristics the salient features of the skeptical account of hypnosis are that hypnotic testimony cannot be accepted at face value (though it is important), hypnotic fantasies do not have (or rarely have) the same sensory content as the content aroused by real stimuli, and trance behavior probably can be matched perfectly well by performance outside the hypnotic state.

The skeptical view of hypnosis is amply illustrated by the work of Barber, Orne, Sarbin, White and others, though Sutcliffe selects White (1941a) as the model for this position. For White, hypnotic behavior is meaningful goal directed striving, the most general goal being to behave like a hypnotized person, as this is structured by the hypnotist and perceived in turn by the subject. White's views are in sharp contrast to those of Erickson whom Sutcliffe takes as the main proponent of the credulous stance. For Erickson (1952), trance is an intrapsychic phenomenon which is totally dependent on internal processes occurring in the subject. Close analysis of Erickson's writings suggests that there is some doubt as to whether he considers that the sensory content of hypnotic experience will always parallel the content accompanying real stimuli, but Sutcliffe's definition of the credulous position is implied at least in Erickson's view of the phenomenon of hypnotic negative hallucination: to Erickson, hallucination involves a reorganization of neuro- and psychophysiological processes capable of withstanding the most searching of test procedures.

The credulous stance as it is formally proposed is an extreme viewpoint, as Hilgard (1965a) and others (e.g., Weitzenhoffer, 1963, 1964) have noted, but some of the value of the theory has been lost amidst overreactions to the connotations that the terms "credulous" and "skeptical" rather naturally evoke (see, for example, Weitzenhoffer's, 1963, 1964, discussion of Sutcliffe's work). Sutcliffe did not mean either term to be taken in any evaluative sense and controversy about what is meant by "credulous" has rather distracted attention away from the sophistication of the skeptical position which is theoretically much more complex and potentially fruitful as a source of useful hypotheses about how hypnotic phenomena might be explained.

The term "skeptical" has also created some confusion in the literature. There are, in fact, two distinct skeptical approaches to hypnosis which Sutcliffe outlines and the distinctions he draws can be easily overlooked when viewing the theoretical possibilities of his model. In its most uncomplicated form the skeptical account merely asserts that a subject is complying knowingly with the suggestions that the hypnotist is administering; directly akin to voluntary responding, the hypnotic subject given a suggestion to hallucinate acts as if the suggested object is present, but knows in fact consciously that it is not. The alternative approach is much more sophisticated in its theoretical stance (and consequently much harder to operationalize). According to this second view the hypnotized subject complies with suggestions despite the fact that his experience does not demonstrate the same consequences as those which accompany real stimuli; significantly, he does not know reality is otherwise than the hypnotist is suggesting. According to this account, the hypnotic subject experiences some kind of delusion but its presence does not assume parallel sensory content and so a skeptical account is essentially indicated. The element of conviction, however clearly distinguishes hypnotic response from simulation.

Sutcliffe's own data imply acceptance of this second, more sophisticated skeptical stance: hypnosis does not reinstitute the sensory content of real stimuli, but it nevertheless is distinct from voluntary responding and deception. The hypnotized subject is genuinely subjectively convinced that the state of affairs truly is as the hypnotist is suggesting and he believes, contrary to the evidence, that the world around him is other than it is. Asked to imagine a shock being administered (which it is not), he will testify that he feels it–despite the fact that he responds physiologically as if the shock is truly absent Similarly, asked to hear voices around him he will be convinced that he hears them, though, in fact, careful test of the consequences of the suggested hallucination will indicate that he does not.

This delusion which the hypnotic subject experiences is said to reflect an aberration of self-consciousness or self-knowledge. The model asserts that the hypnotic subject is deluded about his "relationship to the real world" rather than the real world as such; the hypnotic subject does know the external world as it exists, but does not know that he knows, and it is the attitude of the subject that reflects the nature of his delusion, not the pattern of his objective response. The delusion may have its basis either in the genetic constitution of the subject or in his past experiences: "On the genetic side the delusory form of thinking may be related to brain mechanisms which can be affected by drugs disease, endocrine imbalance, and the like. In terms of past experience, psychoanalytic notions such as repression and the primary process may be relevant [Sutcliffe, 1958, p. 216]." The theory carefully points out that the conviction shown by the hypnotic subject is not peculiar to the hypnotic context–it may, for instance, arise out of normal life experiences. Further, hypnotic suggestion may undermine an existing delusion or merely superimpose another.

Analyzed within an historical context, Sutcliffe's theory of hypnosis constitutes a strong reaction against the early historical notion that the power of the hypnotist and the influence of his suggestion are the salient determinants of hypnotic response. For Sutcliffe, the success of hypnotic suggestion primarily depends on qualities possessed by the subject himself. The hypnotic relationship established between hypnotist and subject represents a situation favorable for the subject to reveal the natural predispositions be brings with him to the hypnotic session and the communication between hypnotist and subject (what we know as "suggestion") is the eliciting condition which facilitates natural display of the subject's aptitude(s) for trance. The procedures of hypnotic induction serve the function of enabling the hypnotist to establish the kind of social relationship where normal reality testing can be held in abeyance and fantasy allowed to operate freely. Ability to fantasy, then, is considered as one of the most important parts of the susceptible subject's cognitive repertoire.

Hypnotizability is regarded as a stable and enduring personality trait and hypnotic procedures simply make this trait manifest in both systematic and reliable fashion. The trait-like nature of hypnotizability is underscored in the theory by the fact there seems to be well defined individual differences in the degree to which aptitude for trance manifests itself among subjects. Although not stated directly and explicitly by the paradigm, the model implies that a person will demonstrate his hypnotizability consistently and reliably over both time and context of testing. Consistent with this view, Sutcliffe (1958) argues that training makes relatively little difference to the level of performance displayed on suggestibility tests by hypnotizable subjects. In summary, hypnosis reflects essence-type structures of personality functioning which display a consistency of functioning that is relatively independent of the person of the hypnotist, or the nature of the induction that he adopts. Several features of the so-called "hypnotizable personality" emerge among the data Sutcliffe collected: the hypnotic person may differ from the nonhypnotizable person in being able to experience more vivid imagery, in being more dissociated (as measured by a self-report questionnaire, and judgment of time in trance), more feminine in interests and attitudes, quicker at reversal of perspective, and more suggestible on waking tests of primary suggestibility.

We consider now the particular strategies of research promulgated by the model and the specific design features that it distinctively advocates. Along the way, we will compare these with some of the characteristics of other methodologies of hypnosis.

SURVEY OF THE MODEL'S STRATEGIES OF RESEARCH

Sutcliffe (see Austin, Perry, Sutcliffe & Yeomans, 1963) distinguishes between general and specific designs–frameworks that adopt comprehensive strategies of research, and methods that use only selected procedural controls–suggesting that both kinds of methodologies should be used to eliminate ambiguity. He suggests that selected control procedures should be used in isolation and that where they are adopted careful consideration should be given to their limitations. In the general instance, for example, the treatment of simulation ought to be used with susceptible as well as insusceptible subjects so as to ensure that the pretense condition is unconfounded with any susceptibility differences that might affect inferences about the data.

In its complete form Sutcliffe's paradigm embraces more procedural groups than any other model in the literature. The paradigm advocates a factorial design involving sixteen different experimental conditions, eight of which are additionally replicated across different experimenters. The complete design itself has never been applied in practice, so demanding is it in its entirety. The generality of the paradigm, however, is instructive insofar as it allows us to judge whether or not it is possible to cope with the major problems of hypnotic research using a single methodological framework. The success of the model should strictly be assessed with reference to the claim of its author that it provides a basic design for studying hypnosis—one that establishes the optimal requirements for test of the credulous account of hypnotic phenomena.

Basic Design

Table 5.1 sets out the basic design for experiments on hypnosis using the model. Control (C) waking conditions constitute test of the objectively real state of affairs. Two hypnotic conditions are employed, one with induction alone (HI) and one with induction plus hypnotic suggestion (HIS). A pretense condition (WA) is also advocated with special faking instructions administered to subjects while they are in the waking state. Taking hypnotic hallucination as a test example, each of these four conditions is then administered for fantasied stimuli being present (an object truly absent being hallucinated positively as present) or absent (an object truly present being negatively hallucinated as absent). All of these eight conditions (major comparisons, and stimuli) are then tested with both somnambule (deeply susceptible) and nonsomnambule (insusceptible) subjects. Finally, the eight hypnotic conditons are replicated for independent hypnotists. Table 5.2 illustrates in concrete fashion the symbols belonging to the separate conditions (as listed in Table 5.1) and indexes them specifically in

TABLE 5.1
Basic Design for Experiments on Hypnosis[a]

		Hypnotizability	
Major comparisons	Stimuli	Somnambule	Nonsomnambule
Control (C)	Present	C –	C –
	Absent	C +	C +
Hypnotic induction (HI)	Present	HI –	HI –
	Absent	HI +	HI +
Hypnotic induction plus suggestion (HIS)	Present	HIS –	HIS –
	Absent	HIS +	HIS +
Acting when awake (WA)	Present	WA –	WA –
	Absent	WA +	WA +

[a] Adapted from Sutcliffe (1961). Copyright 1961 by the American Psychological Association. Reprinted by permission.

relation to the phenomenon of esthesia (hypnotic anesthesia representing the suggested absence of pain, and hypnotic paresthesia representing the suggested presence of pain).

Features of Design

The model schematically outlined in Tables 5.1 and 5.2 represents an attempt to specifically answer two major questions: (a) Is hypnotic behavior akin to playing a role and does it represent a form of voluntary behavior?, and (b) (more

TABLE 5.2
Major Comparisons of Sutcliffe's Model
Illustrated with Reference to Esthesia

Condition		Description
Control	C –	Subject linked to GSR-shock apparatus and receives shock, in fact. No suggestion or hypnotic induction given. Subject is fully awake.
	C +	Subject receives no shock though linked to the GSR-shock apparatus. No suggestion or hypnotic induction given. Subject is fully awake.
Hypnotic induction	HI –	Parallels the objective conditions of C – (shock is present, in fact). Trance is induced but no specific suggestion is given.
	HI +	Parallels the objective conditions of C + (shock is absent, in fact). Trance is induced but no specific suggestion is given.
Hypnotic induction plus suggestion	HIS –	Parallels the objective conditions of C – (shock is present, in fact). Trance is induced and in addition suggestions for anesthesia (no pain) are given by the hypnotist.
	HIS +	Parallels the objective conditions of C + (shock is absent, in fact). Trance is induced and in addition suggestions for paresthesia (pain from shock) are given by the hypnotist.
Waking acting	WA –	Objective conditions same as for C – (shock is present, in fact). Instructions for pretense given–subject is asked to pretend as if shock were absent. Subject is fully awake.
	WA +	Objective conditions same as for C + (shock is absent, in fact). Instructions for pretense given–subject is asked to pretend as if shock were present. Subject is fully awake.

consistent with the dichotomy Sutcliffe draws between "credulous" and "skeptical" accounts of hypnosis) Does hypnotically suggested behavior follow a pattern of response directly comparable to actual sensory reactions to real stimuli? The waking pretense condition effectively answers the first question, but the appropriate comparisons for test of the second question (the credulous position) are more complicated. Table 5.3 sets out in summary form the appropriate design comparisons for basic test of both the credulous and the skeptical positions.

Selecting esthesia again as our example, let us consider the pattern of results which completely confirms the credulous stance keeping in mind the proper identification of symbols as listed in Table 5.2. Always for test of the credulous position, whenever one is concerned with behavior under positive hypnotic fantasy it must be compared with behavior under negative control conditions; alternatively, behavior under negative hypnotic fantasy must always be compared with positive control behavior. Tenability of the credulous stance, for example, requires that when anesthesia is suggested for the effects of shock (HIS–) the behavior of the hypnotic subject should be comparable with the behavior of the control subject who physically receives no shock (C+). Alternatively, when the presence of pain is hypnotically suggested (when shock is truly absent) the credulous position cannot be supported unless the behavioral effects following from this condition (HIS+) are directly comparable to those obtained for waking subjects physically receiving shock (C–). These two sets of comparisons must then be considered in relation to the data obtained for waking-pre-

TABLE 5.3
Basic Design Comparison for Credulous and Skeptical Viewpoints

Experimental outcome[a]	Viewpoint: Credulous	Viewpoint: Skeptical
HIS+ = C–, HIS– = C+ and HIS+ ≠ WA+, HIS– ≠ WA–	Complete confirmation	Complete disconfirmation
HIS+ = C–, HIS– = C+ and HIS+ = WA+, HIS– = WA–	Ambiguous	Ambiguous
HIS+ = C+, HIS– = C– and HIS+ = WA+, HIS– = WA–	Complete disconfirmation	Complete confirmation

[a]Symbols representing conditions in this table are as identified in Tables 5.1 and 5.2. The table is adapted from one that appears in Sutcliffe (1958).

tense subjects. For the credulous position to be unequivocally upheld, hypnotic subjects must not only differ in behavior from their appropriate control group but they should show a pattern of response that cannot be faked. Waking subjects instructed to pretend that the suggestions being given are effective ought not to be able to duplicate their behavior.

The essential comparisons of the model, then, are (a) C+ versus HIS− versus WA− for suggested absence of stimuli (for example, hypnotically suggested anesthesia when shock is truly present), and (b) C− versus HIS+ versus WA+ for suggested presence of stimuli (for example, hypnotically suggested paresthesia when shock is truly absent). The hypnosis-without-suggestion conditions (HI−, HI+) are not crucial; they simply allow the experimenter to investigate whether the differences found in the major set of comparisons occur independent of the specific suggestion that is given—if pain–response data are comparable for HI and HIS conditions, for example, then induction per se is obviously not critical to the occurrence of anesthesia. The independent variable of hypnotizability is also relevant to the design (see Table 5.1). It is introduced to highlight test of the most favorable conditions for the hypothesis; if aptitude for trance is important one would normally expect that the phenomenon in question would be apparent for somnambulists, but not for unhypnotizable subjects.

Other variables such as the experience of the subjects being tested, their age, sex, and the depth of trance they can achieve are also recognized as relevant to the model but they are not formally incorporated into its design. The experimenter is expected to control for them in ways that he sees appropriate, either through matching groups prior to testing or preselecting subjects in some systematic and controlled fashion. Certainly, as far as the selection of subjects for hypnotizability is concerned the model's criteria are stringent. Somnambulists on first and subsequent hypnotic sessions should manifest complete posthypnotic amnesia, be able to demonstrate hallucination, show an ability to remain in trance with eyes open, and express positive motivation. The criteria for insusceptible subjects are that they should show obvious contact with reality, demonstrate no suggested amnesia, respond only voluntarily (if at all), but also express positive motivation.

At this point the formal features of the model can be summarized. Sutcliffe (1960) first insists that normal waking behavior should be used as a control: "It could be a mistake to attribute automatically any given behavior that occurs in trance to hypnosis; it may occur as readily without [p. 74]." Second, independent groups of subjects should be selected for the waking and hypnotic groups; Sutcliffe considers that subjects employed as their own controls may be compromised by being made aware of the hypnotist's expectations, and knowledge of performance in one condition may always affect behavior in another. Third, the design formally advocates the use of a homogeneous pool of hypnotizable subjects from which random samples are drawn, to be allocated either to a hypnotic group or to a waking condition. Fourth, the model attempts to analyze the process of hypnosis into component parts insofar as it chooses to separate out hypnotic induction procedures from the suggestions that routinely accompany them. (Relaxation is another feature of induction—see Edmonston, 1972—that is noted by Sutcliffe, but not incorporated into his design.) Fifth, "presence" and "absence" of stimuli are included as formal conditions of the model. Here, the paradigm aims explicitly to study hypnotic phenomena which are traditionally conceived of as either "positive" or "negative"—phenomena, for example, such as paresthesias and anesthesias, positive and negative hallucinations. Study of stimulus conditions is useful in several ways; it serves as an inbuilt control providing baselines for evaluating hypnotic test performance and it challenges additionally the effectiveness of the experimenter's measuring instrument. If subjects react similarly to the presence and absence of stimuli then the measures being adopted in the study are either irrelevant or they are inherently unstable.

The selection of "hypnotizability of the subject" as a variable for explicit study argues the relevance of enduring personality characteristics to understanding the behavior of the hypnotic subject, and such a trait outlook is quite consistent with the model's underlying emphasis on hypnosis as a state (see Chapters 2 and 9 of this book for general discussion of this relationship). Further, the model insists on a faking control condition. Strategies for faking, however, were formulated prior to Orne's (1959) "Artifact and essence" paper, but Sutcliffe (see Austin *et al.*, 1963) acknowledges Orne's detailed procedures of simulation as a significant extension of the design requirements of his own model.

A major characteristic of the design pertains to the small number of subjects which perforce must be run under the model's time-consuming set of multiple conditions. In practice, Sutcliffe allocated as few as four subjects to each of his experimental conditions. Sensitivity of a study is ordinarily a function of sample size and it was essential therefore that he take steps to increase the probability of his model being able to detect real differences when present. The paradigm handles the problem by adopting an alternative form of random replication; it takes repeated observations on each subject, thus reducing measurement error and enhancing the sensitivity of the test. It also attempts to match groups subject by subject, on selected pretest scores wherever possible. In his experiment on hallucination, for example, Sutcliffe (1958) matched subjects on four levels of arithmetic ability (distraction on the test was later measured after sounds were hallucinated)—"subject variation as a 'treatment' replaced random subject variation [p. 296]."

The final feature of the model that should be mentioned refers to the fact that additional testing with independent hypnotists is advocated formally. Replication of the eight hypnotic conditions (using different hypnotists) aims not so much to establish generally increased confidence resulting from the repetition of a particular body of findings, as to demonstrate that the hypnotist himself (viewed as a potential source of systematic error) did not artifactually influence the original set of data. This demand for replication is quite unique to the model; no other framework of hypnosis argues formally for repetition of its experimental conditions.

Relation to Other Models

The model taps characteristics of the designs of both Barber (1969) and Orne (1959) and parts of the theory underlying it bear considerable similarity to the hypnotic responsivity and subject-oriented theorizing of E. R. Hilgard (1965a). Its generality, in a sense though, is somewhat illusory; no researcher can ignore the massive time and effort it would take for him to apply the model in practice. Somewhat akin to Barber's design, and unlike Orne's methodology, Sutcliffe's paradigm chooses to analyze a variety of component factors in the hypnotic situation—namely hypnotizability, effect of the set of induction procedures independent of the hypnotist's suggestion, and the hypnotist as a systematic source of error. But these particular variables are chosen as relevant while others are laid aside—for example, relaxation as a factor affecting hypnotic response, experimenter-bias influences on waking response, and attitude of the subject to the test situation. The model, as does Hilgard's Same-Subjects design, carefully analyzes the reaction of both susceptible and insusceptible subjects to hypnosis, yet it also formally incorporates within its framework a comparison condition (waking pretense) similar to that advocated in principle by Orne's paradigm (simulation; see Chapter 6 of this book for detailed elaboration of its features). Barber rejects waking role playing as an essential control procedure while both Sutcliffe and Orne vigorously assert its importance, and Hilgard views the issue neutrally. From this brief review we can see that Sutcliffe's model is obviously far more general than the paradigms of Orne, Hilgard, and others but in its choice of selected "relevant" variables it nevertheless manages to remain specific at one and the same time.

We turn now to consider those problems which the model seems best equipped to answer and to review critically the evidence which relates to it.

Problems Associated with the Model

Theoretically speaking, the model is primarily orientated to test of the credulous position, but empirically speaking, this emphasis is best rephrased to state that the paradigm is optimally directed to demonstrating those differences which occur between responses to suggestions within hypnosis and responses to actual physical stimuli. As Hilgard (1965a) has noted, the latter formulation is not necessarily restricted to specific theoretical arguments about the occurrence or nonoccurrence of "parallel sensory content."

The areas of study which are most relevant to the model are obviously those relating to situations where the sensory content of the subject's response is relatively unequivocal. When vivid patches of color are imagined, for example, they may institute retinal adaptation processes which can be subsequently illustrated by the presence of negative after-images; likewise, age regression may reinstitute earlier modes of response which can be verified by comparing them with real life historical records. In both these instances specific consequences of suggested stimulation can be defined in terms of the known content of real stimuli. The model, however, has considerably less application to other aspects of hypnosis—such as the stability of posthypnotic behavior. In the case of the durability of posthypnotic response, for instance, the notion of "real stimuli" is technically not at issue; it would indeed be valuable to contrast the duration of postexperimental response following hypnotic suggestion (HIS) with duration under pretense instruction (WA) or waking suggestion alone, but strictly speaking, there is no sensory content in the absence of the posthypnotic suggestion to make Sutcliffe's waking stimulus present (or absent) condition really pertinent.

There are a number of specific problems indirectly associated with the model by nature of the strategies it adopts and its underlying assumptions. It is considerably important to the model, for example, that simulating subjects are able to stay out of trance; such an assumption is critical since susceptible and insusceptible subjects are tested in its waking pretense condition. Also, the model is peculiarly attuned to the notion that susceptible and insusceptible people have empirically distinct sets of personal attributes that they bring with them to the hypnotic situation and which ultimately determine the nature of their response—the general question of the personality correlates of trance, then, is also very relevant to its concerns.

Evidence suggesting hypnosis has state-like properties is pertinent to this model as it is to others (see Orne, 1959; Hilgard, 1965a; Reyher, 1962). But the state issue is much more complicated in its relationship to the model than is generally recognized. Acceptance of the credulous viewpoint implies quite definitely that hypnosis is a special state of consciousness, one that reinstitutes the physiological processes accompanying naturally occurring stimuli. The skeptical account, however, may equally imply the presence of a special "state" of consciousness. If hypnotic response is perfectly akin subjectively and objectively to waking pretense behavior then hypnosis as a special entity is obviously contraindicated, but a distinctive state of consciousness is very definitely evidenced by a hypnotic subject who behaves comparably to waking reality but nevertheless remains utterly convinced or deluded that he is responding otherwise.

In the following section we will review the evidence from Sutcliffe's own studies and examine the extent to which his experiments satisfy the stringent requirements of his own model. We will also review relevant evidence relating to the physiological aftereffects of suggested stimuli and the faking ability of susceptible subjects, and, as well, consider some of the data in support of the notion that there are distinct correlates of trance.

EVIDENCE RELATING TO THE MODEL

Sutcliffe's Studies

Overall, the impact of Sutcliffe's (1961) own evidence is clearly that reactions following hypnosis are similar to those found in the waking state; this finding is a most important one for the understanding of hypnosis. Generally speaking, the data firmly indicate that subjects perceive stimulus situations as they are physically present despite the hypnotist's communication that they should be otherwise. Sutcliffe found, for example, that GSR to real shock occurred regardless of suggestion that the pain would be absent, and performance on an arithmetic task showed a decrement due to auditory feedback delay despite suggestions that the voice being relayed would not be heard. His evidence overwhelmingly rejects the credulous viewpoint.

Sutcliffe's results suggest that the distinguishing feature of hypnosis is the subjective state of the subject, the main feature of the hypnotized subject's experience being that he is emotionally convinced, or deluded, that the world is not as it is physically present, but is as suggested by the hypnotist. In a series of studies testing the phenomena of hypnotically induced esthesia, hallucination, and delusion, subjects consistently stated that they believed events were as suggested. Somnambulists asserted they were not shocked when they truly were, and reported they could not hear their own voices when they were actually talking aloud; their testimony, however, was always in marked contrast with physiological reaction. The single exception to this general pattern of results was that hypnotic subjects refused to accept the experimenter's instruction that they were of the opposite sex—a finding which suggests that any delusional property of hypnosis is operative only within specifiable limits as defined perhaps by the hypnotic relationship that exists in the testing situation. If delusion characterizes hypnosis, then, there do appear to be restrictions which affect its operation.

Table 5.4 illustrates the conclusions of the program of research with respect to esthesia. In this experiment subjects were connected to a GSR circuit and received either buzz without shock or a buzz with shock simultaneously. The experimental conditions for the study were as set out in Table 5.2; for the "+" (e.g., C+, HIS+, and WA+) conditions a buzz did not accompany shock while for the "−" conditions (C−, HIS−, and WA−) a buzz and shock occurred together. For the waking pretense conditions subjects were asked to respond when they heard a buzz as if a shock had been received (WA+) or respond to the buzz as if there was no shock (WA−). Considering the basic design comparisons outlined in

TABLE 5.4
Mean Changes in GSR Expressed as Log Conductance Change[a]

	Somnambule		Nonsomnambule	
Condition	Nonshock (stimulus absent)	Shock (stimulus present)	Nonshock (stimulus absent)	Shock (stimulus present)
Control	3.3 (C+)	18.1 (C–)	10.8 (C+)	19.7 (C–)
Hypnosis	8.7 (HIS+)	19.4 (HIS–)	9.1 (HIS+)	18.9 (HIS–)
Acting	16.6 (WA+)	18.1 (WA–)	13.3 (WA+)	18.5 (WA–)

[a] Adapted from Sutcliffe (1961). Copyright 1961 by The American Psychological Association. Reproduced by permission.

Table 5.3, results showed that HIS+ was much more akin to C+ than to C– (as the credulous viewpoint would assume); and similarly, HIS– was more comparable to C– than to C+. Data, in all, supported the skeptical viewpoint much more obviously than the credulous hypothesis. The results for faking were most ambiguous: where shock was present but not when it was absent, the hypnosis and acting groups performed comparably. And when shock was actually absent results showed that insusceptible subjects faked the presence of shock (WA+) more convincingly than susceptible subjects.

Close analysis of the procedures used in his series of three experiments reveals a number of irregularities in Sutcliffe's application of the formal strategies laid down by his model. He tested a common pool of subjects for esthesia, hallucination, and delusion, allocating subjects among experimental groups in different ways from one experiment to the next; a C– subject, for example, could have been a HIS– subject in the second study and an acting subject in the third. Although the allocation of subjects was strictly random, independence would have been much better preserved had separate sets of subjects been used across the series of three experiments. Further, there was no replication of the hypnotic conditions using separate hypnotists; thus no inference was possible about the potential biases attached to the single hypnotist who tested subjects. Such bias could have been present for other groups as well, particularly since pretense instructions were given by the same person who also administered hypnotic induction.

Results in Table 5.4 indicate that there was relatively poor faking performance by the WA groups employed in the design. Data show, for example, that neither susceptible nor insusceptible subjects acted effectively as if they weren't shocked (when in fact they were). More importantly, however, faking subjects could not even pretend very convincingly that a shock was present (when in fact it was not). Comparable results occurred in the other two studies. In test of hallucination, for example, subjects asked to pretend that they were distracted (when real distraction was absent) performed on a level with control subjects—thus demonstrating quite poor faking performance. It is plausible that role players actually being distracted might have found it hard to pretend that interference didn't exist, but there seems no reason other than ineffective pretense to explain why faking subjects not distracted could not have pretended to be so and manage to show a reasonable lowering of objective test performance on a relatively simple distraction task. The data suggest that the faking subjects employed by Sutcliffe were not playing their role particularly well and that they were actually insufficiently motivated for their task. Further, the wisdom of asking susceptible subjects to fake seems challenged to the extent that it was generally the nonsomnambules who overplayed their role and somnambules who experienced more difficulty with acting than insusceptible subjects.

Table 5.4 serves also to indicate that the model as outlined above and formulated by its author was incompletely applied—results for twelve not sixteen conditions are tabulated and no independent sets of subjects were run on induction alone (HI). This design gap was handled in practice by Sutcliffe adopting alternative strategies of research. For the experiment on esthesia, two additional design features were included involving somnambules only; C+ and C– somnambules, for example, were run again under HI+ and HI– test conditions, and susceptible subjects from the hypnotic and acting groups were retested under control (C) conditions. For test of hallucination the strategy varied; in this study HIS+ and HIS– somnambules were later retested and given hypnotic induction alone.

The above additional controls perhaps illustrate what Sutcliffe means by "specific" design features: these represent isolated controls used to supplement procedures dictated by the general design. Although they help to refine inferences about data they nevertheless represent compromises in good experimental method; they cannot enter in any interactive fashion, for instance, into the factorial nature of the total design and, in addition, they involve the retesting of subjects—thereby introducing the risk of series effects, and artifact arising from subjects' perceptions on the experimenter's use of them as their own controls. But despite their limitations they help to bridge the gap between the formal scope of the model's multiple strategies and the practicality of a workable, limited set of methodological rules and principles.

We will not make any attempt in this chapter to review all of the evidence in the literature bearing upon the credulous viewpoint; Sutcliffe's (1960) own review of the literature is more than adequate in this regard, and suffice to say that no further evidence has come to light which unequivocally supports the credulous hypothesis. Rather we will consider some of the more specific issues relating to the model—in particular, the evidence associated with the physiological aftereffects of fantasied stimulation, the capacity of susceptible subjects for faking, and subjects' varying aptitudes for trance.

The Physiological Aftereffects of Fantasied Stimulation

The credulous position basically asserts a structural similarity between the physiological processes accompanying hypnotically fantasied events and processes associated with perception of real stimuli. Not all stimulus situations qualify for relevant test of such a notion, however. Extending an argument that has been made elsewhere (Sheehan, 1972) two conditions must be satisfied before one can infer that there is similarity of structural process between perception and hypnotic fantasy: the behavioral product of the hypnotic fantasy being investigated must be typically a well defined, observable, and relatively unique product of the actual perceptual stimulation which corresponds to that fantasy; and further, the fantasy response itself must be genuine, that is, not simply due to any expectation in the subject about what kind of behavior is wanted by the hypnotist. The occurrence of real negative after-images (indexed by distinctive physiological processes) following suggestions of hallucinated colors would satisfy both these criteria. Similarly, study of suggested stimulation paralleling the content of actual perceptual illusions lends itself peculiarly well to test of the structural similarity, or credulous hypothesis. Both situations have yielded conflicting results and represent one of the few remaining areas of research where the credulous position has not been negated.

Binet and Féré (1888) claimed long ago that afterimages could be aroused by images, but Downey (1902), studying the imagery responses of well trained subjects, failed to find convincing evidence for the phenomenon. Much later (in an oft quoted study), Erickson and Erickson (1938) found evidence for the occurrence of negative afterimages to hallucinated colors but Hibler (1940) in turn yielded discouraging results. The most comprehensive study that has been conducted on afterimages to imagined stimuli—and one that demonstrates the full complexity of the phenomenon—has been conducted by Sutcliffe (1972). Working with both adults and children, Sutcliffe found very little evidence to support the structural similarity hypothesis; afterimages following imagery differed in very many features from the afterimages to real stimuli and subjects' knowledge of the phenomenon was clearly related to the findings that were obtained; only one subject showed afterimages to imagined stimuli consistently and she was both a graduate student of psychology and suggestible by personality. In order for subjects to image a colored patch in accord with their instructions they were required to project an image externally. Sutcliffe reports that half of the adult sample was able to image colors appropriately yet this proportion of successful instances of externalized imagery far exceeds the incidence of projected imagery reported for European samples elsewhere (Haber

& Haber, 1964; Leask, Haber, & Haber, 1969; Sheehan, 1973b). The issue, in a sense, still remains open.

Data for other perceptual after-phenomena are also controversial. Parrish, Lundy, and Liebowitz (1968), for example, showed that suggested hypnotic regression produced observable changes on the Ponzo and Poggendorff illusions which paralleled the normative functions of children. But attempted replications of their findings have been unsuccessful (Ascher, Barber, & Spanos, 1972; Miller, Hennessy, & Leibowitz, 1973; Perry & Chisholm, 1973; Porter, Woodward, Bisbee & Fenker, 1972). Perry and Chisholm, for example, corrected a number of faults in the first study's design and additionally tested a group of simulating subjects; results, however, showed no significant differences among any of the groups on either illusion effect.

Recently, a series of studies reported by Sheehan and Dolby (1975) indicated that hypnotic subjects, as opposed to TM and waking control subjects, counteracted a previously well entrenched tendency to view an ambiguous stimulus in a certain way, to change their perception to view the same stimulus anew exactly as the hypnotist was suggesting. Data further showed that the influence of perceiving change in the stimulus "carried over," as it were, to later perceptual testing in the waking state. Other evidence gathered in an altogether different testing situation (Graham, 1969) also implies that hypnotic suggestions may have genuine sensory aftereffects. Further work is needed, however, to fully develop the claim.

Faking Ability of Susceptible Subjects

An essential requirement of Sutcliffe's paradigm is that somnambules can fake trance without entering hypnosis. A number of studies have used susceptible subjects under pretense control instruction (for example, Austin *et al.*, 1963; Johnson, Maher, & Barber, 1972; Overley & Levitt, 1968; Troffer, 1966; see also Table 6.6 in Chapter 6 of this book), but with mixed success. The data certainly are by no means unequivocal in their demonstration of the capacity of susceptible subjects to fake adequately, and more evidence needs to be collected before the model can be unambiguously confirmed in this respect. Austin *et al.* (1963), for example, reported affirmatively on the question. Their design tested nine subjects across four different conditions (hypnosis for real subjects, faking without training for real subjects, and faking with training for both susceptible and insusceptible subjects). A blind experimenter (psychiatrist) tested subjects postexperimentally for spontaneous amnesia and response to posthypnotic suggestion, and in addition probed subjects' feelings about their simulation. Results showed that susceptible subjects could indeed simulate to the extent that the psychiatrist did not suspect faking but a number of aspects of the data suggest caution about the consequences of instructing real subjects to pretend. Across the five faking "susceptible" subjects tested in the study there were 15 instances where a subject reported either responding involuntarily or in uncertain fashion about his response. In marked contrast across the two insusceptible subjects who were tested, there was no instance where a subject reported voluntary or semivoluntary responding. In addition, three out of the five faking susceptible subjects reported they had hypnotic experiences (though fleeting), whereas neither of the insusceptible faking subjects showed a similar effect. Finally, the five faking susceptible subjects reported finding their task difficult and somewhat unpleasant, and felt guilty about the deception in which they were involved. These aspects of the data suggest that susceptible subjects may not only fake less adequately than insusceptible subjects but also may experience their pretense distinctively.

Personality and Hypnosis

Evidence relating to the question whether there are stable cognitive and personality characteristics lawfully defining the hypnotizable personality has been reviewed quite fully elsewhere (see Barber, 1969; Deckert & West, 1963; Sheehan, 1972; Wachtel & Goldberger, 1973). The issue is still a contentious one and is unresolved. In his theorizing about hypnosis, Sutcliffe asserts that subject characteristics set obvious limits on hypnotic phenomena (Sutcliffe, Perry, & Sheehan, 1970) and his view naturally leads one to search for enduring aptitudes for trance that determine hypnotic response. Sutcliffe's own data indicated that somnambules were distinct from nonsomnambules in several aspects but no cross-validation study was done to support the pattern of findings which he found. Evidence, however, tends at least to support the notion that imaginal capacity is one aptitude lawfully associated with trance and its relevance is now quite generally acknowledged (Barber, Spanos, & Chaves, 1974; Hilgard, 1974a; Spanos & Barber, 1974; see also Chapter 9 of this book). Data have, in fact, been surprisingly consistent in demonstrating that such an aptitude plays a significant part in the everyday waking experiences of good hypnotic subjects (for example, Barber, 1960; Barber & Glass, 1962; Sarbin, 1964). In his original set of experiments, for instance, Sutcliffe (1958, 1961) found that susceptible subjects generally reported more vivid imagery than insusceptible subjects, the latter finding being replicated in an independent study (Sutcliffe *et al.*, 1970). In this last experiment, a positive curvilinear relationship between vividness of imagery and hypnotic susceptibility was found, absence of imagery being very closely associated with insusceptibility to hypnosis. The relationship gained further (indirect) support from evidence gathered in a third study (Sutcliffe, 1972) which investigated the association between imagery ability and capacity to arouse after-images to imagined stimuli—vivid imagery appeared necessary for this phenomenon to occur.

It seems that the processes of imagination are theoretically very important to proper understanding of suggestion phenomena; a wide variety of theoretical positions argue their significance (for example, Arnold, 1946; Barber, 1969, 1972; Hilgard, 1975; J. Hilgard, 1970, 1974; Sarbin, 1950, 1964; Spanos &

Barber, 1974; Sutcliffe, 1958). The experimental evidence in support of the relationship is by no means uniformly positive (see Sheehan, 1972, for comprehensive coverage of the data bearing on the issue), but collectively results suggest that Sutcliffe's emphasis on the importance of the imagination-fantasy component in hypnosis is a valid one. Distinctively, he has stressed ability characteristics and the definite cue characteristics conveyed by hypnotic procedures which clearly summon hypnotic subjects to imaginatively involve themselves (Sutcliffe *et al.*, 1970).

In summary, results gleaned from Sutcliffe's own studies and those that he reviews argue convincingly that the credulous account of hypnosis, as a general theory explaining hypnotic phenomena, is quite an untenable one, although the issue does not appear to be finally resolved with respect to the occurrence of aftereffects of fantasied stimulation. But while data clearly tend to refute the credulous account, they bear rather ambiguously on the skeptical viewpoint—and this ambiguity is accentuated by the possible inadequacy of the model's simulation control. The evidence that is available suggests that it may still be premature to propose a design where deeply susceptible subjects are expected to fake successfully. Procedures for testing the credulous hypothesis are clear-cut and well designed; the model, however, has yet to delineate procedures which will *objectively* differentiate a state-like (delusory) account of hypnotic phenomena from a social compliance one. Finally, the data appear to support in limited fashion Sutcliffe's notion that correlates of hypnosis (namely, of a cognitive kind) do exist which can be isolated and meaningfully related to hypnotic response.

SUMMARY EVALUATION OF THE MODEL

This model takes up a specific hypothesis concerning hypnotic events and within a single comprehensive factorial design formulates multiple research strategies to test it. The model especially acknowledges the importance of taking account of individual differences among subjects in hypnotic susceptibility and it attempts, in rigorously systematic fashion, to unconfound unwanted interaction of treatment variables by factorially analyzing the effects of hypnosis and role-playing instruction across groups of both susceptible and insusceptible subjects. The issue of individual differences in susceptibility is conspicuously absent from many designs and Sutcliffe's paradigm attempts to focus on this variable. It is important to note that it does so by attempting to avoid the problem the real-simulating model faces in confounding treatment differences with personality variation among its groups of subjects (see Chapter 6 of this book) and by attempting to overcome the problems other designs face when they employ subjects as their own controls (see, for example, Chapters 2 and 4).

The major difficulty with the model is that its practicality is undoubtedly limited. The model is a particularly "expensive" one. The full design has never been applied in practice, even by the person who formulated the paradigm originally, so demanding is the time and effort required to put the full set of its strategies into operation. As originally proposed by Sutcliffe, the complete paradigm requires the testing of 24 independent groups of specially selected subjects. Some conditions nevertheless appear more indispensable than others. The treatment which seems least necessary in practice is "hypnotic induction without suggestion." It is this treatment that Sutcliffe omits in his own application of the model, perhaps for the reason that one does not need to test the effects of induction alone if the effects of induction plus suggestion are not apparent. As Sutcliffe (1958) acknowledges, however, we seldom know in advance what the outcomes of our treatments will be and the hypnotic researcher has little option but to act cautiously in the meantime. Further, with respect to the general utility of the model, separate conditions for testing the effects of stimuli present and absent are not relevant to many hypnotic phenomena, including catalepsy response, certain aspects of posthypnotic suggestion, and hypnotic phenomena which simply do not carry clear-cut consequences as to precise behavioral outcomes.

Despite the model's comprehensiveness and the rigor of its strategies there are a number of important methodological controls that it omits to include and these inevitably prevent one from adopting the paradigm as a suitable model for investigating hypnotic phenomena generally. The paradigm, for example, offers us no procedures for checking the spontaneous entry of control subjects into trance (as Hilgard's model offers). This problem seems particularly pertinent in light of the evidence that is available that some susceptible subjects have difficulty in faking. Further, the procedures of the model relating to role playing are relatively inexplicit and data suggest that the level of pretense associated with the paradigm is not optimally effective. Also, the model curiously omits recognition of the possibility that E-bias factors may operate upon waking as well as hypnotic response; strictly speaking, the framework should argue for the use of independent experimenters across the full range of its experimental and control conditions—there seems little reason to believe that hypnotic subjects are any more prone to the influence of demand characteristics than waking subjects, though some do argue otherwise (for example, Green & Reyher, 1972).

Replication is a particularly demanding strategy for coping with experimenter bias, and its value is limited (Webb, Campbell, Schwartz, & Sechrest, 1972). As a rarely adopted research strategy it is viewed with cardinal respect in the literature on experimental design; repeating results seems to convey a guarantee almost that the results which are obtained are especially accurate. Replication of identical procedures, however, may repeat the same artifactual influences as occurred in the original test—a point that is made most cogently by Webb, Campbell, Schwartz, and Sechrest (1972). Replication is most usefully supplemented by other strategies. Specific sources of artifactual contamination (inevitably conveyed by all test procedures) can be effectively overcome through independent test of the same hypothesis by altogether different procedures and variable strategies of research. This kind of replication which has been termed elsewhere "heteromethod replication" (Campbell, 1969) is immensely valuable for increasing our confidence in the results we have obtained and complements classical replication in the search for both valid and reliable effects. What is actually required by Sutcliffe's model is not only independent hypnotists working with the same set of methods but also separate experimenters approaching test of the credulous (and skeptical) viewpoint by distinctively different methods. Multimethod convergence on the same hypothesis eliminates a host of rival explanations of the original results in a way that "classical" replication does not (see Chapter 8 of this book for further extension of this argument). The point being made is by no means distinctively relevant to Sutcliffe's model—the principle of convergence as a general rule of scientific method should be brought to bear on whatever methodology of hypnosis the social scientist is applying.

Finally, we note some of the more subtle implications of Sutcliffe's selecting particular variables to be incorporated within the general framework of his design. Separation of suggestion from hypnotic procedures leaves unanalyzed a host of part components of the induction process, for instance; the individual study of susceptibility differences expresses a theoretical bias about trait-like predispositions being central to the organization of personality functioning. Why just these variables and not others should enter into a single, "comprehensive" design has not been well argued by the model and in this sense the generality of the model as a universal paradigm for hypnotic research is substantially limited.

We turn now to considering some specific directions for future research. Investigation of the paradigm and application of its combined strategies has been virtually at a standstill since Sutcliffe originally formulated the model in the early 1960s. Perhaps part of the reason why the model has not been actively employed since, is not just the demanding nature of its procedures, but also the fact that it was first formulated in relation to the credulous hypothesis which has been very largely discredited by a wide variety of sources, including Sutcliffe's original program of research. Far too few people, however, recognize the value of the design as a means of rigorously studying the behavioral differences that can occur between hypnotic subjects' fantasy and their perception of real stimulus events.

IMPLICATIONS FOR FUTURE RESEARCH

There are many relevant areas of study to pursue in relation to this model. The most immediate task, considering the theory of hypnosis underlying the framework and the several implications of the data that Sutcliffe himself collected, is to examine the nature of delusory thinking occurring inside (and outside) the hypnotic context. Sutcliffe (1958) lists a variety of problems very worthy of our attention: we need to know, for instance, much more about the nature of delusion as it occurs hypnotically, the properties of the delusory personality, and what conditions specify delusory thinking exactly. As a general area of study virtually no work has been done to analyze systematically the "nature of belief and its relation to action [Sutcliffe, 1958, p. 218]."

The strength and validity of delusion behavior might be tested in the future by examining the extent to which a subject's hallucination report is affected by the way in which the hypnotist–experimenter probes the subject to try and find out how convinced he is about the experience. The precise wording of suggestions could be carefully manipulated along the lines of the experimenter suggesting the fantasied event "is there," "seems to be there," or "looks as if it is there." If the subject's reports covaried uniformly with the ambiguity of the hypnotist's communication one would begin to doubt the veracity of the delusion that is being reported. Work of this kind has been advocated by Barber (1964) and others but research has advanced surprisingly little to date.

There are many aspects about delusory thought specific to Sutcliffe's theory that have not been analyzed empirically at all. Research needs to decide, for example, whether imagery (as it is related to hypnosis) is a result of the delusion occurring in hypnotic subjects, or whether it is simply a manifestation of it (Sutcliffe, 1958). It is quite possible, though, that questions such as these cannot be answered simply by applying the present procedures of the model. New strategies of research will have to be devised so that one can tease out the precise nature of the special cognitive state that Sutcliffe is hypothesizing. Hilgard (1973a, 1974a, b, 1975; see also Chapter 2 of this book) has attempted something like this task by proposing his "hidden observer" technique which specifically analyzes the discrepancy between subjects' subjective report and the nature of their physiological response to hypnotic suggestion. Formulating his "reference experiment" Hilgard has studied hypnotically induced analgesia to pain in which secondary report of the experience is made through automatic writing or automatic talking. Procedures of such a kind should serve very usefully to index something of the nature of Sutcliffe's delusion response. Finally, work obviously needs to determine what are the defining properties of the hypnotizable personality; research here should be directed to isolating conjoint attributes rather than single correlates of trance (Sutcliffe *et al.*, 1970; Sheehan, 1972).

One of the special strengths of an operational approach to hypnosis such as the account Barber (1969, 1972) offers is that restrictive assumptions are at a minimum. The new look at personality currently in the forefront of psychology (see, for instance, the influential text of Mischel, 1968) argues cogently that observable differences in subjects' reactions should be examined not by assuming underlying structures of the personality, but by looking closely at the specific nature of the stimulus situation in which the behavior is invoked. Situational determinants of human reaction are obviously important. A growing body of evidence appears to support now the view that transituational variability exists with respect to much of personality response. Sutcliffe's model, as well as Hilgard's, must thus argue persuasively why assumptions about enduring traits and aptitudes serve a useful purpose in the study of hypnosis. Specifically, they must demonstrate why it is that in hypnosis traditional concepts of personality should still stand.

6

Real-Simulating Model of Hypnosis: The Methodology of Martin T. Orne

> The observation that even highly trained hypnotists cannot reliably distinguish subjects pretending to be hypnotized from deeply hypnotized individuals without special procedures in no way challenges the genuineness of hypnosis or the subjective reality of the hypnotized individual's experiences. It does, however, force a careful reevaluation of a great many claims made for hypnosis, and challenges common beliefs in the infallibility of good clinical judgment [Orne, 1972a, p. 442].

Experimental subjects are sentient, active, cognizing, persons whose perceptions, attitudes, and expectancies may integrally affect the nature of experimental outcomes. No subject taking part in a study is motivationless and subjects are rarely, if ever, neutral to an experimental outcome. Insofar as they care about the outcome, their perceptions of the role and of the hypotheses being tested may be significant determinants of their behavior. Neisser (1967) has noted that the procedures of experimental psychology tackle the problem of knowing what the subject is trying to do by sheer brute force. In any routine learning experiment, for instance, the subject is assumed to be motivated by the single motivation of "getting on with the experimental task," and solving what he is asked to solve. The richness and variety of response so characteristic of ordinary life is assumed to be absent even in experiments where higher mental processes are obviously involved.

More than any other model of hypnosis, the real-simulating methodology pays specific attention to the possibility that hypnotic subjects artifactually respond to the experimental treatments that are administered to them. Its relatively unique concern for the social psychology of the human subject entering the experimental setting gives the model its distinctive emphasis. Theoretically speaking, Orne considers that hypnosis is best explained by appeal to internal states and he holds to the view that the essence of hypnosis lies in the subjective experiences of the susceptible subject (Orne, 1959, 1969, 1971, 1972a, 1974b). The methodology he proposes seeks behavioral consequences of the hypnotic state which are unconfounded by possible artifact adhering to the nature of the context in which hypnotic testing is conducted.

The model's attention to the problem of artifact exemplifies its basic scientific spirit. Artifact is one of the most essential concerns of psychology for it demands that we know exactly in what way our treatment conditions are distinct and what exactly specifies our groups one from another. This specification requirement, as Boring (1969) argues, raises the question of discovery of all sorts of conditions—for the most part social in nature—that affect or influence the experimental variables that we want to study. Essentially, artifact challenges the validity of the propositions that we wish to test. It is the "irrelevant detail" of specification which offers an alternative explanation of our effects and such irrelevancies abound in the social setting of the psychological experiment.

There are actually many ways we can view the social psychology of the human subject who enters the experimental setting and the real-simulating model views in just one particular way the role that experimental subjects may play. As Weber and Cook (1972) outline the problem, four distinct roles of the experimental subject can be formulated: the good subject (Orne, 1959), the faithful subject (Fillenbaum, 1966), the negativistic subject (Cook, Bean, Calder, Frey, Krovetz, & Reisman, 1970), and the apprehensive subject (Rosenberg, 1969). Orne argues consistently for the position that the experimental subject attempts to give responses which will validate a given experimental hypothesis. His notion is distinct, for example, from the concept of the faithful subject who believes that a subject's major concern should be to follow conscientiously any instruction that he is given even to the point of avoiding acting on the basis of suspicions he has about the true purpose of the experiment. And his view is altogether opposed to the negativistic role Cook *et al.*, (1970) ascribe to their subject when they argue that an experimental subject may attempt to confirm an hypothesis other than the experimenter's or try to give responses that are clearly no use to him. Orne views the hypnotic subject as an active participant in a socially defined interaction who is in fact eager to please and contribute to science (Orne, 1959, 1962a). His view is not altogether incompatible with the notion (as Adair & Schachter, 1972, argue) that this participant may also be apprehensive about the treatments that the experimenter will apply and concerned at how the experimenter will evaluate him personally (Rosenberg, 1969). In a sense, Riecken (1962) sums up Orne's general position most succinctly. In the human experimental setting "processes of negotiation" operate between the experimenter and subject through which they both attempt to arrive at a mutual understanding about how to behave in the situation and these processes make human psychology ripe, as it were, for the operation of artifact.

Orne's model, like most frameworks which acknowledge a particular role that experimental subjects have to play implicitly conceptualizes this role as a two-stage process. The first stage is the arousal of motivation to adopt the role in question (that of the "good" subject); and the second is the perception of cues that direct or steer behavior and bring it into accord with the aroused motivation. Central to his framework is the concept of "demand characteristics," a notion reflecting subjects' perception of all of the cues which exist in the situation as to the experimenter's intent. Demand characteristics are the aggregate of cues which implicitly convey the experimenter's hypothesis to the subject and they depend on the subject's preconceived attitudes about the experiment, on the nature of the setting itself, and on the cues which emanate from the experimenter and the procedures he adopts. Orne views the subject in an experiment as contributing to research to the extent that his participation is useful in making the study "work"; and for an experiment to work means that the experimenter should demonstrate what he sets out to prove.

Orne's (1959) classic paper, "The nature of hypnosis: Artifact and essence" presents strong evidence for his general position and demonstrates that subjects' preconceived notions about trance are, in fact, strong determinants of hypnotic performance. Experimental subjects were lectured on hypnotic behavior and shown instances of dominant hand catalepsy which was described as an essential feature of hypnosis. Compared with subjects in a control group (who received no such demonstration) those in the experimental group demonstrated actual dominant arm catalepsy. A second study in the program showed that cues implicit in an experimental design can be effective determinants of performance and they can act to challenge the relevance of the term "hypnosis" to explaining results. Here, Orne replicated an experiment by Ashley, Harper, and Runyon (1951) which was concerned with the effect of economic status on perception. Ashley *et al.*'s original study induced artificial life histories (rich, poor, and normal) by means of hypnosis. The same subjects were run under all conditions, and suggestions of hypnotic amnesia were used to block out all previous life histories. Orne aimed to test the hypothesis that demand characteristics could be largely responsible for the results obtained by Ashley and his co-workers, and to demonstrate how misleading it is to accept their grounds for asserting that values are significant variables affecting perception. In their study, subjects who were told they were rich, for example, behaved quite differently with respect to coin matching from subjects told they were poor, or simply themselves. Orne argued that the original experiment failed to determine whether subjects' perception of the demand characteristics was responsible for their behavior, or whether their performance truly reflected changes in their psychological organization. To answer this question he included a control group that was prevented from feeling rich or poor by their inability to experience hypnotic phenomena (including amnesia), but was exposed to exactly the same demand characteristics as the experimental group. The group selected was a special role-playing group of insusceptible subjects tested by an experimenter who was unaware as to their hypnotic identity (real or faking); subjects were highly motivated to deceive and to fake trance before another experimenter who administered "poor" and "rich" suggestions before testing subjects on the coin matching task. Results for experimental and faking subjects were the same and reproduced the findings of the original study; in all cases coin judgments in the poor state were the largest; judgments in the rich state were the smallest and judgements in the "normal" state fell inbetween. Data strongly supported Orne in his contention that it is possible for a design presenting the same demand characteristics to omit the crucial treatment (here, hypnotic amnesia) yet elicit similar behavior to that shown by Ashley's subjects. Orne's experimentation effectively challenged the methodology of Ashley *et al.*'s original (1951) study and his data argued strongly for the position that before an effect can be attributed legitimately to hypnosis, it is necessary to show that it is not simply a function of the demand characteristics operative in the experimental setting.

This early study by Orne was the first formal application of the real-simulating model of hypnosis. The control group used in the study was labeled by Orne, "simulator," and comparison of this group with real, susceptible subjects affords the single major comparison of the model. This study demonstrates also the special concern of the real-simulating model with the problems of artifact—in particular, those psychological factors arising from consideration of the social psychology of the psychological experiment.

With this brief introduction to the nature of the model, let us move now to discussion of Orne's theoretical account of hypnosis and then to consideration of the model's research strategies. Such will help us to assess the overall adequacy of the paradigm as a systematic framework for investigating the nature of hypnotic phenomena. As with other theories we have examined in this book, subtle conceptual changes have occurred in relation to the model since the framework was first formulated.

THEORETICAL POSITION

In the early stages of the model's formulation, Orne (1959, 1962a) conceptualized several "essence" features of hypnosis where the term "essence" was taken to specify the residual effects of hypnosis that remained after role playing and increased motivation to respond to the wishes of the hypnotist were accounted for. He expressed uncertainty about how best to view the change in motivation implied by the increase in suggestibility that typically follows induction. The increase in suggestibility was viewed on the one hand as possibly reflecting factors (for example, simple compliance) which equally as well may apply to other experimental situations, including those not involving hypnosis. But, on the other hand, Orne (1959) also expressed the view that possibly "the hypnotic state as such increases the motivation of the subject to comply with the wishes ('suggestions')–both explicit and implicit–of the experimenter [p. 282]." The influence of demand characteristics seemed to be confounded in hypnotic research with the state of consciousness being investigated; both, it seems, may lead hypnotic subjects to be especially cooperative and eager to please. The model took the ambiguous stance of ascribing the motivation of real subjects not just to their perceptions of the cue characteristics of the testing context but also to the drive arousing properties of the actual trance state.

Several essence features were incorporated into this initial formulation, hypnosis being conceptualized as an altered state of consciousness, nonpathological in nature but distinct from ordinary, waking experience. The principal features of the state were held to be those changes in subjective experience characterized by a discontinuity from everyday waking experience; a lack of volition in the subject's ability to respond to the hypnotist; his ability to experience as subjectively real distortions of perception, feeling and memory that are in direct opposition to reality; and the ability he shows in being able to tolerate logical incongruities that would ordinarily be disturbing to the normal, waking subject. The most important of these characteristics–and the ones that are consistently reinforced by the model (Orne, 1972a; Hilgard, 1975)–are the ability of the hypnotized subject to tolerate logical absurdities (illustrated, for example, by trance logic) and the feelings of compulsion that typically characterize the deeply susceptible person's response to hypnotic suggestion. Quite independent of the various features that characterize any trance state, however, Orne insists that hypnosis must be viewed as occurring in a specific context where there are implicit rules of the game operating between experimenter (hypnotist) and subject. Subjectively real alterations of perception and memory take place in accord with cues gathered from the hypnotist while the subject strives to "play the role of a 'good subject' or, in other words to validate the experimental hypothesis [Orne, 1962a, p. 778]."

As far as the strategies of the model are concerned, alterations in subjective experience characterizing hypnotic trance are important only insofar as they accompany changes in *behavior.* Specifically the model aims to detect those differences in observable response that cannot be attributed to the demand characteristics existing in the experimental situation. The real-simulating model in its application, is a rigidly scientific one and strictly behavioral in orientation, but Orne's theoretical appeal is clearly first and foremost to the private experience of the hypnotized individual. The universal effect of hypnosis on any subject in deep trance can only be delineated in terms of his subjective experience (Orne, 1959, p. 297). Theoretically speaking, then, the nature of the experience of the hypnotized subject must be an integral aspect of the study of hypnosis and herein the essence features of the phenomenon supposedly lie.

The significant emphasis of the model on subjective processes has led many to criticize the paradigm. Barber (1969), for instance, criticizes both Orne and Hilgard for their unscientific appeal to private events as criteria of the genuineness of hypnotic phenomena. In doing so, however, the critic too easily overlooks the actual logic of the real-simulating model. The paradigm was primarily designed to scientifically eliminate one particular source of artifact as explanation of the specific patterns of performance that susceptible subjects might show. Obviously, then, testimony of trance may assert the reality of hypnosis for hypnotized subjects. Testimony alone, though, is evidence which the model does not regard as scientific enough to convince others of the meaningful nature of hypnotic (as distinct from nonhypnotic) response. Its theoretical basis aside for the moment, the real-simulating model in strict scientific fashion seeks data which will provide *objective* evidence bearing upon hypnotic effects.

In his later work Orne (1965b, 1969, 1972a) laid down new emphases for his model. He expressed, for example, a willingness to stay much closer to the descriptive level when talking about hypnotic events. There was a move away from the theoretical speculation of his 1959 paper to the expression of concern about delineating those responses which are hypnotic from those which are not. Even if there could be no acceptable definition of hypnosis Orne felt that there might be agreement at the descriptive level as to when hypnosis was involved and he suggested that it was premature to attempt to *define* hypnosis by analyzing antecedent conditions in systematic fashion. Although Orne had consistently focused on the nature of hypnosis (as distinct say from the study of the nature of induction, or the correlates of hypnotizability) some of the characteristics he mentioned earlier as typical of hypnosis began to receive less obvious mention. Two primary features of hypnosis, though, tended to be retained: the effect of hypnosis in distorting the perceptions and memories of susceptible individuals, and the compulsive nature of hypnotic experience whereby the subject abrogates his ability to act volitionally—the phenomena most relevant to analyzing these consequences of induction being those involving suggestions of challenge, hallucinations, amnesia, and posthypnotic behavior.

There were also subtle changes in Orne's conception of the Experimental Subject. Orne's (1959, 1962) notion of the Experimental Subject saw the subject as attempting to validate the experimenter's hypothesis. His current conception (Orne, 1969, 1971, 1972a, 1973), however, views the "good" subject as meaning something more than this. The Experimental Subject came more to be viewed as someone who gives a response which is characteristic of intelligent subjects, responds in accordance with his self-perception and—"if the experimental task is such that the subject sees himself as being evaluated he will tend to behave in such a way as to make himself look good [Orne, 1969, p. 145]." This broader concept of the role of the experimental subject is an important change for it incorporates many of the features of the good subject and the apprehensive subject into a single notion, thereby giving greater generality to the sources of artifact conceptualized by the model.

Another significant change in Orne's theory was his reassessment of the importance of the level of motivation in hypnotic subjects. His earlier theorizing (Orne, 1954, 1959) extrapolated the views of White (1941a, b) and argued for an increase in motivation as a consequence of the hypnotic state. The implicit assumption of the model seemed to be that the hypnotic subject is more compliant than can normally be expected of an experimental subject. Later work (Orne, 1966), however, began to evaluate this question more critically and found no evidence for hypnotic subjects being especially motivated to please. The early assumption by the model of an especially high level of motivation in hypnotic subjects justified, in a sense, the paradigm's selection of simulators as its major control group. Here is a group of insusceptible, role-playing people who are maximally motivated for their task. It would have been highly inappropriate to choose a group less motivated than this to compare with hypnotic subjects if it was true that the state itself substantially increased subjects' motivation to please and willingness to respond to the hypnotist.

Orne remains convinced that if he were unable to find a single well established difference between real and role-playing subjects, deep hypnosis could still be conceptualized as a phenomenon different from simulation, or simple compliance. The "hallmark of the hypnotic phenomenon . . . is the nature and quality of the concomitant subjective events [Orne, 1972a, p. 421]." As far as Orne's theory of hypnosis is concerned, it is theoretically important to assert that the subjective experience of a subject while carrying out a posthypnotic suggestion (say) is markedly different from that accompanying a waking request even though research has shown that differences in behavior cannot be demonstrated between these two sets of conditions (Damaser, 1964). The theory behind the real-simulating model stresses specific qualities of experience and Orne offers suggestions as to those that ought to be identified objectively. The model, however, gives no real indications about how to achieve this goal. It is not clear, for example, how one would assess the ability of the susceptible subject to experience an imagined event as if it really did exist other than by appeal to the subject's testimony. As far as the real-simulating methodology is concerned it is clear that the verbal testimony of the susceptible subject is far from adequate as the sole source of evidence on which to base our diagnosis of "hypnosis," yet the strategies of the model fail to orient themselves as fully as they might to this aspect of data collection. In talking of hallucinating experiences Orne (1972a) argues that if ". . . the subject behaves as if he has these experiences, reports having these experiences and, as far as it is possible to ascertain, actually believes he has these experiences, one may say he is hypnotized [p. 401]." The real-simulating model is excellently equipped to analyze subjects' patterns of behavioral response, but it lacks specific strategies that aim toward meeting the requirement that testimony should be truthful.

In conclusion, the real-simulating methodology of hypnosis directs itself toward careful and specific analysis of the behavioral performance of real, susceptible subjects. In quite penetrating fashion it analyzes one particular explanation of their response in terms of factors relating to the social psychology of the psychological experiment. The hypnotic subject interacts in a special way with the hypnotist as experimenter and the model is designed to answer the important question of how artifact arising from this interaction can be distinguished from possible essence features of hypnosis. The reality of hypnosis is consistently indexed by Orne's theory in terms of the subjective experiences of the hypnotized individual; and the particular experiences which best illustrate the hypnotic state are those involving distortions in memory, cognition, and feeling. The critical importance of these processes is accentuated in recent statements of theory (Orne, 1974b; Orne & Hammer, 1974). Perceptual distortions come into quite distinct focus. The truly significant aspects of hypnosis are viewed as those which pertain to the characteristics of the subjects' induced experiences: "Hypnosis . . . is a collaborative enterprise in which the inner experience of the subject can be dramatically altered [Orne & Hammer, 1974, p. 138]." Specifically, Orne considers that when the subject is hypnotized he comes to accept as real the distortions of perception and memory that are suggested by the hypnotist, a feature Sutcliffe stresses also in his own account of hypnosis (see Chapter 5 of this book). Orne, in fact, has subsequently defined hypnosis in explicit fashion as a state of "transient delusion" (Orne, 1974b).

SURVEY OF THE MODEL'S STRATEGIES OF RESEARCH

General Features of Design

The real-simulating model of hypnosis typically employs independent groups of subjects allocated to two experimental conditions, "real" and "simulating." Both groups receive the same set of hypnotic procedures and undergo identical treatment by the hypnotist. The real group, however, is made up of subjects who have established their deep susceptibility to hypnosis, this having been indexed usually by the high level of their performance on standard hypnotic test scales. The simulating group, on the other hand, is a group of insusceptible subjects who have established in similar fashion their inability to experience routine trance phenomena. Procedures for the role-playing group differ from those for the real group in that before hypnotic treatment is commenced the former group are motivated by a second experimenter to deceive the hypnotist into thinking they are genuinely susceptible to hypnosis; real subjects receive no preexperimental instruction.

Simulators are drawn from the same population as susceptible subjects with respect to the level of their information, expectation, belief, and knowledge about hypnosis. Real subjects, though, must be highly susceptible to hypnosis because as Orne (1972a) argues, in order to approach a poorly defined phenomenon one must be completely sure that the ability of the subject guarantees at least that the phenomenon will be present in the situation. Simulating subjects are meant to seek out and respond to any available cues that will help them in their deception and it is very important to the logic of the paradigm that they are immune to the actual treatment effects of hypnosis. The absence of subjective experience of hypnotic phenomena in these subjects is a necessary assumption of the model for if role-playing subjects report experiencing trance in any way it is then quite impossible to know the extent to which their response is simply a function of the cues they were especially instructed to detect.

Real subjects may respond by reason of hypnosis and/or because of the artifact that may exist in the experimental situation while simulators are meant only to respond on the basis of the cues available as to the experimenter's intent. It is important to note that the model makes no assumption about any similarity of variables existing between these two conditions, hypnosis and simulation. Variables relating to the subjects' simulation task are, in fact, acknowledged by Orne and his associates as distinctly different from those involved in induction. The model argues simply that its role-playing comparison condition is primarily designed to establish the adequacy of the hypnotic procedure as one that the real subject cannot "see through." The simulating condition is meant to investigate whether or not the hypnotist's manipulation for the real subjects is a valid one and whether or not the manipulation in question can be applied to real subjects without fear of contamination from potential sources of artifact. Emphasis on "adequacy of test procedures" clearly draws attention away from concern about potential differences between real and simulating subjects, and focuses instead on the demand characteristics that may affect the experimental group alone. Once the demand characteristics have been demarcated by the simulating group, however, the model essentially requires other strategies to focus directly on the assumed hypnotic quality of what real subjects do.

Whenever the same subjects are tested across conditions we have already seen (see Chapter 2 of this book) that distinctive order effects can occur, and strong argument can obviously be made that separate groups of subjects should in fact be tested in the real and simulating conditions. Pattie (1950) has argued, as Sutcliffe (1960) has also, that if a subject in the waking state is asked to simulate his earlier hypnotic performance, successful execution of the task could not help but convey in some way to the subject that his previous trance performance was not genuine. If the order of experimentation were reversed the design carries the alternative risk of a subject gaining experience in the control session which might facilitate successful simulation in the trance that follows. The use of independent groups, however, also runs some risk. There is the possible danger of the experimenter treating real subjects differently from the way he treats simulating subjects, and this is especially apparent if the experimenter is in anyway aware of the differential susceptibility to hypnosis of the subjects he is testing. To meet this problem the model requires that the experimenter who conducts the hypnotic testing of both real and simulating subjects must be blind as to subjects' true identities. This design feature of the model acknowledges the importance of the hypnotist treating susceptible and insusceptible subjects alike. If an experimenter, for any reason, knows with certainty that a subject is real or simulating then the standards of the model are violated.

In summary, the purpose of the real-simulating model is to explore the behavioral responses of deep hypnotic subjects and to investigate specifically whether or not their behavior can be accounted for on the basis of their perceptions concerning the experimental procedures themselves. The model is based on the well justified assumption that any subject brought to the experimental context, whether he be susceptible or not, is a sentient, cognizing being (Orne, 1959, 1962a, 1969, 1970, 1972a) whose behavior may not reflect, in fact, the influence of the treatment that the experimenter (in this case, the hypnotist) applies.

Orne's adoption of the simulating technique followed careful consideration of other methodological strategies that control in part for possible artifactual response by the experimental subjects. These procedures will now be discussed briefly before we turn to close analysis of the simulation task which is the single, major condition chosen by the model for purposes of control comparison.

Strategies Promulgated by the Real-Simulating Model

One must at the outset realize that the problem of demand characteristics and their potential influence can never really be eliminated. Subjects' perceptions of the experimenter's intent represent a constant and systematic source of error requiring recognition and the adoption of an appropriate methodological tool of inquiry. Two techniques that were considered by Orne (1965a) as possible means of investigating demand characteristics were the *postexperimental inquiry* and what Orne terms the "preinquiry," or "nonexperiment." Both these inquiries constitute "quasi-control" conditions; in both cases, subjects are requested to participate actively in revealing information about likely artifactural effects. The term quasi-control is appropriate to the postexperimental inquiry because the subject steps out of his role, as it were, to reflect upon his earlier performance in an attempt to assist the experimenter in determining the cause of his behavior. The second strategy, the preinquiry, is of a similar nature. Here a group of subjects from the same population of people as would be used in the actual study are asked to pretend they are subjects of the experiment. They are given exactly the same information experimental subjects receive and they are asked to produce the data that would result from receivlng the actual experimental treatment. As before, the strategy represents a quasi-control condition because the control subject cooperates with the experimenter in guessing what another person (a real subject) might do.

Neither of these inquiry strategies is able to prove that any given result is a function of demand characteristics, but they yield information about the possible cue characteristics of experimental procedures and they ultimately allow the design of better treatments. Despite these advantages, however, their usefulness is limited. As far as the postexperimental inquiry is concerned the reported perceptions of the subject may come from the inquiry itself rather than the treatments reported upon; and with the preinquiry strategy there is no guarantee that the guesses of subjects would be the actual determinants of true subjects' behavior. In quite conservative fashion the model has developed a technique to establish those actual behavioral effects based solely on response to demand characteristics–it has constructed a method which directly demonstrates the evidence available for influence by subjects' perceptions. This procedure set down by the model to satisfy its demands is known as the "simulating" technique. Mistaken acceptance of simulators as a normal control group has led to considerable misrepresentation among hypnosis researchers of the adequacy of the real-simulating model of hypnosis. Most of the communication difficulty has surrounded the model's task of simulation which we will now analyze in some detail.

The Simulating Technique

It is instructive at the outset to review the basic elements of the technique. Simulating subjects are preselected for their insusceptibility to hypnosis and are instructed by one experimenter to stay out of trance and to "role play" hypnosis before another experimenter (the hypnotist) who is kept deliberately unaware of the subject's actual susceptibility to trance. Two experimenters must be involved. The first experimenter highly motivates subjects to do whatever the hypnotist will ask and requests them not to ever reveal to the second experimenter that they are not truly hypnotized. They are told the hypnotist will stop the experiment if he finds out they are faking and they are asked not to drop their role until they come back to discuss the study after the hypnotist has concluded the experiment. After simulation instruction they are taken to the hypnotist who administers identical procedures to both real and simulating subjects. Real subjects usually do not know that simulators are being used in the study but simulators obviously know of real subjects' existence. Finally, both sets of subjects receive a postexperimental inquiry by the first experimenter after formal testing has been completed.

The details of this technique are expounded and discussed elsewhere by Orne (1971, 1972a) and others (Sheehan, 1970, 1971a, b, c). Several features of the technique, however, need to be emphasized, since they would be important in any attempted replication of the simulation task. First, the hypnotist must be blind as to the subject's identity and the subject must be aware that the hypnotist does not know how susceptible he is. In this respect, the simulation task is distinct from ordinary role playing in which the subject may pretend to be hypnotized but the experimenter usually is conscious of the subject's role status. It is important also to acknowledge that although the hypnotist does not know to which treatment condition the subject has been assigned (real or simulating) the subject himself knows which treatment he is receiving; in this respect, the simulating condition is "single blind" in orientation and distinct, for example, from the "double blind" drug placebo control in psychopharmacology where both subject and experimenter are blind as to the treatment (drug, or no drug) that has been applied. Second, simulators must perceive that they have a definite choice of fooling the hypnotist and the importance of their contribution must be emphasized to them. Third, simulators should have no special training and should operate with the same background experience as real subjects. Fourth, the special instructions to simulate must be administered immediately prior to hypnosis. And fifth, the inquiry that is arranged afterwards (with the experimenter who first instructed subjects) should be used to carefully screen any role-playing subject who has inadvertently slipped into trance during the hypnotic session. On the question of subject exclusion the model dictates also that any subject whom the experimenter perceives "with certainty" is faking ought also to be rejected. Exclusion of simulators on the grounds that trance is present is relatively rare, because the model dictates that subjects should be screened for their immunity very carefully–ideally by independent hypnotists who have brought them to a plateau of hypnotizability.

It is important to note, as Orne (1971, 1972a) does, that simulating subjects differ from hypnotized subjects in the fact they are operating under distinctly different instructions; the two groups of subjects clearly differ both in the nature of their task and the mental set they bring to it. Viewed in this light, simulating subjects are most appropriately considered as a special comparison group that helps us to find out what highly motivated subjects would do in the same situation the real subjects are in when the only reason for their action is the information available as to the experimenter's intent. The simulation condition precisely gives us an exact estimate of the capabilities of subjects who we know are not in hypnosis; it tells us what the hypnotized person could or couldn't do if he had simply tried to figure out what the experimenter had wanted.

The major function of the simulating comparison condition can be illustrated by the results of an experiment conducted by Orne, Sheehan, and Evans (1968) who were concerned with the persistence of posthypnotic response outside the experimental setting. Successful demonstration of persistence has important theoretical implications but proper test of it requires the adoption of carefully considered controls in order to establish that the extraexperimental test is one that will not be perceived by real subjects as in anyways related to the experimenter's purpose.

Fisher (1954, 1955) presented evidence that posthypnotic behavior is purely dependent upon the presentation of a cue in a particular type of setting. He aimed to establish an informal test of posthypnotic suggestion in the study he conducted by arranging for the experiment to be interrupted by a confederate and for the cue word to be then used in casual conversation. Susceptible subjects ceased responding during the interruption and Fisher inferred from this that posthypnotic behavior was limited to the experimental setting. Close analysis of his instructions, however, shows that the suggestion itself could have been interpreted by subjects as one that was in fact limited only to the context in which it was subsequently observed. Orne, Sheehan, and Evans (1968) gave subjects a much less ambiguous set of suggestions and tried to test response in a setting totally unrelated to the experimental context. They scheduled people for two sessions, one day apart. The experimenter delivered the posthypnotic suggestion to respond compulsively to the cue word "experiment" and tested the suggestion formally on both days. The informal test (the critical one) was administered by the secretary–receptionist who casually dropped the cue word in conversation to subjects as they departed on the first day and as they arrived again the following day for the second session. The real-simulating model was adopted to evaluate whether the secretary's test was actually perceived by subjects as one that was irrelevant to the experimenter's concern. Here, the simulating condition probed intensively for the success of the deception the experimenter intended toward real subjects, the condition being used to establish unequivocally the truth of the statement that the receptionist's test was "extraexperimental." If highly-motivated unhypnotized subjects alerted to all the cues that were available failed to perceive the relevance of the waiting room test then it can be assumed that the behavior of the hypnotic subjects to the secretary's use of the cue word is validly representative of extraexperimental behavior; the adequacy of the procedural manipulation is thereby established. Data showed that simulators were actually more alert to the cue word than hypnotic subjects (responding, appropriately, for example, to the experimenter's casual use of the word as he talked to them informally before beginning the second session), but failed to perceive the secretary as a surrogate of the experimenter. Five (out of 16) hypnotic subjects responded consistently away from the experimenter; no simulator demonstrated comparable behavior. Simulators' behavior shows us that the deception was successful, but it is important to realize that it gives us limited information about why hypnotic subjects continued to respond compulsively. The pattern of difference really tells us only that hypnotic subjects did not respond because they perceived the experimenter's intent. Such a result is important, however; it indicates that adequate theorizing about hypnotic events must come to grips with the fact that posthypnotic suggestion in hypnotized subjects carries over to situations where the hypnotist cannot know how a subject will respond.

In another experiment, Orne and Evans (1966) employed the real-simulating model to test the prediction that the disappearance of the hypnotist (following a simulated power break-down interrupting the experiment) would not lead to the immediate termination of hypnosis in real subjects. The prediction was based on the hypothesis that hypnosis is more than simply a role relationship existing between experimenter and subject. The disruption of an experiment and the subsequent disappearance of the hypnotist are manipulations the authors assumed would end the social relationship between hypnotist and subject. According to their theory, it was predicted that termination of this kind would have no immediate impact on the hypnotized subject. In the study, simulating subjects continued to fake hypnosis throughout the power failure in the absence of the hypnotist. The experiment is a particularly interesting one because it reports the use of a deception procedure that was clearly inadequate. No conclusion could be drawn at all in the study about the hypnotic nature of the behavior of the susceptible group. Results simply tell us that real subjects may have also performed according to their perception of the cues existing somewhere in the situation. Evans and Orne (1971) later modified the methods of their earlier study making it considerably more difficult for subjects to suspect the genuineness of the experimental procedure. Results from this follow-up study showed that simulating subjects ceased faking as soon as the hypnotist left the room while real subjects slowly but spontaneously terminated hypnosis with considerable subjective difficulty. It is important to note here that what the simulators' responses do not tell us are the reasons for hypnotized subjects' gradual rather than abrupt termination of hypnosis. But the data do tell us that real subjects didn't slowly wake up simply because they thought the study was actually still progressing.

Finally, we will conclude this discussion of the simulating technique by considering the results of a study where the conclusions drawn from the data would have been much more acceptable had a simulating comparison group been employed. Discussion of this study hopefully serves to further reinforce the value of the simulation task as a methodological tool of inquiry.

Nace and Orne (1970) investigated the fate of an uncompleted posthypnotic suggestion (see also Coe, 1973b, for discussion of this issue) in a study designed to test the possibility that subjects who resist completing a posthypnotic suggestion may, at a later time, and in a situation which is not seen as related to the hypnotic session, carry out the earlier suggested behavior. The critical test occurred after the hypnotic part of the experiment was over and involved an activity which was meant to be independent of the hypnotic session and the hypnotist. Nace and Orne took pre- and posttest measures (the hypnotic suggestion was that the subject would take up a blue pencil to play with) to investigate whether a person who failed to carry out a posthypnotic suggestion would nonetheless show a subsequent tendency toward the suggested behavior. They employed three sessions; pretest measures (choice of color of pencil) were taken in the first two sessions and in the third session the suggestion was given and tested formally by an experimenter who then left the room asking the subject to complete a few questionnaires while he was gone. The experimenter then observed the subject through a one-way screen. Results showed a relation between hypnotizability and the tendency to complete the posthypnotic suggestion. Within the medium range of hypnotizability subjects were found who did not complete the posthypnotic suggestion but subsequently, in the extrahypnotic settting, behaved in accordance with the earlier suggestion. Low hypnotizable subjects also failing the item in the formal setting did not demonstrate any subsequent action tendency.

The Nace and Orne (1970) study was concerned with the issue of adequacy of procedure. It was important that the final (posttest) testing was seen by subjects as unrelated to the experiment, irrespective of the nature of their early pretest choices. No simulating group was used, however, and no postexperimental inquiry was conducted into the perceptions of subjects. The authors argued that if subjects wanted to merely comply they would surely have passed the formal test of the posthypnotic suggestion, not failed it. However, the salience of the posttest if it was perceived, would have been such that it might have been very important to subjects no matter how they had performed previously. The findings reported in this study are interesting; they indicate that posthypnotic suggestion may create in subjects the need to carry out or complete the item of behavior. Coe (1973b), however, has shown that simulators are quite likely to complete uncompleted suggestions.

The absence of effective controls in the Nace and Orne study—the very ones that the real-simulating model so consistently advocates—renders any inference drawn from the data of the study about the state-like features of hypnotic subjects' behavior quite equivocal. The contrast between the methodological procedures of this experiment and the others conducted by Orne and his associates elsewhere, highlights the stringent standards of the real-simulating paradigm. The authors' findings that the relationship varied with the range of susceptibility of subjects adds credence to their conclusions but the data are not sufficient to overcome the essential weakness of the study—the failure to establish unequivocally the "adequacy" of the experimenter's test procedure.

This brief consideration of some of the studies that have employed the real-simulating paradigm reveals implicitly the subtlety of the logic that is associated with the model. Because of this subtlety the rationale of the model can be easily misinterpreted. We turn now to examine the logic of the paradigm in close detail and to comment also on some of the major misconceptions associated with it.

The Logic of the Real-Simulating Paradigm

Two major features describe the task of simulation. First, the simulating subject is required to be deeply involved in a task of pretending to be in hypnosis and is instructed accordingly; and second, trance is not in fact experienced by him. The first characteristic emphasizes the fact that simulating subjects are asked to do something quite different from real subjects and the second draws our attention to the fact that the two groups in question differ quite markedly in suggestibility. Both these features affect our inferences when the model is applied. Interpretation tends to be most affected, however, when behavioral differences rather than similarities, are found between the two groups (Sheehan, 1971a).

If real and simulating subjects perform similarly during hypnotic testing then the logic of the model dictates the interpretation that the results for the hypnotic group may be due to the demand characteristics of the experimental situation. The performance of role-playing subjects who are not hypnotized but who satisfy the hypnotist's requests in the same way real subjects do, clearly demonstrates that the concept of hypnosis need not be invoked to account for the behavior of the hypnotic group. The comparison in question offers no proof that results for the hypnotic subjects are artifactual, it simply states that an alternative explanation of what hypnotic subjects do is possible. The model is unable to say, with any certainty, whether the pattern of behavior that has been found represents genuine "essence" which can be faked or whether we have really located artifact that is adhering to the hypnotic condition. However, the fact that real and simulating subjects perform similarly offers conclusive demonstration that "given the identical treatment, unhypnotized subjects can figure out the kind of responses that appear appropriate on the experimental tasks [Orne, 1972a, p. 418]." As we saw in our discussion of Orne and Evans' (1966) initial failure to demonstrate differences between real and simulating subjects (the case of the disappearing hypnotist) the behavior of the real subjects can only be regarded as equivocal when they perform the same as simulating subjects. Hypnotized subjects' behavior simply cannot be attributed to hypnosis while we know that nonhypnotized subjects placed in the same test situation are able to perceive an experimenter's intention well enough for them to behave in exactly the same way. Bowers (1966, 1973a) expresses essentially the same point of view when he argues that successful application of the simulating technique can never prove the assumption that hypnotic behavior is attributed to demand characteristics; the model can only firmly indicate the converse, that is, a hypnotic effect is *not* attributed to these cues.

Leaving aside for the moment the question of similarities let us move now to considering the problems the model faces in interpreting behavioral differences between real and simulating subjects.

When differences occur, the pattern of results tells us unequivocally that the behavior of real subjects is not a function of the cues provided by the hypnotist or his procedures, and simulators, as we have seen, allow firm test of the adequacy of the hypnotist's test procedures. The two main features of the simulation task outlined above prevent us from making stronger conclusions of the kind that "the obtained differences index unambiguously the effects of hypnosis." We know, for example, that there are demonstrable consequences of insusceptible subjects being given faking instruction (Sheehan, 1970, 1971c), the results obtained suggesting that the differences between real and simulating subjects may in certain circumstances be due to the nature of the specific psychological situation that simulating subjects are in rather than to the effects of hypnotic suggestion on the real, susceptible group. Logically, it is also pertinent to argue that since real and simulating subjects differ in level of suggestibility then personality differences between the two sets of subjects may be the real determinants of their varying pattern of response. Attitudinal and motivational differences may also relate to the two distinct groups (see Austin *et al.*, 1963). Detailed argument has been put forward elsewhere (Sheehan, 1971a), however, that personality differences between real and simulating subjects are relatively unimportant. Faced with the task of interpreting differences, it seems more useful to ascertain when and in what fashion faking performance is peculiarly influenced by the treatment effects of insusceptible subjects alone receiving instructions to simulate. Not until these effects are known and discounted can the real-simulating model be used to argue that the behavior of the hypnotic group is related unequivocally to the presence of "trance."

In the normal fashion of establishing control groups, the experimenter aims to set up a condition which is comparable to the experimental group with which it is being compared except with respect to the treatment under study. It is important to recognize that the real-simulating model makes no attempt at all to establish a condition of this kind. The model compares two quite different treatment conditions—"hypnotic" and "simulating"—which have their own distinctive consequences and predictable outcomes. However much the simulating condition is defined as "quasi-control," though, we cannot overlook the implications of control that do exist simply because one group is able to respond to the treatment under scrutiny (hypnosis) while the other group cannot. The situation is somewhat analogous to the conditions of control existing in drug research where it is argued (see Orne, 1969; Ross, Krugman, Lyerly, & Clyde, 1962) that the true action of a drug can never be fully evaluated. All one can really do is to compare placebo ("demand characteristics"?) effect plus drug ("hypnosis"?) effect with placebo effect without drug and draw appropriate inferences wherever possible. Comparison conditions inevitably differ in so many ways that our confidence in any experimental outcome, not just the effect of hypnosis, can only be established through the gradual elimination of alternative explanations of the data we obtain. The specific contribution of the real-simulating model (when group differences are observed) is that the model soundly eliminates one such viable form of alternative explanation.

The logic of the real-simulating model can be perhaps most usefully illustrated by comparing it with the logic of Barber's paradigm of hypnosis. Table 6.1 summarizes the main points of comparison. Both frameworks embrace the logic of "alternative explanation" (see Chapter 3 for extended discussion of this rule) and both models investigate the possibility that hypnotic subjects are responding in the way that they do for reasons that are unrelated to hypnosis. But whereas Orne's framework investigates specifically the potential effects of subjects' responding to the demand characteristics naturally occurring in the situation,

TABLE 6.1
Comparison of the Logic of the Real-Simulating and Operational Paradigms of Hypnosis

Real-simulating model	Operational paradigm
Aim is to eliminate an alternative hypothesis oriented around demand characteristics as an explanation of obtained hypnotic result.	*Aim* is to establish an alternative explanation of hypnotic events in order to illustrate the expendability of the trance concept. Motivational elements of a nonhypnotic kind existing within induction procedures, for example, are examined for their effects.
Employs "Simulators" as quasi-control subjects. The task of simulation itself shares nothing procedurally in common with hypnotic induction.	Employs (primarily) "TM" subjects as control subjects. This condition shares elements procedurally in common with the hypnotic condition.
Model assumes, procedurewise, no equivalence of variables across experimental and quasi-control conditions. The logic of alternative explanation, by which the model operates, is quite independent of any procedural similarity.	Model assumes, procedurewise, equivalence of particular variables across experimental and control conditions. Logic of alternative explanation depends for its validity on the acceptance of this equivalence.
Simulators are highly motivated for their task which is to respond to whatever cues are available as to the experimenter's intent.	Task-motivated subjects are highly motivated for their task which is to cooperate and try to experience the suggested effects.
Simulators and real subjects are instructed differently but are tested by the same suggestion procedures.	Hypnotic subjects receive instructions which subsume those given to task-motivated subjects. Both groups are tested by the same suggestion procedures.
Quasi-control subjects are *selected* for their immunity to hypnotic treatment. Real subjects are highly susceptible.	Control subjects are *unselected* for their immunity to hypnotic treatment as also are experimental (hypnotic) subjects.

Barber's model analyzes the potential effects of particular elements (task motivational) of a nonhypnotic kind that are typically contained within standard hypnotic-induction procedures. Procedurally speaking, Orne's simulating condition is designed to be quite distinct from his hypnotic condition, whereas Barber's TM condition is presumed to share particular variables in common across conditions. The "logic of alternative explanation" ("a rival hypothesis may account for so-called hypnotic effects") applies to both models. For Barber, however, success of the application of this logic is dependent on acceptance of the "logic of equivalence" ("variables must be shared in common with hypnotic procedures"); for Orne, no such dependence exists.

To the extent that the real-simulating model is more cautious in the inferences it draws from its data its conclusions are often more acceptable. If simulators and real subjects behave similarly, Orne's model simply infers that hypnotic subjects could be responding for the same reason as unhypnotized (role-playing) subjects. The model argues logically that we may still need the concept of hypnosis to explain what real subjects do, but the similarity of response indicates there is considerable room for doubt. On the other hand, if TM subjects perform similarly to hypnotic subjects, Barber argues for the expendability of the trance concept. Providing that the logic of equivalence holds for his model this inference may be justifiable but to the extent there are distinctive attributes of the TM condition that are not shared to the same extent by the hypnotic condition then this inference breaks down. Finally, the unselected nature of the subject sample attached to Barber's model leaves open the possibility that some of his control group subjects may inadvertently be responding for the same reasons his hypnotic group subjects do, while Orne's model takes special precautions to guarantee the immunity of his comparison group to hypnotic effects. The established immunity of simulating subjects tightens considerably the logic of the inferences that can be drawn from application of Orne's model, for differences between real and simulating subjects could not even begin to be attributed to hypnosis if the role-playing subjects in any way were capable of responding to hypnosis.

The above logic of the real-simulating model which is summarized in Table 6.1 is frequently misrepresented by hypnotic researchers and there is a great deal in print which attacks Orne's conception of hypnosis and his associated methodology. Critics, however, are often far from fully aware of the full implications of the logic behind the model. For the purposes of demonstrating this point we will take four misconceptions about the real-simulating model and discuss them briefly in turn.

Misconceptions

The first and most common misrepresentation arises from the premise that the model asserts that differences between real and simulating subjects reflect genuine essence features of hypnosis. Coe (1971, 1973a), for example, generally offers a sensitive account of the logic of the real-simulating model but misrepresents Orne on this major point. He states that the model views differential behavior as hypnosis specific; differences between the two groups are taken to indicate essence while similarities are taken to index artifact. Similar conclusions are drawn in error by other authors who apply the real-simulating model and make the prediction that performance differences signify the unique effects of hypnosis. Scheibe, Gray, and Keim (1968), for instance, adopted the real-simulating model to study the effects of hypnotically induced deafness. In their study real and simulating subjects performed the same in a delayed auditory feedback test (DAF) following suggestions of deafness, and they concluded that "there is as yet no evidence that hypnotically induced deafness is functionally unique in modifying DAF effects [p. 158]." Their inference, in fact, is a sound one but the rationale behind their study was unfortunately based on the premise that found differences would be firm evidence for unique hypnotic behavior. Orne's model makes no such claim for any differences that it might locate. Discrepancies in performance are said to be possibly related to hypnosis but "essence" is far from necessarily demonstrated. Nevertheless, the stated relevance of the term "essence" to observed differences does place the onus on Orne's model to make clear what the concept actually means, even if it is not necessarily indicated.

The second misconception looks at the other side of the coin, as it were. Reyher (1972) argues, for example, that application of the model retards progress because the concept of hypnosis is never invoked whenever simulating and hypnotic subjects perform the same. Coe (1971) conveys the same implication when he argues that nondifferential responses between the two groups are the artifacts in the situation. Here, again the subtle logic of the model is overlooked. Similarity in performance tells us only that hypnotic subjects *may* be responding because of the influence of artifact; the model definitely admits that essence features can explain the performance of the real subjects even though simulating subjects are performing in the same way. If both simulators and reals report seeing an object which isn't there, the reals may obviously be indicating what is required by the situation in which they are placed, but they also may be genuinely hallucinating. The patterns of similarity between the two groups of subjects leaves us no way to judge, however. The logic underlying the model is strictly that of the "logic of alternative explanation."

The third misrepresentation is a corollary, as it were, of the two that we have discussed. This is the misconception that the real-simulating model takes an either/or look at hypnotic phenomena. Bowers (1973a) argues, for instance, that the simulator paradigm assumes from the outset that hypnotic behavior is attributable either to the state of the organism or to the demand characteristics inherent in the situation. In fact the model says only that one possible explanation of what hypnotic subjects do is in terms of the influence of the demand characteristics that they perceive and that the real-simulator design can effectively eliminate this one alternative account of the data. Other explanations, though, are quite possible, for example, the differences found may be due to the variation in personality across the two groups or to the specific consequences of one group being asked to fake. Bowers does point, though, to a danger inherent in any use of the real-simulating paradigm: hypnotic behavior attributable to suggestion will obviously look to the unsophisticated observer less convincingly hypnotic if it can be also demonstrated by a group motivated purely to respond on artifactual grounds. The danger, though, reflects an understandable misperception of the observer rather than a flaw in the logic of the paradigm.

The final misrepresentation, in contrast to those above, paradoxically deals with assertions that limit the application of the model more than is necessary. Evans (1971), for instance, argues that when differences are found between real and simulating subjects that "the nature and mechanisms of these behavioral effects of hypnosis require subsequent hypothesis testing experimentation using different methodologies [p. 13]." Evans here is too restrained by his appeal to the quasi-control nature of simulation. There is no reason why the real-simulating model cannot effectively be used to narrow inferences about the actual mechanisms of hypnosis. The specific effects of faking instruction, for example, can be investigated across a variety of stimulus contexts by applying the model and probing for cross-situational consistency in the pattern of behavioral differences found. Research of this kind—application of multiple methods and test procedures in pursuit of consistency of data—represents a major goal for the social research scientist (see Chapter 8 for detailed discussion of the strategy).

With the logic of the real-simulating paradigm formulated in this way, we turn now to the problems that are typically associated with the model and to the empirical evidence that bears upon the paradigm.

Problem Areas Relevant to the Real-Simulating Model

Orne (1972a) states that "whenever an investigator wishes to make assertions about what subjects could not conceivably do without hypnosis because they would not have the ability or knowledge to do so, it behooves the investigator to test his belief, using the blind real-simulator design [p. 420]." The reference to ability and knowledge indicate two major uses for the real-simulating paradigm. First, the model is especially suitable for investigating the assertion that hypnosis leads to a transcendence of normal volitional capacity. Traditionally (Hull, 1933), such a problem has been the concern of other paradigms (see Chapter 2 of this book for discussion of the Same-Subjects design) but the real-simulating model seems peculiarly well equipped to answer the question precisely. The reason for this is that application of the simulating technique guarantees a particularly highly motivated group oriented to do exactly what the experimenter wants and if the performance in question is executed successfully by the model's unhypnotized subjects the question raised is answered with as much unequivocality as science can muster. Evidence, in fact, has overwhelmingly supported the position that transcendence of normal capacity is far from being a necessary attribute of hypnosis (Barber, 1969; Orne, 1959; Sutcliffe, 1958, 1960). Nowhere has it been found that hypnotic subjects perform in a way that waking or role-playing subjects cannot.

The second related issue to which the model is selectively attuned is represented by the question "do behavioral effects exist that are specific to hypnosis"? As we have seen, the uniqueness of behavioral response is something many have mistakenly assumed can be answered affirmatively by applying the model. The major use of the paradigm, however, lies in its capacity to negate such a claim. If simulating subjects perform identically to real subjects then the experimenter can be certain that the effect he is investigating is not at all specific, or unique to hypnosis. Differences between the two groups, however, do not establish that specificity exists and the application of the real-simulating model is only the first step toward the claim that uniqueness has been found. Before specificity can be inferred the investigator interested in the effects of hypnosis must carefully eliminate as many alternative accounts of the pattern of differences found as possible in the search for influences other than demand characteristics which might explain the results.

The simulation task is uniquely suitable for assessing how much of an experimenter's intent is actually implied by his procedures. One of the most primary purposes of the model–one that has already been discussed–is the adoption of the simulator paradigm as a means of assessing the adequacy of the experimenter's manipulations. Whenever an experimenter attempts to deceive hypnotic subjects as to the true nature of his intent, the real-simulating paradigm of hypnosis is especially called for. Evans and Orne's (1966, 1971) case of the disappearing hypnotist and the manipulation by Orne *et al.* (1968) of an "extra experimental" context concretely illustrate the point.

The question of whether an individual in hypnosis will perform in a way that he would refuse to do otherwise is a problem requiring deception by the experimenter and it is one which, by definition, pushes the subject to the limits of his control. No responsible experimenter, for example, would ask any subject to injure himself or others, or to commit antisocial acts. The whole problem of antisocial behavior places the hypnosis investigator in a dilemma (Orne, 1972b) and this area of inquiry raises a question which is very relevant to the concerns of the real-simulating model as it is to other paradigms (for example, Sarbin's, Chapter 4; Sutcliffe's, Chapter 5 of this book) as well: "What is the extent of control possible without hypnosis?" It is hard to see, however, that the contribution of standard experimental design to the problem can ever be a positive one. How can the deception necessary for a study of antisocial behavior ever be instituted in the experimental setting when the hypnotist–experimenter must convince the subject of the genuineness of a request that obviously oversteps the limits of his role? The real-simulating model would be in the peculiar position of struggling to establish a group of quasi-control subjects who are sensitized to do what the experimenter wishes, but also to set up a group of subjects which is expected to deny one of the major reasons assumed to lie behind its participation in the study—involvement in *responsible* pursuit of scientific knowledge. The problems associated with research into antisocial influences of hypnosis are highly complex. The study by Orne and Evans (1965), which adopted the real-simulating model, set the stage, as it were, for psychology to solve the issue. Others have analyzed the problem (for example, Coe, Kobayashi, & Howard, 1972; Conn, 1972; Kline, 1972; Parrish, 1974; Watkins, 1972a), but resolution has never been achieved.

Finally, as with other paradigms analyzed in this book the issue of whether there are particular features which characterize hypnosis is one of special relevance to this model as it is to others. Any differences that distinguish real subjects from simulating subjects are potential indicators of essence characteristics of the hypnotic state. Consideration then of the differences that have been found between real and simulating subjects is obviously highly relevant to proper evaluation of the model. The next section therefore reviews results which are offered in support of the differentiation of trance and artifact and looks closely at the data available to justify the simulation task as an efficient tool of inquiry. Finally, evidence will be considered which bears upon the limitations of the inferences that can nevertheless be drawn from the model when it is applied in practice and behavioral differences are found.

EVIDENCE RELATING TO THE REAL-SIMULATING PARADIGM

In outlining the theory lying behind the real-simulating model we considered the implicit assumption of the paradigm regarding the motivational accompaniments of hypnosis. We saw how some uncertainty has been attached to the model regarding whether or not an increase in motivation is a product of the trance state. The evidence bearing on this issue suggests in fact that hypnosis does not generally produce a special willingness in hypnotized subjects to carry out the hypnotist's requests, but that in some hypnotized subjects there nevertheless does exist a particular desire to satisfy the hypnotist's demands. Recent work, however, has isolated a placebo component that is related to hypnosis (McGlashan, Evans, & Orne, 1969; Orne, 1974a), so any claims regarding "essential" motivational features must be analyzed carefully.

As Orne (1963, 1966) has acknowledged there seems ample evidence in the clinical literature to suggest that hypnosis per se enhances motivation, but there is considerable experimental evidence to suggest the contrary. Data show that prior to induction insusceptible rather than susceptible subjects demonstrated superior performance on a physical endurance task (Rosenhan & London,

1963a; see also Shor, 1964; London & Fuhrer, 1961; Chapter 7 of this book for detailed analysis of this issue). Evidence on the effectiveness of posthypnotic suggestion is also relevant. Damaser (1964), for instance, found that fewer subjects given a posthypnotic suggestion to send a postcard to their hypnotist every day did so as compared with a group given a simple waking request. At a more anecdotal level, Orne (1963) reports that insusceptible subjects are more reliable and punctual than susceptible subjects in keeping appointments. Evidence has built up, in fact, from a variety of such sources to indicate that, far from hypnosis necessarily increasing the motivation of subjects to carry out requests from their hypnotist, a subject who is less susceptible to hypnosis may in some senses be more willing to comply than a subject who is deeply susceptible.

The available data, however, are not entirely clear cut. Measures of motivation can be misleading because it is difficult to know how exactly one ought to index "increased motivation." The susceptible subject may choose a lower level of shock (Shor, 1964), or be late for appointments, and show less persistence in his postexperimental behavior than waking subjects do but nevertheless he may care very intensely about what the hypnotist wants and it is involvement of this kind that could constitute the motivational impact of hypnosis. Supporting evidence for this claim has been presented by Sheehan (1971b) who found that real susceptible rather than insusceptible simulating subjects were prepared to contravene a preconception about trance in order to do what their hypnotist really wanted. After subjects had been led previously to expect that a response would continue automatically, real and not simulating subjects stopped responding to the hypnotist's use of an appropriate cue word when he subtly communicated to subjects that he no longer really expected them to respond. Data suggested that some real subjects were especially desirous to please while other susceptible subjects were not and that the differentiating factor was the personality of the subject. Further, susceptible subjects who countered their expectation in order to accord with the experimenter's implied intent were consistently more deferent and submissive in their characteristic patterns of interpersonal relations than those who did not contravene their preconception.

This motivational issue underlying the theoretical formulations of the model is still as yet unresolved. There is certainly far from overwhelming evidence to suggest that the link between heightened motivation and hypnosis is a necessary one which reflects an essence feature of the state. Yet Orne's theorizing may well have been correct in borrowing initially on some of White's (1941a, b) early notions about motivations in hypnosis. Recent evidence has suggested there is a particular desire to please in some susceptible subjects and the importance of the intent of the hypnotist has now emerged as a major factor to be considered in our understanding of hypnotic events (Sheehan, 1971b; Sheehan & Bowman, 1973; Sheehan & Dolby, 1975).

We turn now to considering the major sources of differences that have been observed in the literature between real and simulating subjects. These differences must be considered carefully—the logic of the paradigm indicates that it is here where the essence features of the trance state most probably lie.

Real versus Simulating Behavior

Hypnosis researchers frequently record how difficult it is to obtain differences between real and simulating subjects (Blum & Graef, 1971; Bowers, 1966; Orne & Evans, 1966; Scheibe, Gray, and & Keim, 1968; Sheehan, 1969, 1971a; Shor, 1964); simulators rarely are distinguished in their behavioral response from susceptible subjects. Damaser, Shor, and Orne (1963), for example, showed that physiological alterations in real subjects involving heart rate and GSR were comparably present in simulating subjects following hypnotic suggestions of particular mood states. Sheehan (1969) also found equivalent patterns of performance across a wide variety of psychological tests after both real and simulating subjects received anxiety conflict suggestions. O'Connell, Shor, and Orne (1970) conducted a comprehensive study on age regression and found that simulating subjects yielded behavior which in every respect could not be discriminated from that shown by susceptible subjects. Differences between the two groups are clearly the exception rather than the rule and when one grasps the procedures of the paradigm it is not difficult to understand why this should be so; the simulation technique is a highly motivating one. For this reason, the model is much more likely to yield similarities rather than differences in response, or if differences do occur they nearly always indicate nonstandardized application of the simulation technique, or the overzealousness of the simulators in their role—insusceptible simulating subjects, for example, often perform better than hypnotic subjects (Barber & Calverley, 1966; Orne & Evans, 1966; Orne, Sheehan, & Evans, 1968; Sheehan, 1971b).

Leaving aside for the moment discussion of the patterns of performance found when the real-simulating model as formulated in this chapter has not been applied (for example, Graham & Schwarz, 1973; Greene & Reyher, 1972; Moore, 1964; Perkins & Reyher, 1971; Reyher, 1967; Reyher & Smyth, 1971; Rokeach, Reyher, & Wiseman, 1968) four major areas of study have indicated performance differences between real and simulating subjects. The classification does not do justice to all instances in which group differences have been observed (for example, Graham & Schwarz, 1973), but our categorization orders the majority of them. To summarize briefly these differences: real subjects have responded posthypnotically outside of the experimental context (Orne, Sheehan, & Evans, 1968) and countered preconceptions about compulsive responding (Sheehan, 1971b) while simulators did not. Real subjects showed evidence of trance logic while insusceptible, simulating subjects did not (Orne, 1959); the finding, though, has not replicated consistently (for example, Peters, 1973). Real subjects showed frequent instances of source amnesia while simulators did not (Evans & Thorn, 1966) and susceptible subjects have appeared to demonstrate distinctive cognitive styles of coping with material that was blocked from memory (Evans, 1972). Finally, real subjects failed to terminate hypnosis when the hypnotist disappeared from the test setting while simulators ceased responding immediately (Evans & Orne, 1971).

We have already discussed some of these differences elsewhere in this book. Johnson, Maher, and Barber (1972), for example, found evidence of trance logic behavior in simulators—a pattern of results quite contrary to the early observations of Orne (1959), but which is consistent with the data of Blum and Graef (1971) and some of the results of McDonald and Smith (1975) and Peters (1973), whose work indicated the absence of differences between good hypnotic subjects and poorly susceptible simulators across a range of individual measures of trance logic. Studies have clearly varied in the extent to which trance logic is evident among hypnotic subjects. Insofar as trance logic is regarded by Orne as "one of the major characteristics of hypnosis [Orne, 1959, p. 296]"—although not *the* defining characteristic (see Orne, 1974b)—it seems fair to say from the evidence that the conclusiveness of this assertion has yet to be demonstrated. Data seem to show that the contribution of hypnosis to tolerance of incongruity in deeply hypnotized subjects still remains somewhat indistinct from the influence of subjects' expectations and prior knowledge about appropriate ways of responding (for further discussion of this issue see Chapter 3 of this book).

Let us consider again for the moment the case of the disappearing hypnotist (Orne & Evans, 1966; Evans & Orne, 1971). Evans and Orne argued that the disappearance of the hypnotist would automatically and immediately terminate hypnosis if the trance state did not exist beyond the simple relationship existing between experimenter and subject. The study misinterprets Sarbin's account of hypnosis (see Chapter 4 of this book), but represents an interesting experiment which highlights an often-cited source of real-simulating differences.

Attacking a role-enactment conception of hypnosis, Orne and Evans inferred from their finding that simulators terminated while hypnotic subjects did not, that hypnosis produced changes within the real subjects which were not at all predictable in simple social–psychological terms. A variety of normal social processes, however, may explain the pattern of results that they found. Barber (1972) comments that similar findings would have emerged if Evans and Orne had simply asked a group of subjects first to relax with their eyes closed. This explanation aside, a more plausible account of their results comes from Bowers (1973a) who implicitly suggests that the differences found can be explained in terms of attribution theory. Following Bower's line of argument, it seems reasonable to assert that simulators would perceive their behavior as controlled and maintained by external factors whereas real subjects attribute behavior to themselves rather than to outside influences. Davison and Valine (1969) found that if a person perceives his behavior as determined by external factors then his behavior will change as external influence changes. A ready explanation of Evans and Orne's data thus becomes available. If real subjects self-attribute behavior, a significant alteration in the external environment such as the disappearance of the hypnotist would not necessarily have immediate implications for their behavior which (as Bowers states) may quite naturally persist well beyond the termination of the demands that initially engineered their performance. Simulators who are immune to the experience of hypnotic events would not self-attribute behavior and hence would respond much more quickly to the change in external contingencies.

Bowers, in fact, argues on other grounds that trance effects can be formally distinguished operationally from the effect of demand characteristic variables. In a rather ingenious study (Bowers, 1966) he took the presence or absence of "volitional quality of response" as the criterion of the presence or absence of an altered state of consciousness, hypnosis. In his design an experimenter (E_1) hypnotized subjects and administered a posthypnotic suggestion that they would begin all sentences in an experimental Taffel-type task with "he" and "they." Susceptible and simulating subjects were employed but there were some unusual departures from the routine procedures of the real-simulating model. Simulators were awakened prior to the critical suggestion and asked to role play subsequently. A second experimenter (E_2) then tested real and faking subjects on the task and ostensibly concluded the study. E_1 returned, however, and asked if subjects would speak to a third experimenter (E_3), who was doing some pilot research in an experiment on verbal behavior. In the postexperimental inquiry conducted by E_3, simulators, but not reals, reported the voluntary nature of their earlier response to testing on the Taffel-type task. All simulators testified that their use of "he" and "they" was voluntary, whereas 12 of 14 hypnotic subjects made no such testimony. Bowers argued that his design placed trance and demand characteristic variables in opposition with each other. The significant fact was that neither real nor faking subjects received any information about how to behave after the study had formally concluded, yet the supposedly identical alteration in demand characteristics (it now being all right to "confess") did not affect the two groups similarly. The evidence is presented as offering hard line support for the existence of an hypnotic state.

Bowers' results for his hypnotic group are interesting: they show that hypnotic subjects who are requested to report honestly are still not willing to assert any voluntary feature of their response. Results for simulators, however, could well be a function of the special set of instructions that they received initially. Differences could have been as much an artifact of the factors peculiarly affecting simulating subjects as they were of hypnotic influence on real subjects. The simulating group, contrary to the real group, was asked to pretend their response was genuinely hypnotic, that is, to pretend that they knew (and E_1 knew) that their response would be otherwise. It seems plausible to argue that it is as reasonable to expect the simulator will say after the study is concluded and when his specific role is terminated, that "it was all voluntary," as it is to expect he will say "it was all involuntary" when the role is obviously in operation during the experiment proper. If role-playing variables do pertain to the behavior of the hypnotic subjects, it is highly unlikely that the procedures of the study demarcated the limits of role playing for real subjects nearly as obviously as they did for faking subjects.

Without reviewing all of the evidence in detailed fashion it is clear from consideration of just these few studies that when differences between real and simulating subjects are obtained, they are suggestive of "trance effects" rather than unequivocal demonstrations of them. The logic of the real-simulating paradigm strictly argues for results that *may* be due to hypnosis, it seems pertinent therefore to stipulate that when differences emerge any model of hypnosis aiming to be comprehensive should routinely conduct validity checks and systematically eliminate as many rival, alternative explanations as possible. To the extent that such validating operations are successful, an experimenter can then have increasing confidence that the group differences he has found truly reflect essence features of hypnosis.

There are rival approaches to the occurrence of hypnotic role-playing differences that have yet to be fully explored. Reyher (1972), argues, for instance, for the provocative notion that the direction of simulation is asymmetrical; if hypnosis is in fact an altered state of awareness, he claims that hypnotized subjects will not be able to simulate the waking state as well as waking subjects are able to simulate hypnosis. It would be interesting in this regard to test whether the pattern of performance on a given task that distinguishes insusceptible simulating subjects from real subjects would disappear when a set of susceptible subjects are instructed to simulate waking performance on the same task. If the features of trance performance found earlier nevertheless remain the same for the real subjects it would be tempting to accept the original data as evidence which offers quite strong support for either a state or trait theory of hypnosis. An initial attempt to explore this valuable hypothesis has been attempted (Reyher, 1973), but the procedures employed were inadequate to firmly attest the point.

Because it appeals so strongly to the logic of alternative explanation, it is critical as far as the real-simulating paradigm of hypnosis is concerned to explore empirically the major limitations on the inferences that can be drawn from the model when group differences emerge. As we have seen above, two major limitations exist: differences may be due to the personality variation among the two groups by reason of subjects' differential susceptibilities to hypnosis, or differences may be due to the psychological consequences of the insusceptible group alone receiving faking instruction. Very little work has explored the former possibility, but recent evidence bears directly upon the latter and it is to this that we turn now.

Evidence Relating to Limitations on the Model's Inferences Concerning Essence Features of Hypnosis

Studies have failed to reliably differentiate susceptible from insusceptible subjects in terms of personality characteristics (Deckert & West, 1963; see also Chapters 2 and 5 for discussion of this issue); nevertheless, the possibility remains that such differences could exist and so influence simulators to perform differently from real subjects. Two methodological alternatives could be said to meet the problem. First, one might simply avoid the issue entirely by requesting susceptible subjects to simulate. The real-simulating model, however, insists on guaranteed immunity from hypnosis for its quasi-control group and the assertion that highly susceptible subjects are always able easily and comfortably to resist trance has received scant support (Austin *et al.*, 1963). The second alternative, and the more indirect one, is to investigate what differences in personality exist between real and insusceptible subjects on those dependent variables relating to the hypotheses under study. The appropriate design to test this second alternative must determine personality differences among subjects before simulators are asked to fake or susceptible subjects are hypnotized. Complete independence of the two testing contexts—test for personality and test for hypnotic susceptibility—is normally quite difficult to achieve. Studies have aimed at some degree of separation (London, Cooper, & Johnson, 1962; Melei & Hilgard, 1964) but have been incomplete in their attempts. Two experiments (Sheehan, 1970; Zamansky & Brightbill, 1965) have achieved the independence in question, however, and both found no personality differences between susceptible and insusceptible subjects on the particular variables that they considered. There seems little justification in the current literature for the assertion that actual differences in personality between real and simulating subjects would confound the interpretation of group differences that are observed in the hypnotic context.

The implications for interpretation of one group being given faking instruction and the other not are much more important to the real-simulating model. Consider for the moment the pattern of results which was found for real and simulating subjects who performed on a word association task before and after the hypnotist had administered anxiety conflict suggestions (Sheehan, 1969). Table 6.2 shows the average number of unusual word association responses (words not reported anywhere by a normative sample) given by real and simulating subjects. Data indicate that hypnotic subjects showed less originality of response in the conflict condition while simulators showed more. One possible interpretation of this pattern of findings is that there was a true hypnotic effect of the anxiety suggestions, hypnosis creating a loss of spontaneity in susceptible subjects. Close perusal of the task of simulation, however,

TABLE 6.2
Average Number of Original Responses for Subject Groups in the Preconflict and Conflict Conditions

	Group	
Condition	Hypnotic	Simulating
Preconflict	3.79	.85
Conflict	3.31	2.08

[a]Adapted from Sheehan (1969). Copyright 1969 by the American Psychological Association. Reproduced by permission.

indicates a highly plausible alternative account. Simulators–somewhat analagous to malingerers in military service (Rosenberg & Feldberg, 1944)–may have simply constricted their response in the preconflict condition, because they were quite unsure of themselves as to what they could do that would satisfy the hypnotist (who at that time had given subjects no special instruction of any kind). Looked at in this way, their first response could have been an attempt to avoid giving themselves away and to give the safest response possible. On the second condition the instructions of the hypnotist implied much more clearly how they were to respond and simulators would have picked up the obvious cue that some change in response was required. The increase in original response, then, could have been a function of the specific demand characteristics arising from simulators' perceptions of the change in test conditions. If this analysis is correct the apparent loss of the hypnotic subjects was more a function of the situation simulators were in than of the influence of hypnosis on real subjects. What is at issue here is the existence of special treatment aspects of simulation. It is essential that research establish what these "treatment" aspects of simulation are, and the extent to which their presence affects the legitimacy of the experimenter's inferences.

Sheehan (1970, 1971c) reports data on the existence and determining conditions of these simulation effects. In the first of his experiments real and simulating subjects were tested inside and outside of the hypnotic setting. The testing outside hypnosis was completely divorced from the hypnotic setting; subjects had not at that time been approached for any hypnotic participation and personality tests were administered entirely for a neutral purpose. Subjects were later recruited by another experimenter for hypnosis and the real-simulating model was applied to conduct a study ostensibly relating hypnotic susceptibility to performance on a battery of tests "fortuitously" including those tests subjects had done previously. Real and faking subjects were appropriately instructed and taken to the hypnotist who without further ado simply asked subjects to complete the required battery of tests. The hypnotist then induced hypnosis and asked subjects to repeat the battery of tests once more. A postexperimental inquiry was conducted to determine subjects' perceptions of the study and no subject was found to be aware of the link between the first and second testings. The critical comparison was between simulating subjects' performance outside hypnosis (before they were asked to role play) and their performance on the same tests in the hypnotic setting just prior to induction (after role-playing instructions had been given but before the hypnotist had given any special instructions to indicate what he wanted them precisely to do). The evidence indicated that real subjects performed the same across the two testings, but simulators showed much lower adjustment scores (indicating less conflict and negative affect) on a sentence completion test inside the hypnotic setting as compared to outside it. The data suggest that the simulators were faced with a poorly defined task and in the absence of any indications from the hypnotist they performed "securely" by responding in a way which minimally revealed themselves personally. The second of the two studies (Sheehan, 1971c) showed that this effect was related to performance on unstructured rather than structured tasks. Together the two studies in the program of research showed: (1) that simulation effects do, in fact, exist and may therefore be influencing the behavior of simulating subjects; and (2) that there are nevertheless specifiable conditions which determine the presence or absence of these effects. Task structure, however, may not be the only determining influence–perceived difficulty of the task, and extent of "feeling lost" (Sheehan, 1971a) may also be related to the effects in question.

The artifactual consequences of an experimenter's procedures–typified by the above analysis of simulation effects–are very easy to overlook. Orne and Scheibe (1964), for example, found that subjects exposed to the "trappings" (demand characteristics) of a sensory deprivation experiment reported deprivation effects while those not exposed to the selected cues showed far fewer effects, performance measures being taken on both motor and cognitive tasks. Both groups were isolated for four hours but not assumed to be sensorily deprived. Results were interpreted as reflecting the influence of the cue characteristics present in the situation but close consideration suggests that the differences found between experimental (cues present) and control (cues absent) subjects are in fact equivocal. Control subjects were told they were control subjects and could therefore have inhibited any real deprivation effects that might in fact have existed for the experimental group. Furthermore, as Weber and Cook (1972) point out, Orne and Scheibe's findings may have resulted simply from anxiety aroused by the medical apparatus in conjunction with the social isolation to which all subjects were exposed. The study is a good illustration of the axiomatic fact that even carefully selected procedures of comparison have unintended consequences that may themselves contaminate the meaning of data that are collected.

After considering the evidence which directly bears upon the model's inferences–in particular, those results relating to simulation–we move now to consideration of the effectiveness of the simulation task as such. We have reviewed its methodological value as a tool of inquiry and its limitations by way of inferences when the technique is applied. We turn now to the evidence which is available to support its adequacy as a comparison condition. Here, the relevant factors are (a) the actual success of simulation as a motivating technique, (b) the extent to which the condition constitutes a standardized task, and how readily simulation can be distinguished in its effectiveness from other role-playing techniques.

Effectiveness of Simulation

There is ample evidence to document how well simulating subjects detect and respond to the cues that are available to them. Johnson *et al.* (1972) found simulators showed greater response to hallucination suggestion than real subjects and Williamsen, Johnson, and Eriksen (1965) in their study of amnesia found simulators *more* effective than real subjects, as did Orne, Sheehan, and Evans (1968) in their study of posthypnotic responding. Simulators show as much tendency as susceptible subjects to tolerate painful stimuli without flinching (Shor, 1964) and are equally able to recall material from the past (O'Connell, Shor, & Orne, 1970). Across the entire range of hypnotic tasks there seems to be no routine behavior manifested by the hypnotized subject that cannot also be produced by the simulator. The broad spectrum of evidence illustrating behavioral similarities between real and hypnotic subjects in itself attests the motivational efficacy of the simulating condition.

The alleged usefulness of the simulator comparison group stems partly from the fact that the model assumes it is a reliable standard against which the performance of real subjects can be assessed. The model implicitly assumes that simulators will not only perform well as a group in the hypnotic setting but will also be motivated to respond uniformly well to the cue characteristics associated with hypnotic test procedures. Overley and Levitt (1968), however, have directly challenged the adequacy of the simulating control in this regard. In test of the expected homogeneity of "simulator" performance Overley and Levitt found marked evidence of strong variability among their role-playing subjects in performance on standard tests of hypnotic susceptibility. Table 6.3 lists their results for two groups in simulating subjects: Group A (insusceptible to hypnosis) and Group B (subjects capable of at least moderate response to hypnotic suggestion). Results in Table 6.3 clearly demonstrate heterogeneity of performance for faking subjects; both sets of role-playing subjects were far from reliable in their task of simulation. It is important to note that even though simulators were indistinguishable from real subjects in their overall performance, the lack of uniformity in their response basically undermines the adequacy of

TABLE 6.3
Performances on 14 Suggested Behaviors
Under Voluntary Control

	Susceptible subjects	Simulator group A	Simulator group B
	9	12	11
	10	12	12
	8	13	3
	10	10	12
	9	13	14
	13	0	6
	13	8	10
	10	14	8
	11	7	
	9		
N:	10	9	8
$\bar{X}$:	10.2	9.9	9.5
SD:	1.57	4.40	3.62
Range:	8–13	0–13	3–14

[a]From Overley and Levitt (1968). Quoted from the October 1968 *International Journal of Clinical and Experimental Hypnosis.* Copyrighted by The Society for Clinical and Experimental Hypnosis, October 1968.

the simulating technique. Only some simulating subjects, it seems, can really be expected to carry out their experimental purpose adequately.

Sheehan (1973a) repeated the essential conditions of Overley and Levitt's (1968) study and found comparable results. However, in addition to the attempted replication he specifically tested the hypothesis that the set of faking instructions and procedures associated with the instructions used by Overley and Levitt in their original experiment were not really adequate and proper for the task of simulation. Close consideration of Overley and Levitt's method indicated that in contrast to the procedures typically adopted for the simulation condition they did not give the exact same instructions nor did they instruct their subjects to fake immediately prior to hypnotic testing. They administered their instructions, in fact, some weeks before hypnotic assessment and it is conceivable that a delay of this kind could have diminished the level of motivation of their subjects and so reduced the quality of their faking performance. Sheehan investigated the effect of the delay variable by administering the exact set of instructions laid down by Overley and Levitt to comparable groups of susceptible and insusceptible faking subjects, either immediately prior to or two weeks before hypnotic testing. The experimental design generated four groups of faking subjects and the results of these groups on standard hypnotic susceptibility tasks are reported in Table 6.4. For comparison purposes this table also includes results for real and simulating subjects tested in exact application of the real-simulating model on the identical tasks. For the purpose of discussion the term "simulating" distinguishes those subjects tested according to Orne's procedures from "faking" subjects who were tested under the procedures laid down by Overley and Levitt (1968).

Results in Table 6.4 show that heterogeneity of faking performance characterized the response of "faking" but not "simulating" subjects. The major findings of Overley and Levitt represented in Table 6.3 were replicated for the faking subjects who were significantly heterogeneous in their pretense, some of these subjects clearly failing very badly in their task. Systematic variation of the factors of "delay" and "susceptibility" clarified the full meaning of Overley and Levitt's original set of data. Table 6.4 shows that susceptibility to hypnosis was associated with variable faking performance quite irrespective of the period of delay in subjects receiving instruction. Insusceptible subjects, nevertheless, yielded variable performance when faking instruction was separated in time from hypnotic testing. The most significant aspect of the evidence is that the simulating subjects were appreciably more successful role players than any of the faking groups. They were not only homogeneous in their pretense behavior, but passed significantly more items than the best of the four faking groups ($p < .05$). The results for simulating subjects clearly indicated that it is a mistake to regard Overley and Levitt's evidence of heterogeneity as in any way relevant to the simulating condition as laid down by Orne (1959, 1969, 1971, 1972a).

When simulators' performance in Table 6.4 is considered closely it is apparent that neither of the factors of delay or susceptibility can entirely explain the relatively poor level of performance of "faking" subjects. Interpretation in some way has to account for the fact that the best faking group in the study still performed less well than simulating subjects. It appears that the nature of Overley and Levitt's faking instruction is a necessary third factor relevant to the quality of their subjects' role-playing performance. Table 6.5 sets out in serial order the essential characteristics of both sets of instructions–Orne's "simulating" instruction and Overley and Levitt's "faking" instruction. Aside from the observation that the simulation set is obviously the more explicit set of instructions the analysis indicated three substantial points of difference. First, the task of "avoiding hypnosis" is described as easy for the subject in both instructions but the task of pretending is defined as difficult only for the simulating group. Second, simulating but not faking subjects are told the experimenter knows some subjects are faking in the study. Third, simulators are alone told that

TABLE 6.4
Performance of Real, Simulating, and Faking Subjects (Low and High Susceptibility) Operating under Delay and No-Delay Instructions on 12 Suggested Behaviors in the SHSS:C[a]

	Simulating (insusceptible) subjects	Real (susceptible) subjects	Faking low-delay subjects[b]	Faking low-no delay subjects	Faking high-delay subjects[c]	Faking high-no delay subjects
	10*	11	7	10	11	9
	9	10	9	8*	9	5
	12	9	10	11	10	0*
	11	9	7*	10	2*	11
	11	12	11	11	4*	5*
	11	5	10	9*	6*	11
	10	8	11	10	8*	11
	11	9	8*	10	7*	10
	11	10	11	10*	11	8
	11	11	3*	9	11	8
$\bar{X}$:	10.70	9.4	8.7	9.8	7.9	7.8
SD:	.68	1.95	2.54	.92	3.14	3.55
Range:	9–12	5–12	3–11	8–11	2–11	0–11

Note: An asterisk* denotes those faking subjects who in the hypnotic setting failed to pass any item available for change (that is, failed by them in the screening session).

[a]From Sheehan (1973a). Quoted from the July 1973 *International Journal of Clinical and Experimental Hypnosis*. Copyrighted by the Society for Clinical and Experimental Hypnosis, July 1973.

[b]This group corresponds to Group A simulators in Table 6.3.

[c]This group corresponds to Group B simulators in Table 6.3.

TABLE 6.5
Analysis of the Features of "Faking" and "Simulating" Instructions

Faking set (Overley & Levitt, 1968)

[a]1. Pretend to be hypnotized and stay out of hypnosis.
[b]2. The task of staying out of hypnosis is easy.
[c]3. Fool the hypnotist and make him believe you are hypnotized.
[d]4. The hypnotist will terminate the session if he finds out; you are deceiving successfully if he carries on.

Simulating set (Sheehan, 1973a)

[b]1. You have tried to enter hypnosis before. It was difficult; others are more responsive.
[a]2. Pretend to be (deeply) hypnotized and stay out of hypnosis.
[c]3. Fool the hypnotist and make him believe you are hypnotized.
4. Use all the cues you can to help you in your task.
5. The hypnotist knows some subjects are simulating in the study but doesn't know who they are.
[d]6. The hypnotist will terminate the session if he finds out; you are deceiving successfully if he carries on.
7. The task of simulation is difficult.
8. Intelligent subjects can handle the task successfully.

Note: Comparable features in the two sets of instructions are marked by a similar prescript (*a*, *b*, *c*, or *d*).

"intelligent people can handle the deception successfully." These differences suggest why simulators should be more motivated for their task of deception than faking subjects. The experimenter stresses to this group alone that their role-playing task is difficult but possible, individually challenges their intellect to meet the problem at hand, and imparts more knowledge to them than to faking subjects about the extent of deception involved in the experiment. Under simulating instruction, subjects may be better able to fool the hypnotist–experimenter simply because they feel they have more accurate ideas about the "odds" against their disclosure. This discussion points importantly to the critical need to acknowledge the intricacies of instructions to subjects and the variable nature of the effects that can be associated with them.

The efficiency of the simulating technique can be further assessed in terms of the ease with which simulators can be detected in their pretense. Orne (1959) argued that experienced hypnotists testing subjects "blind" find it impossible to reliably discriminate real from simulating performance. Blum and Graef (1971) tested six subjects including one male and one female simulator and maintained that simulation becomes apparent as sessions continue. In their study, however, they failed to control for the effect of their changing opinions of subjects' identities on subjects' subsequent test performance and they argued post hoc without attempting to cross validate the differences that were found. Generally, the evidence on the detection of simulation reinforces the evidence available elsewhere on the adequacy of the simulating condition. When in the small number of instances simulators are detected it is nearly always because they are overzealous in their task.

Variability of Faking Procedures: Simulation as a Standardized Task

The adequacy of the simulation condition must be assessed on the basis of those procedures standard to the real-simulating model and not on other procedures which, as we have seen, lead to varying quality of role-playing performance. Taken collectively, Tables 6.3, 6.4, and 6.5 indicate that (1) the task of simulation is highly effective for its purpose, and (2) simulation as laid down by Orne's model achieves markedly better quality of performance than other faking procedures. But only when procedures are replicated precisely can the task of simulation, as an integral part of the real-simulating methodology of hypnosis, operate as an efficient tool for investigating the phenomena of trance in the way that it was intended. The tremendous variability of procedures extant in the literature–many of them located falsely under the label "simulation"–attests, in a sense, the chaotic methodological disorder of much of contemporary hypnosis research.

Studies differ markedly in their choice of susceptibility for the subjects who are asked to fake; hypnotizable subjects, for example, are used regularly for purposes of role playing (Barber, 1969; Johnson *et al.,* 1972; Katz, 1973; Overley & Levitt, 1968; Schofield & Reyher, 1974). This and other departures from uniform procedure (for example, delay in instruction) lead one to question seriously whether results across studies can be legitimately compared at all. Reyher (1962, 1967), for example, has developed a distinctive paradigm around "simulation" as a strategy of control, but the procedures which define that concept for Reyher are vastly different from those which define it for Orne. Variation in method clearly can account for the fact that differences between simulating and real subjects reliably occur for one theorist, but not for another (for detailed discussion of the procedural implications of Reyher's paradigm, see Levitt, 1963, Reyher, 1969, and Sheehan, 1971d).

It is clear that there may be no validity at all in contrasting the absence of differences in one study with the presence of differences in another when entirely different comparison procedures have been adopted. Studies employ quite varying procedures to index the same label given to their pretense subjects (Moore, 1964; Schofield & Reyher, 1974; Zimbardo, Marshall, & Maslach, 1971) and, as well, omit significant details of procedure from their reporting (for example, Graham, 1969; Lennox, 1970; Rokeach, Reyher, & Wiseman, 1968; Scheibe, Gray, & Keim, 1968) thus making cross reference of studies virtually impossible. Our argument in this regard is perhaps most forcibly illustrated by presenting a procedural analysis of the studies reported in a 1971 issue of the *International Journal of Clinical and Experimental Hypnosis* which was formally devoted to discussion of the use of the simulator control. The studies reported in this issue all used and worked with the term "simulation." Excluding an opening paper by Orne (1971) which reviewed the task of simulation, five data-oriented studies were represented in the journal (Blum & Graef, 1971; Evans & Orne, 1971; Hunt, 1971; Levitt & Overley, 1971; Sheehan, 1971c; Solomon & Goodson, 1971). Table 6.6 sets out an analysis of these studies in terms of the major rules of the simulation condition that were violated or obscured in the research that these authors reported. (Sheehan's study which has already been discussed in some detail has been excluded.) The analysis shows an alarming disparity of procedures in studies all presumably aiming to establish a similar technique of comparison. The enormous lack of uniformity of method across these experiments quite categorically excludes valid comparison of the separate sets of results that were obtained. Methodologically speaking, the variability evident in Table 6.6 (which taps only a small sample of research studies in hypnosis employing role-playing subjects) should be profoundly disturbing to the scientific researcher. One catches a glimpse of science involved in the futile task of attempting to disengage endless possibilities of procedural artifact from the multitudinous claims of authors that essence has or has not been found.

SUMMARY EVALUATION OF THE MODEL

This model, of all those that we have considered, is most thoroughly cognizant of the limitations of its techniques and of the exact nature of the logic that underlies its application. It is primarily oriented to eliminating the threat to validity from artifact and in so doing it moves us toward greater certainty of inference about hypnotic events. For the real-simulating model there is no such thing as the ideal experiment and the model itself is based on the premise that all of psychology—not just the pursuit of hypnosis—is stricken with the problem of the surplus meaning of its concepts and the ambiguities of the treatments that we adopt to measure them. The true quality of the real-simulating model lies not in the fact it advances a variety of essence-type hypotheses about hypnosis which are then tested rigorously by hypnotic-faking comparison, but in the fact it works against itself to check the validity of the inferences that might be drawn from the data that are found.

Caution is its password and therein lies the root of the frustration many feel toward the model. The paradigm is regarded by many as too limited and as a framework that involves the experimenter in a task of diminishing returns. Bowers (1966), for example, argued that the model restricts itself excessively to the similarities between real and role-playing subjects and so is concerned far too little with the clarification of differences between the two groups. This criticism is based on an error of interpretation, but it reflects the widely held feeling that the paradigm promulgates the notion that hypnosis cannot be responsible for real subjects' behavior if simulating subjects perform in the same way. The logic of alternative explanation which underlies the model is quite clear on this point—when similarities occur, effects *may* be due to artifact or they *may* be due to the true consequences of hypnosis. Misrepresentation of the logic of the paradigm, though, is not at all restricted to the interpretation of similarities of response. Behavioral *differences* between real and simulating subjects are similarly misjudged. The only correct inference to be drawn from the model's application when differences occur is that the behavior of the real subjects may be due to hypnosis but more certainly we know that the real subjects' behavior is *not* due to the influence of demand characteristics.

We have reviewed many studies which attempted to demonstrate essence characteristics of hypnosis, but in most cases the arguments on the data were too strong for the controls that were applied. Researchers who adopt the real-simulating model of hypnosis must take a great deal more care not to jump from using the technique of simulation as a method for testing the adequacy of their experimental procedures, or assessing the potential influence of demand characteristics, to adopting the method as a way of guaranteeing certainty of inferences about the hypnotic state. Part of the problem no doubt is that Orne's theoretical approach to hypnosis is biased in favor of internal process concepts, but the model he has proposed is thoroughly behavioristic in the flavor of the strategies it adopts. The nature of the model is such that the differences that are found between real and simulating subjects can never be invoked to argue unequivocally for the existence of different psychic mechanisms operating among the susceptible and insusceptible groups; mere consistency of data with the theory in question can only ever really be demonstrated. It is curious that the model works toward delineating the behavioral consequences of subjective processes but has nevertheless failed to institute rigorous procedures for examining the validity of subjects' verbal reports about what they are in fact experiencing. The model accepts at face value, for example, the validity of the preselected simulating subject's report that he has failed to experience hypnosis and also the preselected real subject's report that he has indeed experienced trance.

Closer scrutiny of subjects' postexperimental inquiry responses could add to the power of the model's inferences. An experimenter, for example, could routinely analyze real subjects' perceptions of his hypothesis to test whether they are meaningfully related to the way they behaved in the test setting. As we have already seen, when similarities occur we have no proof at all that demand characteristics are responsible for hypnotic subjects' behavior, but where real

TABLE 6.6
Summary of Simulation Studies in the
International Journal of Clinical and Experimental Hypnosis
(December, 1971)

Author(s)	Aim of study	Major rules of simulation violated	Independent or related groups used	Susceptibility of simulators	"Blindness" of the experimenter	Similarity of instructions to those used in real-simulating model	Detection of simulators	Other unusual features
Blum and Graef (1971)	Detection of simulators over time	a. Second experimenter not completely "blind" b. No exclusion of subjects the identity of whom the experimenter was certain	Independent	Low (1–3)	Partial	Similar	Yes (post hoc)	Instructions applied over an extended period of time
Solomon and Goodson (1971)	Hypnotic age regression	a. Simulators received training in their tasks	Related	Moderate (5–8)	Complete	Instructions not reported	No	The experimenter did not know any subjects

		b. Susceptible subjects were asked to fake						were simulating partial counterbalancing of groups
Levitt and Overley (1971)[a]	Hypnotic versus simulator differences	a. Instructions were delayed* b. Susceptible subjects were asked to fake	Independent	Low (0–4) and moderate (5–9)	Complete	Dissimilar	Not reported	The experimenter did not know any subjects were simulating
Hunt (1971)	Spontaneous speed effects	a. Random allocation of unselected subjects b. Insusceptibility of simulator not guaranteed	Independent	Unselected	Not clear	Instructions not reported	Not reported	Simulators given more hypnotic instruction and time to relax than real subjects
Evans and Orne (1971)	Effects of termination of trance	—	Independent	Low (0–4)	Complete	Similar	Not reported	—

[a]This information was derived from another article reporting further details of this study's procedure (Overley & Levitt, 1968).

and simulating subjects perform similarly and in addition real subjects' perceptions (reported postexperimentally) are positively related to the pattern of their own test behavior, we can at least argue confidently that the demand characteristic hypothesis has been strengthened by report data. Even though the postexperimental inquiry method itself is limited, the use here of multiple strategies supporting each other and converging to the same result must lead inevitably toward some increase in assurance about why susceptible subjects behave as they do.

Some Theoretical Implications of the Model

Theoretically speaking, the real-simulating model was originally developed from the premise of others (Gill & Brenman, 1961; White, 1941a, 1941b) that hypnosis leads to an increased motivation to please, but the evidence, as we have seen supports this contention only partially–certain types of hypnotic subjects, namely those of a deferent personality, display this kind of motivation within the trance setting (Sheehan, 1971b). If different motives are at work among hypnotic subjects it is especially important to the model that they be isolated in systematic fashion. It is still not entirely clear to what extent the real-simulating model regards the motivations of hypnotic subjects as reflecting essence features of the hypnotic state, or simply the conative aspects of the typical Experimental Subject.

Basically, the model assumes that experimental subjects generally adopt the role of a "good" subject and there is ample evidence to illustrate this point; data show that in some contexts, the cooperative experimental subject is characteristically motivated strongly enough that even the effects of posthypnotic suggestion are slight by comparison (Damaser, 1964; Kellogg, 1929; Orne, 1965a; Patten, 1930). The precise motivations of experimental subjects in these instances still remain unclear, however. The problem is highlighted to some extent in the controversy argued by Sigall, Aronson, and Van Hoose (1970) and Adair and Schachter (1972) where both sets of authors attempted to discriminate precisely the role attitudes that specifically motivate experimental subjects. Their work demonstrates the enormous difficulty of empirically differentiating subjects' varying role-taking attitudes, and how much ambiguity among dependent variables has to be eliminated in order that proper inferences can be drawn about particular adopted roles. Perhaps, as Weber and Cook (1972) argue, subject roles should be integrated into better developed theories and experimenters forced to specify the testable antecedents of the roles that they postulate. To date the real-simulating model has explained the behavior of experimental subjects within the context of a role as yet poorly differentiated from other roles the subject could also be adopting, and not until these testable antecedents are specified can we be really confident that the appropriate methodological controls have been developed. The problem of definition is an important one for the model. The real-simulating paradigm uses its major control condition (simulating technique) to analyze the implications of the "good" subject role for hypnotic subjects, but the evidence is not altogether clear as to how widely that specific role ought to be applied to experimental subjects generally.

Methodological Assumptions

The real-simulating model has outlined very carefully a number of procedures which relate to its strategies and in doing so it has made many assumptions by way of rationale that have conceptual backing but relatively little empirical support. Consider for example, the following rules of procedure that it advocates: real subjects should not know that other subjects are simulating (Orne, 1972a, p. 410); knowledge of a postexperimental inquiry to follow will help to motivate simulators in their task (Orne, 1972a, p. 412); simulation is more effective if the role-playing subject believes the experimenter is actually unaware of his identity (Orne, 1972a, p. 410); and the role of a hypnotized subject must be legitimately ascribed to a subject by significant figures whom he accepts as qualified to ascribe the role to him (Orne, 1965b, pp. 321–322). These and other assumptions that have been made by the real-simulating model appear plausible but there are surprisingly few data which directly bear upon them. The lack of empirical justification for procedural details of these kinds partially explains, no doubt, the inadequate attention hypnosis researchers have given to careful and precise replication of the model's strategies (see Table 6.6). Quite clearly, the essential elements of procedure need to be carefully listed and the evidence tabulated which attests their significance. Just as Zamansky, Scharf, and Brightbill (1964) investigated the important implications of "holding back"—a phenomenon highly pertinent to Hilgard's model—and Bowers (1967), and Sheehan and Dolby (1974) have investigated artifactual characteristics of Barber's standard set of procedures—so also further work is needed to explore the empirical justification of the extensive rationale the real-simulating model offers to support its adopted procedures. Relevant work has been conducted on simulation effects (Sheehan, 1969, 1971a, b) and isolated variables such as "awareness of faking" (Sheehan & Marsh, 1974) have begun to be studied, but the efficacy of simulation is now established well enough that we should know much more about the reasons why simulators (as opposed to reals) perform precisely in the way that they do.

To take an illustration of a methodological procedure not explored nearly as fully as might be by the real-simulating model and one that is germane to its rationale, let us consider the blind procedure of hypnotic testing that the model advocates so strongly. Here, the model states explicitly that the hypnotist who is testing real and simulating subjects must be kept unaware as to subjects' actual hypnotic identities. Two problems exist in this regard. The first reflects the fact that the hypnotist conducting the testing may fail to maintain blindness; experimenters will always guess as to subjects' identities and their guesses will inevitably affect behavioral outcomes. The real-simulating model copes with this problem by arguing that subjects are excluded if the hypnotist is certain of the susceptibility of the subject he is testing, but there are no procedures laid down which check for the consequences of an experimenter's emerging awareness as to subjects' identities. Guy, Gross, and Dennis (1967) suggest that the problem of maintaining blindness can be dealt with easily by arranging for a separate group of experimenters to assess subjects after they have been administered an experimental treatment. The procedure that they recommend is far too costly in terms of normal research resources, but they usefully draw attention to the fact that minimizing involvement in some way inevitably reduces bias and produces a more objective appraisal of behavioral outcomes.

The second problem that arises with respect to the experimenter-blindness strategy stems from the fact that the procedures advocated by the real-simulating model are designed to work most effectively when the hypnotist who is conducting testing actually expects that differences will emerge. Orne's procedures were formulated to cope with the possibility that the hypnotist will affect subjects differentially if he knows that the subjects he is testing are distinct. The blind-experimenter procedure guarantees then (as long as the experimenter maintains blindness) that subjects will not be treated differentially, at least in any systematic fashion that would affect the dependent variables under scrutiny. Yet many applications of the real-simulating model are designed to show that no differences between groups can really be expected to emerge (Orne, 1959; Sheehan, 1969) and in such a situation any attempt to establish blindness in the experimenter who is conducting testing is, technically speaking, unnecessary. A hypnotist who believes real and simulating subjects will perform the same does not have to be blind in order to inadvertently influence the subjects he is testing to perform in similar fashion. The "conviction of the experimenter" is obviously an important variable in the design of any hypnotic experiment and the real-simulating model fails to recognize this variable sufficiently. The data of Fisher, Cole, Rickels, and Uhlenhuth (1964) further illustrate the point. These authors found that enthusiasm by an experimenter for a drug's effect was an influential determinant of results even though the study conducted was run using a double-blind control. The evidence indicates that "real" drug effects may be inhibited when they are tested without conviction on the part of the physician who is administering the treatment. It seems plausible to argue that the procedures of the real-simulating model will be most relevant (and effective) only when the hypnotist who is conducting the testing is convinced that group differences will truly emerge.

Demand characteristics are important only insofar as they interact with variables under investigation and while they can never be eliminated it is nevertheless essential to investigate the nature of their interaction. We need to know the defining properties of the situations where they are truly influential. Orne's model makes no discrimination among situations where demand characteristics are operative and those in which they are not. The problem of defining the conditions when such variables are influential has to date been solved in psychology more by accident than by design. Relevant areas of influence that have arisen are those pertaining to the arousal of aftereffects of imagined stimuli (Singer & Sheehan, 1965), the effect of attitudes on conditioning (Cook & Harris, 1937; Mowrer, 1938; Silverman, 1960); lie detection (Gustafson & Orne, 1965); antisocial behavior (Orne, 1962b, 1972b); and hypnosis. A review of the literature suggests that the role of demand characteristics is crucial when widely different results have been found in the same area and also when similar results are found in widely different areas. It is clearly not good enough, however, to define the areas of special methodological interest by the variance and confusion of results that emerge. Recent work by McDonald and Smith (1975) has suggested that data discrepancies concerning the phenomenon of trance logic can be explained in terms of the differential cues hypnotists and their procedures convey to subjects. Future research involving cue manipulation would advance the model theoretically, if the status of phenomena like "trance logic" could be unequivocally resolved.

It seems particularly necessary not only to demonstrate when social, artifactual influences are not at work in any experimental situation, but also to state how artifact is best controlled once its possible presence has been indicated—we could, for instance, cut down the cues available to subjects to the point where real subjects keep on performing but simulators no longer go undetected (Perry, 1963). Possibilities for the control of artifact have not been formally considered within the framework of Orne's model. Generally, the obvious solution might be for research to be conducted in the naturalistic setting, but the limitations of such an approach have been well catalogued elsewhere (Weber & Cook, 1972). Another solution is the "disguised experiment" illustrated, for example, by a study of the effects on a group of observers of the manipulation of a variable when the observers in question do not know their reactions are being assessed. It is hard though to achieve the kind of study (Rosenzweig, 1933) whereby the purpose of an experiment is kept from a subject who is ignorant of the experimenter's technique and modus operandi. Even if such an attempt were successful it is difficult not to side with Boring (1969) when he asserts that a deception of this kind probably creates as many problems as it solves.

In conclusion, the real-simulating model contributes to our knowledge of hypnosis by posing a sensitive, effective and reliable method for investigating potential sources of artifact. Its procedures are immensely well formulated, and its logic subtle (hence open to much misinterpretation) but virtually unassailable. The weaknesses of the model lie not in the looseness of the inferences drawn from its application—for these are remarkably tight if the model is applied correctly—but in the fact it fails to go far enough to isolate the true nature of differences which could be reflecting genuine essence features of hypnosis. Additional strategies have to be formulated once the demand characteristics have been isolated, if "essence" is to be ever delineated. The simulation technique does accurately determine the adequacy of experimental procedures, but other conditions—those providing effective control comparison—have to be adopted if the model is to determine those features which characterize the hypnotic state. The claim others have leveled at the model—that it leaves the "trance state" as the residual explanatory variable (Johnson *et al.*, 1972) can only be met by Orne and his associates pointing to ways in which "essence" rather than alternative accounts of the data can be validated. As Orne (1970, p. 251) himself acknowledges, quasi-control strategies such as simulation do not permit any definite inference to be drawn about dependent variables. Only the application of future research strategies can resolve the uncertainty.

IMPLICATIONS FOR FUTURE RESEARCH

One of the major areas for research developments as far as the real-simulating paradigm is concerned is the systematic analysis of the methodological assumptions underlying the model; empirical detail is needed to support datawise those essential elements of method which must be repeated if the real-simulating model is to efficiently achieve the purpose for which it was designed. When applying this or any other model, the heterogeneity of methods evident in the literature tells us that researchers must simply be more uniform in the procedures that they adopt.

Further work needs to be conducted on the possible treatment effects of simulation which reflect one of the major sources of limitation on the model's inferences. The consequences of simulation are a source of potential artifact that the model creates inadvertently by instituting its preferred procedures of control, and research must establish where and when artifact of this kind contaminates the inferences that it wishes to draw. It is surprising in a sense how little is known about the actual task of simulation. It obviously can be distinguished from other forms of role-playing in the effects that it produces (Sheehan, 1973a) and there appear to be specifiable characteristics which distinguish the simulators' role-playing performance from other forms of pretense (Sheehan & Marsh, 1974). But we still know relatively little about the parameters affecting the simulators' task and what it is exactly in the procedures associated with the model that is responsible for the adequacy of their performance.

Further, it is important to note that potential artifact is introduced into the model through the presence of the differences in suggestibility associated with the model's two comparison groups. Orne (1972a) argues that the problem of personality variation among subjects limit some but not all applications of the model but those applications where the problem is relevant need to be delineated quite clearly from those where it is not. Surprisingly little work has been conducted to determine just how well susceptible subjects can simulate effectively. Work has been done (Austin *et al.*, 1963) to suggest that the task for hypnotizable subjects is a difficult one but systematic programs of research are needed which will determine when and when not we ought to accept the report of susceptible role-playing subjects that they are not in trance.

Finally, the model needs to carefully list the kinds of situations where demand characteristics are operative; in particular, the phenomenon of trance logic should be analyzed closely in this way. Orne (1962a) recognizes the problem generally:

> Delineation of the situations where demand characteristics may produce an effect ascribed to experimental variables, or where they may obscure such an effect and actually lead to systematic data in the opposite direction, as well as those experimental contexts where they do not play a major role, is an issue for further work [p. 780].

The logic of the model is such that it draws attention through the treatment condition of simulation to the possible existence of demand characteristic effects, but, as we have seen, when similarities occur these effects might not really exist for real subjects. It is especially important then that supporters of the model work independently to determine when demand characteristics are influential and what situations are especially susceptible to their influence. The simulating technique in itself is not equipped to indicate when cues are operative for real subjects or even how such cues are transmitted once they are present. The model itself tells us only that cues can be picked up which may lead to the experimenter's expected response providing that hypnotic subjects are sufficiently motivated to be alert for them to respond accordingly.

There are, in fact, many important areas of research which are relevant to the model. Additional work needs to be done, for example, on the question of social control and the extent to which this actually adheres to the hypnotic setting in particular. Research ought also to explore the degree to which hypnotic subjects literally accept whatever suggestions the hypnotist gives them. Orne argues cogently for experimental subjects as sentient, cognizant beings but little work to date has analyzed just how sentient the hypnotized subject actually is—the degree to which, for example, he is willing to cognitively restructure, on his own initiative, the suggestions that he receives. These and many other questions that one can readily ask attest the enormous research productivity of the real-simulating model.

The most important methodological development as far as this paradigm is concerned is clearly the construction of techniques which will reinforce the theoretical underpinnings of the model. These techniques—ones which will presumably index "essence" features of hypnosis–lie most obviously for Orne (Orne, 1974b; Orne & Hammer, 1974) in the area of validation of subjective states viz., delusion. The study of hypnosis can contribute significantly to our general understanding of psychological phenomena through accentuating the need to describe and quantify subjective experiences. Greater comprehension of these through the application of sophisticated research methodology would contribute greatly to psychological knowledge.

7

The Effects of Hypnotizability, Hypnosis, and Motivation on Hypnotic Behavior: The London–Fuhrer Design

> ". . . hypnosis is a situation with potentially variable effects which interact per susceptibility status *per measuring instrument.* Thus, it is not surprising that different experiments in the same area produce conflicting results both since previous research has not commonly concerned itself with the susceptibility dimension and since generalizations about the effects of hypnosis have been offered without much consideration of the limitations of different measuring instruments. This argument suggests that it is improper to define hypnosis for experimental purposes or to generalize about its effects without consideration of the susceptibility of the *S*s and the limited scope of the experimental tasks [Rosenhan & London, 1963b, p. 33]."

The movement of hypnosis as an object of study from the field situation to the laboratory has created a set of problems that are unique to experimentation. Some of these we have already looked at (see Chapter 6 on Orne) in terms of the problem of demand characteristics—the, at times, disconcerting ability of experimental subjects to respond to implicit cues in design and/or procedure, rather than to the experimental stimuli themselves.

There are other problems of artifact that are dependent mainly upon certain inherent ambiguities in the concept of hypnosis. Hypnosis has been variously conceptualized as both a *trait* and a *state,* and very few investigators have attempted to reconcile a number of paradoxes that result from these two alternate ways of looking at hypnotic phenomena. The trait formulation recognizes the long-established belief in stable individual differences in hypnotizability. The state view places its emphasis upon the as equally well established reports of hypnotized subjects that their subjective experience in response to hypnotic instructions is in some way different from ordinary subjective experience.

From these two different lines of observation the gist of the paradox emerges. If there are stable individual differences in the trait, certain difficulties arise in conceptualizing the state (these are taken up by us in more detail in Chapter 8). Some experimenters (for instance, Orne and Sutcliffe) attempt to deal with this problem by making extreme group comparisons between high and low susceptible subjects. The assumption is that high susceptible subjects can experience a lot of the state, whereas low susceptibles are unable to experience any of it. These extreme groups constitute roughly 20–30% of the total range of susceptibility, and there is a problem of what to do about the majority of individuals (70–80%) who fall between these extremes and are labeled medium susceptibles.

The most important problem emerging from the state–trait paradox is that of interpreting any differences found between comparison groups of subjects who are selected for being high and low on the trait. Can these differences be attributed to different manifestations of state, or may they be due to preexisting differences in trait? Or is there a very complex interaction between state and trait components of hypnotic performance whose surface has yet to be scratched? Since a person appears to need to have the trait in order to manifest the state, there is a question of what can be validly inferred from experimental data; there exists the problem of knowing what is due to being hypnotizable versus being hypnotized.

A further difficulty concerns other aspects of hypnotized performance, given that trait differences exist. Many investigators have been puzzled by the motivational components of hypnotic performance. Orne (1959), for example, has noted that highly susceptible hypnotic subjects tend to be particularly cooperative, almost eager participants. Further he has argued that there is reason to suspect that hypnosis, as such, increases the motivation of the subject to comply with the wishes ("suggestions")—both explicit and implicit—of the experimenter. Indeed, in his classic paper of 1959, Orne set out a schematic representation of a working model of hypnosis in which he included an "Increased Motivation Artifact." He described this artifact as follows: "The sources of increased motivation are not defined. They represent a major area of future inquiry. *Probably some aspects will prove to be a component of 'essence'* (of hypnosis) [Orne, 1959, p. 278, italics added]."

The sorting out of this motivational component has subsequently proven to be a highly complex business. To the extent that the motivational component of hypnotic behavior involves greater eagerness to comply with hypnotic suggestions, it has been found in many situations that unhypnotized subjects seemingly show greater amounts of such motivation than do hypnotized subjects. For instance, in investigations of posthypnotic behavior, Kellog (1929), Patten (1930), and Damaser (1964), using a variety of posthypnotic tasks, tested up to three months after either a posthypnotic suggestion or a waking request was given, and uniformly reported similar findings. These studies found that an unhypnotized (or, alternatively, a low susceptible) group carried out the behavior requested more frequently than an hypnotized (or a high susceptible) group. From this, there appears to be a clear discrepancy in certain situations between the frequently reported eagerness and high motivation of highly hypnotizable subjects to comply, and their failure to match the performance of less susceptible and unhypnotized subjects.

A third problem, over and above these difficulties associated with the state–trait distinction and the motivation issue concerns the testing of subjects in a same-subjects design where a subject may receive both an hypnotic and a control condition during the course of an experiment. There is a long standing impression that good hypnotic subjects believe that their performances on a variety of tasks are enhanced by hypnosis. And because they believe, it is thought that they often do better in an hypnotic condition for this reason alone, rather than because of any inherent properties of hypnosis itself. There are various formulations as to how this can come about ranging from the notion that good hypnotic subjects "hold back" in control conditions (see Chapter 2 for discussion of this problem) to the view that the mere instigation of an hypnotic induction is sufficient to initiate motivations that are ordinarily latent in nonhypnotic conditions. According to the latter view, the performance of a good hypnotic subject in hypnosis is analagous to that of a conscientious professional athlete—one who works hard in practice, but gives optimal performance only under actual game conditions.

From these long-recognized problems, and the paradoxes they generate, a major attempt at resolution has emerged. The techniques that have developed in order to deal with these problems have become known as the "London–Fuhrer Design." It is called this because the first formal application of procedures to cope with the issues was set out in a paper by Perry London and Marcus Fuhrer in 1961. However, several other investigators have been closely associated with the use of the same model, as a bibliography of studies using the design indicates (London, Conant, & Davison, 1966; London & Fuhrer, 1961; London, Ogle, & Unikel, 1968; Rosenhan & London, 1963a, b; Slotnick, Liebert, & Hilgard, 1965; Slotnick & London, 1965). We shall refer to this technique as the London–Fuhrer design on the grounds of usage of the term among investigators, even though it is not universal. Sarbin and Coe (1972) refer to this technique of investigation as the *interaction design* since it is concerned particularly with disentangling the effects of hypnosis, hypnotizability, motivation, and orders of presenting experimental conditions.

THEORETICAL POSITION

The London–Fuhrer design was suggested initially by certain unresolved discrepancies among findings in the literature concerning the effects of hypnosis on enhancing muscular performance. A large number of studies have found evidence of enhancement of performance using measures like the hand dynamometer as the criterion measure of enhancement. An equally large number of studies has reported no evidence of enhancement. In such situations, it is common to dismiss discrepancies as due to differences in experimental instructions, procedure and/or measurement technique. The initial force of the London–Fuhrer technique was that it sought to resolve such discrepant findings in terms of design characteristics. It is in their choice of comparison groups that an implicit theoretical position toward hypnosis comes through, though the theory behind the model has never been set out formally. Nevertheless, certain features can be observed that express a definite point of view towards hypnosis.

In analyzing prior discrepant findings, London and Fuhrer observed that all of the studies involved utilized a design that indicated a shared assumption about the nature of hypnosis. This assumption was that "hypnosis may have some kind of special, positively motivating effect on subjects which induces them to perform more strenuously than they otherwise would (London & Fuhrer, 1961, p. 321]." The design they proposed sought to test this assumption, by providing a set of experimental conditions that would bear explicitly on the issue of enhanced motivation. From this, the beginnings of a theoretical position can be discerned—they believed that motivation may be very important for hypnotic performance and this is a view shared by several other investigators as well (for example, Barber and Orne).

Motivation, however, can mean many things, and different things to different people. What makes the London–Fuhrer position distinctive is the attempt to distinguish various sources of motivation that may be operating in an hypnotic situation. Their emphasis is upon disentangling these differential effects, since hypnotic behavior, as it is usually observed, may represent an interaction of motivations derived from a variety of different sources.

Firstly, there is the experimental situation itself. London and Fuhrer (1961) observed that the fact that insusceptible subjects are able to fake hypnotic behavior when appropriately motivated, and without special training, suggests that "some of the effects of hypnosis may represent performances that are neither maximal for those *S*s nor unique to the hypnotic state (London & Fuhrer, 1961, p. 321]." In this respect, they follow Orne (1959) in seeing demand characteristics as not merely artifacts in experiments to be controlled, but as potential sources of motivation in their own right.

Further, they suggest that an hypnotic induction itself may be inherently motivating; there is "an aura which surrounds the experimental situation and implies to *S* that improved performance is expected after exposure to a series of impressive incantations (London & Fuhrer, 1961, p. 322]." This location of the hypnotic induction procedure itself as a source of motivation merges, to some extent, with demand characteristics, but it can become very subtle indeed. Behavior alterations may result "from the very idea that hypnosis will sometime in the future, be used in the experiment [Rosenhan & London, 1963a, p. 78]."

To complicate the issue additionally, there may be differential motivational effects for high and low susceptible subjects. High and low susceptible subjects may perceive an hypnotic induction differently, and this may be further reinforced by differential treatment of those subjects who respond well to an hypnotic induction as compared with those who do not. Thus, the interpersonal aspects of the hypnotic situation may have a bearing on hypnotic outcomes by subtly altering the motivations of subjects.

Over and above these considerations, there is an awareness by London and Fuhrer (1961) that the motivations produced by an hypnotic situation may be generated equally well by other nonhypnotic means. Whenever the major concern is to test hypotheses of enhancement of performance using hypnosis, there exists always a possibility that comparable increments could be elicited equally as much by specific motivating instructions. Thus the London–Fuhrer design has shown sensitivity to the issue of control, and has often sought to compare hypnotic performance to that obtained under explicit motivational instructions given in an unhypnotized condition. Obviously, such comparisons can only clarify the role of motivation in the hypnotic context.

A second feature of the London–Fuhrer position that implies a distinct theoretical stance is their concern with individual differences in hypnotizability. The crux of the design is concerned with extreme group comparisons between high susceptible (or what they call tranceable) subjects and low susceptible (or untranceable) subjects. Comparisons are made between these two groups with special emphasis on the possibility of differential effects on hypnotic and various control instructions on each. This position has a number of interesting ramifications, especially as they have made these comparisons over a number of disparate tasks (for example, various measures of physical endurance, rote learning, etc.).

The design has consistently sought to examine differences between Ts and UTs (tranceable and untranceable subjects) in base-rate performance, suggesting that its authors, like Sarbin (Chapter 4) believe that some of the differences obtained in hypnosis may somehow interact with preexisting differences between the two susceptibility levels. Their procedures for establishing base rates are relatively unstandardized in that the issue of what is the appropriate base rate has never been worked out clearly. (In this respect, however, they are not unique.) They typically obtain base rates in an unexhorted condition, though sometimes, the base rate is obtained prior to the subject having knowledge of the experiment's hypnotic nature and sometimes not. This procedure differs markedly from that of Sarbin (see Chapter 4) who has sought to make the same point by comparing the performance of an unhypnotized group with that of hypnotized subjects in a prior experiment conducted by another investigator. By comparing hypnotized and unhypnotized base rates in the same experiment, the London–Fuhrer design is able to make tighter inferences.

Further, the differences occurring between Ts and UTs tend to depend upon what base rate is obtained and upon the type of task being investigated. Thus,

UTs have been found to typically perform better (though not often significantly so) than Ts on endurance tasks, whereas Ts have tended to show superior base-rate performances to UTs on learning tasks. This, as we shall see, has led proponents of the design to emphasize the role of the situation in which hypnosis occurs as a major factor limiting generalization about hypnosis. This position has been stated more elaborately by London, Conant, and Davison (1966) who observe that it is reasonable to conclude that there are stable differences in personality (broadly conceived) between Ts and UTs. Paradoxically, however, the large body of data that has accumulated over the years on personality correlates of hypnotizability has failed to reveal anything substantial. Given this, these authors (1966, p. 78) propose that "the underlying differences between these groups might be sought in the anticipatory sets of dispositions towards situations in which performance normally varies with different aspects of preparatory instructions, such as the manner in which they are given or the complexity of their content." In other words, the stable individual differences in hypnotizability, regularly reported, may be based more upon differential reaction types or patterns to variations in instruction, than upon underlying static personality variables. In this respect, London and Fuhrer's design clearly advocates an interactionist position (Ekehammer, 1974), one which views behavior as a product of the interaction between situational variables and the person's perception of his immediate environment.

Elsewhere, a variation of this hypothesis (London, Ogle, & Unikel, 1968) has been suggested. On the basis of differences found between Ts and UTs in a heat stress situation, they suggested that differences might be explained in terms of initial motivations between the two groups, particularly when these levels of motivation are high to begin with, and a stress situation is involved. In each case the emphasis of task requirements interacting with dynamic personality variables (whatever these may turn out to be) gives the position a certain distinctiveness.

A further implication of this account is that there are differential effects from baseline to hypnosis conditions for Ts and UTs. While these differences have proven to be elusive (and appear also to depend upon different task requirements), the notion that hypnosis affects the performance of Ts and UTs differentially may be of considerable importance for the understanding of hypnosis. This particular stance has one further implication which is of considerable interest. Contrary to what has been believed traditionally by experimental investigators, there are indications from the use of this design that unhypnotizable (UT) subjects are affected to some degree by hypnotic induction procedures. Obviously, the effect is not as great as for highly susceptible (T) subjects, but it suggests that UTs, while not very susceptible to hypnosis, are none the less amenable to suggestion. For many years during the late 19th and early 20th century, hypnotizability was identified closely with suggestibility (see Chapter 1). A position that emerges from the use of the London–Fuhrer design is that hypnotic susceptibility, if it is indeed a form of suggestibility at all, is only one form of it. Equally important is the observation that low susceptible subjects, though relatively unaffected by an hypnotic induction, may manifest other forms of influence to suggestive techniques.

In all, the theoretical position underlying the London–Fuhrer design has developed primarily (but not exclusively) as a result of experience following its experimental use. Obviously, the initial attempt to differentiate "being hypnotized" from "being susceptible to hypnosis" indicates that London and Fuhrer (1961) began with an implicit theoretical position oriented toward discrepancies in data generated by prior investigators who had not always made this important distinction between "trait" and "state." Likewise, the early emphasis on the importance of differential motivational effects did not emerge from a vacuum. However, it is only through experimentation, and the findings of conflicting results that a broader position has developed. This position sees hypnosis as "a situation with potentially variable effects which interact per susceptibility *per measuring instrument.*" Further, "it is improper to generalize about its effects without consideration of the susceptibility of the *S*s and the limited scope of the experimental tasks [Rosenhan & London, 1963b, p. 33]." Over and above this, experimental instructions are seen to have a crucial role, and it is possible that "the hypnotic condition somehow functions to make a subject more receptive than he has previously been to *certain kinds* of maximal performance instructions[Slotnick & London, 1965, p. 45]."

SURVEY OF THE MODEL'S STRATEGIES OF RESEARCH

As London and Fuhrer (1961, p. 322) pointed out, with reference to performance enhancement by hypnosis, there has been no study "which has attempted to demonstrate the interactions between unhypnotized, hypnotized, and otherwise positively motivated performance in a single experiment." The London–Fuhrer design has developed from these perceptions of what constitute the major variables in hypnotic experimentation. Most of the studies stemming from the design have been concerned with enhancement of muscular performance (London & Fuhrer, 1961; Rosenhan & London, 1963a; Slotnick, Liebert, & Hilgard, 1965; Slotnick & London, 1965). One further study (London, Ogle, & Unikel, 1968) has been concerned with heat stress, and two others (London, Conant, & Davison, 1966; Rosenhan & London, 1963b) have involved the study of rote learning.

The experiments on enhancement of muscular performance illustrate the strategies well. Typically two independent groups of extreme responders are employed, selected on the basis of scoring either low (1–4) or high (8–12) on the SHSS:A or an equivalent group hypnotic performance measure. These comparison groups are intended to assess the effects, if they exist, of hypnotic susceptibility, and are referred to respectively as the Untranceable (UT) and Tranceable (T) groups. These groups are compared in a repeated measures design on a variety of instructional conditions, one of which is usually hypnotic, and the other(s) of which constitute exhortative, involvement, or analgesia instruction conditions.

One major strength of the design is the attempt to obtain base-rate measures of performance both for hypnosis *and* nonhypnosis prior to experimental intrusion. In addition, the model points sensitively to how the appropriate base-rate performance should be obtained. London and Fuhrer (1961) for example, obtained base-rate measures from subjects who knew that in a subsequent experimental session, hypnosis would be used. Aware that this knowledge in itself might affect their performance (and might affect it differentially for UT and T groups) Rosenhan and London (1963a) collected base-rate measures from subjects as part of a statistical assignment in an introductory psychology course prior to any request for volunteer participation in an hypnosis experiment. Thus the design has attempted to evaluate the effects of knowing that hypnosis will be a part of the experiment in determining relevant base-rate measures. However, it has not reached any firm conclusions as to which base-rate collection technique is most appropriate for hypnosis research. Table 7.1 summarizes some of the comparisons that have been made using the design. As can be seen, the general strategy of the design is not to make every comparison conceivable, but rather to select out cells that appear particularly relevant to the question being asked on any particular occasion.

The most important methodological innovation of the design is its attempt to minimize differences in subsequent motivations of subjects found to be of low susceptibility in the initial training session. The most detailed description of the instructions given to all subjects after screening for hypnotizability (but which are aimed at making the less susceptible subjects feel that they have performed successfully) is provided by Slotnick and London (1965). Subjects were told:

> Most people when they undergo the kinds of hypnotic experiences which you have had here previously, wonder just how well they have been responding to the suggestions that are given. They are concerned about whether or not they have been performing as they were expected to, and whether or not they are really good hypnotic subjects. Perhaps you have had these same questions in connection with your earlier experiences here. The fact is that your performance earlier indicated clearly, in some of its significant details, that you would be an excellent subject for the purposes of the experiment we are doing now. Because you *are* a good subject, we want you to participate in the hypnotic phase of this experiment. . . [p. 40].

The efficacy of such instructions when given to low hypnotizable subjects will be discussed in a later section. For the present, it is important to note that these instructions are designed to overcome a difficult problem. When a subject has passed four or fewer hypnotic items out of 12, there is more than a strong possibility that he may feel that his hypnotic performance is inadequate. Any differences between the performance of such subjects and more highly susceptible subjects in subsequent hypnosis sessions may be due to perceptions of one's hypnotic worth alone rather than to the effects of any experimental procedure

TABLE 7.1
Summary of Comparisons made by Studies Employing the London–Fuhrer Design

	Base Rate		Experimental	
	Hypnosis	No hypnosis	Hypnosis	No hypnosis
Tranceable (T)	A, C_1C_2,[a] D F	A, B,[b] D E, F	A, B, C_1, D[c] E, F[c]	A, C_2, D[c] F[c]
Untranceable (UT)	A, D F	A, B,[b] D E, F	A, B, D[c] E, F[c]	A, D[c] F[c]

Muscular enhancement studies

A = London and Fuhrer (1961)
B = Rosenhan and London (1963a)
C = Slotnick, Liebert, and Hilgard (1965)
D = Slotnick and London (1965)

Rote learning studies

E = Rosenhan and London (1963b)
F = London, Conant, and Davison (1966)

[a]The study used two groups of Tranceable subjects—C_1 and C_2. The base rate was obtained under an exhorted condition.
[b]Unhypnotized base rates were taken both before and after subjects knew that the experiment involved hypnosis.
[c]More than one group was run in the experimental condition.

subsequently employed. One of the main emphases of the design is its attempt to equate motivations, sets, and the differential perceptions of high and low susceptible subjects from the very outset.

A further important feature of the design is that it generally attempts to take more than one measure of the dependent variable being examined; multimeasurement of the kind it adopts can be an important tool of scientific inquiry (see Chapter 8). For instance, in the case of the hypothesis concerning the effect of hypnotic and various control instructions upon enhancement of physical performance, three different tasks have been used, each dealing with a separate aspect of the physical strength dimension—strength, endurance, and hand–eye coordination. For strength, the subject is required to squeeze a hand dynamometer as hard as possible to yield a measure of grip strength. For endurance, he is required to hold a 2.5-lb flat weight strapped to the hand at arm's length, for as long as possible. For hand–eye coordination (a more subtle but potentially more relevant measure, which can also be seen as a measure of steadiness), the subject is required to hold a metal stylus at shoulder height and at arm's length in a hole, without touching its sides. By these means, several dimensions of physical performance can be evaluated under the same susceptibility, hypnotic and motivational conditions, thus facilitating a more detailed appraisal of the particular hypothesis than would be possible using any single measure.

Further refinements are added to the design by testing half of the untranceables on the hypnosis condition first and the other half on the control condition first. Serial effects may not be eliminated in this way, but they are at least evenly spread over the T and UT group. Further, their effect on outcomes can be evaluated separately. A final feature of the design is the frequent retesting of subjects at the end of the study for hypnotizability, using the same measuring scale employed initially to screen subjects for the T and UT groups. By this means a validity check can be obtained on this initial allocation of subjects to their respective groups.

In summary, the typical strategy of the design consists of four separate stages. The first two stages involve screening subjects for the T and UT groups, and obtaining base-rate measures in the hypnotic and nonhypnotic condition. The order in which these initial stages are completed depends upon whether the experimenter requires base rates prior or subsequent to the subjects having knowledge that the third stage actually involves hypnosis. In the final stage hypnotizability is retested as a validity check on initial screenings of subjects into the T and UT groups.

The London–Fuhrer design has the major advantage of being both tight and flexible. Data from its application are also readily amenable to scrutiny by analysis of variance, thus enabling interactions among the main variables to show up, should they exist. At the same time, there are many ways in which hypnosis can be presented to the subject, so that many experimental and control groups are possible. The design is thus able to cope with analysis of the combined effects of hypnotic instruction, susceptibility measure, motivational, and control procedures once the experimenter has determined what particular comparisons ought to be relevant.

EVIDENCE RELATING TO THE MODEL

The outcomes of experiments using the London–Fuhrer design indicate the many difficulties inherent in the experimental study of hypnosis. We have already pointed to the intrinsic merits of the London–Fuhrer approach, in particular its explicit attempt to resolve prior discrepant findings by means of an improved design which has the virtue of systematizing comparisons that often were left confounded in previous studies. Procedurally it represents an important advance in its attempt to treat insusceptible subjects in a way as identical as possible to the way highly susceptible subjects are treated, by telling them at the end of the screening session that they are "very good subjects for the purposes of the experiment." Despite these clearly desirable methodological and procedural features, there is very little uniformity of outcomes across studies, though a contrary impression is sometimes given by the treatment of nonsignificant results that "approach significance" in the direction predicted as favorable outcomes. What follows is a review of some major conclusions drawn from the use of the London–Fuhrer design in the investigation of enhancement of physical performance, rote learning, verbal learning, and resistance to heat stress.

The Superior Performance of Untranceable Subjects over Tranceable Subjects in Base-Rate Conditions

One of London and Fuhrer's (1961) major findings was that UT subjects performed significantly better than T subjects on both the hand dynamometer and the weight endurance test. Data for hand tremor were not reported in this study because of an error in its administration. This result was particularly striking, since it held for both base-rate and experimental conditions suggesting that UTs and Ts may well start off being initially different in many situations even before any experimental manipulation is attempted. Since heights, weights and ages of subjects were almost identical, there is little likelihood that this finding was an artifact of differences in physical strength between the two groups. The subjects in this initial study were all females; a subsequent study by Rosenhan and London (1963a) used an all male sample, and despite differences in the manner of obtaining base-rate data, it yielded results that were interpreted as consistent with London and Fuhrer on the dynamometer and weight endurance tests. Separate analyses of variance, however, revealed no significant effects for the T–UT variable for *any* of the three measures of physical performance. The conclusion of consistency of findings was based upon the fact that UTs scored higher in all conditions than Ts, though not significantly so.

A third study (Slotnick & London, 1965, p. 44) was said to reinforce the conclusion of the two previous investigations, demonstrating once again that "UTs manifest greater initial performance ability than T subjects" on weight endurance and dynamometer. However, again, in this study the superiority of UTs over Ts was not statistically significant in either the hypnotic or nonhypnotic base-rate conditions. The basis for this conclusion was "a *trend* for the UT group to do better than the T group on the tremor task *in both waking and hypnotic states,* and on the dynamometer and weight endurance tasks *in the waking states* [Slotnick & London, 1965, p. 42, italics added]." Likewise, in the main experimental session subsequent to the obtaining of base rates, there were no significant differences between T and UT subjects for the weight endurance and dynamometer tasks in both waking and hypnotic conditions. On the tremor test, however, Ts performed significantly better than the UT subjects in both the hypnosis and waking conditions in two of the three experimental conditions.

A careful replication of London and Fuhrer's (1961) study by Evans and Orne (1965) revealed a similar finding. There were no significant differences between T and UT subjects for any of the three weight endurance tasks in either the hypnotic or the waking condition. However, the means for the tremor and dynamometer tests were higher for UTs than for Ts in both the hypnosis and waking conditions. The reverse was true for the weight endurance test. Evans and Orne (1965) used a counterbalanced order of presentation of the hypnosis and waking conditions. They found some reversals of the general trends just reported depending upon whether the hypnosis or waking condition had been administered first.

To complicate matters further, Rosenhan and London (1963b), in a study involving the rote learning of nonsense syllables, obtained a diametrically opposite result. In the base-rate condition, T subjects performed significantly better on the memorization task than UTs. A subsequent study by London, Conant, and Davison (1965) repeated this observation, with T subjects again performing significantly better than UTs in the base-rate condition. Both of these studies used male subjects; however, Schulman and London (1963) used female subjects in a study of acquisition (rather than retention) and found no significant differences in base rates of T and UT subjects. In a final study using the London–Fuhrer design, this time to investigate the effects of hypnosis and exhortation on performance under heat stress, London, Ogle, and Unikel (1968) again found that the UT group performed better than the T group in base-line sessions for both normal temperature and increased heat, but again the difference was not significant.

In all, the results of these several studies clearly lack the consistency necessary to demonstrate the superiority of UTs over Ts in base-rate conditions. While some of these differences may be due to the type of task used (for instance physical endurance versus rote learning), and may be confounded with sex differences and methods of obtaining the baseline, only one study actually showed a superiority for UTs over Ts in base rate that was statistically significant. While it is intriguing to find statistically insignificant superiority of UTs over Ts in several of the studies, false positives are less likely to be generated by adhering to alpha levels of $p < .05$ as ultimate criteria for determining that preexisting differences between UTs and Ts are, in fact, real. Notwithstanding, the London–Fuhrer design's emphasis on base-rate performances is an important one; it is quite possible that more intensive investigation of baseline conditions and of sex differences will clarify the issue of whether, and when, such base-rate differences are present.

Improved Performance of Tranceable Subjects and Depressed Performance of Untranceable Subjects in Hypnosis

The collection of base-rate performances for Ts and UTs permits comparison of these respective groups from pretest to experimental conditions. The initial London–Fuhrer study (1961) reported that although hypnosis did not significantly affect performance on any of the tasks, there was an interaction between hypnosis as an experimental treatment and hypnotizability on the endurance task. The UTs were found to give poorer performance when hypnotized than when not; the Ts tended to give better performance when hypnotized than when not. Even at this early stage the result was not entirely clear-cut. While it is true that this finding held overall, the UTs actually performed better in the hypnotized exhorted condition. Further, on the dynamometer measure, the results went in another direction; both Ts and UTs performed better in the nonhypnotic than in the hypnotic condition. London and Fuhrer (1961, p. 329) argued that the endurance test as compared to the hand dynamometer has "general greater sensitivity" and is a "more pure test of motivation" to explain this discrepancy of outcomes between tasks.

Be this as it may, Rosenhan and London (1963a) were not able to repeat this finding on the endurance task, although there were differences in experimental procedure for this later study. Base rates were obtained prior to subjects being informed of the hypnotic nature of the experiment, males were used as subjects instead of females, and there was an exhorted condition. It was found on the tremor test, however, that Ts made considerably fewer errors in the hypnotized condition than when unhypnotized, and UTs made slightly fewer errors in the unhypnotized than the hypnotized condition.

A somewhat similar finding was reported by Slotnick and London (1965), this time using female subjects, and comparing experimental conditions of analgesia, exhortation, and a combination of both. Once again there were no significant differences on the weight endurance and dynamometer tasks between Ts and UTs in either the hypnotic or waking conditions, for any of the experimental instructions. For the tremor test, however, T subjects showed significantly greater improvement than UT subjects in hypnosis from base-rate to experimental instruction condition regardless of whether the instruction was analgesia, instruction, or combined. In other words, the performance of both groups improved in hypnosis, but the Ts improved more than the UTs.

Once again the rote-learning studies (London, Conant, & Davison, 1965; Rosenhan & London, 1963b) have provided contrary evidence on this point. The latter found a significant interaction between hypnotizability and the hypnotized versus the control conditions. This time, however, the finding was in the opposite direction to that found in the phyiscal performance studies. The performance of T subjects declined during hypnosis while that of the UT subjects improved. In the former study, separate groups of Ts and UTs were run under conditions of hypnosis and exhortation. In both it was found that the performance of Ts declined, while the performance of UTs increased from base rate to experimental condition. The patterns of increases and decreases, however, were small and insignificant. Finally, in the heat stress experiment of London, Ogle, and Unikel (1968) using a pursuit rotor task under conditions of normal temperature and increased (98°) heat, there were increases in performances for both Ts and UTs from base rate to the experimental condition and they were slightly (but not significantly) larger for the Ts.

Once again there is a lack of stability of outcomes from these studies to justify the belief that hypnosis reliably increases the performance of Ts and likewise depresses the performance of UTs. This instability appears to be very much the product of the type of task studied—in particular, the use of tasks where learning is involved and asymptotes are uncertain, so that any sort of instruction, be it hypnotic or exhortative, is likely to improve performance. These findings are somewhat in line with the impression one gains from perusing the main comparisons of the design that hypnotic behavior (or any behavior, for that matter) is most profitably understood as an interaction between subject characteristics, motivations, experimental conditions, and task requirements. This assumes, however, that all other things are equal, and that there are no other extraneous variables operating in experiments utilizing the London–Fuhrer design. While many of the discrepant findings may be due to such situational, subject, and task requirements variables, there may be other ingredients contributing to subject performance which could account equally well for the pattern of conflicting findings that have been obtained thus far.

SUMMARY EVALUATION OF THE MODEL

The original thrust of the model came from its attempt to resolve discrepancies in experimental outcomes in studies investigating the effects of hypnosis on enhancing muscular performance. These discrepancies were perceived by London and Fuhrer (1961) as being due to inadequacies of previous experimental designs rather than to the deficiencies of specific experimental procedures. The fact that the London–Fuhrer design has itself generated a series of conflicting experimental outcomes has led investigators using the design to argue that hypnosis is a situation with potentially variable effects which interact with both susceptibility status and the measuring instrument, so that generalizations about the data must consider carefully the level of the susceptibility of subject and the limited scope of the experimental tasks on which he is performing (Rosenhan & London, 1963b; Slotnick & London, 1965).

This statement is itself a generalization about hypnosis, and it raises the issue of whether it is a verifiable statement or a post hoc rationalization of discrepant outcomes. The evidence is not all in, and thus it seems reasonable to probe at issues stemming from the use of the design, before accepting this conclusion at face value. In doing this, we do not wish to detract from the obvious methodological innovations that the London–Fuhrer design has produced. It is very clear that the design has made explicit certain distinctions that need to be made—in particular, the distinction between "being hypnotizable" and "being hypnotized," the concern with base rates, and the analysis of motivational aspects of the hypnotic situation into finer, more detailed components. Nonetheless, some hesitiation is called for when application of a methodology leads to the very sort of discrepant experimental outcome that the design was invoked to resolve. At the very least, it suggests that one should explore residual procedural difficulties that may account for the inconsistent findings, before concluding that variability of outcome in hypnosis experiments is the rule rather than the exception. An analysis of this question would appear to us to center on three main issues: the issue of what is an appropriate baseline measure for hypnosis, the effect of telling UTs that they are good subjects, and the problem of pitting suggestions of relaxation against instructions to enhance performance. We will now consider each of these briefly in turn.

Baseline Measures of Hypnosis

Perhaps the most vexatious issue raised by the London–Fuhrer design is the problem of determining what the true baseline for hypnotic performance actually is. The emphasis upon obtaining base-rate measures is, as we have observed, one of the design's several commendable features. The process of attempting to obtain base-rate measures has produced, however, its own set of intricacies. The problem, of course, is not unique to hypnotic research; the recent literature on alpha feedback training is an illuminating example of how difficult it is to ascertain base rates once one has decided that they are worthy of collection.

The characteristic solution of investigators using the London–Fuhrer design has been to obtain a measure of some dependent variable task (such as strength of hand grip) in base-rate conditions prior to the introduction of an exhorted hypnotic condition. This has usually been done in situations where subjects knew that hypnosis would subsequently be used in the experiment (London, Conant, & Davison, 1966; London & Fuhrer, 1961; London, Ogle, & Unikel, 1968; Rosenhan & London, 1963b, Slotnick & London, 1965), but in one study (Rosenhan & London, 1963a) base rates were obtained prior to subjects knowing that hypnotic procedures would, subsequently, be utilized.

It is difficult to make comparisons across these studies, since they used a variety of dependent variable measures. The findings of the Rosenhan and London (1963b) experiment, however, indicate that preknowledge that subsequent testing will involve hypnosis has an effect on some baselines. In this study, which involved male subjects, both T and UT subjects performed significantly better on the weight endurance and significantly worse on the tremor test in the preknowledge than in the postknowledge condition; they held the weight longer in a control condition, that was represented to them as a statistical exercise relating various physical and endurance measures (preknowledge), than in an unhypnotized condition which they knew as part of a study that would subsequently involve hypnosis (postknowledge). Paradoxically, they performed worse on the tremor test in the preknowledge than in the postknowledge condition. To add a further complexity, there were no significant differences from pre- to postknowledge on the dynamometer test. While some of these differences of outcome may be task specific, the general problem of *when* and *how* one obtains baseline measures is obviously a serious one deserving further extensive treatment. Many of the inferences drawn by the London–Fuhrer design involve comparisons of baseline with subsequent hypnotic and TM performances; it is thus important to have some normative notions of what baselines are being used. As matters stand, the evidence indicates that on two measures out of three, differential baselines were obtained depending upon whether or not subjects knew that hypnosis would be used in a later phase of the experiment.

Information Given to Untranceable Subjects on the Adequacy of Their Hypnotic Performance

An integral feature of the design involves telling UT subjects, who have scored 4 or less on SHSS:A (or on an equivalent group measure), that their performance indicates that they would make excellent subjects for the purposes of the ensuing experiment. This technique represents one of several innovative features of the design for reasons we have already discussed. The design, however, makes little attempt to evaluate whether such instructions are credible to a person who has experienced negligible effects in response to an hypnotic induction procedure. To the extent that a subject perceives the explicit purpose of an hypnotic experiment as relating to becoming hypnotized, such verbal reassurances may not be consonant with his own subjective impressions. Only one study has attempted to obtain measures of subjective depth on hypnosis for Ts and UTs. In this study (Evans & Orne, 1965), "although the instructions stressed that each *S* was a good *S* for the purpose of the experiment, and although opportunities to test objectively the depth of hypnosis were carefully avoided [p. 112]," the T subjects reported significantly greater depth in hypnosis than the UT subjects. This experiment utilized an additional group of medium susceptible subjects who, interestingly enough rated themselves as even more deeply hypnotized than the highly susceptible group. Though it may be premature to base conclusions on a single study, it is tempting to suggest that some of the variability of outcomes using the London–Fuhrer design may be the result of differential perceptions among less susceptible subjects of the verbal reassurances they receive.

Orne (1972, p. 430) has suggested that for the London–Fuhrer design to be fully effective, an important modification is needed—"It is essential to somehow convince the unhypnotizable group that they can, in fact, respond to hypnotic suggestions." In essence, this involves going beyond mere verbal reassurance to UTs of their excellence as subjects for the task at hand. A study of McGlashan, Evans, and Orne (1969) used an ingenious technique for achieving this end and provides an interesting illustration of how this requirement might be fulfilled. In a study comparing the effects of hypnotic analgesia and placebo on pain tolerance, insusceptible subjects received an apparent demonstration from an independent experimenter of their ability to experience some hypnotic effect, namely hypnotic analgesia. In an hypnotic session prior to the main session, these subjects were given an electric shock to the hand and told that they would be given the same shock while hypnotized following analgesic instructions. In fact, the second shock was only one half the intensity of the initial shock. All but one insusceptible subject were convinced that they had indeed experienced a significant degree of hypnotic analgesia. Postexperimental inquiries by both the independent experimenter at the end of this session and by a different experimenter at the end of the study, were used to determine that the insusceptible subjects had been convinced by the pseudoanalgesia. A similar tactic involving pseudohypnotic items was used by Perry and Mullen (1975) in an attempt to equate subjects for potential differential motivations stemming from their perception of their degree of hypnotizability. As with the study of McGlashan *et al.* (1969), postexperimental inquiries revealed that low susceptible subjects reported themselves as having "experienced hypnosis."

While this procedure of providing an actual demonstration of the subject's ability to experience hypnotic effects (as an alternative to verbal reassurances) might be difficult to implement in all situations, the principle is sound. Although it has yet to be demonstrated with finality, such a procedure appears more likely to minimize differences among subjects of varying susceptibilities by convincing them of their respective hypnotic worth. By using such a procedure, some of the discrepancies of outcome among studies using the design may indeed be reduced.

Relaxation Sleep Instructions to Enhance Muscular Performance

Studies using the London–Fuhrer design have typically used SHSS:A, or the Group Hypnotic Susceptibility Scale (an adaptation of SHSS:A&B by Rosenhan & London, 1961), to permit group administration of hypnosis. In most of the investigations using the design, the nature of the instructions have not been set out in very great detail. Slotnick, Liebert, and Hilgard (1965) described part of the induction as telling subjects that they would feel themselves going "deeper and deeper asleep," but reported that sleep was being used metaphorically while other parts of the hypnotic instructions emphasized that "sleep" was being used to promote a state differing from nocturnal sleep. The most detailed description of hypnotic instructions used in any study that has utilized the London–Fuhrer design is reported by Slotnick and London (1965). In this study, suggestions included statements like:

> As you relax there, very deep and very drowsy you find it easy just to let things ride by your mind without attending very much to them . . . in fact your attention becomes so fixed on what I am saying that you can completely forget about anything else . . . you listen to me, very carefully, without any real effort on your part. . . . In a few seconds, we shall begin working some tasks . . . you have already performed all of them. But this time, throughout everything you do, you will not come out of this state until I tell you . . . [p. 40].

At the same time, in most of the studies employing the London–Fuhrer design, subjects receive exhortative, motivational, or involving instructions to perform optimally on various strength, endurance, or learning tasks. While many of these investigations have conducted postexperimental inquiries, none of them have taken up the issue of subjects' perceptions of the hypnotic instructions, and the possibility that suggestions to be sleepy, drowsy, or relaxed may be antagonistic to suggestions of enhanced performance. Subjects in many of the studies cited may perceive themselves as receiving conflicting messages from the experimenter. Evans and Orne (1965) report postexperimental comments by subjects which suggest that this possibility may be a factor influencing the contradictory outcomes associated with the studies that have been cited. They state that many subjects commented that the special emphasis on drowsiness and deep relaxation in the induction procedure affected their performance adversely. One subject described his experience as follows: "In hypnosis I felt weakened. I want to please the hypnotist, but the harder I try to comply the more I wake up. When you work your muscles, you are working against your own cause [Evans & Orne, 1965, p. 113]." In this study moreover, the mean self-rated depth of hypnosis for the hypnotizable subjects (3.9 ± 3.0, on a 10-point depth scale) was surprizingly low. As these authors point out, the subjects did not see themselves as very deeply hypnotized during the performance tasks; though surprizingly they saw themselves as even less deeply hypnotized on a subsequent administration of SHSS:C. There is thus the possibility that instructions to perform optimally interfered with hypnotic instructions that define the state as relaxation and drowsiness. Such contrary indications to the subject of what is required of him may variously disrupt performance and/or the degree to which he feels hypnotized, depending upon how such messages are perceived. They may in themselves be just as responsible for discrepant findings obtained by the model as any inherent property of hypnotic induction procedures to be variable in their effects.

DIRECTIONS FOR FUTURE RESEARCH

The London–Fuhrer design has had a significant impact on hypnosis research; like many important techniques, its innovations have raised research questions associated with the model's application to the very problems it was devised to illuminate. The model's characteristic concern with base rates of nonhypnotic performance is a clear methodological advance which has opened up the problem of interpreting initial pretest differences between T and UT subjects; these may be of major importance in evaluating the differences subsequently found between them when hypnosis is applied. The ascertaining of such base rates, however, clearly brings up issues of what the appropriate baseline measure for hypnosis should be, and how it can be obtained without pretesting itself becoming a variable which influences subsequent hypnotic performance.

In similar vein, the use of special instructions to convince UTs that they have performed well in hypnosis raises issues of whether such instructions provide information that is counterfactual to the low susceptible subject's private individual experience. We have already noted one elegant attempt (McGlashan, Evans, & Orne, 1969) to improve upon this innovation; a study of the effects of the procedures which meet this problem may not merely add to the model's applicability, but may lead also to some interesting theoretical distinctions between suggestibility and hypnotizability. The few applications of the model to this question strongly suggest that UTs, while insusceptible to hypnosis, are nonetheless amenable to other forms of suggestion.

The distinction made by the model between hypnotizability and being hypnotized brings with it some prospects that a reconciliation of trait and state concepts will, after 200 years, start to merge into a comprehensive theory of hypnosis. At present, no such amalgamation exists so that there is still no intelligible answer to the basic question of what hypnosis is. However, more systematic and widespread use of hypnotic and nonhypnotic (control) instructions with subjects of different susceptibilities may help to resolve some of the paradoxes currently existing in the respective state and trait literatures.

When some of these issues pertaining to the practical application of the model have been resolved we will no doubt be in a position to better assess the role of motivation in hypnosis. The London–Fuhrer design has always held with it the hope that some of the traditional issues concerned with hypnosis and motivation might be unraveled, but the variable outcomes that have stemmed from use of the model do not presently permit one to generalize with certainty on most of the questions. It is still a matter of further research to determine (among other things) whether hypnosis constitutes a form of motivation equivalent to various kinds of motivating and exhortative instructions, and, if it does, to assess whether similar mechanisms are involved. Likewise, the question of whether increased motivation constitutes part of the essence of hypnosis, or is an artifact adhering to elements existing within the hypnotic situation still remains undecided.

Clearly, the London–Fuhrer design has, up to this point, raised more questions than it has answered to a number of theoretically important questions. Rather than see this as the model's epitaph, we see it as evidence of promise that has yet to be fulfilled. Like many major innovations, the fruitfulness of the approach has not been immediately apparent in terms of sudden new insights into the nature of hypnosis. But its long term effects on thinking about hypnosis will almost surely be worth waiting for.

8

Validity of Inference and the Application of Convergent Strategies: The Implications of Cross-Paradigm Check

> To the extent . . . that two scientific schools disagree about what is a problem and what a solution, they will inevitably talk through each other when debating the relative merits of their respective paradigms. In the partially circular arguments that regularly result, each paradigm will be shown to satisfy more or less the criteria that it dictates for itself and to fall short of a few of those dictated by its opponents [Kuhn, 1962, pp. 108–109].

Up to this point we have considered some of the historical antecedents to modern contemporary research and have discussed six distinct models of hypnosis. We have analyzed the respective contributions of each of the models to our understanding of hypnosis, both in terms of the methodological strategies they adopt—specfically to answer the problems associated with them—and in terms of the theory that implicitly, or explicitly, underlies them. Each model clearly has utility in so far as it gives us insight into how to solve problems not associated with alternative models. In all, three essential concerns have dictated the kind of discussion we have offered. We have tried to analyze closely (a) the validity of inferences associated with each of the paradigms taken up, (b) the potential artifacts associated with the models individually, and (c) the distinctive contribution each model makes to our understanding of hypnotic phenomena.

Models or theories of hypnosis must always be evaluated in terms of the validity of inferences they draw from data and we have consistently attempted to outline alternative explanations of performance which the proponents of each model would need to discount if their distinctive interpretations of data are to be affirmed. This approach to validity—the checking of alternative explanations to establish the correctness of an inference—is a process which should be generalized to hypothesis testing as a whole. Validity checks by means of systematic elimination of rival explanations of obtained effects is one of the essential goals of science itself: the greater the strength of reduction of alternative accounts of the data that is possible, the more confidence one can place in the accuracy of the inferences that are drawn.

It is not coincidental at all that discussion of validity and artifact go hand in hand. One of the major threats to validity—in the social sciences, in particular—comes from the artifacts that are distinctively associated with the procedures that experimenters choose to adopt. The methods of hypnotic researchers are no exception to the rule that the specification problems involved in the testing of humans are extremely complex and varied. Let us consider an example from a field altogether different from hypnosis to illustrate the point. It is a basic axiom of learning theory, for example, that extinction is related to the omission of reinforcement. Humans extinguish quickly, but they are also known to develop strong cognitions about the experimental situations in which they are placed (Spence, 1966) and the influence of these demonstrates the presence of potential artifact. It appears that extinction, in fact, is so rapid in some instances that its rapidity cannot be due just to the absence of reinforcement, but must also reflect the fact that subjects become acutely aware that the situation in which they are being tested has changed and the response they gave previously is no longer expected. In such circumstances, the pattern of results for extinction is inconclusive because the validity of the reinforcement hypothesis is challenged in part by the presence of an alternative hypothesis arising from the assumption that experimental subjects cognize about the situation in which they are tested. The validity of the original interpretation can be tested. The original hypothesis can be checked (as Spence acknowledged), by effectively reducing subjects' "inhibitory cognitions" through establishing a procedural context in which the differentiation between the acquisition and extinction period is not so easily detectable. The artifact in question can thereby be discounted, though others may still remain.

The influence of artifact and its challenge to validity is pervasive. When we analyze human behavior it is not easy to find out how best we can "understand those features of persons, situations, and events that are unintentionally present or introduced into the process of data collection and that are responsible for unexpected variation in the behavior of subjects [Riecken, 1962, p. 26]." As Boring (1969) states, we are faced with really the oldest scientific meaning of the word "control." The experimentalist is very much obligated to check to see whether an experimental variable adheres to its stated or intended specifications—such is the essential challenge of artifact. Artifact may be defined in terms of the statement that "the independent variable of $y = f(x)$ is contaminated, often unwittingly, by additional unspecified determinants that affect y [Boring,

1969, p. 3]," and concern for its detection is basic. The problem demands we know exactly in what way our treatment conditions are distinct and what exactly specifies our control groups as different from our experimental groups. The specification requirement raises questions of discovery of all sorts of conditions—for the most part, as Boring emphasizes, social in nature—that affect or influence the experimental variables we take up to study.

Plausible rival accounts of the data need to be formulated, tested and eliminated before confidence in the truth of an experimental outcome can really be affirmed. The problem pertains directly to the accuracy of our inferences, but validity is not simply an internal matter relevant to the stimuli being applied. One can ask not only does the experimental treatment make a significant difference (intended or unintended) in any particular study, but also to what extent other samples, situations, and contexts would yield an identical pattern of findings. This latter formulation raises the important question of the extent to which a given set of findings in hypnosis, or any other area of inquiry, can be generalized to different settings or contexts of testing. This issue of external validity relates obviously, for example, to the problem of differentiating "clinical" from "experimental" outcomes.

In this chapter we will look at a sample of strategies of hypnosis and consider them collectively, in order to analyze some of the major threats to validity of inference that relate to hypnotic treatments and to illustrate ways in which these threats might be resolved. The problem of artifact and its potential effects conveying threat to accuracy of inference has been explicitly recognized by most of the researchers covered in this book in one way or another; however, ways of coping with the general problem and the need to "guarantee" accuracy of inference has never been examined by any of the models in broad perspective. It is the specific aim of this chapter to look back over the models we have considered and to focus on the validity issue in particular, and to discuss ways in which greater certainty of inference about the effects of hypnotic treatments can be attained.

In analyzing specific threats to validity and outlining the sources of potential artifact associated with each of the models that have been discussed, it has been necessary to consider each paradigm individually. This approach would subtly appear to acknowledge that the procedures of one paradigm are best applied in isolation from the procedures of another, if full understanding is to result from the data that are collected. That is not necessarily the case and this chapter proposes to argue this point in some detail. We would indeed assert that the nature of a problem must ultimately dictate the methods an experimenter should adopt, but there is definite value in the application of multiple sets of procedures when the problem facilitates such an approach—and most investigators ignore this fact.

In summary, this chapter briefly reassesses those sources of artifact which adhere to two particular paradigms that we have considered previously (Barber's and Orne's paradigms of hypnosis). It attempts also to aggregate thereby some of the threats to validity that models in general may pose—those that challenge, in fact, the very nature of research endeavor as we traditionally conceive of it. The chapter focuses specifically on the value that accrues to bringing multiple sets of strategies to converge on the same hypothesis and the specific example of this approach we will discuss is a cross-paradigm analysis of a problem arising from theorizing about hypnotic rapport. The multiple application of specific paradigms to the same issue is instructive in two ways. First, it illustrates the potential advantages of convergent inquiry by pointing in illustrative fashion to the kinds of artifact that are necessarily eliminated by such a strategy. Second, through analysis of the artifact that remains after multiple strategies have been employed we can assess some of the major threats to validity which characterize experimental testing (not just hypnotic) in general. All of the experimental paradigms we have considered to date (and any others we might have included) are premised on the implicit assumption that both the hypnotist–experimenter and the subject being studied are engaged in a formal research contract—one that subtly emphasizes relatively ritualized cooperation between unequal participants who take part in a specialized form of social interaction. Prior to formulating our conclusions on the models that we have discussed in previous chapters it seems pertinent to glance, then, over strategies considered collectively in order to analyze the specific threats to validity that this traditional "research contract" stance necessarily conveys. The solution to the difficulties that are integrally associated with such an approach usefully forces us to come to grips with some of the basic problems characterizing contemporary study of the methodology of the social sciences.

ARTIFACT AND THREAT TO VALIDITY

Survey of Major Sources of Artifact

Each of the models we have considered in this book applies distinctive treatments to subjects, labeled "control" as well as "experimental," and in every case features of the procedural applications exist which potentially contaminate the kinds of inferences that can be drawn about hypnosis. A brief survey demonstrates the point.

Consider Barber's operational paradigm of hypnosis (Chapter 3), for instance. This model employs a set of instructions (TM) which subtly pressures subjects to socially conform (Bowers, 1967; Hilgard, 1973b; Sheehan & Dolby, 1974). Demand for honesty by the experimenter may counteract such a tendency, but the evidence tells us that other undefined characteristics of this comparison condition also exist—TM instructions come to be perceived as "hypnotic" by subjects, even though this is not intended. Such unintended specification features of the condition can be expected to yield quite complex behavioral effects.

The problem of artifact is to some extent unresolved with respect to Sarbin's model of hypnosis, as we have indicated in Chapter 4. Sarbin's theory of hypnosis emphasizes not just role enactment, but considers it important to take account of the total hypnotic setting in which hypnotic behavior occurs. The onus is therefore on proponents of this model to distinguish carefully those variables which are, in fact, artifactual in its distinctive explanation of hypnotic events from those which reflect true and genuine influences on hypnotic outcomes. Practice in *as-if* behavior, or experience at role enactment, for example, may or may not be a confounding variable in terms of the model's particular framework of thinking; the precise nature of the variable's influence, though, needs to be established to confirm the validity of the theory that is being proposed.

Role playing represents a comparison condition used by several paradigms of hypnosis which carries its own distinctive sources of artifact. When behavioral differences occur between role playing and hypnotic subjects, these differences may be due to the treatment peculiarities of role-playing instruction as much as they may be due to the influence of hypnosis. Work with Orne's real-simulating model (Chapter 6), for instance, has shown that behavioral consequences of the act of simulation can indeed be demonstrated; simulating instructions, for example, have the effect of making role players less obligated to reveal themselves personally, and more prone to indicate "safe" responses particularly when the task they are completing is an unstructured one (Sheehan, 1970, 1971c). If the investigator using this model wants to explore group differences it is possible, then, that behavioral differences occurring between real and simulating subjects can be attributed to the treatment aspects of simulation as well as to the treatment consequences of hypnotic induction. The logic of the same argument can be equally as well applied to the interpretation of differences found in application of Reyher's clinical paradigm of hypnosis which ordinarily employs susceptible faking subjects (Reyher, 1962).

Sutcliffe's model of hypnosis (Chapter 5) has been presented in this book as aiming toward a general, comprehensive methodology of hypnosis, and this paradigm inevitably achieves by the very scope and variability of its procedures the elimination of many potential sources of artifact, but it is vulnerable nevertheless. Its role-playing condition seeks to eliminate (as for other models) the rival plausible hypothesis that hypnotic subjects are complying socially with the experimenter's intent and are responding for reasons that do not reflect the nature of the treatment "hypnosis" at all. Generally speaking, request to susceptible as well as insusceptible subjects to fake creates distinctive problems in both instances. Insusceptible faking (as opposed to simulating) subjects are not sufficiently motivated for adequate comparison with real subjects, and the evidence suggests that some susceptible simulating subjects find their task a particularly unpleasant one (Austin *et al.,* 1963). Problems such as these raise immediate difficulties with respect to this and other paradigms (for example,

Reyher's) regarding the meaning of the interpretation that can be made of performance differences between faking, susceptible subjects and real, hypnotized subjects.

Base-line measurement represents a most important feature of several paradigms. Prehypnotic testing, however, is associated with many potential sources of artifact that can affect interpretation of experimental data. Employment of subjects as their own controls conveys certain strengths, but the procedure introduces possible serial effects which can contaminate those outcomes associated with the experimental treatment(s). Campbell (1957) comprehensively lists the sources of error that may be related to designs employing pretesting. Possible errors include the maturational effect of pretesting which can be systematic with the passage of time. The effect of pretesting itself on experimental performance can change the very thing one is trying to measure. Also, "instrumental decay" (Campbell, 1957, p. 299) may occur.

London and Fuhrer's model (Chapter 7), for instance, has to cope with the specific threat to validity that arises from subjects who are tested repeatedly coming to realize that future experimentation will involve hypnosis. The problem of when and how base-line measurement should be taken remains a distinctive one for this model as well as for others. Further, with respect to this paradigm, there remains the possibility that some insusceptible subjects simply will not accept the hypnotist's instructions that they will be adequate hypnotic performers. For the validity of the model's obtained effects to be argued, it is essential that procedures guarantee that the verbal instructions of the experimenter in this regard will tally, in fact, with the subjective experience of the subjects being tested. This model, as does others, faces the essential problem of specifying fully the consequences of its various treatment conditions.

Hilgard's paradigm (Chapter 2) is distinctively prone to the influence of serial effects resulting from the administration of different conditions to the same subjects and we reserve discussion of it till last in this survey in order to focus on unpublished data which highlight the problem. Routine strategies are available to control for serial effects and one such technique is that of counterbalancing. The apparent simplicity of this strategy, though, may create a fresh set of complexities of its own. Table 8.1 reports the results from an unpublished study (Connors, 1976) that indicate the presence of subtle interactive effects which relate to counterbalanced sequencing of the basic conditions employed by Hilgard's methodological framework. Following closely the procedures outlined by Hilgard and Tart (1966) and Tart and Hilgard (1966), order of conditions was counterbalanced by Connors for subjects with respect to hypnotic (H) and waking (W) instructions, and also with respect to hypnotic and imagination (I) instructions; testing took place on two consecutive days and independent groups of subjects were used for each of the four comparisons, or paired sequencings (H–W, W–H; H–I, I–H). When simple waking instruction was adopted as the control, mean performance scores on the SHSS:C as reported in Table 8.1

TABLE 8.1
Mean SHSS:C Scores for Subjects Tested under Different Sequencing of Conditions (Hypnotic and Nonhypnotic) on Two Successive Days

Comparison group	First condition (Day 1)		Second condition (Day 2)	
1	Waking (W)	3.2	Hypnosis (H)	5.6[a]
2	Hypnosis (H)	5.8	Waking (W)	3.2[a]
3	Imagination (I)	3.95	Hypnosis (H)	4.05
4	Hypnosis (H)	4.93	Imagination (I)	3.27[a]

[a]Denotes the presence of an appreciable enhancement ($p < .05$) effect associated with the difference in SHSS:C scores obtained across successive days' testing for separate comparisons (Group 1: W/H; Group 2: H/W; Group 3: I/H; and Group 4: H/I)

indicate that comparable hypnotic scores were obtained which were appreciably different from simple waking scores regardless of the particular day on which the hypnotic instruction had been administered. When imagination instructions were selected as the control, however, there was a complex interactive order effect. Results demonstrated that imagination instructions were inferior in their effect to hypnotic induction *only* when induction preceded imagination testing. Both hypnotic and imagination conditions yielded similar behavioral effects when induction of hypnosis appeared second in the sequence of testing. These results convey obvious implications for choice of an appropriate waking comparison condition if control suggestibility testing is to precede experimental testing. Specifically, they indicate the limited enhancement of hypnotic responsiveness one can expect when particular conditions (viz., waking imagination instructions) and orders of test sequence (viz., I–H, rather than H–I) are adopted for subjects who act as their own controls.

This survey is in no way exhaustive. Rather, we have focused attention only on some of the major attenuating factors affecting the validity, or accuracy of inferences related to the effects of hypnotic treatments (as associated with each of the paradigms we have considered in this book). Particular sources of artifact have been outlined and threats to validity categorized. In all, one concludes that the essential problem facing the researcher is that he must consistently provide ways and means of increasing confidence in the accuracy of the inferences he wants to draw about the data he collects. We turn therefore to discuss, in principle, three viable ways of coping with the problem of artifact. All represent feasible methods for eliminating some of the "essential ambiguity" (Sheehan,

1973c) that can arise from the treatments which hypnotic researchers (and other investigators) apply.

Methods for Refining the Validity of Inferences about Data

Perhaps the most obvious way of refining the accuracy of the statements we wish to make about data is to investigate the artifacts associated with our treatments as variables in their own right, and simply adjust our inferences accordingly. The treatment effects of simulation, for instance, serve to illustrate the point. We know data indicate that differences between real and simulating subjects are more likely to occur on unstructured rather than structured tasks; any differences that do eventuate, then, between these two groups of subjects will be most meaningful when the task employed is a relatively structured one, seeing that differences rarely occur in structured situations. Inferences we wish to draw about hypnosis could be strictly limited to tasks of this kind, our statements thereby simply taking account of the knowledge we have acquired about the artifact's effects. Inferences which take account of the limiting factors affecting hypnotic data in this way, however, are especially cumbersome. Arguments about the complex interactions that might be occurring between artifactual variables and experimental treatments may easily become too specific to be useful.

An alternative way of coping with the detected presence of artifact has been termed in the literature "altered replication strategy" (Rosenberg, 1969). In this instance a study is replicated with essential variations in procedures which allow us to recognize the possible influence of the suspected artifact. Consider Barber's paradigm, for example, and the fact that this model needs to come to grips more fully with the potential influence of the cue characteristics adhering to its set of TM instructions. Accordingly, the procedures of the operational paradigm may be repeated so as to render more equivalent the experimental (hypnotic) condition and its control (TM comparison) condition. TM instructions are characterized by "behavioral constraint." To cope with this problem in terms of experimental design social pressure may be either "built into" hypnotic instructions to equate them with TM instructions, or the experiment may be repeated with behavioral constraint eliminated entirely from the comparison set of instructions. Both kinds of replication essentially serve the same basic principle of control: the experimental, hypnotic (*X*) group is equated more exactly with its control, comparison (non-*X*) condition in a way which highlights more sharply the particular treatment (*X*, hypnosis) about which inferences will be drawn. The formal logic of such an approach strictly emphasizes that every condition, be it control (non-*X*) or experimental (*X*), is equally demanding of specification and lends itself in equivalent fashion to systematic manipulation for purposes of more rigorous control. Consequently, a hypnotic condition may be expanded to include a source of contamination present in its comparison condition, just as a nonhypnotic comparison condition may be changed to eliminate the source of artifact in question. Logically speaking, both kinds of altered replication serve the interests of more precise control and move us toward refining our inferences about data.

A third way of coping with the problem of artifact and multiple threats to validity is that of "heteromethod replication" (Campbell, 1969), but it is a method rarely adopted in practice in any comprehensive way. Defense of this strategy has been made by those working in areas quite unrelated to hypnosis. The strategy is defined in terms of a variety of measures and/or procedures being brought to bear upon a single hypothesis; and it exemplifies the principle of multiple operationism (Webb, Campbell, Schwartz, & Sechrest, 1972) in which one set of methods is supplemented by other methods to focus, through their separate idiosyncratic weaknesses, upon the same notion under test. Webb *et al.* (1972) view the strategy as a particularly fertile means of searching for validity and argue that accuracy of inference will inevitably grow as a hypothesis survives the confrontation of a series of complimentary methods of testing. Instead of viewing hypnotic amnesia, for instance, as a phenomenon to be studied by just one set of measures or procedures (for example, number of items recalled) the argument is that our inferences concerning its nature will be sharpened if we approach it procedurally from different directions (for example, taking both a "savings" score following relearning, and measuring the transfer of learning that is apparent on a similar task).

A uniform, primary feature of these three suggested ways of coping with artifact is that the checks on validity are conducted within the confines of the human laboratory test setting. All the paradigms we have considered work within this traditional mode. Whenever such a context of testing is employed, however, there exists the possibility that the very act of testing itself is reactive, thus leading to unintended changes in the behavior of the samples of subjects that are being tested. Further, a considerable number of rival hypotheses about psychological phenomena would be reduced if we could eliminate entirely those social psychological processes that are specific to the formal context of testing in which laboratory test behavior is traditionally measured. The multitude of contaminating test taking attitudes, for instance, that can arise when subjects are aware that they are taking part in a psychological experiment (Weber & Cook, 1972) would then create no problem. The most obvious solution to such difficulties and to the reactivity issue in particular, is to test hypotheses in the natural, nonlaboratory setting where steps can be taken to ensure that the subject is unaware that he is being observed. Such a method of analysis, however, would appear to have relatively little relevance to the study of hypnosis. The hypnotist must necessarily be a participant–observer in the phenomena that emerge in order to understand them fully. Also, leaving aside the ethical problem of the deception which needs to be involved to establish "unreactive" test, most field experiments simply cannot control for the extent or variety of variables that need be studied in order that a given effect can be specified exactly.

TOWARD CONVERGENT INQUIRY

Historically speaking, the impact of the sophisticated research strategies in hypnosis that have been developed, as indeed with modes of inquiry in other major fields of psychological study, has been to search for single sets of increasingly refined procedures which attempt to capture the essence of a given set of phenomena. Most of the procedures discussed in relation to each of the models taken up in this book are detailed and well specified (although not completely). The proponents of the models argue distinctively for the legitimacy of their procedural applications and their own accounts of hypnotic phenomena. The value inherent in the separateness of these various approaches is realized optimally when one conceptualizes the different problems and issues that are explicitly, or implicitly, evoked by the paradigms. As we have outlined in the preceding chapters, Hilgard's model emphasizes individual differences in hypnotic responsivity; Barber's operational paradigm focuses exclusively on the nonhypnotic determinants of suggestibility test performance; Sarbin's model focuses on the relevance of subjects' role skills and aptitudes; Orne's model attempts to discriminate those features of hypnotic performance which may reflect simple response to subjects' perception of their experimenters' demands; London and Fuhrer's model analyzes the impact of equating the motivations of subjects of different susceptibilities.

One decided advantage of this pursuit of distinct and well defined sets of procedural strategies is that the domain of hypnotic study can be widened considerably as research reveals new and interesting data which raise further issues to be explored. But one disadvantage in pursuing separateness of approach is that procedural preferences become too firmly demarcated and theory tends to polarize around particular viewpoints and strategies of research. Penetrating analysis of phenomena is put at some risk when inquiry focuses only on a limited number of ways in which inferences about data can be checked.

In earlier discussion (see Chapter 2, Figure 2.1) we indicated by means of set theory analysis some of the advantages of applying the logic of convergent operations to the study of hypnotic phenomena. If only one measure was permitted in the study of hypnosis our choice would have to be "verbal report," for only this measure directs the investigators' attention to different areas of content, often simultaneously (Webb *et al.,* 1972). Conceptual analysis indicates, however, that verbal testimony considered alone, is too restrictive a way of approaching the study of hypnotic phenomena; and such a measure clearly should be considered in conjunction with other measures. Applying the logic of multiple operationism to the broad domain of hypnotic study, the interests of precision in inference and genuine openness of inquiry (Hilgard, 1972b) can be furthered distinctively by applying separate methodologies collectively to the study of hypnosis where multiple strategies fit the problem being considered. Heteromethod Replication as argued by Campbell (1969) and others (Webb *et al.*, 1972) is a way of coping with artifact which moves us toward the breakdown of any polarization of procedural preferences, and it emphasizes the potential methodological value of approaching hypnosis by adopting alternative modes of inquiry. The technique effectively blurs the confrontation that often emerges between different frameworks of thinking, while, at the same time, it eliminates many of the multiple threats to validity that are posed by strategies when they are considered separately.

Within the context of our argument that particular threats to validity can be eliminated by convergent, impartial inquiry, we turn now to examine, in particular, the consequences of heteromethod replication as a viable means of coping with artfact. Our discussion will focus briefly on (a) the contribution different methodologies may make collectively to the understanding of hypnotic events, and (b) the threats to validity that nevertheless remain. To illustrate the argument we will consider in turn the relevance of imagination processes to hypnosis, and the question of the extent to which some hypnotic subjects appear especially willing to please the hypnotist with whom they are interacting.

The Relevance of Imagination to Hypnosis

One of the most important cognitive processes relating to hypnosis is that of imagination (see Chapter 9 for development of this conclusion) and quite separate models argue strongly for its significance (for example, Hilgard, Barber, Sarbin, Sutcliffe, and Orne). Procedurally speaking, Hilgard's concentration on the imagination comparison group as a suitable control condition highlights the particular significance he attributes to this process within the formal constraints of the Same-Subjects model. Barber, in his choice of TM instructions for his major comparison condition emphasizes the distinctive role imagination plays in determining the nature and function of suggestion response, as does Sarbin who substantially appeals to such processes also within his paradigm. Any model, in fact, which involves pretense, or *as-if* behavior, for purposes of comparison (for example, Sutcliffe and Orne) must ultimately appeal to this process for relevance.

Generally speaking, the search for the cognitive and personality correlates of hypnotizability has been a relatively fruitless pursuit to date, but "imagination capacity" has emerged as one of the few correlates showing any real consistency of data. Subjects' capacities to respond positively to hypnotic suggestions and their utilization of their cognitive aptitude for imagination have not always been in one-to-one correspondence, but regardless of paradigm affiliation there has been a general shift in perspective among contemporary researchers of widely varying orientations toward recognizing the particular relevance of imaginative capacities to the explanation of hypnotic events. And a large variety of research approaches have, in fact, contributed toward this conclusion, as has been noted elsewhere (see Spanos & Barber, 1974). Some studies, for example, have been correlational in emphasis and measured directly the relationship existing between hypnotic responsivity and specific indications of imaginative capacity such as vividness of imagery. Situational factors have been found to influence the kind of relationship that is obtained with vividness of imagery and some negative instances have also emerged (Morgan & Lam, 1969; Perry, 1973). Nevertheless, the consistency of data coming from investigations using a variety of measures of imagining (for example, Barber, 1960; Barber & Glass, 1962; J. Hilgard, 1970, 1974; Palmer & Field, 1968; Sarbin, 1964; Sutcliffe *et al.*, 1970) has been more convincing than for any other single capacity or aptitude measured. Studies have generally confirmed that a positive correlation exists across a range of different self-report test measures. Another approach adopted by researchers with quite different procedural emphases (for example, Barber, Spanos, & Chaves, 1974; Spanos & Barber, 1972; Spanos, De Moor, & Barber, 1973) has demonstrated consistent data; here, procedures orientated to the study of goal-directed fantasy have shown that suggestions explicitly structured within the hypnotic setting to elicit an imagination response from subjects are more likely to be experienced successfully than suggestions which are not so structured.

In measurement of imagination both within and without the trance context, results appear to generate the same conclusion: performance on hypnotic test tasks is a positive function, in part, of subjects' capacities to involve themselves in imagined events. As argued elsewhere (Sheehan, 1972), this association between imaginative capacity and hypnotizability can be formulated in a number of different ways so that it is compatible with either a "state" or "nonstate" account of hypnosis. Theoretically speaking, the relationship is not decisive, but the point to note in the present context is that the special relevance of imaginative processes to hypnosis is most strongly established, in fact, by the cohesiveness of the evidence that has been derived from the application of multiple strategies of research—much more so, than could possibly be the case from the application of any single method, or set of measures, taken alone.

The Influence of the Hypnotist's Intent

Work in only one area has brought altogether different paradigms collectively to bear on the same hypothesis under test. This area concerns the transference-like involvement some subjects appear to have with their hypnotist. We turn now to consider this problem in some detail in order to assess the strengths and weaknesses of the validity check provided by cross-paradigm application of multiple research strategies. The approach will be examined with respect to the investigation of the particular notion that the hypnotist's intent is especially significant for subjects who are susceptible to hypnosis.

For all the importance that social influence processes have played in modern formulation of hypnotic theory, we have noted in the course of this book that the psychology of the interaction between hypnotist and subject has received remarkably little attention from hypnotic researchers. Emphasis on imagination as a correlate of trance and of variables like "absorption" as conceivably related processes (for example, Tellegen & Atkinson, 1974) have indirectly reinforced its relevance, but the cognitive, motivational, and affective features of the hypnotist–subject relationship have been analyzed much more closely in theory than in practice. From a developmental viewpoint about hypnosis, for example, concepts such as transference, dissociation, and regression provide ready means of relating the "residues" of early developmental experiences to current social interactions (J. Hilgard, 1970, 1974). The concept of transference is readily reconcilable with the view that hypnosis is an altered and regressed state. Gill (1972), and Gill and Brenman (1961) argue, for example, for the subjects' involvement with the hypnotist through surrender of his autonomy; they maintain that the needs of both participants fuse together in hypnosis essentially entailing as it does a multilevel, dynamic, and interpersonal relationship interlocking both subject and hypnotist (Conn & Conn, 1967). Wolberg (1948) talks in related fashion of the hypnotist becoming cloaked in a mantle of authority that instils the subject's faith in his ideas and communications and that the very nature of the hypnotic process induces feelings of closeness not possible using other techniques. Watkins (1954) goes so far as to argue that a true science of hypnotizing can only be based on a deep and intimate knowledge of the personality structure of the patient and his transference needs.

Those arguing for the theoretical importance of transference to the understanding of hypnosis (for example, Ferenczi, 1910; Gill, 1972; Gill & Brenman, 1961; J. Hilgard, 1970, 1974; Kubie & Margolin, 1944; Schilder, 1927; Shor, 1962; Wolberg, 1948) nearly always highlight the clinical aspects of hypnotic phenomena and draw attention to features of hypnotic response which are much less readily observed in the laboratory than in the therapeutic context. Transference-like processes reflecting particular states of motivation (viz., intense rapport) are simply not easily reinforced by the constraints of the formal research setting. The human laboratory test context routinely works to minimize rather than enhance personal involvement of subject with the experimenter. In any "experiment," the parties involved work in a formal, relatively ritualized interaction normally contracted so that both subject and experimenter will participate impersonally in the joint enterprise of contributing to science. Many contemporary researchers would prefer not to appeal to such processes at all in fact, not simply because of the apparent inappropriateness of these processes to their usual context of testing, but also because the connotations of the term "transference" are often vague and difficult to index objectively. It is clearly easier to try to work with other more denotable social process variables such as setting characteristics, and subject attitudes and expectancies.

If transference-like processes are important to hypnosis in any way—evoked by the situation, or brought to it by the subject himself—it follows that hypnotic subjects should have a special wish to please the hypnotist and that his communications will have singular importance for them in the trance setting. Such a notion suggests that "motivation to please" is itself an essence feature of the hypnotic process. Focus on communication of the hypnotist's intent as a special motivating force working in the trance setting can also be seen as a limited first step toward systematically studying the more subtle properties of the hypnotist–subject interrelationship. Results from the application of two distinct methodologies to this problem will now be discussed with a view to highlighting the particular contribution of Heteromethod Replication to coping with major threats to the validity of inferences about hypnotic data.

First, we will consider results from a formal application of the real-simulating model of hypnosis. In this program of work (Sheehan, 1971b), real and simulating subjects (before selection for the hypnotic part of the study) were given a lecture demonstration concerning appropriate ways to respond during hypnosis. Two expectations were induced in the demonstration: observers were told good hypnotic subjects always demonstrate catalepsy of the dominant hand only, and that good hypnotic subjects also uniformly respond thoroughly automatically and compulsively to cues being offered by the hypnotist (such as the word "psychology") right up until hypnosis has actually and finally been terminated—regardless of how and when the cue word is used by the hypnotist. Following this demonstration, real and simulating subjects were recruited for experimental testing and procedures were applied strictly according to Orne's paradigm (1959, 1972). In the experiment proper, the hypnotist formally (that is, obviously) tested both suggestions, administered intervening test items and then told subjects he was about to terminate hypnosis, implying that all suggestions previously administered would be no longer effective. At this point, the hypnotist reminded subjects of the cue word and went on, just as subjects expected him to, and told them they need no longer respond. The prediction of the study was that when the cue word was used in this context—just prior to actual removal of the suggestion—hypnotic subjects would counter the particular preconception about compulsive responding that they had acquired in the lecture demonstration while simulating subjects would not. It was argued that the implicit desire of the hypnotist would be experienced by real subjects in a way that would restructure their commitment to favor personal involvement with him in the trance setting. Table 8.2 shows the results of the experiment. Where no conflict of communication between the lecture demonstration and the hypnotist's intent was involved in any way (that is, on the arm catalepsy item), real and simulating subjects demonstrated equally the fact that social expecta-

TABLE 8.2
Frequency with Which Hypnotized and Simulating Subjects Responded "Appropriately" in the Trance Setting When Tested by the Hypnotist[a]

I. No conflict between "lecture demonstration" and "hypnotist's intent"

Subject group	Behavior: Responded according to the lecture demonstration	Did not respond according to the lecture demonstration
Hypnotized	10	4
Simulating	10	4

II. Conflict between "lecture demonstration" and "hypnotist's intent"

Subject group	Behavior: Responded according to hypnotist's intent	Responded according to lecture demonstration
Hypnotized	10	6
Simulating	2	13

[a]Adapted from Sheehan (1971b). Copyright 1971 by the American Psychological Association. Reproduced by permission.

tions influenced their behavior strongly. Where there was a conflict of communication (that is, on the compulsion item just prior to waking), however, real and simulating subjects performed quite differently. Results clearly supported the hypothesis that involvement with the hypnotist carried special impact for the susceptible group alone; only the real, susceptible subjects satisfied the intent of the hypnotist with whom they were interacting when a choice was subtly forced upon them to decide which was the more appropriate way to respond.

Now we will consider Barber's operational paradigm as applied to the same problem. As before, the rules of procedure were exactly as laid down by the model being adopted (Barber, 1969). A task was incorporated into the paradigm which provided a unique test of the hypothesis. Epstein and Rock (1960) have isolated an exact set of conditions in which the influence of subjects' expectancies about events are actually counter-demanded in favor of the influence of events perceived most recently. Epstein and Rock worked, among other stimuli, with Boring's ambiguous wife/mother-in-law figure which is perceived by subjects as either a young (Y) or an old (O) woman. Figure 8.1 illustrates the structured and ambiguous (Y/O) test displays which subjects were shown.

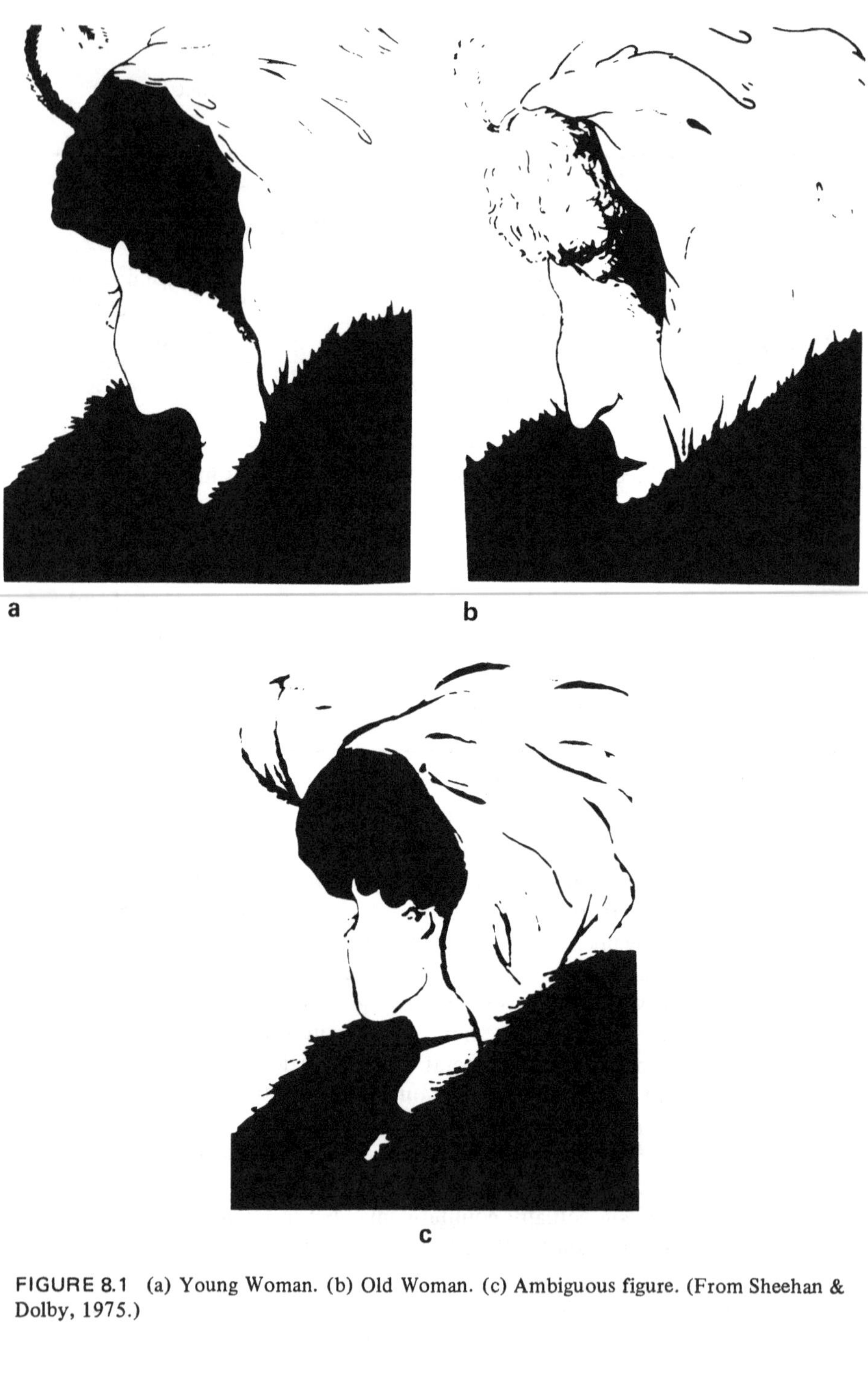

FIGURE 8.1 (a) Young Woman. (b) Old Woman. (c) Ambiguous figure. (From Sheehan & Dolby, 1975.)

Subjects were routinely shown a sequence of four slides (YYY–Y/O) and told that one of the slides in series would be different while all of the others would be the same. Accordingly, subjects received three actual presentations of the young woman exposed for .5 sec only; the fourth display, which was the critical one, was the ambiguous slide and was exposed for .2 sec. Subjects were thus led strongly to expect by the end of the series that the last slide was the one that would be different. Under such procedural conditions Epstein and Rock showed convincingly (and consistently) that subjects typically reported seeing the young woman not as they were led to expect (that is, as old), but as they had most recently perceived it (that is, as young). The argument they used to explain the data was couched in terms of trace theory; trace of the preceding percept supposedly played back to structure final organization of the ambiguous slide.

This situation of Epstin and Rock provides a uniquely sensitive means of testing the impact of the subjects' involvement in trance events. The importance of hypnotic events would be decisive indeed if an expectancy effect was distinctively evident for hypnotic subjects when ordinarily recency determines peoples' perceptual responses. For test of this hypothesis (Sheehan & Dolby, 1975) subjects were first tested for recency (versus expectancy) response in the waking setting and no subject proceeded to the experimental phase of the study who did not demonstrate recency response every single time he was tested in the waking state. In the experimental phase, three sets of 27 unselected subjects were allocated according to Barber's rules of procedure–one group to a hypnotic condition, another to a TM condition, and the third to a waking control (imagination) condition–in strict application of the methods stipulated by the paradigm. Table 8.3 abstracts the results of this main study; data are reported for the ambiguous slide appearing last in the series of slides showing the young woman, and for an actual young-woman-slide shown in its place (in a final test of the consecutive series employing a YYY–Y sequence). Further, data are tabulated only for those subjects who insisted in a postexperimental inquiry that they actually saw the figure they reported. Contrasting with the marked effectiveness of task-motivated response reported uniformly elsewhere throughout the literature, data on the perceptual task differentiated the three groups of subjects. For the routine suggestibility test items that were considered in the study, task-motivated subjects performed just as well as (and often bettern than) hypnotic subjects, but on the slide series task (with ambiguous or young figure occurring last) expectancy dictated the response of the hypnotic group almost exclusively. Further, expectancy behavior was associated most distinctively with those subjects who indicated by their scores on the SHSS:C that they were at least moderately susceptible to hypnosis. Susceptible hypnotic subjects performed in contradiction to the strong reality constraints of the series task and behaved according to the intent of the hypnotist. The reversal from their waking pattern of behavior was dramatic.

TABLE 8.3
Frequency of Subjects Who Gave the "Old Woman" (Expected) Response to the Ambiguous (Y/O) Slide and to the "Young Woman" (Y) Slide at Any Time on the Experimental Test of the Consecutive (YYY) Series[a, b]

Group	Ambiguous slide (YYY–O/Y)	Final Y slide (YYY–Y)
Hypnotic $N = 27$	12 (9) $\bar{X}$ Sus. = 7.1	8 (7) $\bar{X}$ Sus. = 8.1
Task motivational $N = 27$	3 (2) $\bar{X}$ Sus. = 7.0	0
Control waking $N = 27$	3 (2) $\bar{X}$ Sus. = 5.7	0

[a] Adapted from Sheehan and Dolby (1975). in the *Journal of Abnormal Psychology*, Copyright © 1975 by the American Psychological Association. Reproduced by permission.

[b] The series presented three brief displays of the young woman with the test slide occurring fourth in the sequence. Bracketed entries represent the number of subjects who were "susceptible" to hypnosis as diagnosed by their passing 7 or more items on a 10-point modified version of the SHSS:C. Mean hypnotic test scores for each group are also listed.

In summary, application of the procedures of Orne's paradigm showed that real, not simulating, subjects resolved a conflict in communication about "appropriate hypnotic behavior" to favor the personal intent of the hypnotist as transmitted in the trance setting. Separate application of the major strategies relating to Barber's paradigm demonstrated a similar finding; susceptible hypnotic subjects, as opposed to task-motivated subjects, contravened a strong waking tendency to respond on the basis of most recently perceived events in order to satisfy the stated intent of the hypnotist. The two sets of findings are most distinctive in that they yielded behavioral differences–which occur very infrequently in the literature–among the major groups of subjects both paradigms routinely take up to study. It should be noted, however, that additional techniques may be needed to answer the question asked, even when multiple paradigms are employed. In the example we took, for instance, analysis of susceptibility level differences was conducted for Barber's paradigm–a strategy which is not typically associated with that particular model.

Cross-paradigm research of this kind uniquely eliminates several major threats to the validity of inferences that can be drawn about the possible effect of hypnotic suggestion. In the separate chapters devoted to each of these models the strengths and weaknesses of the various methodologies have been discussed in some detail and the limitations of the inferences that can be drawn from application of each of them were made explicit. It was noted, for example, that differences between real and simulating subjects could reflect uncertainty in role-playing subjects about how they should pretend as much as the effects of hypnosis; also, differences found could be due to personality factors associated with the variation in susceptibility which necessarily differentiates real from simulating subjects. On the other hand, distinctive sources of artifact adhere to the procedures of the operational paradigm: differences between task motivated and hypnotic subjects may say as much about the specific characteristics or differentiating features of the TM condition as about the effects of the hypnotic treatment.

Joint application of the two paradigms eliminates all of the above threats to validity—and some others, pertaining to yet undetected treatment artifacts, without the need to formulate them in the first instance. Consider, for example, the differences highlighting the influence of the hypnotist's intent in application of the first paradigm: they cannot be due simply to simulation instructions being used, because the same pattern of differences was found using a quite different treatment manipulation, namely task motivation. Similarly, the same differences could not have been due to personality factors discriminating real from simulating subjects: consistent results were found with Barber's paradigm using unselected subjects who did not differ initially in their suggestibility level at all. On the other hand, the operational paradigm employed no formal strategy to guarantee the "blindness" of the experimenter who conducted testing: an objection of this kind, however, does not seriously rival the validity of the hypothesis that was tested, because the real-simulating model yielded essentially the same pattern of findings when a blind control design was, in fact, adopted. Further, distinctive task motivation artifacts cannot explain results, because data from application of the first paradigm using altogether different instructions converged to a similar result. Several of the major difficulties we have discussed previously in relation to each model's separate evaluation of its data have been eliminated by convergent inquiry.

The possibilities for the presence of artifact are endless and no one strategy of research can ever hope to meet all of the objections that can be raised with respect to a given set of data that is collected. Heteromethod Replication, though, does exemplify our essential argument that the proper way to proceed in science is to eliminate major, plausible rival accounts of the data in systematic fashion. Cross-paradigm research in hypnosis (or any other area of psychological inquiry, for that matter) transcends the boundaries set by procedural and theoretical preferences and is more responsive than any one model considered alone to the demands of open, impartial inquiry.

Convergent inquiry allows us also to refocus on the theoretical implications of our data. The results that have emerged in relation to the prediction discussed above, for example, reinforce the urgency for turning our attention toward the powerful, internal process variables that appear to characterize behavior in the hypnotic setting, at least for some susceptible subjects. And research findings indicate a definite beginning to realizing some rapprochement between experimental and clinical demonstrations of hypnosis. The data that have been discussed could conceivably be formulated in terms of "hypnotist expectancy" as a powerful antecedent factor simply operating to determine socially influenced behavioral outcomes in the hypnotic setting. One could theorize about the data, in fact, without any necessary appeal at all to the concept of hypnotic rapport, or transference. Results nevertheless are altogether consistent with the notion that some susceptible subjects infuse the hypnotist and what he says with a degree of importance that cannot be matched by nonhypnotic subjects, and that these hypnotic subjects are involved with the hypnotist and what he says in an intensely committed way. Such a theory obviously requires more direct test of the real depth of rapport through detailed clinical analysis of individual responsiveness–the processes of transference imply the personal display of dynamic interactional events, for example, and these are very difficult to index. But support so far encourages faith in the clinician's claims regarding what he so frequently observes in the nonlaboratory setting. The fact that the hypnotist's intent is so markedly influential for some subjects, and that the notion is multiply confirmed, begins to unify the claims of the laboratory researcher and the practicing clinician.

THE ESSENTIAL LIMITATIONS OF THE "RESEARCH CONTRACT"

By means of validity checks such as those that have been outlined, laboratory testing can establish confidently whether, or not, the experimental treatment of hypnotic induction creates a significant effect. But no matter how rigorous the research, how refined the controls that are adopted, or what method of validity check is employed, the nature of the human experimental situation is such that the effects that we obtain may be limited to the type of context in which they are established. Discussion of some of the problems of interpretation that remain after multiple sets of strategies have converged on the same problem serves to illustrate this point and raise more general issues pertinent to the methodology of the social sciences as a whole.

Social-psychological analysis of the human laboratory test setting must necessarily affect many of our inferences about phenomena isolated in such a setting, hypnotic, or otherwise. Specific sources of artifact accrue naturally to the laboratory setting. We have argued that the research context, for example, is heavily contractual in nature. Subjects for an experiment routinely know they are participating in a research venture, the relationship between experimenter and subject is invariably one of two unequals (the experimenter as authority has coopted the services of subject as object of scrutiny), and the act of the measurement itself is often reactive. Any amount of validity checking conducted through single application of standard laboratory testing or even multiple instances of its application, fails to escape these essential limitations. Argyris (1968) claims that the more rigorous the research, the more restrictive are the demands of the research contract: the better controlled the experiment, the more heavily obligated subjects simply are to execute the experimenter's chosen task.

There is no easy solution to coping with the restrictions of formalized testing where increased stringency of control serves only to reinforce the basically contractual nature of the research setting. It appears that data must necessarily be limited in the extent to which they can be generalized. This raises the problem of external validity which has been recognized implicitly by hypnotic researchers though the solution they have posed is an unsatisfactory one. Orne (1970, 1973), for example, sets out the criteria for establishing a proper postexperimental inquiry procedure and argues that the subject should become a collaborator, a colleague who helps the experimenter understand the difficult problem of why he has behaved in the way that he has. Role playing has been conceptualized also by others as a particularly feasible solution for changing the status of the experimental subject from object being scrutinized to person as collaborator (Brown, 1965; Kelman, 1967; Miller, 1972).

No traditional postexperimental inquiry or role-playing situation, however, can eliminate the formal, contractual features of the human laboratory test setting. Role-playing instruction, no matter how it is initiated can always be perceived by subjects as an attempt by the experimenter to manipulate their responses for the purposes of study; additionally, deception of a complex kind is implicitly, if not explicitly, involved. Truly active participation is more radically achieved within the humanistic framework of thinking promulgated by Jourard (1968, 1972a, b) and others (for example, Giorgi, 1970). Jourard advocates that both experimenter and subject should be thoroughly open and revealing to each other; a hypnotic subject, for example, would be encouraged to report whatever a suggestion (and his personal response to it) means to him and the hypnotist in turn could then comment on the subject's reaction and his own response to it. The basic motivation assumed to lie behind Jourard's notion of research participation is the intrinsic involvement of the subject in exploring his own individual research experience. In terms of analyzing relationship factors in hypnosis the relevance of such an orientation is obvious; collaborative procedures are much more likely to provide genuine understanding of the subtleties of dynamic interplay between hypnotist and subject than any set of contractual-based procedures. A collaborative framework implies somewhat naively that the best way of investigating the nature of man is simply to ask him (Schultz, 1969). It usefully reasserts, though, the importance of verbal testimony as perhaps the single most valuable measure to adopt in analyzing experimental treatments involving humans. According to such an orientation, the status of the verbal utterances of the hypnotic subject should be of critical importance, because they offer very meaningful testimony about hypnotic processes.

For all the advantages a collaborative framework of testing would actually convey, it is nevertheless seriously limited as a substitute for contractual research; and "collaboration" could, of course, be seen by subjects as just another attempt by an astute experimenter to socially manipulate their behavior. Strategies of a detailed kind have yet to be developed with reference to such an orientation. Few people could handle the role of the experimenter (or subject) in this situation with the ease that is demanded (Carlson, 1971; Schultz, 1969). Few would have the training or the expertise to introspect to such a degree of intensity, and too much evidence exists to tell us that verbal testimony is unreliable as the sole criterion for inferring psychological processes. Finally, sources of artifact and threats to validity of a distinctive kind would obviously characterize collaborative strategies just as they do contractual ones—the nature of the particular threats to accuracy of inference would simply alter, and remain to be detected like those we have already discussed. Viewed within the context of multiple sets of strategies brought to bear upon hypnotic phenomena, however, the application of collaborative procedures (once they are developed in detail) would contribute greatly to more comprehensive understanding of hypnotic events. Relationship processes in hypnosis, multiply confirmed by cross-paradigm research, and the use of collaborative as well as contractual-based procedures, would greatly enhance our confidence in the validity of the inferences we wish to draw about the relevance of transference processes to hypnosis. Many of the peculiar contaminations of the contractual research setting would be cancelled out, in fact, by the contaminations of the collaborative mold, the latter working presumably to create an interpersonal climate in which subject and experimenter—involved with each other—would both feel they were contributing to knowledge equally.

It would have been naive to assume that collaborative testing, as long as an investigation of any kind involving a hypothesis was actually being conducted, would not involve manipulations of which both subjects and the experimenter would be aware. The need does seem clear, however, to develop new strategies of research which attempt to cope with the essential limitations of the "research contract." The move should be towards adopting less formalized and ritualized patterns of interpersonal communication than those utilized in traditional methods of laboratory inquiry to date. The results of the application of these new methods should then be combined with those flowing from the use of the more traditional strategies of control, the several techniques then converging jointly to create a fuller understanding of the psychological processes being considered. Something of a paradigm revolution seems required to meet such a challenge (Sheehan, 1974). Change, though, if it ever did result, ought never to destroy the utility of the strategies that have been developed to date. Collaborative and contractual strategies are not techniques to substitute one for another; rather they must complement each other by converging collectively to focus more intensely on the phenomenon being investigated. Far too important individual differences in hypnotic responsivity are likely to be obscured by restricting our context of inquiry solely to the formalized rules of the interactions adhering to rigorous research, yet the collaborative approach, alone, is very much limited because it presents us with no way of knowing the precise means by which hypnotic subjects behave as they do. Together, however, they can work to bring us toward a richer, more complete understanding of hypnotic events. Such is an awesomely difficult task: the integration of both approaches is a labor for only the most methodologically sophisticated, yet clinically sensitive, of hypnotic investigators.

CONCLUSION

In all research, be it contractual or collaborative, it is essential that we institute the means by which we can efficiently determine the accuracy of our inferences about the data we collect. Validity check in this sense, must be a primary goal. But threats to validity abound in the social sciences and the area of hypnotic inquiry is no exception. Unspecified treatment variables potentially confound data and varying sources of artifact implicitly adhere to every procedure that any particular model of hypnosis may employ, regardless of whether the manipulation in question contains the treatment about which we hypothesize (that is, hypnotic induction) or does not (for example, imagination instruction–Hilgard; TM–Barber; simulation–Orne; or motivational exhortation–London and Fuhrer). The primary task for the researcher is to determine those conditions that yield the greatest control of the contaminations which may exist and every manipulation employed demands full and exact specification–a task that has been given not nearly enough attention, to date. The ideal experiment is not one which aims to achieve complete "purity of control"–that particular goal is unattainable–but one where the experimenter attempts to ensure that the prediction being tested will yield a result unambiguously excluding at least one or more alternative hypotheses about hypnotic events. As others have stated more cogently (Popper, 1959), science really advances by discounting threats to validity, by eliminating plausible rival accounts of the data, and not by attempting to establish proof. Data from studies should yield strong rather than weak inferences (Platt, 1964), where the strength of the inference is determined exactly by the degree to which alternative hypotheses are effectively excluded.

The ways of coping with artifacts, viewed as threats to validity, are many, and a number of different (individual as well as collective) strategies have been discussed in this chapter. Heteromethod replication has been singled out for attention because it distinctively eliminates many, but not all, serious threats to validity which exist when individual strategies are applied. When a problem lends itself to multimethod replication (as does the one we have discussed) the researcher is well advised to consider its strengths. Webb *et al.* (1972) state the reason for the force of the approach succinctly: "If a proposition can survive the onslaught of a series of imperfect measures, with all their irrelevant error, confidence should be placed in it [p. 174]." So long as one model is used to yield data which are then separately compared with the results associated with another paradigm hypnotic researchers can more easily disagree about the problems they find and the solutions which suggest themselves; investigators will be more inclined to talk past each other while debating the merits of their own individual set of strategies. There is more than a hint of warning in Kuhn's (1962) admonition that "in the partially circular arguments that regularly result, each paradigm will be shown to satisfy more or less the criteria that it dictates for itself and to fall short of a few of those dictated by its opponent [p. 109]." Just as for other psychological phenomena, it is altogether too easy to have our vision of hypnotic processes singularly structured by the nature of the procedures we take up to study them.

Contemporary hypnotic research methodology has been based to date on a sensitive awareness of the need to institute careful and rigorous controls and all of the models discussed in this book exemplify that characteristic in one way or another. The tools they use, though, are basically contractual in nature and do create "unintended consequences" (Argyris, 1968) which practitioners in the social sciences in general have also tended to ignore. The world of research engagement should come to be perceived differently and hypnotic investigators, like other researchers, should look further for ways of ensuring that reactive dispositions and spontaneously aroused test-taking attitudes in experimental subjects are minimized, rather than encouraged or supported. The rules of the traditional "puzzle game" (Kuhn, 1962) should not solely dictate any investigator's perspective. When, and if, the standard tools of traditional research methodology are reassessed and alternative (for example, collaborative) strategies come to be developed, then knowledge about hypnotic and other phenomena may grow. New problems will be likely to emerge while others (such as the interpersonal display between hypnotist and subject) will undoubtedly take on new emphases. Scientific pursuit of the meaning of hypnotic phenomena will never advance effectively by persistent use of one paradigm merely to favor another. And when different procedures do come together we would argue they should always converge by complementing each other in the spirit of open, impartial inquiry.

9

Summary and Conclusions: Current Issues and Guidelines to Practice

> Suppose that there were no word or concept such as "hypnosis," and that psychologists then discovered a technique whereby important aspects of a person's belief system could be radically modified, for brief periods, by particular verbal inputs. Clearly, such a startling procedure would be seen to have the greatest of significance for the understanding of belief formation and cognitive processes generally [McReynolds, 1967, p. 175].

The nature of hypnosis is a problem that ultimately must be resolved by observational means. It raises issues both about theory and methodology, since there exists crucial differences in viewpoint concerning both what hypnosis is, and the appropriate methodological strategies for testing hypotheses about it.

This final chapter consists of two parts. The first one is concerned with a number of theoretical issues that underlie the methodologies surveyed in this book which remain both relatively controversial and unresolved. There is no attempt here to survey all of the problems currently existing in hypnosis research. Rather than recapitulate points that have been made in previous chapters, we seek to make explicit some of the implicit differences among the theories and methodological approaches that we have discussed. Our approach now is to attempt integration across general issues rather than specific theories.

A number of prevailing emphases in the hypnosis literature have emerged, historically, in relative mutual isolation. We have seen (in Chapter 1) how certain nineteenth century investigators gave primary attention to the inner workings of the hypnotized person though they differed in terms of the types of mental mechanisms that they postulated. This psychological emphasis developed in antagonism to viewpoints stressing external influence (which was exemplified by the magnetic tradition). Faria's observations on individual differences in hypnotic susceptibility, likewise became influential relatively independently of the external influence and psychological viewpoints, though attempts were made by some nineteenth century suggestibility theorists to reconcile Faria's doctrines with the latter point of view.

These issues continue to underlie many current conceptualizations of hypnosis, though they are formulated now in other terms. Nevertheless, some of the differences to which we have pointed in current methodologies stem from differences in theoretical position with regards to historically important emphases on cognitive processes, hypnotic susceptibility and external influence. Contemporary theorizing regards hypnosis as variously (a) an altered state, (b) an enduring trait of the person, and (c) a product of the situation in which the person finds himself. Because these emphases have developed in relative isolation, they tend to generate certain theoretical paradoxes which become noticeable when any attempt is made to reconcile them. We have sought to isolate these problem areas, and to note developments in current-day attempts to resolve the difficulties they raise.

The second part of this chapter seeks to outline appropriate methodological techniques and strategies that might be adopted by researchers for the purpose of achieving stricter control. The investigation of some issues, undoubtedly requires the development of innovative techniques—that is, unique methodological strategies—in order for them to be evaluated adequately. Nonetheless, some of the controversies running through the book might be more amenable to resolution if certain methodological techniques and practices were adopted and implemented more uniformly.

SOME CONTEMPORARY ISSUES

Hypnosis as an Altered State

During the nineteenth century, suggestibility theory became the vehicle for consolidating a variety of different notions which stressed the internal workings of the hypnotized person. Many of these older doctrines have continued to influence current thinking, even though suggestibility theorizing has itself undergone a decline. In recent decades, investigators whose primary interest is upon inner processes have tended to cluster around the altered state notion, and it may well be that state theorizing is serving similar purposes to suggestibility theory. There has been sharp controversy (see Chapters 2, 3, 4, and 6) concerning whether hypnosis constitutes an altered state, and, if it does, what are its essential characteristics. There appears to be some confusion within psychology, in general, as to what are the necessary and sufficient conditions for labeling phenomena as altered states. As a general rule of thumb, altered states tend to be inferred if there are measurable psychophysiological changes in the person, and if there are behavioral and/or performance increments or decrements. Further, if there are subjective reports from the person that his experience is somehow different, the notion of altered state is usually favored. These criteria are straightforward enough. The confusion arises as to whether any one of them is sufficient of itself to index the presence of an altered state.

This problem of definition is particularly pertinent to the understanding of hypnosis. Despite intensive research efforts, no unique psychophysiological manifestations of hypnosis have been found (Barber, 1970; Sarbin & Slagle, 1972). Further, no behaviors have been indicated that are unique to hypnosis, nor is there any evidence of performance enhancements in hypnosis (as we noted in Chapter 7 when discussing the London–Fuhrer design).

The main reason for considering hypnosis as an altered state stems almost exclusively from the reports of subjects that, while hypnotized, they experienced reality in an uncustomary fashion. Such reports give every impression of reflecting actual experience—an impression which has persisted despite the intensive efforts of people in the nineteenth century to demonstrate that hypnosis is in some way fraudulent. Although the question of sham behavior no longer constitutes a serious issue in the hypnosis literature, a problem remains as to whether such subjective reports are sufficient to infer an altered state. This is an issue that transcends the area of hypnosis; it is, in many ways, fundamental to psychology as a whole. Over the years, despite the attempts of behaviorism to expunge mentalistic concepts from the vocabulary of psychology, many have clung to state formulations to delimit such diverse phenomena as alcoholic intoxication, drug experience, pain, anger, love, meditation, sleep, fever, and hypnosis. In all cases, the common thread running through the formulation of these phenomena as altered states is the notion that they represent relatively distinct changes in subjective experience and in cognitive functioning. On the basis of such widespread usage, it could be that the state notion is too broad to be very illuminating. We may all know what an altered state is until we are asked to define it, at which point irreconcilable differences occur.

A similar point has been made in a very different context. Ryle (1949), in his discussion of dispositional concepts, points to parallel difficulties in ascribing a person as "skillful" or "cunning" or "humorous," and in summoning the requisite propositions which would enable us to say that an animal is "gregarious." The issue is more than just a linguistic quibble, though. Even given a fair consensus that it makes sense to talk of an altered state of hypnosis, there is a need to specify more clearly than hitherto its demarcating features. We will evaluate some of those features that could be said to characterize the hypnotic state after the more general issues have been discussed.

We have reviewed the reasons for Barber's and Sarbin's (Chapters 3 and 4) rejection of the state notion, and for Hilgard's (Chapter 2) endorsement of it as a "domain" for delimiting a set of phenomena requiring explanation. Over and above the issues raised by these investigators there exist other ambiguities in current state notions that have received relatively little attention. One of the most important of these pertains to the legitimacy of the "trait" approach to hypnosis.

The Trait Issue

Following the traditions of Faria, Liébeault, and Bernheim (see Chapter 1), individual differences in susceptibility have been commonly observed. The fact that such regularity has been reported for over 150 years gives some confidence in the position that hypnotizability is a stable trait of the person. (For a detailed review of this literature, see Hilgard, 1965a, 1967.) Despite extensive research efforts over the last 40 years, no reliable basis for accounting for such differences has been found. Hypnotizability has been related to just about every conceivable personality measure, and to a variety of cognitive measures such as imagery, fantasy, and perceptual style. These studies have yielded little in the way of stable correlates, though there is relative consistency (see the previous chapter) in those relating imagery and/or imaginative processes to susceptibility. In general, positive findings have come from "small samples, unusual samples or . . . studies that were not replicated [Hilgard & Lauer, 1962, p. 333]." It appears then, that the bulk of evidence indicates that hypnotizability is a relatively stable trait, but its correlates are elusive. It is still not possible to predict a person's hypnotic performance on the basis of his standing with respect to any of the hypothesized correlates.

Resolution of State and Trait Viewpoints

Experimental studies relating to the state and trait positions have been carried out somewhat independently, and there has been little integration of the two sets of data. Nevertheless, they point to certain theoretical paradoxes (over and above those discussed by Hilgard, 1973b) which can be illustrated by reference to Table 9.1.

State theorists are rarely at a loss in attributing presence and absence of state at the extremes of the continuum of Table 9.1, which uses scores on the Stanford Hypnotic Susceptibility Scale: Form C (Weitzenhoffer & Hilgard, 1962) to exemplify the problem. The customary strategy used by hypnosis researchers is to classify subjects scoring from 10 to 12 on SHSS:C as high susceptibles. Translated into state theory terms, the presence of state is usually inferred unambiguously for this particular group of subjects and not at all for

TABLE 9.1
Correspondences Between State and Trait Notions of Hypnosis, Using SHSS:C as an Example

Hypnotic category	Score on SHSS:C	Item description	State
High susceptible	12	Posthypnotic amnesia	Inferred as present
	11	Negative visual hallucinations	
	10	Hallucinated voice	
Medium susceptible	9	Anosmia to ammonia	Ambiguous
	8	Arm immobilization	
	7	Age regression	
	6	Dream	
	5	Arm rigidity	
	4	Taste hallucination	
	3	Mosquito hallucination	
Low susceptible	2	Moving hands apart	Inferred as absent
	1	Hand lowering	
	0	No response	

insusceptible subjects. One aspect of the London–Fuhrer (1961) data appears to challenge the latter inference, at least partially; in their study it was found that insusceptible subjects reported some degree of subjective alterations. Nevertheless, these changes do not appear to be sufficient to infer the presence of "state."

State theory is particularly vulnerable in what it ascribes to medium susceptible subjects who constitute 70–80% of the population and whose degree of hypnotic response ranges across a broad continuum of item difficulty. In terms of current thinking and terminology about state, little is said about any altered state of consciousness for a subject who progresses as far as the mosquito, or taste hallucination item, and no further, or for a subject who can experience all items up to and including the anosmia for ammonia item, but cannot experience subsequent hypnotic phenomena on the continuum.

Current thinking about hypnosis has been constrained by state and trait notions and, in general, the late nineteenth century notion of hypnotic depth has been neglected by hypnosis researchers. Investigators such as Braid, Charcot,

Liébeault, and Bernheim spoke of various stages which basically incorporated depth notions. Braid spoke of three stages (slight hypnosis, deep hypnosis, and hypnotic coma). Charcot, basing his observations on spurious neurological signs, likewise delineated three stages (see Chapter 1). Liébeault suggested six stages (drowsiness, drowsiness with catalepsy, light sleep, deep sleep, light somnambulism, and deep somnambulism). Bernheim's nine stages were not unlike the gradations in response to items of increasing difficulty now encompassed by the trait notion of susceptibility (see Bramwell, 1906, for further elaborations of these schemes and examples of other categorizations). Such classifications of hypnotic response into stages or depth were able to cope with the altered state notion by simply inferring different degrees of the state corresponding to differential depths reached by subjects on the classifications that were proposed.

To some extent, the trait notion that has developed in recent decades assumes these differences in depth, and recent work by Tart (1970a, 1972) gives some justification for this assumption. Small groups of high, medium, and low susceptible subjects were required to give a depth or state report after each of 12 SHSS:C items on a 0–10 scale (where 0 = normal waking state, 5 = quite strongly hypnotized, and 10 = deep enough to experience anything suggested by the hypnotist). It was found that high-susceptible subjects gave significantly "deeper" state reports than either medium or low susceptible subjects, and there was a slightly greater (but not significant) degree of depth reported by the medium as compared to the low susceptibles.

There would be basically no logical contradiction in postulating an altered state notion based upon different degrees of reported depth. More extensive research could clarify the relationship between degrees of reported state and susceptibility, thereby helping to resolve some of the difficulties we have just outlined that may occur when one applies the altered state notion to the full range of individual differences in test responsivity. There is considerable merit to the notion that "whatever hypnosis is, there will be more of it in people who show more effects of hypnotism [Orne, 1972, p. 430]." To the extent that this assumption can be applied to the altered state formulation, it may be possible to maintain a state notion in terms of differences in depth reported by subjects of varying susceptibilities. Until further research is performed, however, this paradox with respect to the state notion remains.

Certain other theoretical problems exist in connection with the conceptualization of hypnotizability as a trait. Historically, the evidence since the time of Faria appears to indicate that hypnotic susceptibility is an extremely stable characteristic of the person. Recently, though, this assumption has come under critical scrutiny from investigators seeking to modify susceptibility, and from others who attach primary importance to the situation as a major factor determining hypnotic outcomes. Both these emphases are extremely important since they not only challenge the utility of trait theorizing, but suggest also the tenability of a situationist and/or interactionist view of hypnosis–one which gives greater stress to the role of the environment in determining hypnotic response.

Modifiability of Susceptibility: A Contrasting of Positions

The literature on modifiability is both clinical and experimental. Experimental evidence for modifiability stems from designs that pretest susceptibility, proceed to introduce various modification strategies, and then retest susceptibility. Many modification studies are able to report statistically significantly higher group means on retest than for pretest, and it is upon such findings that the claims for modifiability largely rest. Disregarding, for the moment, the methodological and procedural difficulties associated with such studies, the claim for modifiability, taken at face value, raises a number of theoretical paradoxes.

The criteria for modifiability are very poorly specified in virtually all these experimental studies. Further, they tend to have used different criteria of success to clinical studies that have made similar claims. Such clinical studies (Blum, 1963; Erickson, 1952) have used a "strong" success criterion–namely, a low susceptible subject should become highly susceptible (able to experience amnesia and posthypnotic suggestion) as the result of a modification training procedure. By contrast, experimental studies resort to a "weak" criterion of a statistically significant increase in the mean of the modification training group following training. It is somewhat surprizing that these latter studies are not able to produce the sorts of high susceptible subjects demanded by the "strong" criterion of clinical investigations. There is a dearth of experimental evidence, in fact, to indicate that initially insusceptible subjects can be trained to experience amnesia and posthypnotic response as the result of a modification procedure. Further, the very few studies which report correlations between pre- and postmodification scores for hypnotizability (Ås, Hilgard, & Weitzenhoffer, 1963; Cooper, Banford, Schubot, & Tart, 1967; Shor & Cobb, 1968; Tart, 1970a) all show high and significant positive correlations.

These paradoxes have considerable theoretical importance, though they may merely reflect surmountable shortcomings in the techniques that have been thus far employed. To the extent, however, that hypnotic performance represents a continuum, it does seem meaningful that in modification studies, the subject tends to improve his susceptibility only by a limited amount–even though that increase frequently achieves statistical significance. If susceptibility is a truly modifiable characteristic, then training procedures ought to bring a person to optimal performance on this characteristic. The fact that modification studies have so far been unable to do this, coupled with evidence (when reported) of high correlation between pre- and postmodification training scores, suggests that a trait account has yet to be invalidated by this approach.

The fact, however, that some modification seems possible (and there is still the problem of distinguishing reported increases in modification studies from "plateau" susceptibility; see Shor, Orne, & O'Connell, 1966), is important. It may prove to be a major reason why susceptibility studies have characteristically failed to find stable correlates of susceptibility. As well as the unreliability of the measures of the proposed correlates themselves, it could be that the hypnotizability measures themselves typically misestimate hypnotic potential by small but significant amounts.

Situationism and Interactionism in Hypnosis Theory

The inability of investigators to find stable correlates of hypnotizability has contributed to another line of investigation which also challenges the trait notion. This questioning is not unique to hypnosis research; indeed it parallels a *zeitgeist* in general personality theorizing (Bowers, 1973b). Trait theories of personality have failed to account for any more than small portions of the cross-situational variance associated with test scores, and this has led both to predominantly situationist theories of personality (see Mischel, 1968) which view behavior primarily as a function of the situation in which a person finds himself, and more recently to explicitly stated interactionist theories (Bowers, 1973b; Ekehammar, 1974; Endler & Magnusson, 1974). The latter account views behavior most meaningfully as a product of personal characteristics in interaction with situational variables.

A similar influence has been present for some time in the theoretical writings of Barber (see Chapter 3), Sarbin (see Chapter 4), and in the proponents of the London–Fuhrer design (see Chapter 7). The issue has been stated most strongly by Rosenhan and London (1963b) in their conceptualization of hypnotic behavior as an interaction of situation, susceptibility and measuring instrument, and their viewpoint is consistent with characteristic observations associated with application of the London–Fuhrer design. While these investigators retain a trait notion as part of their interactionism, others such as Barber see the interaction as between antecedent induction procedure variables and mediating subject variables (motives, attitudes, expectancies, and imaginative capacities) in which no special attention is given to trait notions. By contrast, to the extent that he conceives of individual differences in hypnotizability as requiring explanation, Sarbin retains the trait notion, but has come to give increasingly greater attention to the role of situational variables interacting with subject characteristics in facilitating role enactment (see Chapter 4).

Thus far, interactionism in hypnosis theorizing has either sought to absorb the trait notion, or else (as in Barber's case) to make it relatively expendable. Apart from the London–Fuhrer design, however, which has taken up some implications of interactionism for hypotheses concerning the effects of hypnosis on enhancing performance, there has been no paradigm or methodology of hypnosis that has been developed formally to test the interactionist position. This is in contrast with the field of personality where special applications of the analysis of variance design has enabled analysis in terms of the percentage of variance due to situations, to persons, and to situation X persons interactions. (See Bowers, 1973b, for a detailed critique of these studies.) Consequently, it is not clear as yet, how major an influence interactionism will have upon theorizing and upon research practices in hypnosis. In particular, the implications of interactionist thinking for trait theorizing appear to be especially uncertain.

Discussion of the modifiability issue serves to illustrate one way in which the relative contributions of trait and situation might be evaluated. Gur (1974), for instance, found that hypnotizability was modifiable only in subjects who possessed some initial degree of hypnotic responsivity. He concluded that although modification procedures led to an enhancement of hypnotizability scores which was "comparable to those found in other experiments reporting success in enhancing hypnotizability, a careful appraisal of the effect on the different levels of initial susceptibility indicates that hypnotizability is largely determined by factors other than situational manipulations [p. 649]." Further studies obviously need to disentangle the separate components of hypnotic response (trait and situation) and determine the extent of their interdependence. It may be, for instance, as Bowers (1973b, pp. 326–327) has suggested, "that stable characteristics of people are situation specific--that high hypnotic susceptibility, for example, will not reveal itself in all situations, but just hypnotic ones." While this is possible, it is scarcely satisfying, especially as there does not exist at present any well formulated position concerning the nature of the interdependence of trait and situation, nor any analysis of those aspects of situation that require special attention. Nevertheless, the refocusing of interest on the effects of situational variables (neglected since the demise of animal magnetism) should be informative in evaluating the relative contributions of internal processes and external influence to the hypnotic process.

Contemporary Formulations of State in Hypnosis

The notion of state as being somehow central to what happens in hypnosis has been often strongly attacked and defended, but it remains basically intact. Neither its critics nor its protagonists have been able to deliver the decisive blow which would settle the issue with finality. Ambiguities and paradoxes in state thinking are nonetheless becoming progressively more apparent. As we have indicated earlier, some of these difficulties have been inherited from general psychology which has tended to use shifting criteria to indicate the presence of state. Within the experimental study of hypnosis these difficulties have been compounded by the coexisting conceptualization of hypnosis as trait and the relative lack of integration between the two bodies of data on state and trait. There are signs within the recent writings of many of the theorists we have discussed in this book, however, that serious attempts are under way to specify the characteristics of hypnosis which have led many investigators to refer to it as an altered state. Of particular interest is the fact that nonstate theorists such as Barber and Sarbin have been as actively engaged in this enterprise as state theorists themselves.

Two main trends are becoming apparent. One trend appears to represent a culmination of a tradition in the hypnotic literature that can be traced back to Binet and Féré (1888) who postulated common mechanisms for imagery and hallucination, and saw imagery as the germ of hallucination. They saw hypnosis as adding a dimension of credence to the image converting it to a hallucination which had reality value for the hypnotized subject. A second viewpoint, which is basically not incompatible with the first, derives its impetus from some interesting anomalies in the behavior of hypnotized subjects which appear to indicate the existence of distinctive modes of cognitive processing other than imagery and imagination.

Imagery and Imaginal Processes

The convergence on imagery and imagination (where these terms are used interchangeably sometimes, and at other times to distinguish vivid mental phenomena with picture-like qualities from fantasy processes that are not necessarily pictorial in quality) is one of the major ways in which the state issue is beginning to be formulated in a way that is more testable. This emphasis is prominent in the theorizing of Sarbin (see Chapter 4), who sees hypnosis as *as-if* behavior in which the hypnotized person's experience is conceived of as "believed-in imaginings." More recently, Barber (see Chapter 3) and his associates have also postulated processes which they have variously labeled as "thinking with and vividly imagining suggested effects" (Barber & de Moor, 1972), "goal directed fantasies" (Spanos, 1971) and "involvement in suggestion-related imaginings" (Spanos & Barber, 1974). The observations which index these concepts are very much in line with the data reported by other investigators (Arnold, 1946; E. Hilgard, 1965a; J. Hilgard, 1970; Sheehan, 1972; Shor, 1959, 1962). The resultant formulations, while converging on imagery and imagining, differ in their degrees of clarity and specificity with which questions about the process and its relationship to hypnosis are asked. It would not be appropriate at this point to distinguish every shade of opinion on the issue, but some of the major formulations merit closer discussion.

The status of the imagery–imagining process itself is particularly important to Sarbin (1950) who initially placed great emphasis on hypnotic behavior as *as-if* behavior. The hypnotized subject responds to verbal stimuli as if they were in some sense real, and hypnotic behavior depends closely upon imaginative processes. Sarbin's more recent formulations (Sarbin & Coe, 1972; Sarbin & Juhasz, 1970) have concretized these earlier notions into what are now called *believed-in imaginings* and it is clear that within his general role-enactment account, such imaginings occupy a central position as an alternative to the state concept. While the conceptualization of hypnosis as role enactment has often been misunderstood (and translated into simple social compliance) it is further evident that Sarbin has consistently seen hypnotic behavior as a type of involuntary alteration which occurs when various self and role characteristics come together in the hypnotic situation. Rather than call this "state," Sarbin has attempted to define the characteristics of this self-role coalescence. The conceptualization of state as believed-in imaginings places primary emphasis not merely on imagery-imagination, but also (importantly) on the status of such imaginings—the fact, for instance, that they have reality value, and are believable to the subject while hypnotized. Through his conceptualization of hypnosis as an individual difference variable which depends upon subjects' skills, Sarbin has reformulated the state issue to ask specifically what makes some imaginings believable. A psychology of both imagining and belief is clearly indicated.

In recent years, several papers from Barber's laboratory have likewise focused upon the central role of imagery–imagination in hypnotic theorizing. This has led to some modifications of Barber's (1969) operational paradigm upon which much of his previous experimental work relied. Constructs such as "thinking with and vividly imagining suggested effects," "goal-directed fantasies," and "involvement in suggestion-related imaginings" are all currently viewed by Barber and his co-workers as cognitive activities that are explicitly designed to function "as an alternative to the traditional trance state formulation of hypnotic behavior" (Spanos & Barber, 1974, p. 505). Indeed the operational model has been categorized most recently as a "cognitive–behavioral viewpoint" (Barber, Spanos, & Chaves, 1974) and imagining is explicitly conceived of as a variable mediating between input and output. It is apparent, too, that the role of imagining is perceived differently by Barber and Sarbin. While the latter emphasizes the "believed-in" quality of such experience, Barber, with his notion of "thinking with and vividly imagining" (and of "involvement"), describes the relevant processes in what appears to be a much more voluntaristic manner. In each case, there is agreement, though, that imagery–imagining constitutes the relevant process. The difference in their accounts lies in how exactly the process is initiated and relates to hypnotic responsivity.

The emphasis on distinctive cognitive processes occurring in hypnosis is also present in the theoretical position of Sutcliffe (see Chapter 5). On the basis of a series of rigorously designed experiments which, among other things, sought to take up the question of the status and reality of the hypnotized subject's testimony, Sutcliffe concluded that a basic issue concerns whether the subject misperceives or misreports the real situation. He indicated support for the former alternative; while hypnotized, the subject appears to misperceive and in some sense he seems to be deluded about reality. Sutcliffe's choice of the term delusion was deliberate, even though the term carries with it certain negative connotations connected with psychopathological processes. He sought to indicate that the distinguishing feature of hypnosis is the hypnotized subjects' "emotional conviction that the world is as suggested by the hypnotist rather than a pseudoperception of the suggested world" (Sutcliffe, 1961, p. 200).

Sutcliffe clearly used delusion in a descriptive sense, and like Sarbin, focused upon the beliefs that hypnotized subjects have about their experience while they are hypnotized. Like Sarbin too, in his posing the question of what may be the antecedent of believed-in imaginings, Sutcliffe was led to ask questions about how delusory conviction is communicated and about the role of the hypnotic relationship in facilitating such phenomena. Although he felt that developmental aspects of the parent–child relationship might clarify some of these conditions of credence, his subsequent thrust was in examining the roles played by imagery, fantasy and dissociation in the hypnotic process. While the data generated by this approach are not conclusive (Perry, 1973; Sutcliffe, Perry, & Sheehan, 1970), the underlying theoretical notion remains compelling and worthy of further exploration. Sutcliffe sees the hypnotic situation as one in which the subject is asked to engage in a type of make-believe or fantasy, and the subject does this to the extent that he has the requisite aptitudes to do so. In contrast to other theorists who have converged upon imagery–imagination as central to the understanding of hypnotic process, Sutcliffe suggests more explicitly that imagery may be one of a multiplicity of cognitive processes and skills that affect the seemingly delusional thinking of hypnotized subjects.

It is very clear that all of these positions represent substantial attempts to index underlying mental processes upon which attributions of altered state may depend. To the extent that they seek, in varying degrees, to account for both individual differences in susceptibility *and* testimonies of altered experience, their thrust is strongly cognitive in direction. They represent a very promising, and potentially fruitful attempt to rephrase the altered state issue in such a way that seemingly essential features of it become formulated in more testable form than hitherto.

Incongruities of Reported Experience

Discussion of the concept of delusion moves us from considering the importance of imagery and imaginal processes for hypnosis to focus on some of the anomalies that exist in the behavior of hypnotized subjects. In some respects, the relevance of the process of delusion illustrates the convergence of investigators upon similar notions, despite their adoption of markedly different methodological perspectives. Orne (1974b) has concluded that the main defining characteristic of hypnosis concerns "the extent to which an individual is able to distort his perception and memory and become subjectively convinced in the sense of a transient delusion [p. 16]." He notes, further, that such delusion is more likely to occur in the context of a trusting relationship with the hypnotist. Orne and

Sutcliffe, however, have arrived at a similar conclusion for almost entirely different reasons. Whereas Sutcliffe postulated delusion on the basis of the discrepancy he reported between objective and subjective states of affairs, Orne's endorsement of the same concept stems from an analysis of distinctive features of the hypnotized subject's subjective report.

Recent research in hypnosis illustrates many interesting developments beyond emphases on just delusional thinking and imagery-imaginal processes. Work is beginning to focus upon many varying aspects of the hypnotized person's experience, and upon quite distinctive "internal-process" mechanisms that may be involved. Some initial ground-clearing is in order, however, before we turn to the distinctive features of some of these developing positions. The direction of hypnosis research over the last forty years appears to have been adversely affected by many of the florid claims made for hypnosis during the nineteenth century. Apart from the more obviously outrageous ones such as the ability of hypnotized people to diagnose, predict, and prescribe proper treatment of physical illness, clairvoyancy, visionless sight and the like, more credible ones concerning the ability of hypnotized subjects to transcend nonhypnotized performance developed and clearly deserved investigation. The evidence for performance increments (which has been extensively researched by Barber and by investigators using the London–Fuhrer design) clearly refutes such a possibility and demonstrates that similar performance enhancements can be obtained without hypnosis. However, in pursuit of the issue of whether hypnotized subjects can perform *better,* attention has been diverted away from the issue of whether hypnotized subjects experience *differently.* Part of the rejection of hypnosis as an altered state has been based on the failure to find any consistent superiority of hypnotic performance over unhypnotized performance and on the considerable evidence that many phenomena thought to be unique to hypnosis can occur without it. There is a real sense in which it could be said that much present-day thinking may have been a victim of earlier traditions of belief in transcendence phenomena as representing the distinguishing feature of hypnosis. By such commitment to performance criteria, the possibility of other, more subtle differences appears to have been lost sight of.

The nature of such differences can perhaps be illustrated in terms of the following anecdote reported by Orne (1974b):

> I age regressed a subject to six years who did not come to the United States until he was eight, and was unable to speak English when he was six. I suggested that he was at his birthday party and his mother was speaking to him and asked him to tell me what she said. 'Do you like your present?' was his response. When I said he should listen more carefully, that she was saying, 'Hast du dein Geschenk gern?' he replied 'Ja.' I then asked him, 'Do you understand English?' 'Nein.' 'Do your parents speak English?' 'Ja, damit ich's nicht verstehe (so that I don't understand it).' 'You mean you can't understand a word of English?' 'Ja.' I then rephrased the question whether he could understand English ten times. Each time he answered in German at the appropriate times verbally asserting that he could not comprehend English yet clearly demonstrating his ability to do so [pp. 5–6].

This example emphasizes a neglected aspect of hypnotic behavior: the apparent stupidity (as Orne notes) of the hypnotized subject in not recognizing the paradoxical nature of his behavior—the phenomenon is similarly illustrated by trance logic and the aspects of age regressed behavior that have just been cited. It is considerations like these, as we have seen, which have led Orne to take up delusion as diagnostic of hypnosis, but the major thrust of this line of thinking focuses on the apparent anomalousness of hypnotic behavior. It is important to note that altered cognitive processing is being inferred from an apparent inefficiency of response, rather than from a traditional emphasis on greater competence.

Recent ongoing work by Hilgard (see Chapter 2) demonstrates a similar point, and highlights in a different way the importance of understanding inconsistencies in susceptible subjects' response. In a number of experiments, subjects have been exposed to experimental pain, either through ischemia or by the cold pressor test, and the effects of hypnotic analgesia in reducing the pain have been explored. In early experiments, certain interesting paradoxes were revealed similar to those reported by previous experimenters (Barber & Hahn, 1962; Sears, 1932; Shor, 1962). In all cases, hypnotically analgesic subjects reported little, if any, pain or distress; their cardiovascular responses, however, were indistinguishable from what was obtained under the nonanalgesic conditions of the cold pressor test. Hilgard subsequently developed techniques to investigate this discrepancy between physiological, verbal, and behavioral evidence, in which he elicited reports of pain and suffering during hypnotic analgesia from what he has termed a "hidden observer" (Hilgard, 1974a, b, 1975).

The reports of the "hidden observer" can be evaluated in terms of what has been cited frequently as a difficulty with the same-subjects design (Evans & Orne, 1965; Sutcliffe, 1960). The general argument is that when a hypnotized subject is given instructions, or placed in an experimental condition which might in any ways conflict or undermine the testimony he gives while hypnotized, he will perform differently in such conditions in order to bolster the reality of his hypnotic performance. The underlying dynamics of such behaviors in control conditions involving hypnotized subjects are probably quite complex; it is not clear whether subjects do this to please an experimenter who believes in such differences or to satisfy his own beliefs concerning the superiority of hypnotic stimuli, or possibly both. Be this as it may, communication with the "hidden observer" can be seen, from the subjects' point of view as designed to undercut his hypnotic analgesia testimony. A priori, one might expect "hidden observer" reports not to differ from the analgesia reports of no pain experience.

The "open" reports given by the "hidden observer" can be said to have the same anomalous quality previously noted with Orne's age-regressed subject. Typically it reports both sensory pain and suffering that has characteristics similar to such reports given under nonanalgesic, base-line conditions. This appears to reflect a "sampling" of ongoing pain by the hypnotized person;

indeed, when retrospective reports are obtained from the "hidden observer," it reports sensory pain comparable to base-line conditions, but no suffering. As with Orne's age-regressed subject, the compelling feature of such reports is that "no play actor would be so stupid as not to recognize this obvious paradox" (Orne, 1974b, p. 6). In this case it is the paradox of analgesic reports of little pain and suffering followed immediately by a "hidden observer" report of pain and (depending on how the reports are collected) suffering similar to nonhypnotic analgesia conditions.

More intensive documentation of the "hidden observer" phenomenon is currently in process. Such "hidden" reports, while contrary to what one might ordinarily expect from the Same-Subjects design, may, as we noted in Chapter 2, reflect another possible difficulty with it. Subjects could be responding to the experimenter's wish for them to both experience and deny anesthesia. Thus only further investigation will tell whether the "hidden observer" represents an ingenious solution to the subject's perception of seemingly conflicting demands by the experimenter. But even if this were demonstrated, the "hidden observer" phenomenon would still appear to have important implications for the documentation of inconsistencies in the hypnotized subject's performance in which major anomalies of reported experience are not recognized.

Overall, the convergence in the hypnotic literature upon altered cognitive processes is an important one and is a worthy alternative to traditional theorizing about state. The latter concept has served an important function in hypnotic theorizing over recent decades by focusing attention upon what has traditionally been seen as one of the most distinguishing features of hypnosis—the verbal reports of hypnotized subjects of subjective alteration. The formulation of cognitive processes such as believed-in imaginings, involvement in and thinking with suggestion-related imagining, fantasy, dissociation, and delusion together with the interest in anomalies of reported experience all provide a fertile field of alternatives. They are bound to be primary areas of hypnotic investigation and the source of controversy in the coming decades.

Holistic Conceptualizations of the Hypnotized Person

Our emphasis on current developments in hypnosis research in the preceding pages draws attention to areas of relative neglect in contemporary theorizing. The most significant omission of all concerns the role of motivation in hypnosis, which has an important place in the theorizing of Barber (Chapter 3), Orne (Chapter 6) and in the rationale of the London–Fuhrer design (Chapter 7). The role of motivation appears to be highly relevant to a proper understanding of hypnosis, and yet there has been little exploration of it in recent years. We have seen, for example, that a special willingness to please may well characterize the performance of some susceptible subjects, and that the relationship between hypnotist and subject should be explored closely for its motivational implications. It is not clear whether the absence of research represents a turning away by present-day investigators from an historically important concept, or whether such investigators are currently more preoccupied with other variables.

The relative dearth of interest in motivation highlights a perhaps more characteristic problem with investigation of hypnosis which has existed since the time of Mesmer. We have seen both with respect to the present and to the past that various aspects of the hypnotized person's performance—cognitive, motivational, affective, situational, and interactive—have been emphasized by different investigators at different periods. While this piecemeal approach is, to some extent, endemic to all research in science, it means that holistic approaches to the experimental study of hypnosis have been traditionally slow to develop. The picture we have of the hypnotized subject is one of a compartmentalized person; the person in his entirety has yet to emerge despite two hundred years of formal investigation.

This state of affairs undoubtedly reflects both the complexity of hypnotic phenomena and the multiplicity of alternate hypotheses about hypnosis that are deserving of scrutiny. It also, however, is a product of the way in which so often throughout the history of hypnosis, opinions have polarized. It has not been common for investigators making conflicting claims to see merit in the positions held by others, or for them to perceive inherent difficulties in the ones that they themselves favor. Perhaps the goal is an utopian one, but we suggest that investigators of the present and future should come much more to see hypnosis as involving interactions of internal process variables of a person in context. A holistic account of the hypnotized person is essential.

METHODOLOGICAL PRINCIPLES: SOME GUIDELINES TO PRACTICE

The second major aim of this chapter is to coordinate discussion of the methodological strategies that have been evaluated in previous chapters and to recommend guidelines to practice for the hypnotic researcher looking for appropriate techniques of study. One of the points that emerges very clearly from previous discussion is that individual paradigms are best suited to answering particular problems. In the process of doing this, they at times raise specific issues, not often emphasized by alternative models. Our orientation throughout this book has been to evaluate the separate models with respect to the adequacy of the particular methodological procedures associated with them. At the same time, we have sought to highlight the distinctive problems and theoretical issues they best seem suited to answer.

The six paradigms discussed have all been analyzed with respect to the individual strengths and weaknesses of the inferences that can be drawn from application of the methodological strategies associated with them. For each of the models considered, important limitations of the interpretation of the data adhering to its procedures have been isolated. Clearly, no one model or paradigm can lay claim to establishing truth or certainty about hypnotic processes. Strictly speaking, the real strength of each model lies in the extent to which the special hypotheses it advocates by way of explanation of hypnotic events establish their own criteria for truth and are convincingly supported by the exclusion of plausible alternative ways of explaining the data. In this sense some models incorporate procedures which are obviously much stronger than others. The real-simulating model, for example, is equipped to exclude a rival account of the data in terms of demand characteristic response most unequivocally, while other strategies aiming towards the same goal (such as Reyher's procedures of control) do not (see Chapter 6).

This chapter does not attempt to reevaluate the models that have been discussed, nor does it aim to propose a comprehensive methodological scheme which will answer unambiguously the problems that other paradigms have been unable to solve. A general methodology of hypnosis does not represent an ideal which is attainable in practice; indeed, it would be altogether misleading to propose it. Models are basically constructed to serve particular purposes and they need to be primarily evaluated in this light. Their relevance and importance can best be judged in terms both of how well they achieve the ends that they propose, and also how successful their procedures are for drawing inferences about the notions they test. It could be said that Sutcliffe (1960) aimed to formulate a general, comprehensive model of hypnosis, but that goal was not achieved; his scheme was at the same time too comprehensive to be practical, and yet too limited to answer many of the issues we know by now are definitely related to a proper understanding of hypnosis. Strategies can really only be chosen as they are appropriate or useful to elucidating the particular claims about hypnosis an experimenter wants to make. The true value of well-defined methodologies of hypnosis lies in the fact that they represent precisely formulated strategies of research which relate procedurally in rigorous manner to illustrate distinct theoretical issues and problems. Looking across the various models, then, it would seem most appropriate to list "methodological guidelines," rather than dogmatically formulated strategies of research to aid the experimental investigator. The primary goals of such guidelines are twofold: they should make both for the enhancement of the probability that valid inferences will be drawn from the data that are collected, and for the accurate realization of the purposes for which the procedures were designed. Rigid adherence to any single set of strategies does not serve objectivity effectively; more often than not, such tenacity violates the spirit of genuine, open inquiry.

To reinforce the argument that one needs to seek procedures which suit the particular research problem at hand, we turn to consider again the issue of whether or not susceptibility can be modified significantly. It has been relevant to previous discussions in this chapter and some degree of consistency is thereby served by pursuing the issue methodologically as well. We will briefly analyze the distinctive strategies the problem demands in order to rigorously confirm the hypothesis, and our discussion will be orientated intentionally toward introducing in concrete fashion the major methodological guidelines that will follow. The example we take is illustrative only of the sorts of principles we take to be important. A variety of other issues can equally as well be used to demonstrate the argument.

The Modification of Susceptibility: An Example of Adopting Relevant Research Strategies

Theoretically speaking, this question is an important one. It raises the issue of the extent to which hypnotizability is stable and durable over time and it challenges the utility value of appealing to a trait account of hypnosis. If a low susceptible subject can be "changed" into a high susceptible one, a situational or interactionist account of hypnotic events seems pertinent and there seems little reason for arguing that there is an enduring predisposition existing in subjects which enables them to respond hypnotically to a hypnotist's communications. Demonstration of such modifiability using rigorous methodology to illustrate the point would lead to a significant revision of the notion that hypnotizability is a relatively stable personality trait yielding consistent response across a variety of test occasions and situations. The problem itself requires specific procedures to answer the question adequately and the issue is an especially important one to Hilgard's paradigm (see Chapter 2) which greatly emphasizes the relative stability of subjects' aptitudes for hypnosis. Other paradigms also take a similar stance (for example, Sutcliffe's, and Orne's; see Chapters 5 and 6). The collective procedures of all these paradigms, however, are not those which would best answer the question. We turn now to examine the set of procedures which would appear most adequate to answering this particular problem.

The first essential requirement in any such design is that we establish meaningful base-line testing to ensure that subjects are brought to a plateau level of hypnotizability. It is well known, for example, that subjects in hypnotic experiments do not always perform at the highest level (plateau) of their hypnotizability at the first induction session that is administered, and many sessions may be required, in fact, to achieve stable performance prior to any attempt at training. Only one study (Shor & Cobb, 1968) has ever aimed to bring subjects to plateau response level prior to attempting modification. In test of the modification hypothesis, then, the effects of training cannot really be regarded with any significance unless a relatively stable level of motivated performance is reached in the first instance. The problem, then, demands base-line testing which establishes "optimal" level of response prior to training.

In studies investigating the modification of hypnotizability (for example, Diamond, 1972; Kinney & Sachs, 1974; London, Cooper, & Engstrom, 1974; Sachs & Anderson, 1967; Tart, 1970b), subjects routinely come to learn the precise purpose of the experiment in which they are participating. The experimental design might incorporate far less direct instructions to inform subjects about the nature of the study in which they are taking part. Further, baseline testing could be conducted without subjects knowing that "training" will be involved. Finally, as a test of the adequacy of the procedures adopted to ensure this state of affairs, simulating procedures may very usefully be employed; they could provide adequate test of whether subjects in the study might have perceived that pretesting and experimental testing were part of the same study.

After baseline testing has been conducted, independent samples of subjects should be allocated to separate comparison treatments; in the illustration we have taken up, the choice of such conditions is precisely constrained by the problem being investigated and separate sets of subjects need to be allocated to an "induction with training" (experimental) treatment, and "induction without training" (control comparison) treatment, these two conditions minimally serving the basic requirements of adequate experimental design. Following treatment application, reevaluation should then be made on the same test of hypnotic responsivity that was used for initial testing. Following reevaluation, it is essential also that follow-up testing be conducted to determine the durability of the posttest level of hypnotic performance over time; "follow-up" is not routinely incorporated into modification studies at all—only the studies by Gur (1974), and Sachs and Anderson (1967) have effectively approached this goal by working to obtain hypnotizability scores later in time using an independent experimenter.

Contrast of the observable effects of Training versus No Training, using an independent subjects design, aims toward highlighting the distinctive consequences of the experimental treatment (training) that is being considered. If differences are observed across the two comparison conditions (providing that baseline level of plateau response is comparable) and these indicate superior performance for the training condition, then other characteristics which could be said to adhere to the hypnotic situation generally (occurring as it does at the same point in the sequence of experimental events) are effectively discounted as offering plausible, rival accounts of the data. Where such differences are evident, the hypothesis is confirmed by results for the experimental condition, and inferences about the effectiveness of training are necessarily sharpened by data arising from application of the control comparison condition in which training was not attempted.

Another essential feature of this design is the basic requirement that individual differences in susceptibility to hypnosis be investigated fully. The question of modification is answered only incompletely unless one looks closely at the degree to which relatively insusceptible subjects may increase substantially in susceptibility to reach optimum levels of responsivity. It is essential, then, that the design incorporate into its framework the means by which diagnostic classification of subjects can be sensitively reexamined following training. Change in classification from "low" to "high" in susceptibility would offer the strongest confirming evidence one could collect in a study of this kind.

Two further features of design need to be accentuated. First, a comprehensive postexperimental inquiry should be conducted, additionally, to investigate subjects' perceptions of the study; such an inquiry is administered most effectively by an experimenter who has not been involved in either the initial testing or the training phase of the study, so as to disallow the possibility that the inquirer's bias inadvertently influences subjects in their reports of how they perceived the experiment. And the potential effects of the wording of the inquiry should be carefully considered. Finally, taking up the point we made in the preceding chapter, multiple measures should be employed in the design, wherever possible. Distinct measures of susceptibility (that is, employment of different test scales for measuring level of hypnotizability) may be adopted both in the pretesting and treatment phases of the study, and varying techniques of "training" may be utilized to investigate the consistency with which they converge together to yield consistent data relating to the single hypothesis being examined.

It should be stated that no study in the literature has actually employed a design such as the one that has been outlined, yet all the features that have been mentioned would seem critical to the success of any very rigorous attempt to investigate the modification issue. In a comprehensive review of the literature on this question, Diamond (1974) concluded that a number of procedures have proved effective for modifying susceptibility; a close look at the research techniques that he surveys, however, reveals copious inadequacies in terms of the strategies adopted by researchers in the past. Not until all of the above conditions have been met can the question of the modifiability of hypnotizability be answered adequately; yet as we acknowledged earlier in this chapter, the question remains as one having considerable theoretical relevance to the understanding of a number of unresolved general issues in the study of hypnosis. No precise application of the procedures relating to any one paradigm–such as Hilgard's, Sarbin's, Sutcliffe's or Orne's–would afford a suitable solution. The problem, at least in part, dictates the detail of the research strategies that need to be employed.

We turn now to outlining some of the methodological guidelines that can be drawn together from the models that have been discussed in this book and which flow in principle from the illustrative example that has just been discussed. Their essential aim is to provide the means by which the accuracy of inferences about hypnosis may be increased. The guidelines primarily pertain to consideration of: (a) the conditions for establishing adequate base-line testing; (b) appropriate sampling of conditions for experimental comparison within an independent (versus Same-Subjects) design; (c) sensitive measurement of individual differences in susceptibility; (d) the value of conducting a postexperimental inquiry; and (e) the importance of adopting a methodologically convergent approach to the problem being examined.

Base-Line Testing

The first guideline asserts the relevance of baseline testing. Whenever the question is asked "does hypnosis have an effect on performance?," pretest measurement of some kind should be conducted. Strictly speaking, it is not particularly meaningful to ask what people do in hypnosis without determining exactly what they are capable of performing outside hypnosis, if it is claimed in any way that the effects of hypnosis itself are under test. Knowledge of preexisting differences in suggestibility performance necessarily sharpens our inferences about the distinctive contribution to behavior of hypnotic processes, but, nevertheless, some problems require base-line testing much more obviously than others. Questions, for example, about the automatic nature of posthypnotic behavior, the qualitative aspects of cognitive responses in hypnosis, the emotional/affective components of regressive behavior can all be addressed by appealing to trance performance independent of the experimenter's knowledge of the level of the nonhypnotic performance subjects may achieve in the waking state. In all of these instances, inferences can be tied legitimately to the descriptive properties of hypnotic phenomena themselves, and such conclusions on the data may be quite meaningful. Knowledge of base-rate response, however, does lead to modification of inferences and the validity of one's conclusion about hypnotic data is necessarily strengthened by disallowing the possibility that experimental (hypnotic) performance reflects naturally existing differences in level of responsivity. We would suggest, then, that base-line testing be conducted, wherever relevant, on the hypnotic tasks that are being examined.

Pretesting should not in any way be viewed as incompatible with the employment of an independent group design when the relevance of separate experimental treatments is clearly indicated. Comparison of nonhypnotic with hypnotic conditions using subjects as their own controls across both kinds of treatment is fraught with the difficulties of coping with subtle and complex series effects. Order effects are not necessarily controlled by counterbalancing and often involve quite complicated interactions between the sequence of testing and the kinds of treatments that are adopted (Connors, 1976). Ideally, base-line testing should be carried out prior to the allocation of independent sets of subjects to selected hypnotic and nonhypnotic treatments and, optimally, such testing should be conducted within a context which the subject does not perceive as associated in any way with later recruitment for a hypnotic study. This property of design is particularly well reinforced by London and Fuhrer's data which highlight the possible contaminating influence on test performance of subjects' prior knowledge that hypnosis will later be involved.

Selection of Comparison Conditions

The "appropriateness" of selection of hypnotic (experimental) and nonhypnotic (control) treatments for purposes of comparison depends necessarily both on the theory that is being tested about hypnosis, and/or the nature of the particular problem that is being considered. If one is concerned to investigate the effects of nonhypnotic variables that may actually accrue to hypnotic procedures (so as to show, for instance, what effects remain after the influence of such factors are accounted for), then the choice is probably some variant of the set of waking or imagination conditions which will function to highlight the differential features of the performance associated with hypnotic induction. The possibilities of selection for such a control group range widely across the various models; they may include simple waking instruction with no special motivating features (for example, see the conditions stipulated in Hilgard's Same-Subjects design, and Barber's operational model), instructions exhorting subjects to perform well (see the London–Fuhrer design), instructions requesting subjects to imagine what is happening (for example, Hilgard's and Sarbin's designs), instructions (motivating or nonmotivating) to simulate or role play being in hypnosis (see Orne's and Sutcliffe's paradigms), and highly motivating instructions requesting subjects to imagine vividly and cooperate to the best of their ability (see discussion of Barber's set of TM instructions). The range of comparison groups in hypnosis research that these conditions represent leads us to formulate general guidelines for making suitable choices.

If the hypnotic researcher is basically concerned with isolating the potential artifact arising from subjects' attempts to please the hypnotist–experimenter, or aims to test for the likelihood of voluntary response, or purports to examine the adequacy or "privacy" of experimental test procedures, then the administration of role-playing instructions is necessarily indicated. The treatment "pretense instruction" requires an independent groups design; as Sutcliffe (1960, p. 125) has indicated, the same subject cannot really simulate in the waking state, especially after being hypnotized, without tacitly admitting that his trance performance is itself an instance of simulation. Ideally, when pretense is to be employed as a treatment manipulation, "simulating" as distinct from a simple, role-playing procedure is the most efficient method to employ, and hypnotic testing should be conducted by a hypnotist who is blind as to the identity of the subjects he is testing. Thorough test and disconfirmation of the plausible rival hypothesis that "hypnotic response is an artifactual effect of subjects' perceptions of what the experimenter wants" is most adequately realized by adopting the most stringent set of pretense procedures available, and these are clearly those attached to Orne's real-simulating model of hypnosis. The evidence in the literature consistently demonstrates that simulating procedures provide a highly reliable and effective means for accurately assessing subjects' perceptions of the experimenter's intent. They provide a strong yardstick for judging the adequacy of the experimenter's test procedures.

Selection of the simulation condition alone, though, as a method of experimental comparison is insufficient of itself for the purpose of providing stringent hypothesis testing about hypnosis. Simulation procedures unambiguously eliminate a rival explanation of hypnotic events, but they only indirectly bear upon the validity of theoretical processes about the so-called "hypnotic state." A design using pretense procedures requires supplementation by additional methods which aim toward making reasonably unequivocal assertions about the processes involved in what hypnotic subjects do and say. Properties of the hypothesized trance state can most effectively be investigated by incorporating procedures which both assert directly the consequences of the features being predicted and allow at the same time the systematic elimination of one or more plausible, alternative accounts of the data that are obtained. No methodology of hypnosis eliminates a rival account of its data with greater precision or internal consistency than the real-simulating model, yet the scope of its two-condition comparison can only be viewed as limited when one considers that the theory which lies behind the model makes definite assumptions about the nature of the hypnotic state. The model itself, though, employs no standard routine procedure to test them. In conclusion, then, our second guideline is that if "pretense" is relevant to the aim of hypnotic research design, then simulation procedures—namely, those advocated precisely by the real-simulating model—are the most adequate ones to adopt; employment of such procedures alone, however, throws insufficient light on the nature of hypnotic processes and, ideally, simulation procedures should be supplemented by other control groups focusing directly on those processes which are theoretically assumed to characterize hypnotic performance.

In terms of what other controls to choose, it is clear that the application of nonhypnotic, waking/imagination instructions necessarily refines inferences about the effects of hypnosis. The use of one's imaginative capacities is highly relevant to the hypnotic situation—most major theorists now recognize this fact—and subjects who respond hypnotically in a way that they cannot when they receive "waking" imagination instructions tells us that one very important category of naturally occurring cognitive processes fails to account for hypnotic behavior. One's choice of imagination instruction, though, must be based on sound assessment of the consequences of the artifacts that are invariably attached to them. Task motivational instructions are perceived by subjects as socially constraining, and where comparability with the hypnotic situation is the experimenter's aim they ought never to be used by him without an accompanying request for honesty of response in which it is emphasized that the subjects should truthfully report the test situation as it, in fact, exists. Hilgard's procedures illustrate a problem of a different kind; data from their application indicate that behavior following imagination instruction must be interpreted with caution if it precedes rather than follows hypnotic testing. Subjects react differently across treatments according to the order in which instructions are employed (see Table 8.1 of this book; Evans & Orne, 1965).

The problems illustrated by these two sources of artifact are not at all unique to imagination instruction. Any experimental treatment that is applied—faking manipulation, imagination instruction, simple waking instruction, or otherwise—can be assumed to have unintended consequences as a result of their application. The most important guideline to the researcher who samples among treatments for purposes of comparison is that he institutes the means to recognize the essential limitations of the procedures that he employs—control, as well as experimental. The search for more complex sets of procedures does not at all provide a solution to the difficulties of achieving adequate control.

Measurement of Individual Differences

A further important guideline in hypnotic research is that individual differences in hypnotic responsivity (which appear to naturally exist among subjects recruited for studies) be scrutinized closely. We are in essential agreement with the point made elsewhere by Hilgard (1965a, 1971) that data arising from hypnosis research must be collected under optimal conditions for the occurrence of the phenomena that are being investigated. If the hypothesis being studied makes positive predictions about hypnotic processes (for example, there is tolerance of logical incongruity evident in trance) then the data collected should provide the opportunity to study the behavior of those people in trance whom we may assume are quite deficient in possessing the characteristic in question (that is, low susceptible subjects), and those also whom we may assume decidedly do possess the trait being studied (that is, high susceptible subjects). The choice of stratified versus unstratified sampling is not the relevant issue. Unselected subjects may be employed within a design (as at times it is advantageous to do), but sufficient subjects should always be tested to provide the means to compare meaningfully distinct categories of suggestible subjects (high, medium, and low). If low susceptible subjects are to be investigated, it may be useful in addition to implement the conditions whereby the group of insusceptible subjects are led to believe that they too are responsive to hypnosis; a manipulation of this kind was suggested by London and Fuhrer (1961) in the formulation of their particular model (see Chapter 7 for more detailed discussion of this point). The point of their procedures was that they tried to guarantee that differential "awareness of susceptibility" did not discriminate the groups of subjects who were studied. To limit effectively the possibility of bias being attached to the assessment of individual differences, pretest measurement of susceptibility should ideally be conducted before actual recruitment for the study when subjects have no particular expectations about what they will later be doing. If, however, susceptibility testing is conducted within the context of the experiment proper, results from measurement prior to the application of the experimental treatment can be checked by conducting posttesting after the treatment is terminated. Differences across the susceptibility testings are likely to highlight any earlier influence of subjects' expectations about "change" in their behavior. Further, experimenters would be well advised to adopt more than one measure of susceptibility so as to ensure that a stable level of hypnotic responsivity has, in fact, been attained.

Postexperimental Inquiry

Hypnotic studies should attempt to incorporate into their design an exhaustive inquiry into subjects' perceptions of the procedures that have been applied, and subjects' individual perceptions of the methods that have been administered should be related systematically to the behavior that they have actually demonstrated in the experiment. It is our judgment that the verbal testimony of subjects about events that have occurred represents crucial data and ought always to be collected in hypnotic research, regardless of the problem that is studied. The privacy of the report may interfere with the process of our coming to know what such testimony means, but such data are invaluable, nevertheless. An experimenter needs to take care that he is not suggesting to subjects what is the appropriate response for them to report considering the performance they have just given. The problem is perhaps most effectively eliminated by employing a different experimenter in the inquiry to the person who conducted hypnotic testing in the treatment phase of the study. Independent of who conducts the inquiry, however, the hypnotic researcher needs to be alert to the possibility that verbal report itself is reactive and that the wording of the inquiry can be extremely influential in determining the nature of the report. Whenever a person begins to pay close attention to his behavior, the possibility clearly arises that his reaction is likely to alter, quite apart from the fact that no change or alteration in response is intended or desired.

Toward Convergence

Finally, we would point to the need to recognize the inherent value of adopting multiple measures and methods in testing any hypothesis concerning hypnosis where the nature of the problem allows multiple strategies to be practically employed. Validation of inferences through open inquiry can be realized effectively by applying different research strategies and bringing them to bear upon a

TABLE 9.2
Summary of Methodological Guidelines for Hypnosis Research

Baseline testing on susceptibility scale and/or dependent variable task(s) (conducted prior to recruitment)	Experimental intrusion by E_1 for groups of subjects tested under Experimental (X) and Control (non-X) conditions[b]		Testing on dependent measure(s)	Posttesting on susceptibility scale and/or dependent-variable task(s)	Postexperimental inquiry
For	*Sample of non-X comparison treatments*				
	(a) Waking-relaxation instruction and/or	*plus*	For/example	(Conducted where	Inquiry into
1. High-susceptible subjects	(b) Waking-Unmotivated instruction and/or	"simulation"	suggestibility testing on one or more standard	necessary, for example, if pre-	subjects' perceptions of the
	(c) Waking-Motivated instruction and/or	procedures	susceptibility test scales, and	testing is carried out when subjects know of	experimenter and his
2. Medium-susceptible subjects	(d) Waking-Imagination instruction and/or	(where	performance measurement	later treatments being applied)	procedures (conducted by
	(e) Task-Motivational instruction (with	necessary)[a]	on additional		independent experimenter E_2
and	demand for honesty instruction)		dependent variable		who is blind as to the

3. Low-susceptible subjects (via stratified or unstratified sampling)	Sample of *X*-comparison treatments (a) Hypnotic induction and/or (b) Hypnotic induction plus suggestion and/or (c) Hypnotic induction plus suggestion plus special dependent variable task(s)	task(s)	subjects and/or conditions)

[a]Simulation is listed here as a supplementary treatment for the purposes of adequate experimental design. When the set of procedures is indicated the method should follow exactly that stipulated by the real-simulating model; only insusceptible subjects, for example, should receive instruction to simulate.

[b]One may select from these conditions either according to an independent or Same-Subjects design.

single hypothesis under test. In this way, a number of major sources of artifactual influences of an idiosyncratic kind–namely, inadvertent contaminations associated with distinctive treatment procedures–are necessarily eliminated, and polarization of procedural (and theoretical) preferences is thereby effectively reduced. Consistency of data flowing from the application of varying sets of procedures strengthens our faith considerably in the validity of the conclusions we can draw about the hypotheses in which we are interested, much more than can be achieved by application of any single set of procedures considered alone.

In all of this discussion about the adequacy of procedures for refining inferences, the essential obtrusiveness of the measurement process itself is a potent source of contamination with respect to the validity of the conclusions that can be drawn. The problem raises the question of the extent to which we can ever generalize past the limited social setting in which the data have been gathered. This potential source of bias is present in all laboratory testing and exists independently of the degree of rigor associated with the procedures that are employed. We discussed this problem in some detail in the preceding chapter where we asserted that all of the paradigms were basically contractual in nature, obligating, as they do, the subject to be responsive to the experimenter. Hypnotic researchers should begin to move further toward coping with the inherent difficulties of the context they take up. We have suggested that they might meet the problem by attempting to develop strategies which are noticeably less contractual in nature–procedures which elicit particular test-taking attitudes less regularly, and which promote a more cooperative, open and honest framework of interpersonal orientation between experimenter and subject and which free research subjects from the strictures of the traditional social contract. Collaborative strategies, however, will have their own special difficulties, as we have seen, and they should not be viewed as methods which replace contractual ones. Heteromethod replication of both contractual strategies (employing distinctly different paradigms) and collaborative strategies (utilizing mutually engaging procedures of participation), would yield stronger inferences about hypnotic events than either set of strategies could achieve alone. One should consider also whether clinical method, too, can be brought to bear in similar fashion upon the particular notion under test; see, for example, Spiegel's (1974) approach to the analysis of high susceptibility.

Convergent inquiry aims toward achieving congruence of data following from application of the various methods that are chosen. The choice of method should not be constrained; laboratory study may converge with unobtrusive measurement, clinical observation, field observation, or even common sense experience. As Orne (1970) states, "applied research may teach us as much about basic psychological mechanisms as laboratory findings may clarify phenomena in the real world [p. 260]." One of the special advantages of adopting multiple sets of procedures is that their application protects the experimenter's basic concern for the phenomena themselves. Heteromethod replication necessarily enhances the possibility that hypnotic phenomena will richly manifest themselves in a variety of ways, not simply in single aspect arising from the specificity of any one method chosen for the purposes of investigation. True concern for phenomena is utterly essential–it is the hallmark of quality of research effort which cuts completely across the application of any single set of procedures, or methodology of hypnosis.

Summary

Table 9.2 sets out the above set of guidelines in schematic outline. The table represents not at all a collection of strategies that we suggest should always be adopted in practice; instead, it depicts a broad set of methodological principles which aim toward guiding the researcher in his selection of suitable methodological procedures for studying the particular problem or theory with which he is concerned. No one set of procedures is suitable for the investigation of all of the aspects of hypnotic phenomena that may emerge; and the listing in Table 9.2 is necessarily limited. Nevertheless, the principles of control explicitly conveyed by these guidelines serve to enhance the accuracy of inferences that hypnotic researchers may wish to draw from their data; they also highlight the potential inadequacies of other procedures which investigators may be tempted to adopt; and, in so far as they borrow heavily from several models, they have the advantage of not being obviously tied to any fixed preference about which theory or hypothesis best explains hypnotic events.

In any application of comparison procedures designed to answer a specific problem, the question automatically arises as to the actual "cost" of introducing the conditions required for purposes of control. It is fatuous to argue, for example, that one can realistically cope with all of the ambiguities arising from the treatments that will be involved. Data emerging from even the widest application of different research strategies cannot yield complete confidence in the hypothesis that is being tested, for, logically speaking, the threats to the validity of our inferences about data are virtually limitless. The proper approach to experimental design in hypnosis, or any other area of study in the social sciences for that matter, is not to aim toward achieving perfect purity of control–that particular goal is unattainable–but rather, to adopt procedures which serve their limited purpose both usefully and accurately, and, above all, elicit recognition of their essential limitations as tools of science.

References

Adair, J. G., & Schachter, B. S. To cooperate or to look good? The subjects' and experimenters' perception of each others' intentions. *Journal of Experimental Social Psychology,* 1972, **8,** 74–85.

Anderson, M. L., & Sarbin, T. R. Base-rate expectancies and motoric alterations in hypnosis. *International Journal of Clinical and Experimental Hypnosis,* 1964, **12,** 147–158.

Archer, W. *Masks or faces?* New York: Longmans, Green & Co., 1889.

Argyris, C. Some unintended consequences of rigorous research. *Psychological Bulletin,* 1968, **70,** 185–197.

Arnold, M. B. On the mechanism of suggestion and hypnosis. *Journal of Abnormal and Social Psychology,* 1946, **41,** 107–128.

Ås, A., Hilgard, E. R., & Weitzenhoffer, A. M. An attempt at experimental modification of hypnotizability through repeated individualized hypnotic experience. *Scandinavian Journal of Psychology,* 1963, **4,** 81–89.

Ås, A., & Lauer, L. A factor analytic study of hypnotizability and related personal experiences. *International Journal of Clinical and Experimental Hypnosis,* 1962, **10,** 169–181.

Ascher, L. M., Barber, T. X., & Spanos, N. P. Two attempts to replicate the Parrish–Lundy–Leibowitz experiment on hypnotic age regression. *American Journal of Clinical Hypnosis,* 1972, **14,** 178–185.

Ashley, W. R., Harper, R. S., & Runyon, D. K. The perceived size of coins in normal and hypnotically induced economic states. *American Journal of Psychology,* 1951, **64,** 564–592.

Austin, M., Perry, C. W., Sutcliffe, J. P., & Yeomans, N. Can somnambulists successfully simulate hypnotic behavior without becoming entranced? *International Journal of Clinical and Experimental Hypnosis,* 1963, **11,** 175–186.

Barber, T. X. The concept of "hypnosis." *Journal of Psychology,* 1958, **45,** 115–131. (a)

Barber, T. X. Hypnosis as perceptual–cognitive restructuring: II. "Post"-hypnotic behavior. *Journal of Clinical and Experimental Hypnosis,* 1958, **6,** 10–20. (b)

Barber, T. X. The necessary and sufficient conditions for hypnotic behavior. *American Journal of Clinical Hypnosis,* 1960, **3,** 31–42.

Barber, T. X. Experimental controls and the phenomena of "hypnosis": A critique of hypnotic research methodology. *Journal of Nervous and Mental Disease,* 1962, **134,** 493–505.

Barber, T. X. Toward a theory of "hypnotic" behavior: Positive visual and auditory hallucinations. *Psychological Record,* 1964, **14,** 197–210.

Barber, T. X. Measuring "hypnotic-like" suggestibility with and without "hypnotic induction"; psychometric properties, norms, and variables influencing response to the Barber Suggestibility Scale (BSS). *Psychological Reports,* 1965, **16,** 809–844.

Barber, T. X. Reply to Conn and Conn's "Discussion of Barber's 'Hypnosis as a causal variable . . .'." *International Journal of Clinical and Experimental Hypnosis,* 1967, **15,** 111–117.

Barber, T. X. *Hypnosis: A scientific approach.* New York: Van Nostrand, 1969.

Barber, T. X. *LSD, marihuana, yoga, and hypnosis.* Chicago: Aldine, 1970.

Barber, T. X. Suggested ("hypnotic") behavior: The trance paradigm versus an alternative paradigm. In E. Fromm & R. E. Shor (Eds.), *Hypnosis: Research developments and perspectives.* Chicago: Aldine-Atherton, 1972. Pp. 115–182.

Barber, T. X., & Calverley, D. S. "Hypnotic" behavior as a function of task motivation. *Journal of Psychology,* 1962, **54,** 363–389.

Barber, T. X., & Calverley, D. S. The relative effectiveness of task motivating instructions and trance-induction procedure in the production of "hypnotic-like" behaviors. *Journal of Nervous and Mental Disease,* 1963, **137,** 107–116. (a)

Barber, T. X., & Calverley, D. S. Toward a theory of hypnotic behavior: Effects on suggestibility of task motivating instructions and attitude toward hypnosis. *Journal of Abnormal and Social Psychology,* 1963, **67,** 557–565. (b)

Barber, T. X., & Calverley, D. S. Toward a theory of "hypnotic" behaviour: Enhancement of strength and endurance. *Canadian Journal of Psychology,* 1964, **18,** 156–167. (a)

Barber, T. X., & Calverley, D. S. An experimental study of "hypnotic" (auditory and visual) hallucinations. *Journal of Abnormal and Social Psychology,* 1964, **63,** 13–20. (b)

Barber, T. X., & Calverley, D. S. Experimental studies in "hypnotic" behaviour: Suggested deafness evaluated by delayed auditory feedback. *British Journal of Psychology,* 1964, **55,** 439–446. (c)

Barber, T. X., & Calverley, D. S. Empirical evidence for a theory of "hypnotic" behavior: Effects of pretest instructions on response to primary suggestions. *Psychological Record,* 1964, **14,** 457–467. (d)

Barber, T. X., & Calverley, D. S. The definition of the situation as a variable affecting "hypnotic-like" suggestibility. *Journal of Clinical Psychology,* 1964, **20,** 438–440. (e)

Barber, T. X., & Calverley, D. S. The effects of "hypnosis" on learning and recall: A methodological critique. *Journal of Clinical Psychology,* 1965, **21,** 19–25.

Barber, T. X., & Calverley, D. S. Toward a theory of "hypnotic" behavior: Experimental analyses of suggested amnesia. *Journal of Abnormal Psychology,* 1966, **71,** 95–107.

Barber, T. X., & Calverley, D. S. Toward a theory of "hypnotic" behavior: Replication and extension of experiments by Barber and co-workers (1962–1965) and Hilgard and Tart (1966). *International Journal of Clinical and Experimental Hypnosis,* 1968, **16,** 179–195.

Barber, T. X., & Calverley, D. S. Multidimensional analysis of "hypnotic" behavior. *Journal of Abnormal Psychology,* 1969, **74,** 209–220.

Barber, T. X., Chauncey, H. H., & Winer, R. A. Effect of hypnotic and nonhypnotic suggestions on parotid gland response to gustatory stimuli. *Psychosomatic Medicine,* 1964, **26,** 374–380.

Barber, T. X., Dalal, A. S., & Calverley, D. S. The subjective reports of hypnotic subjects. *American Journal of Clinical Hypnosis,* 1968, **11,** 74–88.

Barber, T. X., & Deeley, D. C. Formal evidence for a theory of hypnotic behavior. I. "Hypnotic color-blindness" without "hypnosis." *International Journal of Clinical and Experimental Hypnosis,* 1961, **9,** 70–86.

Barber, T. X., & De Moor, W. A theory of hypnotic induction procedures. *American Journal of Clinical Hypnosis,* 1972, **15,** 112–135.

Barber, T. X., & Glass, L. B. Significant factors in hypnotic behavior. *Journal of Abnormal and Social Psychology,* 1962, **64,** 222–228.

Barber, T. X., & Hahn, K. W., Jr. Physiological and subjective responses to pain-producing stimulation under hypnotically-suggested and waking-imagined "analgesia." *Journal of Abnormal and Social Psychology,* 1962, **65,** 411–418.

Barber, T. X., & Ham, M. W. *Hypnotic phenomena.* Morristown, New Jersey: General Learning Press, 1974.

Barber, T. X., Spanos, N. P., & Chaves, J. F. *Hypnosis, imagination, and human potentialities.* New York: Pergamon Press, 1974.

Barber, T. X., Walker, P. C., & Hahn, K. W. Effects of hypnotic induction and suggestions on nocturnal dreaming and thinking. *Journal of Abnormal Psychology,* 1973, **82,** 414–427.

Barrios, A. A. Posthypnotic suggestion as higher order conditioning: A methodological and experimental analysis. *International Journal of Clinical and Experimental Hypnosis,* 1973, **21,** 32–50.

Bentler, P. M., & Roberts, M. R. Hypnotic susceptibility assessed in large groups. *International Journal of Clinical and Experimental Hypnosis,* 1963, **11,** 93–97.

Bernheim, H. *Suggestive therapeutics* (Translated by C. A. Herter.) (2nd ed.) Edinburgh and London: Young Pentland, 1890.

Binet, A., & Féré, C. *Animal magnetism.* (English translation.) New York: Appleton, 1888. (Originally published in French in 1886.)

Blum, G. S. Programming people to simulate machines. In S. S. Tompkins & S. Messick (Eds.), *Computer simulation of personality.* New York: Wiley, 1963. Pp. 127–157.

Blum, G. S., & Graef, J. R. The detection over time of subjects simulating hypnosis. *International Journal of Clinical and Experimental Hypnosis,* 1971, **19,** 211–224.

Boring, E. G. Perspective: Artifact and control. In R. Rosenthal and R. L. Rosnow (Eds.), *Artifact in behavioral research.* New York: Academic Press, 1969. Pp. 1–11.

Bowers, K. S. Hypnotic behavior: The differentiation of trance and demand characteristic variables. *Journal of Abnormal Psychology,* 1966, **71,** 42–51.

Bowers, K. S. The effect of demands for honesty on reports of visual and auditory hallucinations. *International Journal of Clinical and Experimental Hypnosis,* 1967, **15,** 31–36.

Bowers, K. S. Hypnosis, attribution, and demand characteristics. *International Journal of Clinical and Experimental Hypnosis,* 1973, **21,** 226–238. (a)

Bowers, K. S. Situationism in psychology: An analysis and a critique. *Psychological Review,* 1973, **80,** 307–336. (b)

Brady, J. P., & Levitt, E. E. Hypnotically induced visual hallucinations. *Psychosomatic Medicine,* 1966, **28,** 351–363.

Braid, J. *Neurypnology; Or the rationale of nervous sleep considered in relation with animal magnetism.* London: Churchill, 1843.

Braid, J. The power of the mind over the body. London, Churchill, 1846. In M. M. Tinterow (Ed.), *Foundations of hypnosis: From Mesmer to Freud.* Springfield, Illinois: Thomas, 1970.

Braid, J. The physiology of fascination and the critics criticized. Manchester, Grant, 1855. In M. M. Tinterow (Ed.), *Foundations of hypnosis: From Mesmer to Freud.* Springfield, Illinois: Thomas, 1970.

Bramwell, J. M. *Hypnotism. Its history, practice, and theory.* London: Alexander Moring, 1906.

Brown, R. *Social Psychology.* New York: Free Press, 1965.

Buckner, L. G., & Coe, W. C. Imaginative skill, wording of suggestions and hypnotic susceptibility. *International Journal of Clinical and Experimental Hypnosis,* 1976, in press.

Campbell, D. T. Factors relevant to the validity of experiments in social settings. *Psychological Bulletin,* 1957, **54,** 297–312.

Campbell, D. T. Prospective: Artifact and control. In R. Rosenthal & R. L. Rosnow (Eds.), *Artifact in behavioral research.* New York: Academic Press, 1969, 351–382.

Carlson, R. Where is the person in personality research? *Psychological Bulletin,* 1971, **75,** 203–217.

Chaves, J. F. Hypnosis reconceptualized: An overview of Barber's theoretical and empirical work. *Psychological Reports,* 1968, **22,** 587–608.

Coe, W. C. Further norms on the Harvard Group Scale of Hypnotic Susceptibility, Form A. *International Journal of Clinical and Experimental Hypnosis,* 1964, **12,** 184–190.

Coe, W. C. Hypnosis as role-enactment; The role demand variable. *American Journal of Clinical Hypnosis,* 1966, **8,** 189–191.

Coe, W. C. Experimental designs associated with the "credulous–skeptical" controversy in hypnosis. Paper presented at the annual meeting of the American Psychological Association, Washington, D.C., September, 1971.

Coe, W. C. Experimental designs and the state–nonstate issue in hypnosis. *American Journal of Clinical Hypnosis,* 1973, **16,** 118–128. (a)

Coe, W. C. A further evaluation of responses to an uncompleted posthypnotic suggestion. *American Journal of Clinical Hypnosis,* 1973, **15,** 223–228. (b)

Coe, W. C., Allen, J. L., Krug, W. M., & Wurzmann, A. G. Goal-directed fantasy in hypnotic responsiveness: Skill, item wording, or both? *International Journal of Clinical and Experimental Hypnosis,* 1974, **22,** 157–166.

Coe, W. C., Bailey, J. R., Hall, J. C., Howard, M. L., Janda, R. L., Kobayashi, K., & Parker, M. D. Hypnosis as role enactment: The role location variable. Proceedings of the 78th Annual American Psychological Association Convention, 1970, Washington, D.C.: American Psychological Association, 1970.

Coe, W. C., Buckner, L. G., Howard, M. L., & Kobayashi, K. Hypnosis as role enactment: Focus on a role specific skill. *American Journal of Clinical Hypnosis,* 1972, **15,** 41–45.

Coe, W. C., Kobayashi, K., & Howard, M. L. An approach toward isolating factors that influence antisocial conduct in hypnosis. *International Journal of Clinical and Experimental Hypnosis,* 1972, **20,** 118–131.

Coe, W. C., & Sarbin, T. R. An experimental demonstration of hypnosis as role enactment. *Journal of Abnormal Psychology,* 1966, **71,** 400–416.

Coe, W. C., & Sarbin, T. R. An alternative interpretation to the multiple composition of hypnotic scales: A single role relevant skill. *Journal of Personality and Social Psychology,* 1971, **18,** 1–8.

Conn, J. H. Is hypnosis really dangerous? *International Journal of Clinical and Experimental Hypnosis,* 1972, **20,** 61–79.

Conn, J. H., & Conn, R. N. Discussion of T. X. Barber's "Hypnosis as a causal variable in present day psychology: A critical analysis." *International Journal of Clinical and Experimental Hypnosis,* 1967, **15,** 106–110.

Connors, J. Experimental definition of the characteristics of task motivation instructions in the operational paradigm of hypnosis. Unpublished BA Honours thesis, University of New England, Armidale, Australia, 1972.

Connors, J. Empirical analysis of procedures relating to Hilgard's "Same-Subjects" design. Unpublished masters dissertation, University of Queensland, 1976.

Connors, J., & Sheehan, P. W. Analysis of the characteristics of task motivational instructions. *International Journal of Clinical and Experimental Hypnosis*, **1976**, in press.

Cook, S. W., & Harris, R. E. Verbal conditioning of the galvanic skin reflex. *Journal of Experimental Psychology*, 1937, **21**, 202–210.

Cook, T. D., Bean, J. R., Calder, B. J., Frey, R., Krovetz, M. L., & Reisman, S. R. Demand characteristics and three conceptions of the frequently deceived subject. *Journal of Personality and Social Psychology*, 1970, **14**, 185–194.

Cooper, L. M., Banford, S. A., Schubot, E., & Tart, C. T. A further attempt to modify hypnotic susceptibility through repeated, individualized experience. *International Journal of Clinical and Experimental Hypnosis*, 1967, **15**, 118–124.

Dalal, A. S. An empirical approach to hypnosis. *Archives of General Psychiatry*, 1966, **15**, 151–157.

Damaser, E. C. An experimental study of long term posthypnotic suggestion. Unpublished doctoral dissertation, Harvard University, 1964.

Damaser, E. C., Shor, R. E., & Orne, M. T. Physiological effects during hypnotically requested emotions. *Psychosomatic Medicine*, 1963, **25**, 334–343.

Darnton, R. *Mesmerism and the end of the enlightenment in France*. Cambridge, Massachusetts: Harvard University Press, 1968.

Davison, G. C., & Valine, S. Maintenance of self and drug-attributed behavior change. *Journal of Personality and Social Psychology*, 1969, **11**, 25–33.

Deckert, G. H., & West, L. J. The problem of hypnotizability: A review. *International Journal of Clinical and Experimental Hypnosis*, 1963, **11**, 205–235.

Diamond, M. J. The use of observationally presented information to modify hypnotic susceptibility. *Journal of Abnormal Psychology*, 1972, **79**, 174–180.

Diamond, M. J. Modification of hypnotizability: A review. *Psychological Bulletin*, 1974, **81**, 180–198.

Dorcus, R. M. (Ed.) *Hypnosis and its therapeutic applications*. New York: McGraw-Hill, 1956.

Downey, J. E. An experiment on getting an after-image from a mental image. *Psychological Review*, 1902, **8**, 42–55.

Edmonston, W. E. Relaxation as an appropriate experimental control in hypnosis studies. *American Journal of Clinical Hypnosis*, 1972, **14**, 218–229.

Ekehammar, B. Interactionism in modern personality from a historical perspective. *Psychological Bulletin*, 1974, **81**, 1026–1048.

Ellenberger, H. F. *The discovery of the unconscious: The history and evolution of dynamic psychiatry*. New York: Basic Books, 1970.

Endler, N. S., & Magnusson, D. Interactionism, trait psychology, psychodynamics, and situationism. Report from the Psychological Laboratories, University of Stockholm, 1974.

Epstein, W., & Rock, I. Perceptual set as an artifact of recency. *American Journal of Psychology*, 1960, **73**, 214–228.

Erickson, M. H. Deep hypnosis and its induction. In L. le Cron (Ed.), *Experimental hypnosis*. New York: Macmillan, 1952.

Erickson, M. H., & Erickson, E. M. The hypnotic induction of hallucinatory color vision followed by pseudo-negative after-images. *Journal of Experimental Psychology*, 1938, **22**, 581–588.

Erickson, M. H., & Erickson, E. M. Concerning the nature and character of post-hypnotic behavior. *Journal of General Psychology*, 1941, **24**, 95–133.

Evans, F. J. Recent trends in experimental hypnosis. *Behavioral Science*, 1968, **13**, 477–487.

Evans, F. J. Simulating subjects: who is fooling whom? Paper presented at the Annual conference of the American Psychological Association, Washington, D.C., September, 1971.

Evans, F. J. Posthypnotic amnesia and the temporary disruption of retrieval processes. Paper presented at Symposium on Amnesia, Annual Conference of American Psychological Association, Hawaii, September, 1972.

Evans, F. J., & Kihlstrom, J. F. Posthypnotic amnesia as disrupted retrieval. *Journal of Abnormal Psychology,* 1973, **82,** 317–323.

Evans, F. J., & Orne, M. T. Motivation, performance, and hypnosis. *International Journal of Clinical and Experimental Hypnosis,* 1965, **13,** 103–116.

Evans, F. J., & Orne, M. T. The disappearing hypnotist: The use of simulating subjects to evaluate how subjects perceive experimental procedures. *International Journal of Clinical and Experimental Hypnosis,* 1971, **19,** 277–296.

Evans, F. J., & Schmeidler, D. Relationship between the Harvard Group Scale of hypnotic susceptibility and the Stanford Hypnotic Susceptibility Scale: Form C. *International Journal of Clinical and Experimental Hypnosis,* 1966, **14,** 333–343.

Evans, F. J., & Thorn, W. A. Two types of posthypnotic amnesia: Recall amnesia and source amnesia. *International Journal of Clinical and Experimental Hypnosis,* 1966, **14,** 162–179.

Faria, J. C. di, Abbé. *De la cause du sommeil lucide; ou étude sur la nature de l'homme,* 1819. 2nd edition, D. G. Dalgado (Ed.), Paris: Henri Jouve, 1906.

Ferenczi, S. *Introjektion und Übertragung. Eine psychoanalytische Studie.* Wien: Deuticke, 1910.

Field, P. B. Review of T. X. Barber, "Hypnosis: A scientific approach." *International Journal of Clinical and Experimental Hypnosis,* 1971, **19,** 109–111.

Fillenbaum, S. Prior deception and subsequent experimental performance: The "faithful" subject. *Journal of Personality and Social Psychology,* 1966, **4,** 532–537.

Fisher, S. The role of expectancy in the performance of posthypnotic behavior. *Journal of Abnormal and Social Psychology,* 1954, **49,** 503–507.

Fisher, S. An investigation of alleged conditioning phenomena under hypnosis. *International Journal of Clinical and Experimental Hypnosis,* 1955, **3,** 71–103.

Fisher, S. Problems of interpretation and controls in hypnotic research. In G. H. Estabrooks (Ed.), *Hypnosis: Current Problems.* New York: Harper & Row, 1962. Pp. 109–126.

Fisher, S., Cole, J. O., Rickels, K., & Uhlenhuth, E. H. Drug-set interaction: The effect of expectations on drug response in outpatients. In P. B. Bradley, F. Flugel, & P. Hoch (Eds.), *Neuropsychopharmacology.* Vol. 3. New York: Elsevier, 1964, pp. 149–156.

Franklin, B. *et al.* Report of Dr. Benjamin Franklin and the other commissioners, charged by the King of France, with the examination of the animal magnetism, as now practised at Paris. Translated from the French, with an historical introduction (by Wm. Godwin) London, 1785. In M. M. Tinterow (Ed.), *Foundation of hypnosis: From Mesmer to Freud.* Springfield, Illinois: Thomas, 1970.

Friedlander, J. W., & Sarbin, T. R. The depth of hypnosis. *Journal of Abnormal and Social Psychology,* 1938, **33,** 453–475.

Fromm, E., & Shor, R. E. *Hypnosis: Research developments and perspectives.* Chicago: Aldine-Atherton, 1972.

Garner, W. R., Hake, H. W., & Eriksen, C. W. Operationism and the concept of perception. *Psychological Review,* 1956, **63,** 149–159.

Gilbert, J. E., & Barber, T. X. Effects of hypnotic induction, motivational suggestions, and level of suggestibility on cognitive performance. *International Journal of Clinical and Experimental Hypnosis,* 1972, **20,** 156–168.

Gill, M. M. Hypnosis as an altered and regressed state. *International Journal of Clinical and Experimental Hypnosis,* 1972, **20,** 224–237.

Gill, M. M., & Brenman, M. *Hypnosis and related states.* New York: International Universities Press, 1961.

Giorgi, A. *Psychology as a human science: A phenomenologically based approach.* New York: Harper & Row, 1970.

Graham, K. R. Brightness contrast by hypnotic hallucination. *International Journal of Clinical and Experimental Hypnosis,* 1969, **17,** 62–73.

Graham, K. R., & Schwarz, L. M. Suggested deafness and auditory signal detectability. *Proceedings of the 81st APA Conference, Montréal, Canada,* 1973, **8,** 1095–1096.

Greene, R. J., & Reyher, J. Pain tolerance in hypnotic analgesic and imagination states. *Journal of Abnormal Psychology,* 1972, **79,** 29–38.

Guillain, G. J. M. Charcot, 1825–1893. Sa vie, son oeuvre. Paris: Masson, 1955. In M. M. Tinterow (Ed.), *Foundations of hypnosis: From Mesmer to Freud.* Springfield, Illinois: Thomas, 1970.

Gur, R. C. An attention-controlled operant procedure for enhancing hypnotic susceptibility. *Journal of Abnormal Psychology,* 1974, **83,** 644–650.

Gustafson, L. A., & Orne, M. T. Effects of perceived role and role success on the detection of deception. *Journal of Applied Psychology,* 1965, **49,** 412–417.

Guy, W., Gross, M., & Dennis, H. An alternative to the double blind procedure. *American Journal of Psychiatry,* 1967, **123,** 1505–1512.

Haber, R. N., & Haber, R. B. Eidetic imagery: I. Frequency. *Perceptual and Motor Skills,* 1964, **19,** 131–138.

Hahn, K. W., & Barber, T. X. *Hallucinations with and without hypnotic induction: An extension of the Brady & Levitt study.* Harding, Massachusetts: The Medfield Foundation, 1966.

Ham, M. W., & Spanos, N. P. Suggested auditory and visual hallucinations in task motivated and hypnotic subjects. *American Journal of Clinical Hypnosis,* 1974, **17,** 88–101.

Harriman, P. L. Hypnotic induction of color vision anomalies: I. The use of the Ishihara and the Jensen tests to verify the acceptance of suggested color blindness. *Journal of General Psychology,* 1942, **26,** 289–298.

Hibler, F. W. An experimental investigation of negative afterimages of hallucinated colors in hypnosis. *Journal of Experimental Psychology,* 1940, **27,** 45–57.

Hilgard, E. R. Lawfulness within hypnotic phenomena. In G. H. Estabrooks (Ed.), *Hypnosis: Current problems.* New York: Harper & Row, 1962.

Hilgard, E. R. The motivational relevance of hypnosis. In D. Levine (Ed.), *Nebraska Symposium on Motivation.* Lincoln, Nebraska: University of Nebraska Press, 1964. Pp. 1–44.

Hilgard, E. R. *Hypnotic susceptibility.* New York: Harcourt, Brace & World, 1965. (a)

Hilgard, E. R. Hypnosis. *Annual Review of Psychology,* 1965, **16,** 157–180. (b)

Hilgard, E. R. Individual differences in hypnotizability. In J. E. Gordon (Ed.), *Handbook of clinical and experimental hypnosis.* New York: Macmillan, 1967. Pp. 391–443.

Hilgard, E. R. Altered states of awareness. *Journal of Nervous and Mental Disease,* 1969, **149,** 68–79.

Hilgard, E. R. Is hypnosis a state, trait, neither? Paper presented at the 79th Conference of the American Psychological Association, Washington, D.C., September, 1971.

Hilgard, E. R. A critique of Johnson, Maher, and Barber's "Artifact in the 'essence of hypnosis': An evaluation of trance logic," with a recomputation of their findings. *Journal of Abnormal Psychology,* 1972, **79,** 221–233. (a)

Hilgard, E. R. The domain of hypnosis with some comments on Barber's alternative paradigm. Paper presented at Annual Meeting of The Society for Clinical and Experimental Hypnosis, Boston, Massachusetts: October, 1972. (b)

Hilgard, E. R. A neodissociation interpretation of pain reduction in hypnosis. *Psychological Review,* 1973, **80,** 396–411. (a)

Hilgard, E. R. The domain of hypnosis: With some comments on alternative paradigms. *American Psychologist,* 1973, **23,** 972–982. (b)

Hilgard, E. R. Dissociation revisited. In M. Henle, J. Jaynes, & J. Sullivan (Eds.), *Historical conceptions of psychology.* New York: Springer, 1973. Pp. 205–219. (c)

Hilgard, E. R. Book Review of Sarbin, T. R. & Coe, W. C. Hypnosis: A social psychological analysis of influence communication. *American Journal of Clinical Hypnosis,* 1973, **16,** 67–69. (d)

Hilgard, E. R. Neodissociation theory in relation to the concept of state. Paper presented at 26th meeting of The Society for Clinical and Experimental Hypnosis, Montréal, Canada, 1974. (a)

Hilgard, E. R. Toward a neodissociation theory: Multiple cognitive controls in human functioning. *Perspectives in Biology and Medicine,* 1974, **17,** 301–316. (b)

Hilgard, E. R. Hypnosis. *Annual Review of Psychology,* 1975, **26,** 19–44.

Hilgard, E. R., & Lauer, L. W. Lack of correlation between the CPI and hypnotic susceptibility. *Journal of Consulting Psychology,* 1962, **26,** 331–335.

Hilgard, E. R., & Tart, C. T. Responsiveness to suggestions following waking and imagination instructions and following induction of hypnosis. *Journal of Abnormal Psychology,* 1966, **71,** 196–208.

Hilgard, E. R., Weitzenhoffer, A. M., Landes, J., & Moore, R. K. The distribution of susceptibility to hypnosis in a student population: A study using the Stanford Hypnotic Susceptibility Scale. *Psychological Monographs,* 1961, **75** (Whole No. 512), 1–22.

Hilgard, J. R. *Personality and hypnosis: A study of imaginative involvement.* Chicago: University of Chicago Press, 1970.

Hilgard, J. R. Imaginative involvement: Some characteristics of the highly hypnotizable and nonhypnotizable. *International Journal of Clinical and Experimental Hypnosis,* 1974, **22,** 138–156.

Hilgard, J. R., & Hilgard, E. R. Developmental–interactive aspects of hypnosis: Some illustrative cases. *Genetic Psychology Monographs,* 1962, **66,** 143–178.

Hull, C. L. *Hypnosis and suggestibility: An experimental approach.* New York: Appleton-Century Crofts, 1933.

Hunt, S. Spontaneous speech effects in hypnosis. *International Journal of Clinical and Experimental Hypnosis,* 1971, **19,** 225–233.

Janet, P. *Psychological healing: A historical and clinical study.* (English translation by E. Paul & C. Paul.) New York: Macmillan, 1925. 2 vols. (Originally published in French, 1919.)

Johnson, R. F. Trance logic revisited: A reply to Hilgard's critique. *Journal of Abnormal Psychology,* 1972, **79,** 234–238.

Johnson, R. F., Maher, B. A., & Barber, T. X. Artifact in the "essence of hypnosis": An evaluation of trance logic. *Journal of Abnormal Psychology,* 1972, **79,** 212–220.

Jourard, S. M. *Disclosing man to himself.* Princeton, New Jersey: Van Nostrand, 1968.

Jourard, S. A humanistic revolution in psychology. In A. G. Miller (Ed.), *The social psychology of psychological research.* New York: The Free Press, 1972. (a)

Jourard, S. Experimenter–subject dialogue: A paradigm for a humanistic science of psychology. In A. G. Miller (Ed.), *The social psychology of psychological research.* New York: The Free Press, 1972. (b)

Katz, S. Thematic productions under hypnotically aroused conflict in age regressed and waking states. *Proceedings of the 81st Annual Convention of APA, Montréal,* 1973, **8,** 1093–1094.

Kellogg, E. R. Duration and effects of post-hypnotic suggestions. *Journal of Experimental Psychology,* 1929, **12,** 502–514.

Kelman, H. C. Human use of human subjects: The problem of deception in social psychological experiments. *Psychological Bulletin,* 1967, **67,** 1–11.

Kihlstrom, J. F. Order of recall in posthypnotic amnesia and in waking memory. Paper presented at the 43rd annual meeting of the Eastern Psychological Association, Boston, Massachusetts, 1972.

Kinney, J. M., & Sachs, L. W. Increasing hypnotic susceptibility. *Journal of Abnormal Psychology,* 1974, **83,** 145–150.

Kline, M. V. The production of antisocial behavior through hypnosis: New clinical data. *International Journal of Clinical and Experimental Hypnosis,* 1972, **20,** 80–94.

Klinger, B. L. Effect of peer model responsiveness and length of induction procedure on hypnotic responsiveness. *Journal of Abnormal Psychology,* 1970, **75,** 15–18.

Knox, V. J., Crutchfield, L., & Hilgard, E. R. The nature of task interference in hypnotic dissociation. Hypnotic Research Memorandum, Stanford University, 1973, No. 136.

Knox, V. J., Morgan, A. H., & Hilgard, E. R. Pain and suffering in ischemia: The paradox of hypnotically suggested anesthesia as contradicted by reports from the "hidden observer." *Archives of General Psychiatry,* 1974, **30,** 301–316.

Kubie, L. S., & Margolin, S. The process of hypnotism and the nature of the hypnotic state. *American Journal of Psychiatry,* 1944, **100,** 611–622.

Kuhn, T. S. *The structure of scientific revolutions.* Chicago, Illinois: University of Chicago Press, 1962.

Leask, J., Haber, R. N., & Haber, R. B. Eidetic imagery in children: II. Longitudinal and experimental results. *Psychonomic Monograph Supplements,* 1969, **3,** 25–48.

Lennox, J. R. Effect of hypnotic analgesia on verbal report and cardiovascular responses to ischemic pain. *Journal of Abnormal Psychology,* 1970, **75,** 199–206.

Levitt, E. A comment on "A paradigm for determining the clinical relevance of hypnotically induced psychopathology." *Psychological Bulletin,* 1963, **60,** 326–329.

Levitt, E. E., Aronoff, G., & Morgan, C. D. A note on possible limitations on the use of the Harvard Group Scale of Hypnotic Susceptibility, Form A. *International Journal of Clinical and Experimental Hypnosis,* 1974, **12,** 234–238.

Levitt, E. E., & Overley, T. M. A comparison of the performance of hypnotic subjects and simulators on a variety of measures: A pilot study. *International Journal of Clinical and Experimental Hypnosis,* 1971, **19,** 234–242.

Lieberman, C. R. Appropriate controls in hypnosis research. *American Journal of Clinical Hypnosis,* 1972, **14,** 229–235.

Lindquist, E. F. *Design and analysis of experiments in Psychology and Education.* Boston, Massachusetts: Houghton-Mifflin, 1953.

London, P., Conant, M., & Davison, G. C. More hypnosis in the unhypnotizable: Effects of hypnosis and exhortation on rote learning. *Journal of Personality,* 1966, **34,** 71–79.

London, P., Cooper, L. M., & Engstrom, D. R. Increasing hypnotic susceptibility by brain wave feedback. *Journal of Abnormal Psychology,* 1974, **83,** 554–560.

London, P., Cooper, L. M., & Johnson, H. J. Subject characteristics in hypnosis research. II: Attitudes towards hypnosis, volunteer status, and personality measures. III: Some correlates of hypnotic susceptibility. *International Journal of Clinical and Experimental Hypnosis,* 1962, **10,** 13–21.

London, P., & Fuhrer, M. Hypnosis, motivation, and performance. *Journal of Personality,* 1961, **29,** 321–333.

London, P., Ogle, M. E., & Unikel, I. P. Effects of hypnosis and motivation on resistance to heat stress. *Journal of Abnormal Psychology,* 1968, **73,** 532–541.

Ludwig, A. M. Altered states of consciousness. In C. T. Tart (Ed.), *Altered states of consciousness.* New York: Wiley, 1969.
Marx, M. (Ed.) *Psychological theory: Contemporary readings.* New York: Macmillan, 1951.
McDonald, R. D., & Smith, J. R. Trance logic in tranceable and simulating subjects. *International Journal of Clinical and Experimental Hypnosis,* 1975, **23,** 80–89.
McGlashan, T. H., Evans, F. J., & Orne, M. T. The nature of hypnotic analgesia and placebo response to experimental pain. *Psychosomatic Medicine,* 1969, **31,** 227–246.
McReynolds, P. On alternative models of hypnosis: An integration and some new proposals. *Psychological Record,* 1967, **17,** 167–176.
Melei, J. P., & Hilgard, E. R. Attitudes toward hypnosis, self-predictions, and hypnotic susceptibility. *International Journal of Clinical and Experimental Hypnosis,* 1964, **12,** 99–108.
Melzack, R., & Wall, P. D. Pain mechanisms: A new theory. *Science,* 1965, **150,** 971–979.
Mesmer, F. A. Mémoire sur la Découverte du Magnétisme Animal. Par A. Mesmer, Docteur en Médecine de la Faculté de Vienne. A geneve; et se trouve à Paris, chez P. Fr. Didot le jeune, Libraire–Imprimeur de Monsieur, quai des Augustins, 1779. In M. M. Tinterow (Ed.), *Foundations of hypnosis: From Mesmer to Freud.* Springfield, Illinois: Thomas, 1970.
Milgram, S. Behavioral study of obedience. *Journal of Abnormal and Social Psychology,* 1963, **67,** 371–378.
Miller, A. G. Role playing: An alternative to deception? A review of the evidence. *American Psychologist,* 1972, **27,** 623–636.
Miller, A. G., Galanter, E., & Pribram, K. H. *Plans and the structure of behavior.* New York: Holt, Rinehart & Winston, 1960.
Miller, R. J., Hennessy, R. T., & Leibowitz, H. W. The effect of hypnotic ablation of the background on the magnitude of the Ponzo perspective illusion. *International Journal of Clinical and Experimental Hypnosis,* 1973, **21,** 180–191.
Mischel, W. *Personality and assessment.* New York: Wiley, 1968.
Moore, W. F. Effects of posthypnotic stimulation of hostility upon motivation. *American Journal of Clinical Hypnosis,* 1964, **7,** 130–135.
Morgan, A. H., Johnson, D. L., & Hilgard, E. R. The stability of hypnotic susceptibility: A longitudinal study. *International Journal of Clinical and Experimental Hypnosis,* 1974, **22,** 249–257.
Morgan, A. H., & Lam, D. The relationship of the Betts vividness of imagery questionnaire and hypnotic susceptibility: Failure to replicate. Unpublished paper. Hawthorne House Research Memorandum, 1969, No. 103.
Mowrer, O. H. Preparatory set (expectancy)–a determinant in motivation and learning. *Psychological Review,* 1938, **45,** 62–91.
Nace, E. P., & Orne, M. T. Fate of an uncompleted posthypnotic suggestion. *Journal of Abnormal Psychology,* 1970, **75,** 278–285.
Nace, E. P., Orne, M. T., & Hammer, A. G. Posthypnotic amnesia as an active psychic process: The reversibility of amnesia. *Archives of General Psychiatry,* 1974, **31,** 257–260.
Neisser, U. *Cognitive psychology.* New York: Appleton-Century Crofts, 1967.
Norris, D. L. Barber's task-motivational theory and posthypnotic amnesia. *American Journal of Clinical Hypnosis,* 1973, **15,** 181–190.
O'Connell, D. N., Shor, R. E., & Orne, M. T. Hypnotic age regression: An empirical and methodological analysis. *Journal of Abnormal Psychology Monograph,* 1970, **76** (3, Part 2).
Orne, M. T. Die leistungs Fähigheit in Hypnose und im Wackzustand. *Psychologische Rundschau,* 1954, **5,** 291–297.

Orne, M. T. The nature of hypnosis: Artifact and essence. *Journal of Abnormal and Social Psychology,* 1959, **58,** 277–299.

Orne, M. T. On the social psychology of the psychological experiment: With particular reference to demand characteristics and their implications. *American Psychologist,* 1962, **17,** 776–783. (a)

Orne, M. T. Antisocial behavior and hypnosis: Problems of control and validation in empirical studies. In G. H. Estabrooks (Ed.), *Hypnosis: Current problems.* New York: Harper & Row, 1962. Pp. 137–192. (b)

Orne, M. T. The nature of the hypnotic phenomenon: Recent empirical studies. Paper presented at the Annual Conference of the American Psychological Association, Philadelphia, September, 1963.

Orne, M. T. Demand characteristics and their implications for real life: The importance of quasi-controls. Paper presented at the Annual conference of the American Psychological Association, Chicago, September, 1965. (a)

Orne, M. T. Psychological factors maximizing resistance to stress: With special reference to hypnosis. In S. Z. Klausner (Ed.), *The quest for self-control.* New York: The Free Press, 1965. Pp. 286–328. (b)

Orne, M. T. Hypnosis, motivation, and compliance. *American Journal of Psychiatry,* 1966, **122,** 721–726.

Orne, M. T. What must a satisfactory theory of hypnosis explain? *International Journal of Psychiatry,* 1967, **3,** 206–211.

Orne, M. T. Demand characteristics and the concept of quasi-controls. In R. Rosenthal, & R. L. Rosnow (Eds.), *Artifact in behavioral research.* New York: Academic Press, 1969. Pp. 143–179.

Orne, M. T. Hypnosis, motivation, and the ecological validity of the psychological experiment. In W. J. Arnold, & M. M. Page (Eds.), *Nebraska Symposium on Motivation.* Lincoln, Nebraska: University of Nebraska Press, 1970. Pp. 187–265.

Orne, M. T. The simulation of hypnosis: Why, how, and what it means. *International Journal of Clinical and Experimental Hypnosis,* 1971, **19,** 183–210.

Orne, M. T. On the simulating subject as a quasi-control group in hypnosis research: What, why, and how? In E. Fromm, & R. E. Shor (Eds.), *Hypnosis: Research developments and perspectives.* Chicago, Illinois: Aldine-Atherton, 1972. Pp. 399–443. (a)

Orne, M. T. Can a hypnotized subject be compelled to carry out otherwise unacceptable behavior? *International Journal of Clinical and Experimental Hypnosis,* 1972, **20,** 101–117. (b)

Orne, M. T. Communication by the total experimental situation: Why it is important, how it is evaluated, and its significance for the ecological validity of findings. In P. Pliner, L. Krames, & T. Alloway (Eds.), *Communication and affect: Language and thought.* New York: Academic Press, 1973. Pp. 157–191.

Orne, M. T. Pain suppression by hypnosis and related phenomena. *Advances in Neurology,* 1974, **4,** 563–572. (a)

Orne, M. T. On the concept of hypnotic depth. Paper presented at the 18th International Conference of Applied Psychology, Montréal, Canada, August, 1974. (b)

Orne, M. T., & Evans, F. J. Social control in the psychological experiment: Antisocial behavior and hypnosis. *Journal of Personality and Social Psychology,* 1965, **1,** 189–200.

Orne, M. T., & Evans, F. J. Inadvertent termination of hypnosis with hypnotized and simulating subjects. *International Journal of Clinical and Experimental Hypnosis,* 1966, **14,** 61–78.

Orne, M. T., & Hammer, A. G. Hypnosis. *Encyclopaedia Britannica,* Chicago, Illinois: William Benton, 1974. Pp. 133–140.

Orne, M. T., & Scheibe, K. E. The contribution of nondeprivation factors in the production of sensory deprivation effects: The psychology of the "panic button." *Journal of Abnormal and Social Psychology,* 1964, **68,** 3–12.

Orne, M. T., Sheehan, P. W., & Evans, F. J. Occurrence of posthypnotic behavior outside the experimental setting. *Journal of Personality and Social Psychology,* 1968, **9,** 189–196.

Overley, T. M., & Levitt, E. E. A test of the expected homogeneity of simulator performance. *International Journal of Clinical and Experimental Hypnosis,* 1968, **16,** 229–236.

Palmer, R. D., & Field, P. B. Visual imagery and susceptibility to hypnosis. *Journal of Consulting and Clinical Psychology,* 1968, **32,** 456–461.

Parrish, M. J. Moral predisposition and hypnotic influence of "immoral" behavior; An exploratory study. *American Journal of Clinical Hypnosis,* 1974, **17,** 115–124.

Parrish, M., Lundy, R. M., & Leibowitz, H. W. Hypnotic age-regression and magnitudes of the Ponzo and Poggendorff illusions. *Science,* 1968, **159,** 1375–1376.

Patten, E. F. The duration of posthypnotic suggestions. *Journal of Abnormal and Social Psychology,* 1930, **25,** 319–334.

Pattie, F. A. A report on an attempt to produce uniocular blindness by hypnotic suggestion. *British Journal of Medical Psychology,* 1933, **15,** 230–261.

Pattie, F. A. The geniuneness of unilateral deafness produced by hypnosis. *American Journal of Psychology,* 1950, **63,** 84–86.

Perkins, K. A., & Reyher, J. Repression, psychopathology, and drive representation: An experimental hypnotic investigation of impulse inhibition. *American Journal of Clinical Hypnosis,* 1971, **18,** 249–258.

Perry, C. Martin T. Orne: Somnambules and simulators. Unpublished paper presented at the University of Sydney, Sydney, 1963.

Perry, C. Imagery, fantasy and hypnotic susceptibility: A multidimensional approach. *Journal of Personality and Social Psychology,* 1973, **26,** 217–222.

Perry, C., & Chisholm, W. Hypnotic age regression and the Ponzo and Poggendorff illusions. *International Journal of Clinical and Experimental Hypnosis,* 1973, **21,** 192–204.

Perry, C., & Mullen, G. The effects of hypnotic susceptibility on reducing smoking behavior treated by an hypnotic technique. *Journal of Clinical Psychology,* 1975, **31,** 498–505.

Peters, J. E. Trance logic: Artifact or essence in hypnosis. Unpublished doctoral dissertation, Pennsylvania State University, 1973.

Plapp, J. M. Task motivation as an appropriate experimental control. *American Journal of Clinical Hypnosis,* 1972, **14,** 210–217.

Platt, J. R. Strong inference. *Science,* 1964, **146,** 347–353.

Podmore, F. *From Mesmer to Christian Science. A short history of mental healing.* New Hyde Park, New York: University Books, 1964. (Originally published in 1909.)

Popper, K. R. *The logic of scientific discovery.* London: Hutchinson, 1959.

Porter, J. W., Woodward, J. A., Bisbee, T. C. & Fenker, R. M., Jr. Effect of hypnotic age regression on the magnitude of the Ponzo illusion. *Journal of Abnormal Psychology,* 1972, **39,** 189–194.

Rawlings, R., & Hammer, A. G. Scale of hypnotic factors. Unpublished test. University of New South Wales, Sydney, Australia, 1971.

Reiff, R., & Scheerer, M. *Memory and hypnotic age regression.* New York: International University Press, 1959.

Reyher, J. A paradigm for determining the clinical relevance of hypnotically-induced psychopathology. *Psychological Bulletin,* 1962, **59,** 344–352.

Reyher, J. Hypnosis in research on psychopathology. In J. E. Gordon (Ed.), *Handbook of clinical and experimental hypnosis,* New York: Macmillan, 1967.

Reyher, J. Comment on "Artificial induction of posthypnotic conflict." *Journal of Abnormal Psychology,* 1969, **74,** 420–422.

Reyher, J. The real-simulation design and laboratory hypnosis: Two methodological culs-de-sac. Unpublished paper, University of Michigan, 1972.

Reyher, J. Can hypnotized subjects simulate waking behavior? *American Journal of Clinical Hypnosis,* 1973, **16,** 31–36.

Reyher, J. Review of "Hypnotic Phenomena" by T. X. Barber, & M. W. Ham *American Journal of Clinical Hypnosis,* 1975, **17,** 202–205.

Reyher, J., & Smyth, L. Suggestibility during the execution of a posthypnotic suggestion. *Journal of Abnormal Psychology,* 1971, **78,** 258–265.

Riecken, H. W. A program for research on experiments in social psychology. In N. F. Washburne (Ed.), *Decisions, values, and groups.* New York: Pergamon Press, 1962. Pp. 25–41.

Rokeach, M., Reyher, J., & Wiseman, R. Importance of belief as a determinant of organization of change within belief systems. In M. Rokeach (Ed.), *Attitudes, beliefs, and values.* San Francisco, California: Jossey-Bass, 1968.

Rosenberg, M. J. The conditions and consequences of evaluation apprehension. In R. Rosenthal, & R. L. Rosnow (Eds.), *Artifact in behavioral research.* New York: Academic Press, 1969. Pp. 279–349.

Rosenberg, S. J., & Feldberg, T. M. Rorschach characteristics of a group of malingerers. *Rorschach Research Exchange,* 1944, **8,** 141–158.

Rosenhan, D., & London, P. Group Hypnotic Susceptibility Scale. Unpublished manuscript, Princeton, New Jersey, 1961.

Rosenhan, D., & London, P. Hypnosis: Expectation, susceptibility, and performance. *Journal of Abnormal and Social Psychology,* 1963, **66,** 77–81. (a)

Rosenhan, D., & London, P. Hypnosis in the unhypnotizable: A study in rote learning. *Journal of Experimental Psychology,* 1963, **65,** 30–34. (b)

Rosenzweig, S. The experimental situation as a psychological problem. *Psychological Review,* 1933, **40,** 337–354.

Ross, S., Krugman, A. D., Lyerly, S. B., & Clyde, D. J. Drugs and placebos: A model design. *Psychological Reports,* 1962, **10,** 383–392.

Ruch, J. C., Morgan, A. H., & Hilgard, E. R. Measuring hypnotic responsiveness: A comparison of the Barber Suggestibility Scale and the Stanford Hypnotic Susceptibility Scale, Form A. *International Journal of Clinical and Experimental Hypnosis,* 1974, **22,** 365–376.

Rudé, G. *Revolutionary Europe 1783–1815.* London: Collins, 1964.

Ryle, G. *The concept of mind.* Middlesex, England: Penguin University Books, 1973. (Originally published in 1949.)

Sacerdote, P. Clinical and experimental trance: What's the difference? A symposium (discussion). *American Journal of Clinical Hypnosis,* 1970, **13,** 10.

Sachs, L. B. Construing hypnosis as modifiable behavior. In A. Jacobs & L. Sachs (Eds.), *Psychology of private events.* New York: Academic Press, 1971.

Sachs, L., & Anderson, W. Modification of hypnotic susceptibility. *International Journal of Clinical and Experimental Hypnosis,* 1967, **15,** 172–180.

Sarbin, T. R. Contributions to role-taking theory: I. Hypnotic behavior. *Psychological Review,* 1950, **57,** 255–270.

Sarbin, T. R. Role theoretical interpretation of psychological change. In P. Worchel, & D. Byrne (Eds.), *Psychological Change.* New York: Wiley, 1964. Pp. 176–219.

Sarbin, T. R. The concept of hallucination. *Journal of Personality,* 1967, **35,** 359–380.

Sarbin, T. R. Imagining as muted role-taking: A historical–linguistic analysis in P. Sheehan (Ed.), *The function and nature of imagery.* New York: Academic Press, 1972. Pp. 333–354.

Sarbin, T. R., & Andersen, M. L. Base-rate expectancies and perceptual alterations in hypnosis. *British Journal of Social and Clinical Psychology,* 1963, **2,** 112–121.

Sarbin, T. R., & Andersen, M. L. Role-theoretical analysis of hypnotic behavior in J. E. Gordon (Ed.), *Handbook of Clinical and Experimental Hypnosis.* New York: Crowell-Collier, & Macmillan, 1967. Pp. 319–344.

Sarbin, T. R., & Coe, W. C. *Hypnosis: A social psychological analysis of influence communication.* New York: Holt, Rinehart & Winston, 1972.

Sarbin, T. R., & Juhasz, J. B. The historical background of the concept of hallucination. *Journal of the History of the Behavioral Sciences,* 1967, **3,** 339–358.

Sarbin, T. R., & Juhasz, J. B. Toward a theory of imagination. *Journal of Personality,* 1970, **38,** 52–76.

Sarbin, T. R., & Lim, D. T. Some evidence in support of the role taking hypothesis in hypnosis. *International Journal of Clinical and Experimental Hypnosis,* 1963, **11,** 98–103.

Sarbin, T. R., & Slagle, R. W. Hypnosis and psychophysiological outcomes. In E. Fromm, & R. E. Shor (Eds.), *Hypnosis: Research developments and perspectives.* New York: Academic Press, 1972. Pp. 185–214.

Scharf, B., & Zamansky, H. S. Reduction of word-recognition threshold under hypnosis. *Perceptual and Motor Skills,* 1963, **17,** 499–510.

Scheffler, I. Vision and revolution: A postscript on Kuhn. *Philosophy of Science,* 1972, **39,** 366–374.

Scheibe, K. E., Gray, A. L., & Keim, C. S. Hypnotically induced deafness and delayed auditory feedback: A comparison of real and simulating subjects. *International Journal of Clinical and Experimental Hypnosis,* 1968, **16,** 158–164.

Schilder, P. *Hypnosis.* (Translated by Simon Rothenberg.) New York: Nervous and Mental Disease Publishing Co., 1927.

Schneck, J. M. Observations on hypnotic dreams. *Perceptual and Motor Skills,* 1969, **28,** 414.

Schofield, L. J., & Reyher, J. Thematic productions under hypnotically aroused conflict in age regressed and waking states using the real-simulator design. *Journal of Abnormal Psychology,* 1974, **83,** 130–139.

Schulman, R. E., & London, P. Hypnosis and verbal learning. *Journal of Abnormal and Social Psychology,* 1963, **67,** 363–370.

Schultz, D. P. The human subject in psychological research. *Psychological Bulletin,* 1969, **72,** 214–228.

Sears, R. R. An experimental study of hypnotic anesthesia. *Journal of Experimental Psychology,* 1932, **15,** 1–22.

Sheehan, P. W. Artificial induction of posthypnotic conflict. *Journal of Abnormal Psychology,* 1969, **74,** 16–25.

Sheehan, P. W. Analysis of the treatment effects of simulation instructions in the application of the real–simulating model of hypnosis. *Journal of Abnormal Psychology,* 1970, **75,** 98–103.

Sheehan, P. W. A methodological analysis of the simulating technique. *International Journal of Clinical and Experimental Hypnosis,* 1971, **19,** 83–99. (a)

Sheehan, P. W. Countering preconceptions about hypnosis: An objective index of involvement with the hypnotist. *Journal of Abnormal Psychology Monograph,* 1971, **78,** 299–322. (b)

Sheehan, P. W. Task structure as a limiting condition of the occurrence of the treatment effects of simulation instruction in application of the real-simulating model of hypnosis. *International Journal of Clinical and Experimental Hypnosis,* 1971, **19,** 260–276. (c)

Sheehan, P. W. An explication of the real-simulating model: A reply to Reyher's comment on "Artificial induction of posthypnotic conflict." *International Journal of Clinical and Experimental Hypnosis,* 1971, **19,** 46–51. (d)

Sheehan, P. W. Exit magic and enter science into hypnosis. Review of T. X. Barber, "Hypnosis: A scientific approach." *Contemporary Psychology,* 1971, **16,** 15–18. (e)

Sheehan, P. W. Hypnosis and the manifestations of "imagination." In E. Fromm & R. E. Shor (Eds.), *Hypnosis: Research developments and perspectives.* Chicago: Aldine-Atherton, 1972. Pp. 293–319.

Sheehan, P. W. Analysis of the heterogeneity of "faking" and "simulating" performance in the hypnotic setting. *International Journal of Clinical and Experimental Hypnosis,* 1973, **21,** 213–225. (a)

Sheehan, P. W. The variability of eidetic imagery among Australian aboriginal children. *Journal of Social Psychology,* 1973, **91,** 29–36. (b)

Sheehan, P. W. Escape from the ambiguous: Artifact and methodologies of hypnosis. *American Psychologist,* 1973, **28,** 983–993. (c)

Sheehan, P. W. *A neoclassical account of experimental method: Some dilemmas for the social scientist.* Brisbane, Queensland: University of Queensland Press, 1974.

Sheehan, P. W., & Bowman, L. Peer model and experimenter expectancies about appropriate response as determinants of behavior in the hypnotic setting. *Journal of Abnormal Psychology,* 1973, **82,** 112–123.

Sheehan, P. W., & Dolby, R. M. Artifact and Barber's model of hypnosis: A logical-empirical analysis. *Journal of Experimental Social Psychology,* 1974, **10,** 171–187.

Sheehan, P. W., & Dolby, R. Hypnosis and the influence of most recently perceived events. *Journal of Abnormal Psychology,* 1975, **84,** 331–345.

Sheehan, P. W., & Marsh, M. C. Demonstration of the effect of "faking subjects' knowledge that others are aware of their pretence" on perception of role-playing performance: A methodological comment. *International Journal of Clinical and Experimental Hypnosis,* 1974, **22,** 62–67.

Shor, R. E. Hypnosis and the concept of the generalized reality-orientation. *American Journal of Psychotherapy,* 1959, **13,** 582–602.

Shor, R. E. Three dimensions of hypnotic depth. *International Journal of Clinical and Experimental Hypnosis,* 1962, **10,** 23–28.

Shor, R. E. A note on shock tolerances of real and simulating hypnotic subjects. *International Journal of Clinical and Experimental Hypnosis,* 1964, **12,** 258–262.

Shor, R. E., & Cobb, J. C. An exploratory study of hypnotic training using the concept of plateau responsiveness as a referent. *American Journal of Clinical Hypnosis,* 1968, **10,** 178–197.

Shor, R. E., & Orne, E. C. *The Harvard Group Scale of Hypnotic Susceptibility, Form A.* Palo Alto, California: Consulting Psychologists Press, 1962.

Shor, R. E., Orne, M. T., & O'Connell, D. N. Psychological correlates of plateau hypnotizability in a special volunteer sample. *Journal of Personality and Social Psychology,* 1966, **3,** 80–95.

Sigall, H., Aronson, E., & Van Hoose, T. The cooperative subject: Myth or reality? *Journal of Experimental Social Psychology,* 1970, **6,** 1–10.

Silverman, R. E. Eliminating a conditioned GSR by the reduction of experimental anxiety. *Journal of Experimental Psychology,* 1960, **59,** 122–125.

Singer, G., & Sheehan, P. W. The effect of demand characteristics on the figural after-effect with real and imaged inducing figures. *American Journal of Psychology,* 1965, **78,** 96–101.

Skinner, B. F. The steep and thorny way to a science of behavior. *American Psychologist,* 1975, **30,** 42–49.

Slotnick, R. S., Liebert, R. M., & Hilgard, E. R. The enhancement of muscular performance in hypnosis through exhortation, and involving instructions. *Journal of Personality,* 1965, **33,** 37–45.

Slotnick, R., & London, P. Influence of instructions on hypnotic and nonhypnotic performance. *Journal of Abnormal Psychology,* 1965, **70,** 38–46.

Solomon, D., & Goodson, D. F. Hypnotic age regression evaluated against a criterion of prior performance. *International Journal of Clinical and Experimental Hypnosis,* 1971, **19,** 243–259.

Spanos, N. P. Goal-directed fantasy and the performance of hypnotic test suggestions. *Psychiatry,* 1971, **34,** 86–96.

Spanos, N. P., & Barber, T. X. "Hypnotic" experiences as inferred from subjective reports: Auditory and visual hallucinations. *Journal of Experimental Research in Personality,* 1968, **3,** 136–150.

Spanos, N. P., & Barber, T. X. Cognitive activity during "hypnotic" suggestibility: Goal-directed fantasy and the experience of non-volition. *Journal of Personality,* 1972, **40,** 510–524.

Spanos, N. P., & Barber, T. X. Toward a convergence in hypnosis research. *American Psychologist,* 1974, **29,** 500–511.

Spanos, N. P., Barber, T. X., & Lang, G. Cognition and self-control: Cognitive control of painful sensory input. In H. London, & R. Nisbett (Eds.), *Cognitive alterations of feeling states.* Chicago, Illinois: Aldine, 1974.

Spanos, N. P., & Chaves, J. F. Hypnosis research: A methodological critique of experiments generated by two alternative paradigms. *American Journal of Clinical Hypnosis,* 1970, **13,** 108–127.

Spanos, N. P., De Moor, W., & Barber, T. X. Hypnosis and behavior therapy: Common denominators. *American Journal of Clinical Hypnosis,* 1973, **16,** 45–64.

Spanos, N. P., & Ham, M. L. Cognitive activity in response to hypnotic suggestion: Goal-directed fantasy and selective amnesia. *American Journal of Clinical Hypnosis,* 1973, **15,** 191–198.

Spanos, N. P., McPeake, J. D., & Carter, W. Effects of pretesting on response to a visual hallucination suggestion in hypnotic subjects. *Journal of Personality and Social Psychology,* 1973, **28,** 293–297.

Spanos, N. P., Spillane, J., & McPeake, J. D. Suggestion elaborateness, goal-directed fantasy, and response to suggestion in hypnotic and task-motivated subjects. Unpublished paper, Medfield Foundation, Medfield, Massachusetts, 1974.

Spence, K. W. Cognitive and drive factors in the extinction of the conditioned eye blink in human subjects. *Psychological Review,* 1966, **73,** 445–458.

Spiegel, H. The grade 5 syndrome: The highly hypnotizable person. *International Journal of Clinical and Experimental Hypnosis,* 1974, **22,** 303–319.

Stevens, S. S. Psychology and the science of science. *Psychological Bulletin,* 1939, **36,** 221–263.

Stoyva, J., & Kamiya, J. Electrophysiological studies of dreaming as the prototype of a new strategy in the study of consciousness. *Psychological Review,* 1968, **75,** 192–205.

Sutcliffe, J. P. Hypnotic behavior: Fantasy or simulation? Unpublished doctoral dissertation, University of Sydney, Australia, 1958.

Sutcliffe, J. P. "Credulous" and "sceptical" views of hypnotic phenomena: A review of certain evidence and methodology. *International Journal of Clinical and Experimental Hypnosis,* 1960, **8,** 73–101.

Sutcliffe, J. P. "Credulous" and "skeptical" views of hypnotic phenomena: Experiments in esthesia, hallucination, and delusion. *Journal of Abnormal and Social Psychology,* 1961, **62,** 189–200.

Sutcliffe, J. P. The relation of imagery and fantasy to hypnosis (NIMH Project Final Report, United States Public Health Service) Washington, D.C.: United States Government Printing Office, 1965.

Sutcliffe, J. P. After-images of real and imaged stimuli: *Australian Journal of Psychology,* 1972, **24,** 275–289.

Sutcliffe, J. P., Perry, C. W., & Sheehan, P. W. Relation of some aspects of imagery and fantasy to hypnotic susceptibility. *Journal of Abnormal Psychology,* 1970, **76,** 279–287.

Sutcliffe, J. P., Perry, C. W., Sheehan, P. W., Jones, J. A., & Bristow, R. A. The relation of imagery and fantasy to hypnosis (NIMH Project Report, United States Public Health Service) Washington, D.C.: United States Government Printing Office, 1963.

Tart, C. T. Self-report scales of hypnotic depth. *International Journal of Clinical and Experimental Hypnosis,* 1970, **18,** 105–125. (a)

Tart, C. T. Increases in hypnotizability resulting from a prolonged program for enhancing personal growth. *Journal of Abnormal Psychology,* 1970, **75,** 260–266. (b)

Tart, C. T. Measuring the depth of an altered state of consciousness, with particular reference to self-report scales of hypnotic depth. In E. Fromm, & R. E. Shor (Eds.), *Hypnosis: Research developments and perspectives.* Chicago, Illinois: Aldine-Atherton, 1972. Pp. 445–477.

Tart, C. T., & Hilgard, E. R. Responsiveness to suggestions under "hypnosis" and "waking-imagination" conditions: A methodological observation. *International Journal of Clinical and Experimental Hypnosis,* 1966, **14,** 247–256.

Tellegen, A., & Atkinson, G. Openness to absorbing and self-altering experiences ("absorption"), a trait related to hypnotic susceptibility. *Journal of Abnormal Psychology,* 1974, **83,** 268–277.

Thompson, K. F. Clinical and experimental trance: Yes, there is a difference. *American Journal of Clinical Hypnosis,* 1970, **13,** 3–5.

Tinterow, M. M. (Ed.) *Foundations of hypnosis: From Mesmer to Freud.* Springfield, Illinois: Charles C Thomas, 1970.

Troffer, S. A. H. Hypnotic age regression and cognitive functioning. Unpublished doctoral dissertation, Stanford University, 1966.

Underwood, H. W. The validity of hypnotically-induced visual hallucinations. *Journal of Abnormal and Social Psychology,* 1960, **61,** 39–46.

Wachtel, P. L., & Goldberger, N. I. Hypnotizability and cognitive controls. *International Journal of Clinical and Experimental Hypnosis,* 1973, **21,** 298–304.

Watkins, J. G. Trance and transference. *Journal of Clinical and Experimental Hypnosis,* 1954, **2,** 284–290.

Watkins, J. G. Antisocial behavior under hypnosis: Possible or impossible? *International Journal of Clinical and Experimental Hypnosis,* 1972, **20,** 95–100. (a)

Watkins, J. G. Review of T. X. Barber's "LSD, Marihuana, Yoga, and Hypnosis" in *International Journal of Clinical and Experimental Hypnosis,* 1972, **20,** 267–269. (b)

Webb, E. J., Campbell, D. T., Schwartz, R. D., & Sechrest, L. *Unobtrusive measures.* Chicago, Illinois: Rand McNally, 1972.

Weber, S. J., & Cook, T. D. Subject effects in laboratory research: An examination of subject roles, demand characteristics, and valid inference. *Psychological Bulletin,* 1972, **77,** 273–295.

Weitzenhoffer, A. M. "Credulity" and "skepticism" in hypnotic research: A critical examination of Sutcliffe's thesis and evidence. *American Journal of Clinical Hypnosis,* 1963, **6,** 137–162.

Weitzenhoffer, A. M. "Credulity" and "skepticism" in hypnotic research: A critical examination of Sutcliffe's thesis and evidence. Part II. *American Journal of Clinical Hypnosis,* 1964, **6,** 241–268.

Weitzenhoffer, A. M., & Hilgard, E. R. *Stanford Hypnotic Susceptibility Scale, Forms A and B.* Palo Alto, California: Consulting Psychologists Press, 1959.

Weitzenhoffer, A. M., & Hilgard, E. R. *Stanford Hypnotic Susceptibility Scale, Form C.* Palo Alto, California: Consulting Psychologists Press, 1962.

Weitzenhoffer, A. M., & Sjoberg, B. M. Suggestibility with and without "induction of hypnosis." *Journal of Nervous and Mental Disease,* 1961, **132,** 204–220.

White, R. W. A preface to the theory of hypnotism. *Journal of Abnormal and Social Psychology,* 1941, **36,** 477–505. (a)

White, R. W. An analysis of motivation in hypnosis. *Journal of General Psychology,* 1941, **24,** 204–224. (b)

Williamsen, J. A., Johnson, H. J., & Eriksen, C. W. Some characteristics of posthypnotic amnesia. *Journal of Abnormal Psychology,* 1965, **70,** 123–131.

Wolberg, L. R. *Medical hypnosis.* Vol. 1. *The principles of hypnotherapy.* New York: Grune & Stratton, 1948.

Zamansky, H. S., & Brightbill, R. F. Attitude differences of volunteers and nonvolunteers and of susceptible and nonsusceptible hypnotic subjects. *International Journal of Clinical and Experimental Hypnosis,* 1965, **13,** 279–290.

Zamansky, H. S., Scharf, B., & Brightbill, R. The effect of expectancy for hypnosis on prehypnotic performance. *Journal of Personality,* 1964, **32,** 236–248.

Zimbardo, P. G., Marshall, G., & Maslach, C. Liberating behavior from time-bound control: Expanding the present through hypnosis. *Journal of Applied Social Psychology,* 1971, **1,** 305–323.

Author Index

Numbers in *italics* refer to pages on which the complete references are listed.

Subject Index

I

L

M

N

O

For Product Safety Concerns and Information please contact our EU representative GPSR@taylorandfrancis.com
Taylor & Francis Verlag GmbH, Kaufingerstraße 24, 80331 München, Germany

www.ingramcontent.com/pod-product-compliance
Lightning Source LLC
LaVergne TN
LVHW011111300926
849160LV00008B/349

* 9 7 8 1 1 3 8 8 8 4 9 9 1 *